THE RULERS
OF RHODESIA

From Earliest Times to the Referendum

Oliver Ransford

JOHN MURRAY

TO ANDREW

© OLIVER NEIL RANSFORD 1968

Printed in Great Britain for
John Murray, Albemarle Street, London
by The Camelot Press Ltd, London and
Southampton
7195 1822 9

CONTENTS

ILLUSTRATIONS

ILLUSTRATIONS

MAPS

Copyright: National Archives of Rhodesia.
†*Copyright: Rhodesian National Tourist Board.*

ACKNOWLEDGEMENTS

I am grateful to many friends for the assistance they have given me while writing this book. It is impossible to acknowledge them all by name but I would like to make special mention of the unfailing help and courtesy I have received from Mr T. W. Baxter and the staff of the National Archives of Rhodesia, from Mr Roger Summers of the National Museum, and from Mr C. K. Cooke of the National Monuments Commission. All these have been generous with their advice, and although they can in no way be held responsible for my mistakes in interpretation or fact, these errors would have been far more numerous without their help. I am also grateful to Mr R. W. Stacey and Mr N. Johnson, together with their staffs at the two Bulawayo Libraries. Dr J. C. Shee, Mr Peter Gibbs, Mr J. Wakelin and Dr A. O. Ransford kindly read through parts of the manuscript and made a number of most useful suggestions. The bibliography at the end of this study sets out the more important sources on which it has been based, and also bears witness of my debt to previous writers about the Rhodesian past. In addition, I am greatly obliged to all those who have agreed to allow me to reproduce illustrations and also to the following publishers for permission to include quotations: G. Bell & Sons (*Great Days*, Frank Johnson, 1940), William Heinemann Ltd (*From Dan to Beersheba*, A. R. Colquhoun, 1908) and Chatto & Windus Ltd (various selections from the Oppenheimer series).

The endless alterations, erasures and additions to my manuscript were unravelled and then typed out by Mrs A. Hutchings, Mrs M. Dugmore, and my daughters Carol and Charlotte. And at every stage, my wife's cooperation in preparing this book has been such that it is really as much hers as mine.

INTRODUCTION

Interest in Rhodesia today far exceeds knowledge of the country. Many people view it through a Judas hole of misconception and prejudice, wondering why this land should have failed to follow the recent developmental pattern of most sub-Saharan African states. Few observers realise that Rhodesia's history for centuries has run on separate and distinctive lines; fewer still appreciate that although she received her present boundaries during the 'scramble for Africa' they happened for once to coincide with a geographical entity which could look back on a thousand years of nationhood. This heritage of individuality is owed to natural obstacles which have converted the country into a land-locked island. The Zambesi to the north has always been a physical and cultural barrier; on the east the Manica Highlands separate Rhodesia from the low veld of Mocambique; the Kalahari and a broad belt of tsetse country likewise guaranteed her seclusion from the west and south.

Indian and Arab traders ventured into present-day Rhodesia during the first Christian millennium, but not until the sixteenth century was it penetrated by Europeans. Portuguese conquistadors then found it to be a surprisingly well ordered state; they spoke of it as Mocaranga, or sometimes as Monomatapa in deference to the dynastic title of its reigning emperors. But after the Portuguese eviction towards the end of the seventeenth century practical knowledge of Mocaranga was lost by the outside world for the next hundred and fifty years: all that was remembered was its fabled association with the wealth of Ophir; and Mocaranga joined the ranks of other never-never-lands like Atlantis and Lemuria. A century ago, however, an increasing demand for ivory, the discovery of gold in the neighbouring Transvaal, and the mid-nineteenth-century outburst of missionary endeavour in England, all combined to focus appropriate European interest again on the huge blank space on the map beyond the Limpopo river.

Mocaranga accordingly was 'rediscovered' by elephant hunters,

I

prospectors, and missionaries, rather than by the 'professional' explorers of Victoria's reign. Even Livingstone, whose journeys took him all round Rhodesia, only crossed its modern boundaries twice and on both occasions he penetrated no further than a few hundred yards. During the exploitation of Africa which followed its exploration, the far interior of southern Africa became a prize to be competed for by several great powers. It fell at last into the eager hands of Cecil Rhodes and was named after him; although many famous men have been immortalised in the names of towns and cities, very few have given their names to a whole country, and Rhodes took pride in sharing this distinction with Philip II, Amerigo Vespucci, Bolivar, and Columbus.

Rhodesia today is a strange blend of twentieth-century Europe and untamed Africa. She is famous for her unspoiled scenic wonders, of which those lying on the country's periphery—the Victoria Falls, the Eastern Highlands, and the Matopo Hills— are the best known. But none of these Three Graces represent the real Rhodesia for me: when I hear the country's name mentioned the image that leaps into my mind is that of the high veld which runs like a broad backbone through the land. My mind's eye sees an immense sweep of tawny grass leaning in the distance against a blue sky; it sees a sun-drenched prairie so level that even time has not marked it, a landscape which suggests at once vastness and seclusion, and where man's presence is only indicated by travelling columns of smoke or little dwellings which merge as it were with the earth. And in particular it visualises one fragment of this great plateau where it is framed by an iron-stone ridge some thirty miles from Bulawayo. We own a cottage there surrounded by arched veld horizons except on the north where the ridge swells into Litche Hill, which looks for all the world like a stranded brontosaurus.

In a curious way many of the fibres of Rhodesian history run past Litche Hill. The pastures below are littered with stone axes fashioned by primitive men more than 50,000 years ago, and with the tiny microlithic blades used by Bushmen for barbing arrows. Trenches dug along the ridge by modern prospectors encroach upon the gold workings of the Rhodesian 'Ancients'.

An earthwork, made either by a white hunter a hundred years ago or by a seventeenth-century Portuguese trader, stands close to scores of saucer-like depressions in the ground whose origin is still unknown. Lobengula, the last Matabele king passed through these farmlands when he fled from Bulawayo in 1893, and behind him pounded Major Wilson's patrol riding towards immortality on the banks of the Shangani river. Votive offerings are still brought to Litche Hill when the rains are late and laid in a cave-shrine dedicated to the High Deity of the Karanga. Five miles away another hill, Thabas Ikonya, makes a landmark (which African tradition insists must not be pointed at) where the last Rozwi Mambo was skinned alive in 1834 by Zulu conquerors from the south. And at Inyati a few miles further east one can still see the foundations of the first Christian mission to the Matabele. All these shreds from the fabric of Rhodesian history (and many more besides) lie around our cottage, and it seemed fitting that an African artist should have depicted them on one of its walls in a fresco painted in an unusual idiom.

The great plateau constitutes nearly a third of Rhodesia's land area. On both sides of this watershed between the Zambesi and Limpopo rivers the ground drops away through middle veld into the low veld, where a stranger feels an uncanny sense of familiarity and precognition, due, one conceives, to a lingering subconscious memory of the time when its natural orchard permitted his first ancestors to make a living. Until seventy years ago the low veld was so infested with tsetse fly that it formed a pestilential fosse that protected the high Rhodesian heartland from invasion and allowed its successive inhabitants to develop their separate personalities and cultures in seclusion and peace. And some spell lay in this land which endowed its people with strange novelties of mood and spurred them on to new initiatives. That *erdgeist* nourished the Rhodesian Bushmen's splendid artistic talents, and inspired the Karanga to develop a unique and bizarre stone-building technique. The ferment is still present in the country and sets its tone today; modern visitors at once sense the vitality of a frontierland, and here white men and black men believe they will find a way of living together in tolerance and peace.

It may be considered pretentious to seek a pattern in the development of a country, yet it is difficult not to be impressed in Rhodesian history by one recurrent theme that repeats itself like a motif introduced again and again into a Wagnerian opera: each subjugation of the great plateau resulted in it being governed by a new minority élite which was willingly accepted by the lower strata of society and scarcely ever challenged from within. In this book we are not concerned with the ethics of government by a minority except to take notice that from the earliest times successive groups of newcomers were able to dominate a more numerous indigenous people by virtue of their superior cultural or organisational powers. This cyclic pattern was established when a negroid minority subjugated its Khoisan predecessors in the land during the first Christian millennium; one dominant Bantu clan among them then captured secular as well as spiritual power in Mocaranga and came eventually to rule the great empire of Monomatapa. A Portuguese élite next exercised authority until it was replaced by a Rozwi ruling class which governed a nation of bondsmen in a manner made familiar by the feudal seigneurs of medieval Europe. The Rozwi in their turn were supplanted by the aristocratic *abazansi* of a warlike Zulu tribe until they too went down before the greater strength of the white frontiersmen, who, in grasping power, wedded themselves to the land.

This great and curious cycle is the theme of this book, whose purpose is to provide the general reader with a background history of modern Rhodesia. It is written as objectively as possible; but at this time when our conception of the earlier events in central Africa is constantly being revised in the light of current research I have no doubt that some of my interpretations will elicit criticism from professional historians and archaeologists who have used their disciplined skills to erect the factual framework on which I have attempted, gratefully, to build.

The majority of published works on the Rhodesian past have either been sugar-coated to suit the tastes of English readers or written as though the history of central Africa began only a century ago. I therefore make no apology for attempting to paint the picture in deeper perspective and to include in it 'warts and all'. In using this large canvas a certain amount of depth and detail has had to be sacrificed, but at the same time it has allowed me sometimes to focus attention on events which bring the genre of the Rhodesian past to life.

Many snares await the historian of Africa. The Bantu, having no form of writing, largely depended on oral folk-lore for their knowledge of the past, and this has a tendency to telescope events in time or to distort them according to the tribal prejudices of the narrator. There is difficulty too in drawing up a chronological order of the earlier rulers of south-central Africa, since succession and inheritance among the Bantu does not follow the tidy primo-genitural form of Europe. The spelling of African names also presents problems: wherever possible the use of the plural prefix has been avoided, and tribal names have been used in the forms most familiar to English readers. The spelling of names in quoted passages has occasionally been altered to conform with those given in the text.

This book takes the story of Rhodesia up to the granting of internal self-government in 1923. Since then the country's character has somewhat altered; its texture has been stitched together by tarred roads and high-level bridges, by humanism and growing patriotism. But even today the tourist in many parts of this land feels himself to be an explorer and is very conscious of the primitiveness of Africa. Once off the beaten track he can share the sense of heightened living and freedom from restraint which nearly a hundred years ago made another visitor to Rhodesia write 'there is certainly deep enjoyment in going whither you will and where you will, free as air, untrammelled by appointments, unfettered by the *convenances* of society, lord of all you survey, absolute master of all your actions, pure despot among your party, the world all before you, your time your own; choose your path and go where you will. Creation for the time seems to be your slave. Such circumstances cannot but create a buoyancy of spirits, and when striding on, rifle on shoulder, in front of my party, I almost felt a childlike happiness as, when in schooldays, one started on some little trip of pleasure.'

Rhodesians today have undoubtedly been placed in a testing

position which exposes them to adverse criticism. Yet it is often conveniently forgotten that the record of her white settlers compares favourably with those of the colonists of America and Australia, and that they have made Rhodesia a tremendous asset to the Western cause in Africa. Nor are they always given credit for the immense benefit they have brought to the land of their adoption, whose African population has increased since 1890 from 400,000 to 4 million. Although a wholly praiseworthy desire to speed the evolution of democratic government in Africa has nearly everywhere proved to be a death wish for its European settlers, some observers find it reprehensible that white Rhodesians have refused to accept a *fin de siècle* role and still aspire to preserve Christian standards in their country. Nor is it everywhere sufficiently realised that in these efforts to preserve stability they are supported by the large majority of black Rhodesians. For the Africans willingly accept government by an élite, provided that its positions of privilege remain open to them, and that it does not interfere with age-old customs and traditions.

Even though they come from different stocks, all modern Rhodesians feel great pride in their achievements; all are intensely patriotic and resentful of external pressures. They know that their primary task is to find the rapport and compassion which will allow them to share the country for the common good. Sometimes I believe a people are helped in solving the difficulties of the present by a better understanding and respect for what has gone before, and this perhaps more than anything else justifies the writing of yet another book on Rhodesian history. At the same time I would gain particular pleasure if something of the beauty and historical interest of Rhodesia reaches from its pages to readers who have not yet had the good fortune to visit this land-locked island in central Africa.

THE FIRST RHODESIANS

Sometimes when contemplating the course of a country's history it is possible to seize upon a particular period and say 'this was its Golden Age'. A very good case can be made for affirming that Rhodesia's Golden Age occurred during the last millennium B.C. when it was inhabited by a yellow-skinned people whom we know today as the Bushmen or Capoids. For by one of those paradoxes which delight the historian, these first Rhodesians, (who were perhaps the most amiable and worthy people ever evolved) enjoyed quite unusual artistic talents. They used them to blazon Rhodesia's rocks with colour; it was as though they were determined to glorify their demesne by covering it with paintings of the most beautiful animals in creation. In so doing they endowed Rhodesia with its most particular and abiding glory—the Bushman paintings.

There is some dispute as to the origin of the Capoid race, and we are still waiting for the vital piece of evidence which will determine which of two evolutionary theories is correct. Some anthropologists maintain that the Bushmen were evicted from ancestral homelands on the Mediterranean littoral of Africa by Caucasoid expansion. They base their theory on several pieces of evidence: the resemblance shown by Bushman rock art in Africa to that of Spain and southern France, the occurrence of similar paintings in north and east Africa along the postulated route of the Bushpeople's southerly migration, the fact that the Bushpeople were known in dynastic Egypt, and the presence of relict Bushmanoid communities living today in Libya and Tanganyika. They further suggest that the Capoids traversed a well-watered Sahara during the Makalian wet phase which began about 5500 B.C., and that afterwards they were sealed off from the rest of the world by the desiccation of the Sahara; they then scattered through the empty subcontinent, living as it were in a cultural capsule of their own for several thousand years.

The other school of anthropology maintains that the Capoids were an autochthonous race originating in south central Africa, and evolving by mutations from, and interbreeding with, other aboriginal peoples like the tall Boskop folk who correspond to the Neanderthals of Europe.

However they may have originated, the Bushpeople, sometime after the fifth millennium B.C., began to dominate the great Rhodesian plateau, at the expense of the even more primitive men who were unsuccessful 'blue-prints' for homo sapiens. These Bushpeople were only driven away or absorbed by other races of a superior culture in comparatively recent times.

Although nearly all the Bushmen have now disappeared from Rhodesia, our knowledge of them is yet surprisingly precise. It is derived largely from the recordings of their daily lives which their rock artists left behind in more than 1,500 Rhodesian caves and shelters; it is drawn too from archaeological remains found at their living sites, and from studies of the Capoids still living today in Botswana and South-West Africa.

At the same time one must avoid the common fallacy of equating the Rhodesian Bushmen of two thousand years ago with the poor remnants of their race which now eke out a living in the Kalahari. For one thing, the mere struggle for survival in the desert has quite deprived the modern Bushmen of their forebears' artistic genius; they are smaller too in stature, for natural selection has allowed the modern Bushmen to adapt, by dwarfing, to an existence which involves them in a continuous toilsome and uncertain search for food and water, and which puts a premium on litheness and speed.

The Rhodesian Bushmen of their halcyon days may have been materially poor, but they enjoyed tremendous spiritual wealth. Their ethos was based on a remarkably high degree of co-operation and mutual tolerance for each other. Although fighting among them was rare and they never killed except for food, they were most proficient hunters and their natural faculties were perfectly suited to the chase. Their acuity of vision was such that with the unaided eye they could readily distinquish the four major moons of the planet Jupiter, or follow the flight of a swarm of bees to a far distant hive. Their hearing was no less perceptive, and they possessed such skill in tracking that the Bantu who followed them to Rhodesia believed that they had an extra pair of eyes in their feet. But what makes the Bushmen so particularly a race apart is the insatiable passion they had for expressing themselves by painting. Their artists covered every suitable rock they could find in Rhodesia with records of their own lives and likenesses of the animals they admired. Although at first their style of painting was primitive, at its peak it compared in beauty with any school of naturalistic art in the world.

The Bushpeople are members of a race which is different in many respects from the other four subspecies of mankind. These aberrations are seen in the modern Capoids, who like their forebears of the Rhodesian painting era, are more delicately built than other men and women, seldom being more than five feet tall. They are infantile in appearance, having flat faces, bulging foreheads, and prominent cheekbones. Their skin is of a yellowish colour, and an extra slanting epicanthric fold of skin protects their eyes from glare so that it was not surprising that the first Europeans who saw them believed the Bushpeople to be of Mongolian origin. Their hair differs from ours; it grows in tight 'peppercorn' spirals that leave bare areas of the scalp exposed to the air and so facilitates sweating. Body hair is deficient. The Capoid women have bulging buttocks in which they are said (probably incorrectly) to store up nourishment as in a camel's hump, but it is much more likely that, since this condition of steatopygia is highly prized as a physical attraction, it has arisen by sexual selection; the unusual appearance it produces is accentuated by these people's characteristic sway-back due to lumbar lordosis. Young Capoid girls have nipples very much larger than in other races; like those of animals about to mate, the teats become so prominent at puberty that one fanciful observer has described them as 'glowing like orange ping-pong balls'. At maturity the inner lips of the Bushwomen's vulvae become grossly elongated, forming a little apron of skin which sometimes hangs four inches below the perineum. This appendage was considered comely; it was proudly called a *khuae*, or (by Europeans) the *atelier Egyptienne*.* Capoid men are no less unusual in their sexual anatomy: most of them are monorchous,† while their penis is permanently set in a semi-erect infantile position; with no less pride than their women, this distinctive feature is called a *qhwai-xkhwe*, and judging from ancient paintings its appearance was made still more anomalous by infibulation, presumably as some form of moral inhibition.

The Bushpeople differed from other human beings in their psyche as well as in their anatomy. They had developed an unusual social organisation based on an unselfish consideration for each other's needs. Their clans were presided over by acknow-ledged leaders. They obeyed laws which tended to prevent friction with neighbouring clans and which were especially concerned with guarding against trespassing on each other's hunting grounds. Their codes of behaviour were surprisingly rational, and although essentially communalistic, a certain degree of specialisation permitted the existence of priestly figures who conducted complicated ceremonies in which all clan members took part. One has the feeling that they were a very happy people: the Bushmen remind us a little of the Polynesians whom Captain Cook introduced to the modern world, for in them one senses the same engaging qualities of gaiety and artless innocence that could have only existed in a Garden-of-Eden world untarnished by human ambitions and jealousies. Their very name—the *Zhu twa si* or 'harmless people'—sums up their uncompetitive nature which only altered when the outside world caught up with them; then the Bushmen began to exhibit that suspicious hostility to the Europeans encroaching on their homelands by which they have ever since been stigmatised.

No other race of human beings has lived so close to nature as the Capoids: the Bantu and white men who came to make war

---

* The connotation *atelier Egyptienne* is produced as additional evidence of the north African origin of the Capoids. Some reports suggest that the elongation of the labia minora results in part from manipulation.

† An infantile condition where only one testicle descends into the scrotum.

on them thought of these little people more as wild animals than human beings and in one sense they were right: not only has the Bushpeople's knowledge of the plant life of the veld never been even remotely approached by other peoples and races, but they had an astonishing comprehension of the behaviour and anatomy of the animals who shared the country with them. Although examination of the Bushmen's ancient middens has shown that sixty per cent of their diet was vegetable, and that for meat they preferred the flesh of small animals such as hares, mice, tortoises, and lizards, these people were almost mystically obsessed by the study of the larger antelope: they lived with them on terms which were not unlike the feelings reserved by the Bantu for their domestic cattle. They killed only to eat, for Capoid philosophy enjoined the protection of all life provided this was compatible with their own survival, and even today a Kalahari Bushman who has inadvertently dug up an unappetising root will bury it again for the sake of the animals coming after him.

During their halcyon era the Rhodesian Bushmen disdained any form of agriculture and were primarily food gatherers from the natural orchard of their land; they preferred to paint the antelope on the veld rather than kill them, but when they required meat they were the most proficient (and merciful) hunters the world has ever seen.

The invention of the bow had been the greatest breakthrough in the Bushpeople's hunting technique. From their paintings we know that hundreds of years ago in Rhodesia they used bows which are almost identical with those employed today in the Kalahari. The bows were between three and four feet in length, weighed a mere eight ounces, were strengthened by bindings of gemsbok tendons, and strung with plaited eland sinews. The short unfeathered arrows were both flimsy and erratic, having a range of barely twenty-five yards, but the hunters made up for their inaccuracy by loosing them off in volleys. One must presume that the arrows were fabricated then, as now, in four sections; the head was made either of gemsbok horn, bone, or pointed stone, and sometimes it would be barbed with microlithic flakes of quartz attached by mastic; a reed 'sleeve' strengthened by over-lapping sinews attached the arrow-head to a wooden link shaft, some two inches long, which was designed to break off on impact leaving the point buried in the quarry; the main shaft was about seventeen inches long and made from a reed which was nicked at the back to fit the bow string.

Fragile arrows of this sort could only just penetrate an antelope's hide, and their effect depended on the poisons which were liberally smeared over the link shaft. A wide variety of nerve and heart toxins, mainly derived from snakes, beetles, and scorpions, were used for this purpose, and they were usually compounded with irritating fruit saps which made a wounded animal scratch itself and so facilitated the toxin's spread. There were no known antidotes to the poisons, and the Kalahari hunters of today take extreme care to avoid contamination. One wonders in passing how long it will be before future physicians find medicinal uses for these secret drugs, as they have already done with the curare arrow poisons of the South American Indians.

When the Bushmen had to hunt they preferred to do so in the evening, for a wounded quarry did not move far in the darkness, and could be easily found and dispatched next morning. Very little of the animal would have been wasted: all the meat except that part surrounding the arrow wound was consumed in a gargantuan feast lasting several days; blood was made into something resembling a Yorkshire black pudding; tendons were removed to be dried and used as bow strings; the hides were rubbed down with tiny quartz scrapers and then sewn together with sharp bone needles to make cloaks and bags; the bones such as the shoulder blade were preserved for use as digging tools.

The primitive hunting technique of the Bushmen possessed certain advantages over those of the great carnivora and modern men's sophisticated methods. Their weapons were silent and caused the minimum of fear reaction; a wounded animal suffered little pain and dropped out quietly from the herd only after the poison had exerted its effect, often being out of sight when it died. After a kill the antelope were left for several days in peace to get over whatever shock they may have experienced. Nor was a herd ever 'shot out'; rather the game was regularly 'culled' and allowed to remain on their accustomed pasturelands in a condition that was close to domestication.

Separated as they were from all outside influences, it was inevitable that the lives of the Capoids should have developed on lines utterly different from those of other people. In two respects —their hunting expertise, and the development of an ethos based on co-operation and peace—they perhaps advanced beyond any standards attained by mankind's other subspecies. But their very quality of humanism turned out to be a liability when they were eventually confronted with the modern world. Today the Capoid section of the human race is represented by a mere remnant of about 55,000 people, most of whom live in Botswana and South-West Africa. Only a few full-blooded Rhodesian Bushmen are still to be found near the country's western border, although many Bantu/Capoid hybrids exist, and the Tonga of the Zambesi valley show Bushman traits.

But for five thousand years the Bushmen were the masters of Rhodesia. They were most concentrated in the broken kopje country of north-east Mashonaland, the Fort Victoria area, and the Matopo Hills, which all suited their hunting methods and provided them with granite 'canvasses' on which to paint. If only for their skill in hunting, their ethos of moderation, and the opportunity they provide for a stone-age people to be studied in the twentieth century, the Bushmen would be considered a most remarkable people. It is, however, their mastery of naturalistic painting which has lifted them to one of the pinnacles of human achievement and it is this which gives them their especial claim to attention. For rock painting was the *métier* of the Rhodesian Bushmen, and their triumph. The magic of the country touched them in a subtle and exquisite way by allowing them to evolve the purest expression of original art in Africa—but in a form which yet differs entirely from anything that is understood today by 'African art'.

The stone murals they left behind in Rhodesia form a brilliant exposition of the Bushman's eye for beauty, and unveil a primitive people's temperament in a way which is unique. They have tremendous value too as vivid records of Rhodesia's early history, providing a national archive of stone and pigment like a vastly expanded Bayeux tapestry. These paintings bring the onlooker into an almost physical communion with the distant past, and allows him to feel close to participation in the mystique of a forgotten people. Although concentrated in the areas where granite caves provided easily worked 'canvasses', the paintings occasionally appear on sandstone and quartz. Where no suitable stone exists the paintings are sometimes replaced by perhaps even more intriguing rock engravings: a fine petroglyph of a giraffe can be seen near Beitbridge, while at Bumboosie, just inside the northern limits of the Wankie Game Reserve, a single cave contains more than two hundred pecked-out engravings of antelope spoor, and perhaps represents a 'school' for uninitiated huntsmen.

The earliest rock paintings of Rhodesia can with confidence be attributed to the first millennium A.D., but they must only be the end result of a long tradition whose earlier exposition by now is lost. For their canvasses the painters chose cave walls sheltered from the weather but which would catch the light of the rising or setting sun. Before applying their paint early artists painstakingly smoothed down the rockface, but subsequently they avoided this laborious task by spreading mastic over the virgin rock—and by accident hit upon a technique which gave their paintings a lustrous varnish.

The Bushmen artists employed feathers, frayed wood, wildebeest hairs, flexible wooden spatulas, and sometimes their fingers as brushes. They made their paints from plant roots, local rocks, and earths containing iron; haematite and limonite were popular for the purpose, being crushed and heated before being fashioned into brown, yellow, and red crayons. Kaolin and birds' droppings provided the white, and charcoal the black colours. The pigments were bound together with tree gums, animal fats, and hyrax urine, and were so liquid that we can still make out a stone-age artists's brush marks; yet they never ran, nor have they cracked as do paintings in oil.

The Rhodesian artists' favourite colours were variegated browns, purplish black, claret, and white. Blue was excessively rare, and green, surprisingly, never appears. The painters made little attempt to match their colours to the subjects: possibly the Bushman colour-range perception differed from ours, but it seems more likely that, although essentially naturalistic, the Bushman conception of art was yet to some extent impressionistic, and the artists were released in their representations from all conventional links with flesh and blood.

The earliest Rhodesian paintings to have survived are simple outline forms, and they show a certain woodiness; but later, as their technique improved, they took on a vibrant sense of movement. By the time of the European Renaissance the rock artists had mastered the painting of naturalistic polychromes which, even if their pristine radiance has now faded into a time-worn reticence, are still intensely alive and expressive. It is interesting to note that the Bushmen artists may have passed some of the milestones of their craft before European painters: thus the problems of perspective and foreshortening appear to have been mastered in the Matopo Hills before Mantegna, in distant Padua, made his own artistic breakthrough.

The Capoid painters of Rhodesia planned their work with the utmost precision and presented it with crispness and economy of line. There are no signs of erasures or alterations in their friezes, and they have lasted remarkably well considering the adverse conditions to which they have been exposed. No portrayals of extinct animals (with the possible exception of the quagga) are to be seen; but many of the paintings suggest that they were executed during a wetter climate than today's, for hippopotami, fish, elephants, and giraffe are all shown in areas where now they would not survive. The artists were most concerned with depicting the familiar game animals with which they lived in such intimate contact, and tremendous attention was lavished on their accurate representation. Great care was taken too in rendering the carnivores whose hunting expertise the admiring artists considered rivalled their own, but zebras and giraffes are also superbly painted. The smaller buck and rodents, which provided the greater part of these people's animal food, are, however, rarely seen in the cave-paintings.

Convention prescribed surrealistic forms for depictions of the artists' people. Children were rarely painted: usually only adults appear in the paintings, and then in a stylistic manner which has been aptly likened to match-stick figures. The taboo on accurate portrayal of the Bushpeople seems to have been intended to prevent the painters from gaining magical powers over their subjects, and one is reminded here that factual representations of the human face were once also proscribed by Mohammedans and Jews. No such communal fear of sympathetic magic, however, affected the rock artists when portraying 'foreigners', and the racial characteristics of Hottentot and Bantu migrants to Rhodesia were not only represented but even emphasised in the later pictures. The Capoid witch-doctors too were rendered realistically and with concentration on detail, presumably because they were considered to be immune from sorcery.

Convention also determined the forms of some inanimate subjects: landscapes and trees were painted in pale gold and browns, so that they appear in an almost Chinese idiom. Rocks are depicted like ungainly sacks standing on end. Schematic and near-abstract figures appear commonly and their esoteric meanings can only now be surmised. As in Spain and France, outline painting of hands occur in Rhodesia, and some of them show the same finger mutilations which have puzzled the interpreters of European paintings for so long. These representations of hands may have been the artists' signatures, or claims to ownership of a cave and the surrounding hunting ground.

The Rhodesian artists also frequently painted grotesque mythological figures combining human and animal characteristics, and they look like phantoms from preposterous nightmares. Nowhere in the paintings is there the slightest suggestion of obscenity, although some friezes are clearly meant to be humorous. It is remarkable that no try-outs are ever found: the technical skill of the artists is always so uniformly good that one must conclude that only recognised masters were allowed to decorate the Rhodesian caves, while apprentices practised their craft on skins and wood before they were judged sufficiently proficient to be commissioned for work on durable rock. Bushman tradition insists that the masters were greatly revered, and no one was allowed to superimpose new compositions on theirs until all memory of their creators had been lost. The accepted craftsmen, it seems, were itinerant and perfectly free to develop individual styles; it is possible even now to recognise masterpieces from the same hand at distant sites, just as today we can identify an El Greco or a Titian. One gains the impression, without the support of any definite evidence, that the great masters were persons of the highest importance who journeyed far to beautify remote caves and who were endowed too with priestly duties concerned with initiation and rain ceremonies.

Rock murals of a type ancestral to those of Rhodesia are to be found in east Africa along the suggested line of Capoid migration. But in Rhodesia the naturalistic painting forms became stabilised; later they spread across the Limpopo to South Africa and through the Kalahari to South-West Africa, and there they found their most splendid manifestations. But the Zambesi formed a cultural barrier to the north: the rock paintings of Zambia are schematic in type, and quite unlike the naturalistic art forms of Rhodesia.

Why did the Bushmen paint? What inspired their mysterious urge to decorate the Rhodesian landscape so lavishly? These questions have been asked by everyone who has seen their creations of rare intrinsic beauty, and many suggestions have been made in attempts to answer them.

One favoured theory maintains that the paintings were an expression of sympathetic magic and were intended to use the psyche to affect the physical: it suggests that by depicting an eland pictorially, the artist hoped to gain the power to find and kill a real eland. This all sounds plausible enough, especially when it is remembered that until quite recently sophisticated Europeans would attempt to harm their enemies by piercing their wax images with pins; but the theory has lost support with the realisation that the main sources of the Bushpeople's meat were rodents and small buck which are rarely represented in Rhodesian rock art.

Some of the painting no doubt had a totemic significance, for the Capoid clans all believed in their own animal guardian spirits.

The thinness of the domestic deposits in the most profusely decorated caves shows that they were not used as living places, but suggests instead that at least some paintings were inspired by religious motives, for men have always wished to adorn their tabernacles, and in these painted shrines the Bushpeople may well have gathered for festivals, ceremonies, dancing, and recitals of the prowess of their ancestors beside old burial places. Other caves, however, show temporal scenes which are clearly intended to record the day-to-day activities of the Bushmen, the pleasures they took in the dance, and the important events of local history: thus we see representations of memorable hunts, with the hunters' bag laid out for inspection; others show the arrivals of foreigners seeking gold, ivory, and slaves. We see pictures too of the battles fought by the aborigines in the innumerable wars of liberation which they never won.

But no theory, however attractive, explains the cardinal problem of Bushman art—the reason why the larger antelopes provided the masters with their most frequent subjects, and why on them they lavished their most precise care.

Here, one must suppose, the stone-age masters were painting for the love of art, were seeking a way of expressing not only the fairy-like spirit of their people but also their strange affinity for the most graceful of all animals. In these splendid portrayals they seem to have found pleasure in the act of creating, rather than in admiration of the finished product or for any implicit connotations of their work. And although everything about their motives is only surmise I still defend my private hypothesis that the Rhodesian artists of the rocks painted these lovely animals so often and with such tenderness in an effort to improve upon nature itself and to glorify their domain with added beauty.

No one knows what artistic heights the Rhodesian rock painters would have attained had they been left undisturbed for a few more centuries in their chosen milieu. But the story of these gifted people ends on a particularly sad note. Their expressions of *l'art pour l'art* are replaced in the caves by a pictorial narrative of racial tragedy and genocide. By the middle of the fifteenth century the 'classical' paintings begin to be superseded by ones from which the old serenity has disappeared. They are sketchy, hurried, and finally decadent. No longer are they representations of peaceful scenes: as black men from the north gather strength and invade the Bushpeople's ancestral hunting grounds, war and disaster become their dominating motifs. The blissful golden age of Rhodesia and all it inspired in the Bushmen are forgotten as their rare energies are increasingly directed into a grim effort for survival in the Bantu blizzard. The paintings suggest that the artists of Matabeleland were first affected when the Karanga tribes began to exert their authority over the southern part of the country. For a little longer, however, the rock artists in Mashonaland worked on undisturbed; then their work deteriorates as they too are drawn into the vain defence of their hunting grounds.

Most of the Rhodesian Bushmen died royally in battle, neither asking nor giving quarter, but some slave women were spared to spread their genes among the victorious black men; and a few tattered remnants of the race escaped to join their kinsmen to the south and west, where their splendid talents were reprieved and even enhanced for several hundred years. Almost within living memory, however, they too were crushed between the two mill-stones of Bantu and European expansion. In the new age of enlightenment that followed, consideration was increasingly given to the preservation of the wild animals of southern Africa by herding them into giant game reserves, but it is a strange reflection on human behaviour that no effort was made to prevent the near-extermination of one of the most gifted branches of mankind. Some of the names, however, that the Bushmen gave to streams and hills and caves in Rhodesia remain with us, and their tiny microliths are scattered in great profusion in the country. But their true monument lives on in their paintings, which have made the original yellow-skinned Rhodesians articulate with tangible immortality. And somehow in the Matopo Hills these fairy-like little people even now seem very near and far more real than the living remnants of their people who, like human sweepings brushed into a corner, drag out an existence among the sands of the Kalahari. Yet even in these survivors a little of their forebears dogged spirit endures for still they refuse to come to terms with the modern world, and cling to their lithic traditions in the face of challenges from a culture far more formidable than the Rhodesian Bushmen ever had to meet.

* * * * *

Rhodesia is a land of many mysteries, but few are more intriguing than the identity of the people who began to share the country with the Bushmen in the Early Christian Era.

Rhodesians refer somewhat vaguely to these people as the 'Ancients', and tend to think of them as a rather pleasing national enigma—which indeed they are. For no one really knows very much about them.

What knowledge we do possess is owed to archaeological research and the paintings made of the Ancients by Capoid artists. We have learned that the newcomers, unlike the stone-age Bushmen, were an iron-age people, and the cave paintings show them driving flocks of fat-tailed sheep and long-horned cattle. Essentially they were pastoralists rather than food gatherers. They had also mastered the principles of primitive agronomy, and, having thus assured themselves of tomorrow's sustenance, were inclined to be less nomadic than the Bushmen, building semi-permanent settlements of flimsy huts. Above all, the Ancients were skilled prospectors and had learned methods of extracting and smelting metals. Rhodesia in their time must have been a gold-encrusted fairyland; all about them were outcrops of rocks containing visible gold. As they began to appreciate its value and their mining techniques improved, a certain amount of inter-tribal bartering inevitably took place, and the gold finally reached the Arab traders who were already sending their exploring dhows down the east African coast.

The Ancients' competence in gold mining had tremendous long-term consequences for the far interior of Africa. The country for the first time was producing something which other people wanted, and archaeological evidence shows that towards the end of the first millennium A.D. exotic articles of Arab, Indian, and Chinese manufacture were being traded for Rhodesian gold and ivory. The Ancients were also skilled at pottery manufacture. They decorated their pots with impressions from square-toothed combs, and the resulting characteristic 'stamped-ware' has provided the archaeologists with a convenient name to designate them.

The existence of a race so mysterious as the Rhodesian Ancients has of course led to considerable controversy regarding their origin, and although the problem is too wide and too debatable for us to consider here in any detail, we should take notice again of two separate theories concerning their beginnings. The protagonists of the conjectural Bushmen trek from the Mediterranean to Rhodesia suggest a rather similar but shorter migration of 'stamped-ware' folk from a nuclear area round the central African lakes. The Ancients, they submit, were the result of hybridisation between Khoisan Bushman and Caucasoid Hamitic stock, and they have conjectured that they spoke a language allied to that of the Capoids which is characterised by the use of five click consonants. Clans of these hybrid people supposedly followed the earlier migratory tracks of the Bushmen into the green-gold south, carrying with them an iron-age culture and possibly a knowledge of stone-building techniques derived from their Hamite forebears. The migrants, the theory continues, crossed the Zambesi about A.D. 100, and although many settled in Rhodesia, some elements continued the southward march, and the Hottentots whom Bartholomew Dias saw herding cattle when he made his landfall near the Cape of Good Hope in 1488 were their descendants.

The theory is an attractive one and it fits in very well with many of the facts, and particularly with the paintings made by the Rhodesian Bushmen of these strangers along the postulated course of their migration. For the cave artists show the new-comers as tall, peaceful, brown-skinned foreigners with well-developed steatopygia but lacking negroid prognathism; the women are seen to be loaded with metal ornaments, and the men are wearing high pointed hats resembling those worn in ancient Egypt and by the Hottentots of the Cape four hundred years ago.

But a different hypothesis concerning the origin of the stamped-ware folk is an equally valid one: its protagonists point out that the Bushmen were a very adaptable people, that there is evidence of at least some Bushman clans being taller and more robust at the beginning of the Christian era than their descendants who had been affected by a dwarfing mutation, and that iron-age culture could have diffused over the Zambesi long before it was carried across by an iron-age people. Their conclusion follows that the Ancients were members of the original Rhodesian Bushman stock who had abandoned their old ways in favour of a newer and more advantageous economy and technology; the less adjustable clans of the old hunting people, on the other hand, chose to continue their stone-age hunting habits until they were destroyed or driven away in more recent times.

Whatever may have been the true origin of the Rhodesian Ancients, there is little doubt that they were a docile people, who, if the evidence of the Bushman paintings is to be believed, shared the great plateau peacefully with the Capoids for many centuries. Only with the arrival of foreigners with negroid features do battle scenes appear in Rhodesian rock art. For about A.D. 800 family groups of Bantu crossing the Zambesi from the north began to swell into clans and then into whole tribes. And the Bantu were strong, fecund, and militant.

MONOMATAPA

The year A.D. 800—the year which saw Charlemagne crowned Emperor in Rome and watched England groping towards unity under a single king, the year when Haroun al-Raschid was turning his court at Baghdad into the centre of all Arab learning, and a year when the Bantu were pouring into Rhodesia in such numbers that it was becoming certain they would eventually dominate the country's older yellow-skinned inhabitants.

For many centuries before 800, immigrants carrying Khoisan, Hamitic, and Negroid genes had been entering Rhodesia; but now the proportion of Negroid blood had so increased that the newcomers were hardly distinguishable from modern Bantu.

We are uncertain what prodigous stimulus set these Bantu-speaking people migrating southwards from a nuclear region round the great lakes of central Africa. It was a movement which lasted a thousand years and only ceased near the southern extremity of the continent when it clashed with Dutch colonists trekking northwards from the Cape. Often the Bantu diaspora slowed down to a mere trickle; sometimes it halted for long periods; but always it would begin again as more nomadic people followed the winding game trails of tropical Africa, turning sometimes eastwards and sometimes westwards, but always trending south again as though guided by inexorable instinct. It seemed that some vital life force was driving this procession of human beings into one of the largest mass population movements of world history. That movement was not stimulated by the thoughts of plunder which set Asiatic hordes surging through Europe in deliberate wars of conquest, but can be better compared to the spreading out of the American pioneers across the prairies of their own land many centuries later. For the migrants of Sub-Saharan Africa moved south because there they could find limitless land to cultivate and game without number to hunt. Century after century, they launched themselves, like pedestrian astronauts, into earthly space, and in doing so they peopled a subcontinent.

The Bantu entering Rhodesia combined the characteristics of their Negro, Hamitic, and Khoisan ancestors in proportions which varied from clan to clan, but they all spoke a common root language. They had crossed the Zambesi first as families, and now about A.D. 800 as whole tribes. By the end of the millennium the Tonga and Tavara were already settled in the Zambesi valley and according to some authorities the Rozwi had pushed further south and were occupying the southern part of the great Rhodesian plateau. Soon afterwards Sotho and Nguni people passed through the country, crossed the Limpopo, and headed south. They were followed by another tribe whom today we call the Karanga,* but it is doubtful whether these Bantu immigrants used that name to describe themselves at this time. They had not by then developed the same sense of nationality as contemporary Europeans who without hesitation would have told an inquisitive stranger that they were, for instance, Greeks or Frenchmen. Probably the people now entering Rhodesia would have been surprised by any inquiry as to their tribal name, and would have merely answered that they were subjects of their paramount chief, the Mambo. One tradition affirms that the word Karanga had an autochthonous derivation and meant 'the children of the Sun', but another one suggests that it is a word meaning 'maidens' and that it was mistakenly applied to a whole people by an early Portuguese adventurer who, having encountered some young girls, was told that Karanga was the Bantu word to describe them.

Once across the Zambesi, the majority of the Karanga went no further: they settled on the great plateau, subjugating or absorbing the 'stamped-ware' peoples already living there, and acknowledging the Mambo, the head of one of their dominant clans, as the paramount chief. The Karanga brought with them the cult and sacerdotal equipment of the worship of Mwari.† Their concept

---

* The date of the arrival of the Karanga in Rhodesia is conjectural: one authority suggests that it took place as late as 1325.

† An earlier name for Mwari was Musikawanu ('our creator'); in recent times the deity has become known as the M'Limo.

of Mwari was of a peaceful, all-powerful and omnipresent God, and in some ways it resembled that of the ancient Israelites for Jehova; but if there is any truth in the suggestion that the name Mwari is derived from Allah it is conceivable that the Karanga religion was influenced by Islam at an early stage. Mwari was considered to be primarily concerned with the phenomena of nature, but he was not so remote from ordinary human beings as to be inaccessible to supplication and prayer. Some clans approached Mwari through both the Mambo, the divine King, and a theocracy of acolytes known as 'the children of Mwari' practising at recognised shrines which were usually caves, but sometimes prominent trees and boulders. Other Karanga clans, however, made their supplication to the High Deity through the mediation of ancestral spirits, who were themselves approached through spirit mediums or *mondoros*. The *mondoros* were ordinary men and women of the community who were believed to have been 'possessed' by the ancestral spirits, and the approach was usually made at their forefathers' graves. A whole hierarchy of ancestral spirits was recognised, each clan revering one particular intermediary rather in the manner that people in different regions of medieval Europe recognised their own patron saint. The spirit of Chiminuka was believed to be especially powerful as an intercessor and to possess the ability to interpret the squawkings of the fish eagles which carried Mwari's pronouncements. Today the spirit of the Monomatapa Nogomo stands in similarly high repute.

The chief shrine to Mwari, because he was a rain god, was set up by the Karanga on a high rocky hill close to the Nyamungwe river in an oasis-like area that enjoys a consistently high rainfall; close by the huts of the Mambo and 'children of Mwari' went up on the site of an earlier settlement built by the Ancients.

Successive Karanga chiefs were buried near the shrine and the place came to be spoken of as Zimbabwe—the graves of the chiefs. In the course of time Zimbabwe became recognised as the temporal and spiritual capital of the Karanga nation; and later still when the Mambo moved his residence the name was applied to his court as well.

The Mambo derived his power from the acceptance of his

divinity by the Karanga and from his right to monopolise the appointment of all officers of state. His agents were clan chiefs, relatives, and 'the children of Mwari' who were initially employed as religious messengers to the scattered Karanga clans, but who gradually became invested with a second 'political' function as spies and informers.

The Karanga of Rhodesia, like the Ancients before them, were good prospectors and continued to exploit the mineral wealth of their country, but few of their mines went deeper than 100 feet, and the majority were simple open stopes. The gold-bearing ore was hauled out of the mines in baskets, split up by alternate applications of heat and cold, and finally crushed under rocking boulders or in the mortars ground into rocks which can be seen still beside many Rhodesian streams. The Karanga bartered their gold winning directly with Moslem traders and it seems to have been exported at first along a route that crossed the Zambesi near Tete and ended at the port of Kilwa, which the Arabs had established on the coast about A.D. 700. A shorter trade route to Sofala subsequently served the Manica goldfields, while gold from the southern parts of the plateau appears to have been sent down to a harbour on the Sabi river near its confluence with the Lundi. It has been estimated that before the arrival of the Portuguese during the sixteenth century, £75 million worth of gold was taken from the Rhodesian goldfields.

The outcrops of granite which are such a feature of Karangaland happen to laminate very easily into rectangular blocks and they make ideal building material; probably simple stone walls were being set up along the plateau before the advent of the Karanga, and now the earlier technique of their predecessors was developed on a massive scale as the Mambo's state became increasingly well organised. The Arab traders who visited this country in the far interior began to speak of it as Guruhuswa,* Gunuhutwa, Butua and other variants. And as the *laissez-faire* attitude of the Karanga rulers altered during the early fifteenth century, the country became recast in a more military pattern after being exposed to the pressures of Bantu tribes driven out

* Guruhuswa means broad grasslands.

of the Kalahari by its increasing aridity; slowly the Mambo's power increased and the complex hierarchical structure of the future empire of Monomatapa began to take shape. Then, about 1450, a sudden outburst of energy sent the Karanga careering off on wars of conquest which were to extend the boundaries of their state as far as the Indian Ocean.

*   *   *   *   *

It is difficult for us of the twentieth century to appreciate just how important salt was to primitive human communities after they had turned from nomadism to a life based on agriculture. For when milk and raw or roasted animal flesh had formed the foundation of men's diets, there had been no need to supplement it with salt; but after their food became largely cereal and vegetable, life without it could barely be supported. Three pieces of evidence will serve to demonstrate the value placed on salt by the classical world: its association with solemn covenants, the payment of Roman soldiers in salt (whence comes our word salary), and the significance of the great trade routes linking the salt mines of the Libyan desert as described by Herodotus. It should not therefore strike us as one of the more absurd caprices of central African history that the fifteenth-century growth of Guruhuswa into the Bantu empire of Monomatapa originated from a craving for salt. Until 1450 most of the salt used by the Karanga was extracted from burnt grass and animal dung, and only scanty supplies of it were available. The shortage was particularly resented in the relatively sophisticated court at Zimbabwe and it was therefore a very notable event when one of the Mambo's servants about 1440 returned from Tonga country with the dramatic news that salt could be obtained there in ample quantities from Arabs trading in that part of the Zambesi valley known as the Dande. According to tradition Mutota, the reigning Mambo, was informed of this development (in words which seem to be the first ones recorded in Rhodesian history) with the exhortation 'cease now from eating the droppings of goats'.

Mutota moved north at once with a Karanga army (the expedition is so well remembered that even today descendents of the Karanga still sing the commemorative song *Ndende Dande* —'we are going to get salt from the Dande'). He quickly subjugated the Tonga and Tavara living in this part of the Zambesi valley, and the conquered tribes were so impressed by the number of soldiers Mutota was able to put into the field that they called them the Makorekore, or locusts, and spoke of the Mambo himself as Mwene Mutapa—the 'master pillager'.*

Mutota accepted his new designation as a compliment and added it to his dynastic titles, to be preferred to that of Mambo. The Europeans who later visited the far interior were fascinated

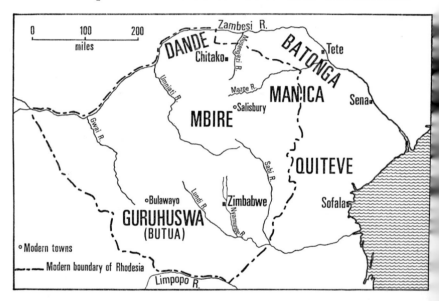

The Provinces of the Monomatapan Empire

by the title; it has appeared in over a hundred different spelling forms and it took on the same sort of aura as that of the Great Mogul and Grand Cham of Tartary. But unhappily for future

* One explanation of the name accepted by some modern Karanga is that it is derived from Munhu-Mutapwa, a praise name bestowed on a chief who was powerful enough to enslave his subjects.

historians the title Monomatapa was used indiscriminately to refer not only to the Karanga ruler, but to his country and his subjects as well.

After the conquest of the Dande the centre of gravity of Karanga power shifted northward and Mutota moved his capital from Great Zimbabwe to a more central position on the escarpment overlooking the Zambesi valley. His new Zimbabwe was built on the slopes of Chitako Hill close to the great pile of Fura, now renamed Mount Darwin. A second stronghold to protect the villages in the lowlands was set up on the Utete river, close to its confluence with the Musengezi. Great Zimbabwe now reverted to provincial status, and (since archaeological evidence suggests that the temple was sacked and burned sometime after 1450, perhaps in a peasant revolt after the Karanga army had moved north) it was probably temporarily abandoned.

Mutota died soon after his conquest of the Dande, and Karanga tradition dwells at some length on the curious manner in which his heir was chosen from among his many sons. According to this story, which must have been told as often as our own Arthurian legends, the Monomatapa's corpse proved too heavy to be raised onto its funeral bier, but the great wife of the dead man revealed that if one of his sons consented to have ritual intercourse with his half sister, Nyamahita, he would be given the strength to raise his father's body, and this would be the sign that he should inherit the Karanga kingdom. A son named Matope was the only one to comply and he was at once acclaimed as Monomatapa II.

One is reminded here of the way the divine kings of ancient Egypt kept their royal blood unsullied by a similar practice of incest. And if in succeeding generations this was to impair the calibre of the later Monomatapas, Matope at least was unaffected by consanguinity and he became one of the great conquerors of Africa. His conquests began soon after his father, the first Monomatapa, had been interred on the sacred hill of Chitako, when according to African folk-lore eight baobab trees were planted round the grave; two of these trees are still alive and today provide a living link with the first of the great Karanga kings.

Matope and Nyamahita—the William and Mary of Rhodesian history—ruled an enlarged Karangaland for the next thirty years. Before he died Matope had expanded his state into an empire which stretched from the Gwai river to the Indian Ocean; it thus included most of modern Rhodesia and a great deal of the southern half of Mocambique. The sheer size of the empire necessitated a certain amount of decentralisation, and relatives or trusted servants were deputed to rule Guruhuswa in the south, Mbire the central province, and the newly conquered lands bordering on the sea. Of all these Karanga proconsuls, we need take note only of Changa, one of Matope's sons by a slave wife.* Changa was an ambitious and capable soldier who was made custodian of the royal cattle herds and thus attained a far-reaching political influence. He chose to make his provincial headquarters at Great Zimbabwe and thus gained the prestigious control of the 'children of Mwari' at this shrine. But if Changa had any ideas about seceding from the empire, he was careful not to show his hand until after his father's death.

Matope died about 1480, and it is impossible to withhold admiration for all that had been accomplished during his reign. On the spiritual side the Mwari cult (which is based on a fundamental belief that although a man's body may die, his spirit lives on) had been so developed that it was later able to withstand the successive impacts of Islam and Christianity. For the Karanga faith developed a true religious sense although it must be admitted that it was perhaps more open to exploitation by an unscrupulous priesthood (especially if its members practised ventriloquism) than other theologies; we find a Portuguese without any condescension comparing the Karanga beliefs to Christianity and writing that they 'acknowledge only one god', and that 'they call upon the royal *Muzimos* or *Mondoros* as we the saints'.

In temporal matters the achievements of the Karanga in Monomatapan times pay tribute to their having attained probably the most advanced cultural level ever seen in Bantu Africa. The ruins of over a hundred stone-building complexes proclaim the

---

* Some authorities maintain that Changa was not the son of Matope, but of a Rozwi chief who had married one of the Monomatapa's daughters.

material prosperity of their country.* A flourishing gold industry, based on more than six hundred identified mines, was developed, and a profitable trade was conducted with Moslems of whom no less than ten thousand are said to have lived in the empire during its heyday; even if this figure may be an exaggeration, there is no doubt that Moslems exerted considerable influence in Monomatapa, for we have evidence that Indian overseers managed the mining operations while Arabs controlled the carrying trade.

The emperor ruled a court which was a strange *mélange* of an African kraal, Imperial Byzantium, and a Gilbert and Sullivan operetta. Much of our knowledge of the Monomatapan *beau monde* comes from the accounts of Portuguese visitors during the sixteenth century, and in them one expects at every page to come across references to the Lord High Executioner, or the Varengarian Guards. According to the Portuguese, a multitude of office-bearers swarmed in the palace bearing such imposing titles as 'The King's Right Hand', 'Keeper of the Royal Relics', 'Major Domo', 'The King's Doorkeeper', and 'The King's Apothecary'. A certain degree of elegance graced the imperial ménage after imported luxuries came into use: graceful ceramics and Chinese porcelain were displayed, probably as tokens of prestige; Persian carpets adorned the Monomatapa's living quarters; and use was made of gold, copper, and tin ornaments. The Monomatapa maintained an enormous harem, ruled by a 'Great Wife'; one of them is credited with espousing no less than three thousand wives but he drastically reduced their number after suffering from severe indigestion on one occasion when he had four hundred of them executed for casting evil spells. Yet there was a certain sophistication among the courtiers: one admiring Portuguese account for instance declares that they talked 'the best and most polished of the kaffir tongues that I have heard spoken. . . . They speak in metaphors with very just comparisons, used most appropriately for the purpose and interest, to which all designs are directed'; another visitor is even more complimentary about their diction for he writes that 'whereas the Moores of Africa

* Although most of the ruins were plundered by prospectors at the turn of the last century, rich rewards await future archaeologists working in them.

and Arabia draw their words out of the throat as if they would vomite, these pronounce their words with the end of the tongue and lips, that they speak many words in a whistling accent, wherein they place great elegance'.

No doubt we should discount many of the more eulogistic Portuguese reports of the polish and cultivation of the Monamatapan élite since many of them were more concerned with impressing Lisbon than with a strict adherence to the truth. But without any doubt they provide us with occasional accurate and vivid glimpses of conditions in Rhodesia four centuries ago. Thus one Portuguese dispatch has this to say about the Monomatapa's palace near the sacred hill of Chitako: 'The dwelling in which the Monomatapa resides is very large and is composed of many houses surrounded by a great wooden fence, within which there are three dwellings, one for his own person, one for the queen, and another for his servants who wait upon him within doors. There are three doors opening upon a great courtyard, one for the service of the queen, beyond which no man may pass, but only women, another for his kitchen, only entered by his cooks, who are two young men from among the principal lords of his kingdom, his relations in whom he has most confidence, and the lads who serve in the kitchen, who are also nobles between fifteen and twenty years of age. These are also employed to lay the food when the king wishes to eat, which they spread upon the ground, upon a carpet or mat, with muslin extended above, and many different kinds of meat are set before him, all roasted or boiled, such as hens, pigeons, partridges, capons, sheep, venison, hares, rabbits, cows, rats, and other game, of which, after the king has eaten, a portion is given to some of his servants who are always provided from his table . . . the king will not be served by those who know a woman, but only by these youths, who are enjoined to observe chastity so long as they serve the king, and if any one is found guilty of the opposite vice he is severely punished and expelled from the king's service.'

All power and influence in the Karanga state was centralised in the emperor. He controlled its entire commerce, just as he directed the craftsmen who built his palaces and temples. And the Monomatapa commanded the most formidable army in the far interior. From Portuguese sources we learn that he was able to put 100,000 men into the field, and that their regimental commanders could be recognised by special banners. Duarte Barbosa, in describing these imperial officers, tells us that 'they carry swords thrust into wooden scabbards, bound with much gold and other metals, worn on the left side as with us in cloth girdles which they make for this purpose with four or five knots with hanging tassels to denote men of rank'. The army included both sexes for another Portuguese report after alluding to the Monomatapa's regiments goes on to say that 'the more valorous of his soldiers are his Legions of Women, who burn off their left Paps with Fire, because they should be no hindrance in shooting, after the manner of the ancient Amazons. Their weapons are Bows and Arrows. . . . The King grants them certain Countries where they dwell by themselves; only they sometimes keep company with men for Generation's sake.'

Just as the Monomatapa's authority was supported by a warrior aristocracy, so in the spiritual field the emperor's position was buttressed by a closed hierarchy of priestly appointees. In sixteenth-century Mocaranga these priests combined with military commanders and cadet members of the ruling dynasty to form a Bantu élite: they were the 'manipulators' of power in political, commercial, and religious spheres alike, and the mere fact that this élite existed bears testimony to the Karanga abandonment of the usual Bantu concept of unrelenting orthodoxy in every aspect of life. Some strain in their blood had allowed them to recognise the inequality of individual endowment and this perhaps was the most significant mental breakthrough made by the Karanga. Here in Monomatapa the aimless repetitive cycle of Bantu life stopped turning over; the customary fatalistic acceptance of a subsistence economy and a sterile preoccupation with the past were both renounced. The members of the élite had something to sell or had inherited power, and they became such material individualists that one feels they would have been at home in feudal Europe and even in a modern capitalistic state. Undoubtedly the ruling class did very well for themselves; they accumulated wealth and succeeded in perpetuating ownership of property. But what is more significant, they developed a capacity for organisation which makes the élite of Monomatapa stand out from the cringing anonymity of Bantu history. Despite all its anachronisms they had evolved a perfectly stable system of government which even if it was a good deal less than perfect and was based to a very large extent on harnessing the humility and easily aroused credibility of their vassals, could also fairly claim to have given the lower classes security and a standard of living higher by far than that endured by the peasants of India today.

There was a stirring of curiosity in the Karanga state, a desire for improvement, and a refusal to suffocate any longer on ingrained habits. In the Monomatapa of its heyday one feels that sorcery and archaic customs did not entirely dominate people's actions. The Karanga even became sufficiently civilised to show benevolence to the unfortunate: the emperor we learn from another Portuguese source 'shows great charity to the blind and maimed, for these are called the king's poor, and have land and revenues for their subsistence'. It was also to their credit that they adopted an original and reasonably accurate calendar, which has continued in use to the present day: 'They have six holidays in every month', our earlier authority tells us, 'which they divide into three weeks of ten days each, counting from the day of the new moon to the last day of that moon, and thus they allow thirty days to each month. In the first week they keep the fourth day of the moon and the seventh; and when the first ten days are done they begin to count another ten, and they keep the fourth, which is the fourteenth day of the moon, and the seventh, which is the seventeenth day of the moon; and when the second ten days are done they begin to count another ten days and keep the fourth, day, which is the twenty-fourth day of the moon, and the seventh which is the twenty-seventh; and when the three tens are done they begin a new month with the appearance of the new moon. In this they are so correct that they never mistake a day of the moon.'

We hear something on this same subject and gain a glimpse of imperial ritual from another source: 'Every month has its Festival

Days, and is divided into three weeks, each of ten days. The first Day is that of the new Moon, and the Festivals the fourth and fifth of each week. On these days they put on their best apparel: and the King gives public Audiences to all, holding a Truncheon about three-quarters of a yard long in each Hand, as it were leaning upon it. . . . On the Day the new Moon appears the King with two Javelins runs about in his House as if he was fighting. The great Men are present at this Pastime, and it being ended, a Pot full of Indian Wheat, boiled whole, is brought, which he scatters about the ground, bidding them eat, because it is the Growth of the Earth. The greatest holy Day is the first Day of the Moon of May. They call it "Chuavo". On this Day, all the great Men, who are a vast number, resort to Court, and there, with javelins in their Hands, run about representing a Fight. The Sport lasts all Day: Then the King withdraws, and is not seen in eight days after; during which time the Drums never cease beating. On the last day he orders the Noblemen he has least affection for to be killed. This is in the nature of a Sacrifice he offers to his Muzimos or ancestors. . . . This done the Drums cease, and every Man goes home.'

Yet for all their advances, no power was ever known in Monomatapa more effective than that of human muscle; even at the height of the empire's vitality neither the wheel nor plough were in use, nor were draught animals employed. All Karanga knowledge depended on experience and the spoken word. They never adopted any form of writing and preferred to polish their culture by a progressive sophistication of archaic skills than to broaden it by imitating alien practices; rather they instinctively and adamantly repudiated all foreign influences.

But still one feels that for a moment of time towards the end of the fifteenth century the subjects of Monomatapa stood trembling on the brink of a spiritual and material progress more dramatic than anything that had been achieved in Bantu Africa before. It was as though they had been affected by the magic of their land and their imagination had become a pliant bow which shot out arrows of bizarre energy at random. For the Karanga were suddenly possessed of originality and creative vitality which were typified in the exuberant and sometimes contorted idioms of architectural style that still intrigue modern visitors to Rhodesia. At the time when the Renaissance was breathing fresh life into Europe, the Karanga too had seized the initiative from their own harsh continent which is always pitiless to the weak and ignorant. We can only guess at the expansion of their psyche had they been able to grasp their opportunity more firmly. But after its brief moment of strength, on Matope's death it seemed that the vitalising energy in Karangaland was suddenly switched off, and the intellect of its people drifted back into the old backwaters. Succeeding emperors dissipated their strength in palace intrigues and civil wars. Yet the ferment which had made the Karanga advance so far still exists in the modern Africans of Rhodesia, and only needs to be reactivated for them to take their proper place in the world.

All Matope's sons, with the exception of the base-born Changa, were weaklings. Already two of them had been expressly excluded from the succession because of indiscretions with their father's wives, and the others were jealous men and constantly at each others' throats. And so after 1480 the customary *danse macabre* performed by the principals in a disputed succession began to shake the Karanga empire to pieces: Mavura I, after reigning for only a few weeks, is murdered; the succession passes to another son, Nyahuma, whom Changa openly defies from his strong position in the central and southern provinces; soon Changa, who now identifies his interests with the Rozwi, initiates Rhodesia's first unilateral declaration of independence by seceding from the empire and proclaiming the new state of Urozwi. As the Monomatapa's power declines, Changa finds allies among the Moslems who flock to his court at the holy city of Great Zimbabwe, and when they address him ingratiatingly as 'Amir' he delightedly fuses the honorific to his own name and assumes 'Changamire' as a dynastic title and mode of address.

The story of the Karanga continues to unfold in a way made familiar to us all by European wars of succession. 'They are nearly always at variance among themselves' explains one disparaging Portuguese chronicler: Changamire attacks Nyamhuma's stronghold, killing him together with most of his family, and usurps the Monomatapan throne; four years later, Changamire in his turn is defeated and killed by Chikuyo Chisamarengu, the only remaining son of Nyamhuma. An account of these reversals of fortune has been given to us almost in biblical prose by a Portuguese chronicler which we can take up when Changa attacks the king Nyahuma: '. . . and when the ameer [Changamire] saw that the king wished to kill him he made up his mind to kill the king in the city where he was, which is called Zimahauhy [Zimbabwe]: and he took with him many people; and when he arrived near the city the grandees who were with the king knew that he was coming, they went to receive him, and when they saw him coming in that way they would not remain in the city but went out of it; and the ameer went to the houses of the king, which were of stone and clay very large and of one storey, and he entered where the king was with his slaves and some other men; and while speaking to the king the ameer cut his head off; and as he killed him, he made himself king; and all obeyed him; and he reigned peacefully four years; and the king left twenty-two children; and the ameer killed them all, except one, the eldest, who was still young, whose name was Kwekarynugo, who is now the king; and this one fled to another kingdom of his uncle; and when he was twenty years old, he took possession of the kingdom with many people of his father, who came to join him; and he marched against the ameer who had killed his father, in a field close to the town. And when the ameer saw that he was coming upon him, he sent many people to fight with him; and the son of the king killed many people of the ameer; and when the ameer saw that they had killed so many people, he came out to fight with him; and the son of the king killed the ameer in the field; and the battle lasted three days and a half, in which many people were killed on both sides.'

Stalemate followed: Chikuyo Chisamarengu was never quite strong enough to evict Changa's son from Great Zimbabwe; the new Changamire was too weak to regain his father's conquests, but his dynasty continued to present a threat to the diminished empire of Monomatapa. The reign of Chikuyo Chisamarengu is, however, notable because during it his court was visited by a

Portuguese adventurer named Antonio Fernandes, and the documented history of Rhodesia began.

From then on increasing numbers of Europeans journeyed into the Monomatapa's country which they called Mocaranga, and there complicated an already complex struggle for power. Although our knowledge of the course of its subsequent developments may be imprecise probably it is as factual as the history of Anglo-Saxon England which was taught to our grandparents. We know that in 1530 Chikuyo Chisamerengu was followed as Monomatapa by his nephew Neshangwe, and that Neshangwe evicted the Changamire of his time from the province of Mbire, and took the additional praise name of Munembire. For a short time it seemed then that he and his successor, Chivere Nyasoro, might restore the glories of the empire. But during the reign of Nogomo Mapunzagutu, the next Monomatapa, Mocaranga was confronting a power stronger than Urozwi, and gradually it became dominated by the Portuguese of Mocambique. Nogomo, a professed Christian, died in 1589, and we are lucky to have an account of the subsequent ritual obsequies which gives us a concept of the ceremonies that attended the death of a sixteenth-century Karanga emperor: the body of Nogomo was first bathed and shaved by his widows, and parings from his finger and toe nails were carefully buried outside the royal hut. The corpse was then placed on a trestle standing inside his chief hut, and six pots placed below it to catch the liquid products of putrefaction (these unpleasant humours were later made into 'medicine' which was smeared over the next emperor to ensure his fecundity). The body was now reverently swathed in a winding sheet, and secured to the trestle by the wrists and ankles to prevent it rising with the dead man's spirit when it left the body. For the next three months the funeral-hut was sealed off and guarded day and night, until the High Priest of Mwari could announce that decomposition was complete.

This was the signal for the holding of a great dance followed by a mammoth beer drink and the prolonged beating of the deceased emperor's war-drum. The ceremony concluded with the Monomatapa's burial inside his hut: with him were interred a beer pot, the body of a greyhound which had recently been presented to Nogomo by the Governor of Mocambique, his weapons, wooden plates, and bundles of washing fibre. The hut was now planted round with thorn bushes. Black bulls were slaughtered, and a solemn announcement stating that 'the mountain has fallen down' was dispatched round the empire.

The long delay between the emperor's death and final interment gave the Karanga elders an opportunity to examine the potentials of his possible successors, and only after some months did the ancestral spirits 'announce' that their choice had fallen upon a member of the royal family named Gatsi Rusere. He succeeded to an empire which by now had shrunk by the secession of border provinces to the size of England; it was coming under increasing Portuguese control, and it was being attacked by the Zimba, a horde of cannibal warriors, who came pouring over the Zambesi. From now on the story of the fragmented Karanga empire becomes a confused and somewhat incoherent record of invasions and bloodshed, of shifting alliances and vandalism. Much of the empire was depopulated; the surviving inhabitants of its eastern marches are known to have taken refuge from the Zimba in the inhospitable mountain country of Inyanga. But help came from the Portuguese; they assisted Gatsi Rusere to repulse the Zimba, yet the moment he felt strong enough the new Monomatapa led a national revolt against the white men. He was crushingly defeated, obliged to cede the rich Chicova silver mines to the king of Portugal, and to accept a Portuguese guard of men-at-arms in his palace. Further fragmentation of the empire followed and its condition can be likened now to that of a train careering down a steep gradient very nearly out of control, with a foreign passenger struggling on the footplate to take over from the incompetent driver as the coaches uncouple one by one and break away.

The remainder of the chronicle of the Monomatapan saga can be quickly told: it became a blood-feud country. Gatsi Rusere's heir, Nyambo Kapararidze (whom the Portuguese called Capracina), led another rebellion against the Europeans and was replaced by a puppet emperor—Mavura II—who reigned until 1652. The names of subsequent Monomatapas continue to read like the index of Gibbon's *Decline and Fall*: Siti Kazurukumusapa, Kamharapasu Mulombwe, Nyamatinde Mhande, Myemyedzi Zenda, Boroma Dangwarangwa, Samatambira Nyamhando, Dehwe Mapunzagutu all reign obscurely one after the other over the dwindling empire, whose very existence is owed to the grace of the Governor of Mocambique. The story of decline and disintegration continues until in 1720 the Monomatapan court finally left Rhodesian soil and moved to the Tete district where it could be protected by Portuguese guns. Like the sycophants of a Bantu Estoril, the tiny Karanga community there continued to make obeisances to a powerless emperor and deeper reverences to Portuguese officials, but its very existence was precarious and by now quite irrelevant to the Karanga people of the Rhodesian plateau. The courtiers remind us of ghostly actors on a darkened stage, who continue to speak their lines although the audience has gone home. In the eighteen-fifties a brief spotlight falls on the set, illuminates the survivors of the Monomatapan *ancien régime*, and focuses on Katuruza, the twenty-fourth Monomatapa, as Dr Livingstone takes grave note of him in his best-selling *Missionary Travels in South Africa*. Only in 1917 does the rule of this incredible Bantu dynasty come to its end when Choko, the twenty-seventh Monomatapa revolts and is deposed by the Portuguese. But the memory of the old heroic glories of the Imperial house linger on in Rhodesia today; the descendants of the Monomatapas who are said to have inherited the rain-making powers of their ancestors are still revered in the Dande, and Chitako remains a nostalgic *genius loci* for the Africans. For the crumbling ruins of Mutota's old palace, half-buried by the bush, is one of those rare places of the world which retains a real aura of the past. It is as though all the piled experiences of human emotion which were once aroused there have soaked their intangible memorials into these scattered stones. And its guardians say that the visitor who lingers after nightfall at Chitako when the moon is new will hear the poundings of Kagurukute, Mutota's great war-drum, which the spirits continue to beat over his grave.

3

THE PORTUGUESE CONQUEST

Sofala, Quiloa, Mocambique, Quelimane, Mocadaco—how exciting their names look on the old maps of the east African coast. They conjure up visions of caravels and dhows, of men in heavy armour sweltering in the tropical sun and sickly white women borne in palanquins by sweating slaves; they speak of Portuguese forts whose culverins and falconets frown from massive stone walls at squalid kaffir huts on the further side of brackish mangrove swamps. These forts are ruined and deserted now, but once they were the stepping stones of conquistadors who expanded Portugal's maritime empire into the Indian Ocean. Each citadel could tell bloodstained stories of siege and massacre, but their sagas all stem from the day in February, 1488, when the flagship of Bartholomew Dias doubled the Cape of Good Hope. For a week Dias had run down the west African coast before a storm and quite out of touch with land. But when the rough weather abated he had steered north-eastwards, looking for a landfall, and early on 3rd February his mariners heard the noise of pounding surf ahead. As the first streaks of light appeared in the sky that day they saw a smudge of darkness which slowly resolved itself into a range of low hills. Later the flagship dropped anchor in an open roadstead, which, after obtaining a glimpse of Hottentots tending their cattle, Dias named Angra dos Vaqueiros —the Bay of the Herdsmen. Today it is known as Mossel Bay. Beyond the bay the coast was seen trending to the east and north, and a warm current flowed down it. Clearly Dias had doubled the southern extremity of Africa and the sea route to the Indies lay open.

Looking back on it now it seems rather strange that the Portuguese did not immediately exploit their breakthrough into the Indian Ocean. Not until 1497 did Vasco da Gama make a real effort to extend Dias' discoveries and pioneer a sea route to India. During his epic voyage da Gama sent home detailed reports of a succession of Arab cities on the east African coast whose material culture, he said, rivalled (and often surpassed) that of contemporary Europe. It seems too that he learned something about a powerful empire in the far interior, and in 1502 a reference is made by another mariner to a walled city there. Da Gama's discoveries in Africa and India were now quickly followed up. In 1505 Francisco d'Almeida set out from Lisbon with a fleet of twenty-one sail and orders to gain naval control of the Indian Ocean. He was also instructed to establish a refreshment and trading station at Sofala near modern Beira, and by the September of 1505 a fort was already taking shape there. It was intended to be not so much a victualling station as a point of departure for the African interior, and an entrepôt which would tap the rich gold trade conducted by the coastal Arabs with the fabled empire of Monomatapa.

It must be admitted that the immediate results which followed the establishment of a Portuguese garrison at Sofala were disappointing since the Arabs found little difficulty in diverting the gold trade to a string of small ports higher up the coast. Presently royal remonstrations were streaming to Sofala from Lisbon and the military governor of the fort was instructed to secure the trade at its source: in 1511 he accordingly dispatched an emissary to Monomatapa's court to spy out conditions in Karangaland.

It was customary during the sixteenth century for the Portuguese to entrust dangerous missions of this kind to convicted felons on the understanding that they would be pardoned if they carried them out successfully. A *degradado* named Antonio Fernandes was chosen for the task of exploring Monomatapa. This convict was the first white man to enter present-day Rhodesia.

One must pause for a moment at this point to consider the magnitude and danger of the undertaking to which Fernandes had been committed. No one had more than the slightest idea of what he would find in the interior and in terms of distance alone the journey called for tremendous stamina and fortitude. Danger could be expected from wild animals, unknown diseases, and Karanga fighting men, and from Moslem traders too who would be certain to resent any threat to their monopoly of the gold trade. But Fernandes was a product of an age when all Portugal was inspired by unbounded faith and dynamic energy: its people accomplished feats which at any other time would have been considered beyond the scope of human endeavour. We glimpse something of this spirit that animated the Portuguese conquistadors of Africa and India in Camoes' *Lusiads* for in this, his country's most epic poem, their exhilaration at having gazed on new horizons finds its perfect expression. Fernandes the *degradado* accomplished his hazardous mission with a proficiency and dispatch which can have been scarcely matched in the annals of African exploration, and one feels pleased that this first white man to know Rhodesia was rewarded with a withdrawal of the order of banishment from his homeland, a knighthood, and—a final honour—the gift of two oxen on instructions from the king himself.

When Fernandes returned to Sofala at the end of his visit to the court of Monomatapa he had an arresting story to tell, and it must be considered fortunate that much of his report has survived the somewhat drastic editing to which it was submitted. Fernandes' account begins prosaically enough: 'These are the kings there are from Sofala to the mines of Monomatapa', he writes, 'and the things to be found in each of these kingdoms'; but he goes on to give us our first panorama of the far interior as seen through European eyes. And no one could complain that it lacked interest: Fernandes for instance tells us that one Karanga chief 'mines a great deal of gold throughout his land, and this man saw it being drawn and he says it can be seen where the gold lies because a herb like clover grows over it and that the greatest he saw mined in one day was a large basket full of bars the size of a finger and large nuggets.' It is difficult for us to make out Fernandes' exact itinerary from his report, but it seems that he first made his way to Embiri where he found the reigning Monomatapa, Chikuyo, living in a formidable fortress which, we learn from this first written description of a Zimbabwe,* 'he is now making of stone

* It is perhaps wise here to remind the reader that Zimbabwe means 'burial ground of the chiefs'. In practice it was applied to the towns—usually stone built —where the Monomatapa lived. In modern times the name has been loosely used to denote the ancient capital of Great Zimbabwe near Fort Victoria.

without mortar'. The place where the Bantu emperor and white adventurer met has been identified with some confidence as Samanyai Hill close to where the Musengezi river pours over the Zambesi escarpment, and all the past and the future of Rhodesia were gathered at the confrontation. Fortunately the two men seem to have got on very well together; Chikuyo was delighted with the muzzle-loaders which 'Furnanda' presented to him, and we can be certain that Fernandes was jubilant at having so easily achieved his most important objective of meeting this pagan emperor. We learn from his narrative that, like the good Catholic he was, Fernandes took the opportunity of giving Chikuyo some brief instruction in the tenets of the Christian faith. Afterwards the white man seems to have gone off on several separate journeys of exploration. We know that he penetrated into the Kingdom of Changamire(who, he states, 'is as great as the king of Monomatapa and is always at war with him'); he also made contact near Sinoia with Bushmen at whose stature and steatopygia he marvels in his narrative and, rather quaintly, remarks in passing that they have 'tails like sheep'. He travelled too as far as the Zambesi, and southwards to the Sabi river. By the time Fernandes got back to Sofala, he was convinced that if the Portuguese established a fort on the island in the Zambesi which was later to bear the fort and huts of Tete, and patrolled the river with a brigantine, they would be able to control its entire traffic: 'If this house was built there,' he declared, the king 'could have all the gold of this land and also that of Monomatapa', and he returns to the subject in another passage when he writes, 'if this house were to be built Your Highness would make the trade of Sofala safe'.

Admittedly Antonio Fernandes' report is sadly laconic, and some tantalising parts are open to several interpretations; nor can he be entirely blamed for having embellished his account of the wealth of the far interior in the hope that the authorities would grant him a free pardon. The important thing was that this unschooled convict's piece of travel literature which, in its own way is as exciting (and sometimes as imaginative) as any modern tourist brochure, had irrevocably committed Monomatapa to the modern world.

It must be considered wholly remarkable that Fernandes was able to travel in safety through the far interior where we would expect every Arab hand to have been raised against him, and one is driven to the conclusion that either the historians have greatly exaggerated the strength of Arab influence in Monomatapa or that Fernandes succeeded in passing himself off as a Moslem. As for the Karanga, there is some evidence that they accepted him, Cortes-like, as a visitor from the spirit world, for one account tells us that by them 'he was adored like a God'. Be this as it may, Fernandes' pioneering journey had opened the way into Monotmatapa and it was quickly followed up. Portuguese records show that within fifty years several European traders were well established at the Karanga court.

One of them, Antonia Caiado, stood high in the emperor's favour, and it is to him that we owe much of our knowledge of the next important event in Rhodesian history—the coming of the first Christian mission to the Karanga, and the martyrdom of the Jesuit priest, Dom Gonçalo da Silveira, at Chitako in 1561.

We possess several contemporary portraits of da Silveira, drawn by different pious hands, but all of them show a head that would have delighted Velazquez: in them we see the conventional aesthetic face with the proud Iberian nose of his genre, the short pointed beard, and the downcast eyes fixed it seems on eternity.

At the time of his arrival in Monomatapa da Silveira was in his middle thirties. His friends later remembered that during his childhood the priest exhibited certain manifestations which they believed clearly pointed to his having been destined for martyrdom: he was heard, they said, to cry from his mother's womb, and he startled everyone in Lisbon at the age of seven by refusing to drink wine. In 1543 the youth entered the newly-formed Society of Jesus, and a little later his novice master was gravely reporting to Saint Ignatius Loyola that his new pupil was '. . . a young man of sound and sober judgement, born to do great things. He has come to realise the truths of eternity, and has been stirred by such thoughts. He seems to have them stamped on his heart. He is strong and robust in body and needs to be restrained in his excessive austerities. But he is very tractable and responsive when corrected. He possesses remarkable gifts.'

For thirteen years after his ordination da Silveira laboured in metropolitan Portugal and during that time more indications of his sanctity were noted and recorded by his acquaintances: he fell into ecstasies; he was seen celebrating Mass with blood covering his hands; and one day he indicated foreknowledge of the manner of his martyrdom by explaining that 'I value this throat of mine above everything else in the world because it will be strangled so completely that my breath will cease and I shall die.'

In 1556 da Silveira received orders to proceed to Goa as Provincial of his order, and there he spent three unhappy years before receiving a missionary call to Africa. It was in response to a request from a native chief living near Inhambane on the coast for a teacher or *kasisi* to instruct his people in the white men's faith. Da Silveira was the obvious choice, and he leapt at the opportunity. He reached Mocambique on the 4th February, 1560, and from there made an adventurous journey to Inhambane. But da Silveira very soon decided that his real task lay in the conversion of the Monomatapa who, he had learned, ruled over a great empire in the interior, and the planting of the faith where it could flourish most abundantly. In the September of 1560 the priest accordingly set out for the Karanga capital. His biographer tells us that he went by sea to Quelimane and was then paddled up the Zambesi to the tiny Portuguese settlement of Sena. From Sena, he sent an envoy to Nogomo Makunzagutu, the reigning Monomatapa, asking for permission to enter his dominions and to sprinkle holy water on his imperial head.

As soon as Nogomo's consent reached Sena, da Silveira engaged carriers and set out on the last lap of his journey. He went by canoe to Tete, one hundred and fifty miles up river from Sena, and then walked to Chitako, probably along the Mazoe valley which was later to become the regular Portuguese trade route into the interior. It was a difficult journey: the rains had begun; he had to cross many rivers and we read that Dom Gonçalo, who could not swim, was pushed over them in a cooking pot. It was the Christmas week of 1560 when da Silveira at last reached Nogomo's Zimbabwe, to be enthusiastically welcomed by Antonio Caiado and the other resident Portuguese traders. But he was disappointed to find that the emperor had moved fifty miles away to a kraal in the Dande, which stood on the banks of the Musengezi just below its confluence with the Kadsi, and almost certainly in Mocambique a few hundred yards beyond the present Rhodesian borders.

On Christmas Day, 1560, at Chitako da Silveira celebrated the first Mass ever to be heard in Rhodesia. Next day, the anniversary of St Stephen the first Christian martyr, he walked down the escarpment to meet the Monomatapa, and to keep the appointment with death which he himself had prophesied.

The two men—the kasisi from across the seas and the pagan emperor—met on the last day of the year. They were utterly unlike each other in outlook and upbringing. Nogomo was to become a ruler of great renown, and to be revered by the Karanga after his death as one of the most powerful of their ancestral spirits, but in 1560 he was still an immature youth, unmarried, and very much under the influence of his mother. The young Monomatapa of course represented a state which, although barbarous in many ways, had yet reached the highest pitch of achievement ever to be attained unaided by Bantu Africa. Da Silveira on the other hand was a man who personified the intellectual fire of the counter reformation and the moral standards of a Church which could look back on fifteen hundred glorious years of history.

Caiado's account gives us a graphic description of this early confrontation of paganism and Christianity in the far interior: the kasisi he writes, is invited to enter the royal hut, and seats himself on a Persian rug beside Nogomo and his mother, while Caiado is ordered to stand nearby and interpret. The conversation, Caiado continues, begins with Nogomo expostulating because his visitor has returned the gifts of gold, oxen, and slaves which had been sent to him on his arrival; the priest in reply takes the opportunity of intimating that all he wants from the Monomatapa are opportunities to speak to him about his God and to sprinkle his head with sacred water which he has carried up from the coast for this very purpose.

As each man's words were interpreted by Caiado, we can be sure that both Nogomo and da Silveira were watching the other man's face very closely and trying to size up each other. They both looked forward to gaining some advantage from their meeting: the Monomatapa thought that his visitor might well become a potential ally in the dispute with a rebellious brother in which he happened to be engaged; Dom Gonçalo da Silveira regarded his host as the vehicle by which he would carry the Gospel into the interior. Privately however, the priest was finding it difficult to conceal his disappointment at the level of culture and intelligence attained by this youth who had been represented to him as a most powerful and enlightened potentate. But both men smile and mumble unmeaning little courtesies to each other and they part on the most cordial terms, the *kasisi* being conducted with some ceremony to a nearby hut which has been prepared for him.

Caiado's narrative goes on to record the somewhat bizarre events of the next few days with increasing gusto: da Silveira, he says, has by now unpacked his few belongings and some Karanga nobles passing his hut are startled to catch sight of the priest and a beautiful white woman at their devotions inside. Their report intrigues Nogomo, and at once he sends a message to the *kasisi* saying that he would like to meet his companion. In response the priest presently emerges from his hut carrying a bundle wrapped in costly cloths and takes it to the imperial presence; it is then unwrapped to reveal a painting of the Madonna.

The Monomatapa is entranced by it; never, he says, has he seen anything so beautiful, and after some discussion he persuades the priest to give the sacred portrait to him. It is reverently placed in Nogomo's sleeping quarters, and for several successive nights afterwards the emperor states that the Madonna in the picture has appeared to him and spoken in a language which he cannot, alas, comprehend. This, of course, was the sort of opportunity for which da Silveira had been waiting, and now the dazzled Nogomo learns that if he is to understand the message of the beautiful lady he must first attend to the teachings of the true Church and submit himself to baptism.

Soaring success now seemed to have blessed the first Christian mission to Monomatapa. Before the month is out, Nogomo, his mother and three hundred of his courtiers have all sought and accepted baptism, Nogomo being christened Sebastian, and his mother Maria. To Dom Gonçalo da Silveira it must have appeared that the flickering flame of faith which had been kindled in central Africa would be safeguarded now by the hands of the great Monomatapa himself, and spread throughout the empire.

But the shadow of dark wings were already over Dom Gonçalo, and the first victory of the Cross in Monomatapa was destined to be short-lived. The conflict of Christian and pagan tenets, as so often in Africa, soon became a subject that engulfed the Karanga court. The Moslem merchants already established there, recognising that any increase in European influence would damage their trade monopoly, were firmly opposed to the *kasisi*'s interests and they proceeded to poison Nogomo's mind against him by saying that he was a spy sent to prepare the way for an invading army of Portuguese, that he was in league with the Monomatapa's usurping brother, and more effective still, that he was a sorcerer who bewitched the Karanga by pouring water on their heads. They even declared that Dom Gonçalo had been seen stealing a bone from the grave of one of Nogomo's ancestors and intended to use it as magic to kill the Monomatapa.

For week after week the credulous Nogomo and his mother listened to charges of this sort, and soon they began to look on their *kasisi* with misgiving as he preached and baptised increasing numbers of Karanga postulants. Caiado's narrative conjures up a picture of Dom Gonçalo holding his services at make-shift altars within the royal and neighbouring kraals, while inside Nogomo's hut close by, a group of bearded brown-skinned men arrayed in embroidered gowns and turbans, huddle round the youthful emperor warning him again and again of the witchcraft that was being practised under his very eyes. Slowly Nogomo's first resolve to protect his white teacher weakened, and in the end he reacted as a man of his background and upbringing was bound to react when the twilight world of his pagan tradition clashed with the ethics of a faith which even denied him the polygamy which was so fundamental to his prestige. In fairness to Nogomo it must be recorded that he made one attempt to save the *kasisi*'s life by commanding him to leave the country; but very soon afterwards that order was rescinded and towards the middle of March, 1561, Nogomo agreed in council that this powerful white sorcerer must be put to death.

All through the hot weeks while Nogomo wavered between his friendship for the white man and his superstitious fear of witchcraft, da Silveira continued his mission to the Karanga and according to Caiado, during March, fifty more Africans accepted baptism at his hands. He was well aware of his danger but steadfastly refused his countrymen's insistent advice that he get away to safety while there was still time. Caiado tells us that Dom Gonçalo patiently explained instead that he could not abandon his converts, and assured one of the Portuguese traders that 'I know that the chief will kill me' but added 'I am delighted to receive so happy an end from the hand of God . . . it is certain that I am more ready to die than the Mohammedans to kill me.'

Although a certain amount of pious myth may have been woven into Dom Gonçalo's biography, Caiado's account of the final death-watch kept by this first Rhodesian martyr bears the ring of truth. We read of him dressed in his white robes pacing up and down in front of his hut on the last day of his life, and of the manner in which he declines his friends' advice to escape: he offers them instead absolution, and the gift of all his possessions except only his cassock, surplice, and crucifix.

It can have been no easy thing after they had gone for da Silveira to wait alone for death in the darkness of his hut. It came to him very early on the morning of Sunday, 16th March, 1561. The assassins chosen for the task entered noisily, threw the priest on his face, lifted him up by his feet and arms, drew a rope round his neck and then, by pulling on each end, strangled him in the fashion prescribed by the Karanga for all sorcerers. When da Silveira was dead they stripped his body of its surplice and of the hair shirt studded with nails which the priest had worn to subdue his living flesh; then they dragged the corpse, bleeding at the mouth, to the banks of the Musengezi and threw it into the river.*

Caiado went to the priest's hut later that morning and found a smashed crucifix and a trail of blood zigzagging from it through the dust to the river bank. His report of da Silveira's martyrdom made a deep impression in Portugal: it stimulated interest in the far interior and dressed it with an emotional desire to carry on his missionary work. Nogomo himself seems to have been deeply affected by the *kasisi*'s murder, less perhaps at first because of any stirrings of his conscience than by the series of catastrophes which now began to afflict the Karanga. Locusts devastated their crops; disastrous floods followed; famine and pestilence then raged for years throughout the empire; worst of all for Nogomo, da Silveira's bodily presence was replaced by visitations of his ghost. Young, and highly strung, Nogomo lost his nerve and, acting on an impulse, ordered the execution of his mother and the Moslems who had turned him against the *kasisi*. Still haunted by the memory of the dead man, he then dispatched an envoy to Sena carrying heartfelt expressions of penitence, together with a request that another Christian priest be sent to minister to his people. But he was not to escape the consequences of da Silveira's death thus easily. The white men had a *casus belli* now and a martyr to be revenged: and very soon plans were being laid at the Portuguese court of Lisbon for the conquest of Monomatapa by force of arms.

* * * * *

In the November of 1568 there was a tremendous stir in the Portuguese palace of Almeirim. Sebastian, the new king, was presiding over his first council of state. When the immediate business had been concluded, King Sebastian, sitting in his high, canopied chair, drew his counsellors' attention to their need to avenge the death of Dom Gonçalo da Silveira in central Africa,

---

* The weight of evidence suggests that Dom Gonçalo da Silveira was murdered some 400 yards inside the present border of Mocambique.

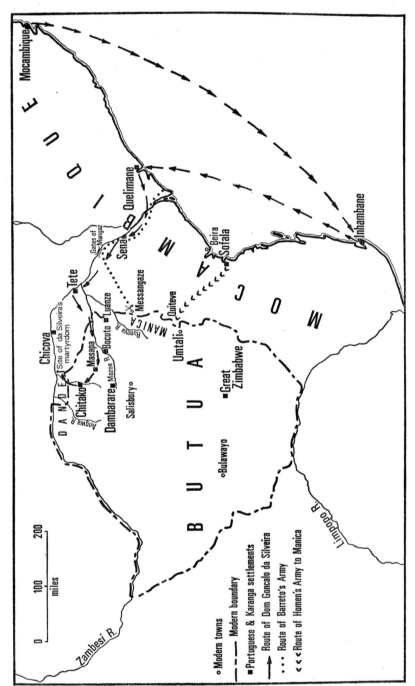

The Portuguese conquest

and he stressed the opportunity it gave their country of gaining control of the Monomatapan empire. This empire, he went on to say, was clearly the Ophir of the Bible whence the Queen of Sheba had drawn her wealth.* His thoughts as he addressed the Council may have been confused by a cluster of interlocking legends, but there was no doubt about his passionate enthusiasm, and it was contagious enough to entrap the minds of his advisers. Before they rose that day they had reached a firm decision to dispatch an expedition to the conquest of Monomatapa, and everyone was certain that they would find such wealth there as would rival the gold mines in the Americas being exploited at the time by the king of Spain.

It is strange that an unbalanced youth's determination to gain distinction for himself should have had such enormous consequences for the future state of Rhodesia. But then everything about the new king of Portugal was unpredictable. There never has been, and now there never can be, another person quite like King Sebastian. All his life he lived close to lunacy. He was only fourteen at the time when he decided on the conquest of south-east Africa, but already he affected the swagger and truculence of a veteran campaigner; his thoughts, which for weeks had been reeling with the knowledge of his own impotence, at Almeirim had become crystallised into a resolve to lead a crusade into Morocco and to win the empire of Monomatapa for the Portuguese crown. At least he achieved his twin ambitions: after incredible hardships and set-backs his countrymen did effect the temporary conquest of the African far interior, and Sebastian led his crusade to Morocco—and died there together with most of his army on the fatal field of Alcazar. It had been wholly fitting that he had chosen as his personal motto a passage in Portuguese which requires no translation: 'Un bel morir tutta vita honora'.

When the royal counsellors at Almeirim in 1568 became resolved on the conquest of Monomatapa, never for a single moment did it occur to them that a variety of circumstances might have combined to give them a totally false impression of the

---

* It was an error into which John Milton fell a little later when writing *Paradise Lost*, Book XI.

wealth of south-east Africa. Each one of them was so much a captive of the age-old fables about King Solomon's mines and the kingdom of Prester John that they had eagerly accepted Fernandes' breath-taking accounts of the gold mines in the interior and the splendid culture of the Karanga; it never crossed their minds that Fernandes might have touched up his report to ingratiate himself with the authorities, or that on very little evidence they were equating a Bantu social system with the civilisations of the Aztecs and Incas. But that was how it was: they had become dupes of their own fantasies, and it was symptomatic of their self-deception that the prints of da Silveira's martyrdom, which even then were circulating in Portugal, depicted his murderers as dressed in rich eastern robes and living in classical palaces resplendent enough to have adorned imperial Rome itself.

Nor for that matter has any other military expedition been founded upon so many misconceptions as the one which six months later sailed from the Tagus to conquer Monomatapa's empire. There were no precedents to the African campaign on which the Portuguese were embarking, and it was perhaps inevitable that they should have made nearly every possible mistake during their preparations. But at least the expedition could be accounted singularly fortunate in having a man of Francisco Barreto's calibre chosen as its Captain-General and Governor of the future conquests. For Barreto was a devout Catholic and an experienced soldier who could be relied upon to conduct the great affair with scrupulous honesty and ability. So popular was Barreto with his countrymen that volunteers flocked from all over Portugal to join his expeditionary force. In the end he selected a thousand fighting men from the applicants for the crusade in southern Africa. Four Jesuit priests were nominated by the king to provide the commander with spiritual guidance; one of them was a dyspeptic, sharp-tongued man named Monclaro who enjoyed Sebastian's absolute confidence and who also happened to be an eager tale-bearer. Monclaro's duties included the preparation of what today we would call a war diary. Although a less biased record of the expedition was also written by De Faria, a great deal of our

Bushman paintings in caves at Marandellas and Mtoko; the lower frieze
represents Hottentot migrants, with skin bags slung over their shoulders

The martyrdom of Dom Gonçalo da Silveira

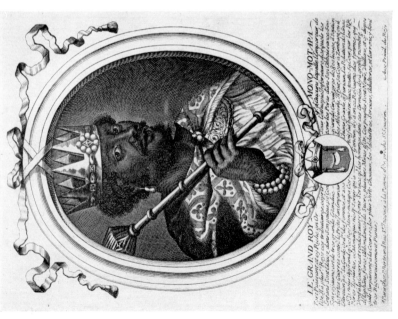

Portuguese portrait of Monomatapa

knowledge of the events during the first Portuguese attempt at the conquest of Monomatapa is owed to the lively narrative that Monclaro wrote for the king's edification. His account is extremely readable, and it gives us a very good insight into conditions in contemporary Karangaland. It must, however, be remembered that Monclaro was by no means an unprejudiced observer, and clearly he never formed a very high opinion of Barreto's military abilities: all through his narrative one can sense the undercurrent of the bickering that he enjoyed with the Captain-General. For Father Monclaro was prodigal with advice about how even military affairs should be conducted and on at least one occasion his 'inspired' recommendations led to disaster. But Barreto generally deferred to him (although sometimes he must have privately wished the perverse priest had been consigned not to Africa but to the deepest pit in hell) and one is left with the impression that he was even a little afraid of this chaplain who had the ear of King Sebastian.

The expedition was launched at last in 1569, and Barreto's lavishly equipped fleet sailed from the Tagus amid scenes of wild enthusiasm. Contemporary chronicles have succeeded in conveying to us something of the excitement that attended the occasion as the sails of the Captain-General's three ships caught the breeze and headed out to sea. There were prayers and sharp trumpet calls and cheers from a great crowd which covered every vantage point, and constrictive fears too among the mariners and their relatives, for the world of southern Africa was almost as incomprehensible to them as outer space is to us today. Most of Portugal's noble families had a representative on board, and Monclaro was not exaggerating when he stated that 'in the opinion of many it was the best and most illustrious company that had ever set out from the harbour of Lisbon'. But progress once they were clear of the Portuguese coast was agonisingly slow; reading about it now, when we are so far separated in time from the leisurely days of sail, one wonders whether the army will ever reach Monomatapa. Soon after setting off, one of the ships ran aground off the Canaries and was ordered home. Near the Equator, the great flagship became separated in a storm from the smaller boat commanded by Vasco Fernandes Homen, and was driven right across the Atlantic until it made a landfall in Brazil. Here at Santos, Barreto had to wait six whole months for favourable winds and only on the 16th May, 1570 did he at last drop anchor in the harbour of Mocambique and regain contact with Homen's ship. For a further year and a half, incredibly, Barreto remained based on Mocambique, leading several diversionary expeditions to explore the east African coast as far north as Malindi, and by the end of that time a hundred crusaders were already dead of mysterious tropical diseases. Only towards the close of 1571, did the Portuguese turn at last to the conquest of Monomatapa and at this late stage it turned out that there was no unanimity among them about the best way of getting there. King Sebastian's clear orders were to march directly inland on Chitako from Sofala, but now Monclaro became insistent that they must reach the interior instead up the Zambesi valley, and for days their argument droned on. It is difficult to understand the priest's motives for wanting Barreto to change the royal plans in this way, but one suspects that among them was a pious anxiety to follow the road pioneered by da Silveira so that he might obtain relics of the martyr's last journey. Whatever the reason may have been, and despite the advice of all his military counsellors, Barreto in the end submitted to Monclaro's persuasion. To begin with all went well but it turned out to be a disastrous decision. The expedition moved slowly up the Zambesi in a flotilla of boats, revelling in all the novelties of native life and the strange sights seen along the banks of the great river. 'The navigation of the river was very cheerful', Monclaro remembered afterwards; 'we had abundant supplies of hens and capons and fish also, as we had nets. The sixty miles of river up to Sena are the most fertile lands I have ever seen except the plains of India. But the cultivators are extremely lazy and their country most unhealthy.'

By the end of 1571 the Portuguese army was safely established outside the Moslem village of Sena, and an envoy was dispatched to Monomatapa offering him terms for a treaty of friendship and alliance. But by now it was the unhealthy season of the year, and dysentery and malaria very soon swept through the camp, while many of the horses on which so much depended died from trypanosomiasis.

A dreadful six months was passed in the pestilential camp at Sena waiting for a reply from the Monomatapa, and a further hundred men perished during this time. The Portuguese were utterly ignorant of the nature of the tropical diseases which had descended on them. The loss of the horses was equally inexplicable, and a very serious mishap too, for without them the Portuguese had lost what amounted to their secret weapon, and the opportunity of exploiting the cavalry tactics which had been so effective during the Spanish conquests in America. Barreto himself believed that his horses had died from toxic herbs growing in the grass round Sena. Monclaro, on the other hand, was convinced that they had been deliberately poisoned by the Moslems living in the area, and after a groom under torture confessed to administering poison to the horses on orders from the infidels, he had little difficulty in persuading the Governor to exact retribution from them.

What followed was both pointless and savage, and one cannot help being appalled at the vengeance taken by the Portuguese. Theirs was the special kind of cruelty reserved for heretics by men who are possessed of religious fervour. The Portuguese in Sena became caught up in a ferocious manhunt which was made all the more frantic by the loot they came across. Monclaro was full of applause for their ardour and he is at his most complacent when he reports to the king on the fate of the Moslems: 'These were condemned', he says, 'and put to death by strange inventions. Some were impaled alive; some were tied to the tops of trees, forcibly brought together, and then set free, by which means they were torn asunder: others were opened up the back with hatchets; some were killed with mortars, in order to strike terror into the natives; and others were delivered to the soldiers, who wreaked their wrath upon them with arquebusses.' A single infidel was permitted to enjoy a comparatively merciful death because, de Faria tells us, 'affirming the blessed virgin had appeared to him, and commanded him to become a Christian, by the name of

Lawrence, he had the favour to be strangled'. Within a week the countryside round Sena had been cleared of Moslems, though it was very frustrating for Monclaro when this successful conclusion had no effect on the mortality among the Christians. We can see now that from a political point of view the cruelty of the Portuguese at Sena was the extreme of ineptitude, for from now on the Moslems in Africa would always tend to regard them as their mortal enemies, to be harmed and molested at every opportunity.

In fairness to Monclaro and Barreto, one must view the outrage in the light of its time and place: this was the year of the St Bartholomew's Day massacre; and the recent conquest,of those parts of the Iberian peninsula settled by the Arabs had been attended by revolting brutalities which had been condoned and even encouraged by the Church. And now here in the Zambesi valley the Portuguese had come into an area which has always brought out the worst qualities in men. The prevailing atmosphere of witchcraft and superstition which one senses there today was no doubt even more oppressive in these pestilential lowlands four hundred years ago, and it was perhaps inevitable that the Christian soldiers of 1571 should have reacted to it in the way they did.

Barreto, during the long wait at Sena during the hot season of 1571, had no inkling of what had delayed the return of his envoys from Monomatapa's court. With them they had carried demands, buttressed by a threat of invasion, that all Moslems be evicted from the Monomatapa's dominions and the Portuguese allowed to trade and prospect freely for gold in Butua and Manica. Nothing for the time being was said about the Captain-General's real design which was to secure effective control of the Karanga capital in the manner which had proved so successful in the cases of the Mexican and Inca empires. At the same time the envoys were instructed to notify the Monomatapa that the Tongas living up river from Tete had been molesting Portuguese traders and that Barreto intended to punish them. His intention of course was to subdue the Tongas and acquire a firm base within striking distance of Chitako before proceeding, if necessary, to armed invasion of the emperor's central provinces. The Tongas by this time were semi-independent of Monomatapa: they were ruled by a chief named Samungazi; Monclaro always refers to them in his narrative as the Mongazes, a modification of their chief's name. In fact, Barreto's envoy to the Emperor Nogomo had been drowned on his journey to Chitako and the Portuguese terms were never presented. Barreto, unaware of this development, was inclined to believe that the delay in answering his letter was due to Nogomo's prevarication and in the end he lost patience and decided to go ahead with the invasion of Monomatapa. His army accordingly left Sena on the 19th July, 1572, and made its way for seventy miles up the left bank of the Zambesi until half way to present-day Tete. This part of the march was slow but it was comparatively prosperous: the weather was cool and the pressing problems of logistics had been dealt with reasonably well. The Portuguese had imported a number of transport camels, and according to Monclaro 'had more than twenty boats laden with provisions, merchandise and ammunition', while 'on land with our company we had twenty-five wagons drawn by oxen of the country, as big as the large oxen of France and very tractable. These cattle came (as I have said) from Butua, and escaped the poison of the Moors.'

Now for the first time in history a European army had launched itself on the invasion of Bantu Africa, and no one can deny that this final, and perhaps most heroic, exploit of medieval Europe was launched with a flourish. Barreto's army made a splendid spectacle: like food for future legend all the panoply and trappings of chivalry were present to grace the occasion. In the van rode twenty-three knights, fully armoured and carrying the banners of Christendom through the African sunlight. They were led by Barreto, 'clad in a thick coat of mail, attending on every side to the good order of the camp'. Beside him went Monclaro, mounted on a mule and holding up a blazoned crucifix. Behind the cavalry marched a solid phalanx of six hundred arquebusiers in the helmets and body-armour of the period which were of course utterly unsuited to tropical conditions. Next came a creaking wagon train drawn by oxen, and a line of swaying litters for the priests and sick, borne by two thousand pressed slaves. Straggling behind them trudged a less impressive mob of eight hundred Indian and half-breed levies, and lines of baggage camels which terrified the Africans watching from the bush, especially after the word had got round that they were fed on human flesh. In the rear came eight small cannon dragged along by reluctant donkeys.

It took over a month for Barreto to get his army up to the Lupata Gorge which Monclaro calls 'the gates of Mangaz'. Here he left the river and marched westwards towards the interior, probably following the Muira river. Almost immediately contact was made with Samungazi's Tonga, whom we learn were 'very warlike and great thieves and highwaymen', and 'more dreaded for their cruelty than the Turks in Italy'.

A few days later, arriving on a plain, where the enemy was clearly preparing to fight, the Portuguese army debouched for battle. Barreto and Monclaro with his great crucifix, halted while the white troops extended into line, and 'two pieces of artillery, namely a swivel falcon and a demi-cannon' were hurriedly brought to the front. At the far end of the plain a dark menacing crescent of warriors was drawn up directly across their line of advance, probably in the vicinity of the present-day village of Messangaze, which is just on the Portuguese side of the Rhodesia/Mocambique border. Never before had the Portuguese seen anything quite so intimidating; they estimated the opposing army to number twelve thousand men.

There is always something very frightening about the unknown, and this first significant armed encounter between Christian Europe and Bantu Africa must have been attended by extreme apprehension and anxiety to both sides. No one really knew just how formidable the others were. Barreto had no idea whether he was facing an efficient fighting machine or a rabble; he had no conception of what novel weapons or tactics might be used against him; all he was certain of was that his army was out-numbered by a fantastic margin. Indeed the sheer novelty of Barreto's situation must be continually emphasised: before that September day in 1572 the Portuguese had been dealing only with fables and conjectures about the fighting powers of the Bantu; now they were face to face with the reality.

The Tonga, of course, were even less mentally prepared for this first clash of arms than the white men; the rumours drifting up to them about the strange people who had come from the ocean had suggested they were sea monsters who floated on it in giant shells and lived exclusively on a diet of elephant tusks. But the morale of Samungazi's warriors had been bolstered that day by their witch-doctors, who had assured them they would contrive an easy triumph by magic, and they watched confidently as 'an old woman' cavorted between the two armies and, according to de Faria, 'scattered some powder towards Barreto's men', having previously persuaded Samungazi that the powder alone would gain victory. Some of their enthusiasm it must be admitted oozed out of the tribesmen, when a lucky shot resulted 'in the old hag being torn to pieces, to the astonishment of the Kaffirs who believed her to be immortal'. But in the event it was the noise and smoke of Barreto's guns which made the most impression on the Tonga.

For an account of this first battle with the Tonga army we cannot do better than follow Monclaro's narrative: 'Their light parties', he tells us, 'were drawn up on either wing and the heaviest force in the middle; and they threw out companies of slaves on either side and had many in ambush who were so well concealed that when they began to discharge their arrows they fell close to the royal standard, but as the wind was against them they came with less force. Against these skirmishers two squadrons of soldiers advanced, who put them to flight with their arquebusses.

'Meanwhile', he continues, 'the main divisions were drawing near, and when they had approached within range of our guns, both pieces were fired among them, killing fifteen or sixteen, and at the same time our horsemen with some soldiers and all our slaves attacked them with loud cries, and put them to flight.'

It was over very quickly: within a few moments of the Portuguese opening fire the Tonga were stampeding off in full retreat. Later that day there was another brush with the enemy. Monclaro takes up the story again as the Portuguese approached a kraal where the Africans were rallying: 'As we were entering it in the same order,' he says, 'the Kaffirs returned to defend it, attacking us in the rear, and as this was the post of the company that contained the fewest Portuguese, I went there with a crucifix with the Governor's leave, to encourage them in the fight, which the enemy sustained very vigorously, attacking our people and darkening the air with arrows. They advanced in the form of a crescent, and almost surrounded us on every side. The colonel ordered no one to fire till they drew nearer, that having closed we might attack them with heavier loss: and this enabled them to wound more than twenty-five of our men, though not dangerously.'

'It was noticed,' the gratified Monclaro continues, 'that wherever I was with the crucifix, although the arrows were numerous, no one was wounded by them within ten or twelve paces of it; and looking up in some fear of the arrows I observed that though many seemed to be falling on my head, the Lord whose image I carried in my hand diverted them, so they left as it were an open space, within which no one was wounded, although I was in the front, and they came with great force, the wind being now in their favour.' Soon after this encouraging manifestation of divine support, the Tonga drew off in confusion, leaving more than five thousand dead on the field.

There was a more serious fight a few days later when Samungazi again attacked the Portuguese column; Monclaro's account of this encounter is curiously evocative of those written more than three hundred years later during the Matabele rebellion of 1896. 'After three days, at dawn in the morning', he says, 'we made ready to set out, and were just leaving when there came like a great dust storm and loud clamour the army of Kaffraria and Mongazes, reinforced with a number which was said to be sixteen thousand men, and with great intrepidity and noise of drums, and more confident in victory, for they had with them a wizard who by the spells he carried in a gourd, which I afterwards saw, had persuaded them that he would deliver us all into their hands, and that our *nafutes*, which are the arquebusses, would be of no use. As sure of victory, he made them bring ropes made of bark of trees, which afterwards served the soldiers as very good match for their arquebusses. These were intended to bind us with, and their war cry was *Funga Muzungo!* which signifies *bind the white man* . . . they attacked us four times that morning, and each time we repulsed them with heavy loss. They tried to break our ranks in eight different places. The smoke was so great from the arquebusses and artillery, for besides the guns before mentioned six small pieces which were in the wagons were also used, of which Francisco Barreto made himself the gunner, that the air was obscured so that we could not see each other, and this was increased as the battle took place in a valley, and there was no wind. At this the enemy was astonished, saying that we were great wizards, since we could turn the day into night.'

Over four thousand Africans were killed in this third engagement and the loss was heavy enough to persuade Samungazi to send envoys to the Portuguese tendering his surrender. An unusual incident which now resulted in Samungazi supporting his submission with a welcome peace-offering of oxen is related by de Faria:

> It happened that one of the camels breaking loose, ran towards the Governor, who stopped him till his pursuers came up: the Kaffirs who had never seen such a creature, admiring to see it stop at the Governor, began to ask some questions. He making his Advantage of their Ignorance, told them he had many of those Animals, which only fed upon Man's Flesh; and having devoured all that were killed, that Beast came from the rest to desire he would not make Peace, because they should then come to want Food: The Blacks, astonished hereat, earnestly entreated, that he would desire the camels to be satisfied with good Beef, and that they would instantly bring them a great Number. He granted their Request, and marched on.

Barreto had lost only two men killed in the fighting, though more than forty soldiers had been wounded. Now, with his army virtually intact, he stood on the borders of Monomatapa's central provinces and within a few days' march of the Inyanga highlands where the soldiers' health might if necessary be recruited.

But on this very brink of success, malaria and dysentery again overwhelmed the Portuguese army. One after another Barreto's men succumbed to disease and Monclaro tells us that 'the sick increased so much that there were no Kaffirs to carry them and of those given to us by Chombe (a friendly chief) sixty of the two hundred had fled, and the sick and wounded were more than a hundred and twenty. Every day we buried two or three, and others fell ill. This land of Mangaz', he goes on to explain, 'is very mountainous and has few plains, and there is a great scarcity of water . . . worse water cannot be imagined, for it is obtained from stagnant pools left from winter, exposed to the sun and covered with green slime; and even this was scarce. This we drank, though it tasted of human filth, and from this bad water, air, and dews, the heat during the day, the bad provisions, and eating so much beef as we had there, the people fell sick of dysentery, with no hope of recovery. As there was no one to carry the sick, we were all obliged to go on foot and even Francisco Barreto carried the sick behind him on his horse.'

Out of all this came tragedy. There was now little hope of the Portuguese following up their victories with a direct advance on Chitako, and although they made one attempt to flounder forwards to the escarpment the realisation soon grew on Barreto that retreat was inevitable. Indeed so desperate were conditions now that he judged himself very fortunate in being able to pull what remained of his army safely back to the Zambesi and from there to the doubtful haven of Sena. The first Portuguese attempt at the conquest of present day Rhodesia, which had started off with such panache, had been defeated, not by arms, but by the pestilential natural dyke of the Zambesi valley which defends the country's northern frontier.

If King Sebastian's great design for the conquest of Monomatapa had failed, the victories at Messangaze had at least impressed Nogomo with the military prowess of the Portuguese, and, back at Sena (where he was also encouraged by news of the Christian victory at Lepanto), Barreto found twelve of the Monomatapa's great officers of state awaiting him with a fawning message of friendship, and a present of fine golden bracelets. Not to be outdone, Barreto at once dispatched three of his own officers to Chitako together with costly gifts and a reiteration of his terms, but they had grown, as so often, with keeping. He demanded again that the Moslems be evicted from the interior, that priests be allowed to enter and preach to the Karanga, and also that certain gold mines be ceded to the Portuguese, together with Samungazi's country on the Zambesi.

On the 24th April, 1573, Nogomo welcomed Barreto's embassy at his Zimbabwe and at once agreed to all the Portuguese conditions, relinquishing the entire Zambesi valley from Tete as far as the sea to King Sebastian without protest. It was one of those rare treaties which pleased both sides; the Portuguese believed they had secured control of another Eldorado, while for his part Nogomo assumed that for the cession of some mines in which he had little interest and the country of the lower Zambesi (which anyway had already cast off allegiance to him) he had gained the help of powerful white allies against his other troublesome vassals.

Barreto was at Mocambique, arranging to take provisions up to the remnants of his army when his envoys returned with their treaty. It seemed that at least some success could be plucked from apparent disaster, and he was back in Sena by the May of 1573. There he was horrified to discover that during his absence lethal disease had again raged through the Portuguese camp. Of the four hundred and fifty soldiers he had left in the settlement, only one hundred and fifty now remained alive, and of these a mere handful were still capable of bearing arms. The blow for Barreto was the end of a fever-ridden dream; within two weeks he himself had succumbed to the prevailing fever. It was widely believed in the camp, however, that his death could be more accurately ascribed to Monclaro's abusive criticism of the Captain-General's handling of the campaign. For the priest now seems to have excelled himself in his tongue-lashing, and Barreto for once hit back at him. It was the quarrel of two men who had been strained too much and it was perhaps enough to turn the scales against Barreto: 'this great man', one of his officers noted sorrowfully, 'having escaped so many bullets . . . fell by the words of a religious man'. De Faria's comment was even more embittered: 'Barreto', he says, 'took the Jesuit's insolence so much to Heart, that he died within two Days, without any other sickness, breathing out his soul in sighs.'

*   *   *   *   *

The command of the Portuguese expeditionary force passed to Fernandes Homen, a steady, hard-working soldier, who at least was spared one of his predecessor's embarrassments, for Brother Monclaro by now had decided to report in person to the king on the situation in south-east Africa, and the shrewish chronicler of the expedition, after burying Barreto with the maximum possible pomp, took himself off by boat to Lisbon.

Scenting glory where Barreto had failed (and no doubt suspicious too of Nogomo's good faith) Homen at once decided to make another attempt to enforce a military occupation of the gold-bearing areas of Monomatapa. He had no intention of using the Zambesi route into the interior again: he proposed instead to march directly inland from Sofala as King Sebastian had originally directed. Some months were spent at Mocambique, filling up the army's ranks with recruits from the ships lying in harbour, and Homen eventually was able to muster a respectable force of four hundred and twelve white soldiers. He would have preferred to wait for more reinforcements, but this would have risked advancing during the rainy season. Accordingly, as he reported later to Lisbon, 'I started off with what I had and I reached Sofala on the sixteenth of March 1575. We at once struck inland, as I had promised the soldiers who had come with me so cheerfully.' He marched up the course of the Buzi and Revue rivers, beckoned on all the time by the sight of the cool blue Chimanimani mountains ahead, and from now on all that had been so mysteriously hazardous about Barreto's crusade was marvellously changed. The army moved forward rapidly through the province of Quiteve, which like Samungazi's country had become semi-independent of the Monomatapa, overcoming only sporadic resistance, and immune apparently from sickness.

Presently the Portuguese entered the mountainous fief of Manica, which was ruled by a chief named Chikanga. Chikanga still paid tribute to Nogomo, and he found it expedient to welcome the Portuguese with a show of cordiality although, if de Faria's account is to be believed, 'rather through fear than love'. Having set up a camp in the vicinity of the beautiful modern city of Umtali, Homen's soldiers next divided themselves up into prospecting parties, and began the exploration of the Manica highlands.

At last they were moving within the frontiers of the fabulous empire about which they had heard and dreamed so much, and which had taken five long years to reach. Everyone was full of optimism, and a fresh note of buoyancy creeps into the dispatches Homen sends home. In one of them, as though it were the end of a chapter, he writes: 'and so we settled down on the mines of the Manicas which Francisco Barreto and I had so long sought'. For it seemed that the fabulous treasure of the Queen of Sheba at last lay within the grasp of the Portuguese conquistadors.

Even now, after all these years, it is not difficult to imagine the delight and excitement with which the Portuguese men-at-arms 'believing they should gather Gold by Handfuls' (the words are de Faria's) scattered through the splendid valleys of Manica-land, searching for the mines of Ophir. It was a tableau which, in a curious historical encore, was to be re-enacted by the British pioneers of 1890. Like their search it ended in anticlimax. Instead of massive outcrops of solid nuggets, all the Portuguese saw were hordes of coerced natives toiling unwillingly in primitive shafts and after several days work producing only a few grains of gold. Homen realised almost at once that the wealth of the Manica mines had been grossly exaggerated; certainly it did not justify the cost of maintaining an army of occupation in Manica, and he decided to withdraw it. But he made the best of the situation: he concluded agreements with both Chikanga and Quiteve to allow white traders and miners free access to the interior in return for an annual emolument of two hundred rolls of cotton cloth. Then he returned to Sofala with the two hundred and thirty soldiers who had survived the campaign.

If the results of the invasion of Manicaland had fallen far short of expectations, Homen had at least secured a qualified success, for the Portuguese became firmly established in Manicaland and from now on a trickle of gold began to reach Sofala. Admittedly the Moslem traders in the interior were able to soften the blow to their commerce by reopening the long and vulnerable trade route across the Zambesi to Kilwa; indeed it was to intercept this traffic, as well as to seize the rich silver mines which had been reported at Chicova up river from Tete, which made Homen, that same year, lead a new expedition up the Zambesi. It ended in complete disaster. Although Chicova was occupied and a fort built there, as soon as Homen's army withdrew, its garrison of forty men was starved into submission by local tribesmen who by now had quite thrown off their allegiance to Nogomo. Homen retaliated by re-occupying Chicova with two hundred soldiers, but they in turn were lured out of the fort and 'all slain by darts and arrows'. With this set-back the tide of Portuguese military advance in south-east Africa temporarily receded. By 1576, all they had to show for much suffering and many deaths was the presence of the few score Portuguese traders and prospectors in Manica.

It was a sad end to all the high hopes which had accompanied Barreto's great expedition, but it paled into insignificance when compared with the disaster on a national scale which struck down metropolitan Portugal only two years later. King Sebastian, as headstrong and fanatical as ever, sailed in 1578 with the pick of his army on a new crusade to Morocco, and led it to a crushing defeat at Alcazar. The king died in action together with eight thousand of his soldiers; the remainder surrendered to the Moslems, and Portugal during the next few years beggared herself in ransoming them. From the time of that rout, the power of the Portugal which had led Europe to her destiny waned. Only two years later Philip II of Spain annexed Sebastian's flagging kingdom, and stiff Spanish sentries mounted guard at Lisbon for the next sixty years.

The effect of the military débâcle at Alcazar did not at once make itself felt in Portugal's south-east African possessions, but they were threatened instead by a more direct danger when hordes of man-eating savages named the Zimbas suddenly erupted from central Africa, poured across the Zambesi into the northern marches of the Monomatapan empire, literally consumed the white traders they encountered in Manica, and drove the Bantu living there to take refuge in the bleak Inyanga highlands. So great was their alarm that these refugees remained in this corner of Rhodesia for several generations and built up the vast complex of forts and agricultural terraces whose relics today are one of the country's chief archaeological wonders.

When the Zimba flood receded again across the Zambesi, Portuguese colonists moved back into Quiteve and Manica where their position had been secured by the treaties negotiated by Homen, and gradually the more venturesome of them penetrated into the central provinces of the empire, bartering trade goods for gold and ivory. Admittedly, the emphasis lay more on commerce than on military conquest, but from now on the European grip tightened on the country as little oases of Portuguese life sprang up in places where a few acres had been ceded by the Monomatapa to the traders. These grants were run rather on the lines of the European concessions in nineteenth-century China; as in their case, the Portuguese took sides when civil wars broke out and were able to assist the Monomatapa in campaigns against his rebellious vassals. In return they obtained the right to recruit their own levies and to fortify their stations, and they began to rule them in the manner of African chiefs.

Markets (which the Portuguese called fairs) were held regularly in these fortified Portuguese settlements, the most important of which was Masapa, situated at the foot of the legendary Mount Fura. Its European commander was styled the 'Captain of the Gates' by the Portuguese, while the Monomatapa honoured him even more by calling him his 'Great Wife'. This official controlled ingress to the empire from the Zambesi, and subjected all merchandise to customs dues which were divided between Nogomo and the Portuguese crown. Stockaded trade concessions were also set up at Luanze between the Mazoe and Ruenya Rivers about a hundred miles south of Tete, at Bocuto in the Mrewa district, and at other sites as far west as the Angwa River. But it was Dambarare,* just north of modern Mazoe, which became the most opulent of all the Portuguese concessions; it was described by a contemporary chronicler as a 'noble settlement and good sized town in the heart of Mokaranga, and has grown to be the centre of that conquest, with many rich inhabitants', and he goes on to say that it is situated in a countryside which was eulogised for the salubrity of its climate and for its rich crops of fruit and vegetables.

The same Portuguese account tells us that the white merchants in Karangaland became so wealthy that some of them owned slaves numbering more than 'three hundred, all Christians', and we know that a great deal of proselytism was undertaken among the Karanga. There seems, however, to have been very little European penetration of Changamire's kingdom, and nothing became known about the gold resources of the southern part of the great plateau until many years later. By the time of Nogomo's death in 1596, the number of Portuguese traders in Monomatapa has been estimated to have reached four hundred, and this is probably a conservative figure for another source gives a number four times larger.

Troubled times came to Karangaland with the succession of Gatsi Ruseri as Monomatapa. Gatsi Ruseri was a notorious dagga smoker who ruled (although misruled might be the better word) uneasily from 1596 to 1627. His reign was marked by alternating civil wars, risings directed against the Portuguese colonists, and defensive campaigns against Changamire. It was a period, one chronicler tells us, of 'abominable treachery' and continual chaos; its intricacies of alliances and betrayals can now only be unravelled by the most ardent and patient of Bantu historians. Some of Gatsi Ruseri's letters have survived as curious pieces of Rhodesiana: in them he uses a special seal, and signs himself with 'his mark' and an impressive 'by the mercy of God, Emperor of Mocaranga as far as the salt waters, Lord of the mines of gold and silver'. But for most of his reign this Monomatapa was little more than a puppet maintained on his throne by the power of

* The site has recently been excavated and a Christian graveyard found.

ne ruined city of Zimbabwe; conical tower

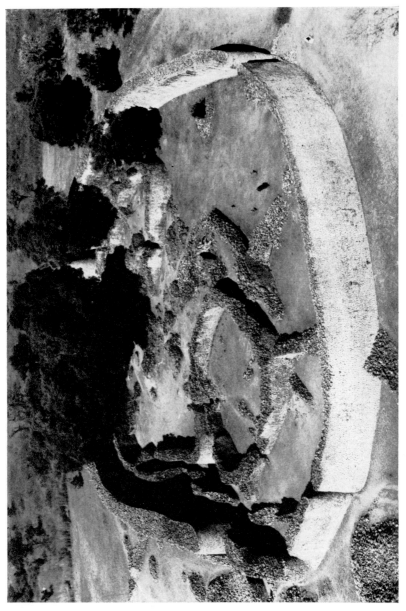

The great enclosure of Zimbabwe

Portuguese muskets, and threatened throughout its course by pretenders. In 1607, he went so far as to make sweeping concessions to the Europeans in a treaty signed on the 1st August of that year which read: 'I, the Emperor of Monomatapa, think it fit and am pleased to give to His Majesty all the mines of gold, copper, iron, lead and pewter which may be in my empire, so long as the King of Portugal, to whom I give the said mines, shall maintain me in my position.'

After the death of Gatsi Ruseri, his son, Kapararidze (whom the Portuguese usually referred to more euphoniously as Capracina) organised a national rising against the European colonists when they decided to support a rival emperor. Four hundred Portuguese died in the rebellion which followed and their records speak in gruesome detail of the martyrdom of two friars named Luis da Espirito Santo and Joao da Trinidado. By 1631, only a handful of Europeans from Mashonaland and Manicaland had succeeded in escaping from Capracina's triumphant armies to the more settled areas on the Zambesi, and the Portuguese position in south-east Africa appeared to be desperate.

Yet the Portuguese had no intention of abandoning the far interior, and it is difficult to withhold one's admiration from the strength and vigour of their reaction to the débâcle of 1631. A punitive expedition of three hundred arquebusiers supported by native levies was hastily assembled, and on the 24th July, 1632, made contact with Capracina's army which was estimated to number 100,000. The battle which followed forms the subject of one of the most picturesque of Rhodesian legends. As the Portuguese put in their attack a resplendent cross was seen shining in the sky, and although the attendant Jesuit priests searched in vain for the heaven-sent wording which had accompanied a similar vision preceding Constantine's triumph at the Milvian bridge, the white men that day secured a decisive victory; if their accounts are to be believed, they inflicted twelve thousand casualties on the Karanga.

It had been a fantastic reversal of fortune. When all hope seemed to have gone, this single battle, in which they had been miraculously assisted, had allowed the Europeans to regain control over the remnants of the Karanga empire, and their position in what is now Mashonaland was unchallenged. 'Now', we read in a contemporary narrative, 'the Portuguese elect and depose kings at their pleasure', and they could fairly claim to be masters of central Africa. Their puppet Monomatapa was reinstalled at Chitako, having agreed to 'make his land free to the Portuguese', and he reigned for the next twenty years as Mavura II, or (even more splendidly after accepting baptism) as Dom Philipe I. The king in far-distant Madrid decreed that Mavura, his brother, should be invested with the Order of Christ, and the bewildered Mavura's investiture in the Order's splendid robes was duly carried out in a ceremony which must have been as bizarre as any ever conducted in Rhodesia. A fort was built at Chitako and a strong Portuguese garrison posted there with orders to supervise the emperor as well as to guard him. Finally a Christian chapel was set up within the royal precincts of Zimbabwe, and the pious Mavura himself carried its foundation stone to the site on his shoulders.

The sky seemed bright with promise now for the Portuguese in south-central Africa. It was the Europeans who gave the orders, and they were strong enough to evict all Moslems and monopolise the gold trade. We learn that two thousand ounces of gold were mined in Monomatapa annually. Encouraging reports reached Lisbon from the mission stations which were established there and the number of converts was large enough to justify the ministrations of fourteen friars. Elaborate plans were now made for the further European colonisation of the great plateau. The settlement of two thousand pioneer families including 'four to six physicians' was envisaged in Mocaranga. 'Except for white colonists', the delighted king was assured, 'the land lacks nothing else, and with this your Majesty will be lord of the world as you deserve to be.' And indeed the history of Rhodesia would no doubt have developed on different lines had the Portuguese ambitions for central Africa been implemented. But the vision, which was so similar to the one realised centuries later by Cecil Rhodes, faded and finally dissolved as Portugal's declining power was used to prop up her possessions in Brazil and India. Yet for some time it still seemed that the Portuguese grip on the interior would tighten rather than weaken. In 1652, the pliant Mavura was succeeded by Kazuru Kumusapa, a professed Christian who had accepted baptism as Dom Dominic. The conversion of the entire Karanga people was now confidently expected, and Rome and Lisbon basked in the prospect of this great victory for the Faith in central Africa. But 1652 proved to be the high-water mark of Portuguese supremacy in the far interior. Dominic was assassinated soon after his accession, and with him died many hopes.

By the remarkable symmetry of history, only a few weeks before the fortunes of the Portuguese in south-east Africa began to decline with Dom Dominic's death an event took place which was ultimately to be of even greater significance to the future of Rhodesia: in the April of 1652, a Dutchman named van Riebeeck successfully planted a victualling station at the Cape of Good Hope; in time it was to develop into a colony whose influence eventually engulfed all south Africa as far north as the Zambesi.

The Portuguese in the end failed to secure central Africa for themselves, but they only just failed, and their temporary subjection of Monomatapa must be considered one of the most remarkable achievements of Europe in Africa, especially when seen in the light of the Portuguese numbers and resources. Indeed it seems a little strange that their conquests in the African interior should have now been so far forgotten, for this first European attempt at colonising Karangaland lasted more than a hundred years. Its failure was perhaps due less to the weakness of metropolitan Portugal than to the effect of the African environment on its conquistadors. The first white settlers in Rhodesia had to face obstacles which have now been overcome by modern science. Malaria, dysentery, and trypanosomiasis were their chief enemies —diseases which today are very largely controlled. They were hampered too by the vast distances which separated them from their sources of power—distances that have shrunk to manageable dimensions in the jet age. But perhaps equally important, the Portuguese of the seventeenth century profoundly misinterpreted the Bantu ethos and their understanding of it was nothing like so broad as it is in Rhodesia today.

There are less obvious reasons which may in part account for the Portuguese failure to maintain and consolidate their position in central Africa. Local authority was placed in the hands of men whose loyalty to the crown was tempered by personal avarice and corruption, and the king was constantly being swindled by his own officials. Few white women came to live in the far interior during the years of Portuguese paramountcy; miscegenation in consequence became common, and the conquistadors were to some extent submerged by the Bantu. And the settlers' allegiance to their homeland weakened after the interests of Portugal had been subordinated to those of Spain: many of them reacted by abandoning their old loyalties, and they set themselves up among the Karanga as independent princelings. The king in Madrid was informed that these bush Caesars 'fear neither God nor Your Majesty', and this sums up their attitude very well. They were perverted by the vast power they wielded in their enormous fiefs, and something of the way they behaved in them comes out in a letter written by Mavura II where he grumbles that they 'do great harm to the natives, killing some, wounding others, stealing their sons and their daughters and cows of their herds, so that each day I have complaints in this my Zimbabwe'. The European and mulatto potentates in short conducted themselves like robber barons and they were very jealous of each other; each one raised his own private army, and added to the chaos in the disintegrating empire of Monomatapa by indulging in successive and completely irrelevant civil wars.

The strength of the Portuguese in south-central Africa had always lain in their flintlocks and in their truculent assurance of the superior merits of white men, Christianity, and western civilisation. Their weakness paradoxically lay in their very apathy towards the Bantu. The Karanga never made such easy converts to Christianity as the South American Indians, and they obstinately refused to assimilate European culture. In consequence the Portuguese always remained alien to their vassals, and they were too far committed to their own faith to adopt a compromise policy which would have gained the real allegiance of their Bantu subjects.

Portuguese rule in Mashonaland still had nearly fifty years to run at the time of Mavura's death, and there was even a surprising resurgence of its power just before the final collapse: in 1667, we find one enthusiastic chronicler, reporting that 'Mokaranga is very healthy, fertile, and verdant, with numberless rivers and fountains, which proves the falseness of the idea that land rich in gold is dry and barren of plants; for Mokaranga is one continuous gold mine', and he goes on to boast of his compatriots that 'with the people of these lands and their *macamos* as they call their troops of slaves, they are more powerful than the king of Mokaranga himself'. A little later, the Portuguese surprisingly were able to extend their influence: they invaded Butua with a Karanga army stiffened by a few European soldiers, defeated the reigning Changamire in the field, and may even have evicted him from his capital at Great Zimbabwe. Relics found at Dhlodhlo, and the evidence of European building techniques at Nalatali, together with oral tradition, all suggest that these Rozwi Escorials and centres of power were temporarily occupied by the Portuguese about this time.

But soon afterwards the familiar rhythm of alternating Bantu and European ascendancy reasserted itself, and finally the advent of a man with military talent to the Rozwi chieftainship decisively tipped the balance against the Portuguese. In 1693, Dombo, the Changamire of his day, led a Rozwi army northwards at the Monomatapa's invitation, and joined him in a devastating attack on the white men. Nothing but their common detestation of the Portuguese could have allowed such hereditary protagonists to form an alliance, and their combined forces were superior to anything that the Europeans could put into the field. The Portuguese army was defeated in a pitched battle at Maungo which is said to have lasted a whole day. Then Dambarare, the jewel of the Portuguese crown in south-central Africa, was surprised and sacked; its garrison of forty soldiers was wiped out, the two resident friars were flayed alive, and all Europeans and Indian civilians living in the settlement were mercilessly hunted down and their bones subsequently ground up to be used as medicine by the witch-doctors. All the other Portuguese concessions except one or two in Manica* were now abandoned and by 1700 Changamire could announce that the whole of Butua and Monomatapa had been cleared of white men. One is not surprised to learn that the Monomatapa, when he invited Changamire north, had conjured up a sorceror's apprentice, and that very soon the Rozwi were ruling over all Karangaland. They proved more formidable enemies to the Portuguese than their predecessors. Although a few merchants from Sena and Manica seem to have entered Karanga country later, they came on sufferance, and the Portuguese never made a real effort to reassert their authority in modern Rhodesia until, during the European scramble for Africa during the eighteen-eighties, they were spurred on to extract concessions from Mashona chiefs as far west as Lomagundi. Yet earlier they had been the country's masters for over a hundred years. What perhaps is most surprising about this long ascendancy is the little impact it made on the Bantu: the Karanga had proved extraordinarily resilient to Western culture, and after they had driven them out of their country the possibility of the white men coming back never even crossed their minds.

Today, the Portuguese conquerors of Rhodesia are almost forgotten: the only realities of their existence seem to remain now in the faded documents of the Lisbon archives, the scant ruins of the fortresses they built in Mashonaland, and a vague recollection in the country of the final staleness of their lives. They had made a magnificent attempt to create a Christian empire in the far interior but they had been too few in numbers and too corrupted by their environment to administer their conquest properly; paradoxically they had been too proud to abandon it voluntarily. The Portuguese had been no more successful as evangelists than as colonists: when white missionaries re-entered Rhodesia in 1859, not one Christian was there to welcome them. The seeds of the Faith which had been so laboriously planted in Rhodesia by the Jesuits and Dominicans by then had quite withered away and not a single trace of them was left.

* In 1832, the Portuguese still maintained a 'fair' in Manica. It was besieged then by the Nguni invaders of Rhodesia; the garrison was reduced to such straits that they cast golden bullets for their guns before being overwhelmed.

4

MZILIKAZI

The Karanga were on their own again, and they sank back with relief into the old Bantu days. For the next one hundred and fifty years they almost lost touch with the outside world, and a strange anonymity enveloped the country. Students have to rely heavily on African tradition and the few rumours that drifted down to the coast from the far interior for their knowledge of Karangaland during the eighteenth century; and the glimpses they do obtain during this enigmatic period are fitful and tantalisingly out of focus, like photographs of the moon relayed back to earth from an orbiting spacecraft whose cameras are not working properly. A certain amount of bartering continued with itinerant traders; gold and ivory was exchanged for Chinese and Persian porcelain and for Portuguese firearms from the coast, but in all Rozwi sites the amount of exotic material found is minute compared with indigenous articles, and so far as Europe was concerned the Karanga might have been living on another planet.

From 1700 to 1835 successive Mambos of the Changamire dynasty reigned over a theocentric nation which comprised most of Rhodesia and part of Mocambique, and also reached across the Zambesi when the satellite state of Barotseland (whose name enshrines that of its founders) was established. The Mambo ruled through a closed hierarchy of Rozwi nobles, and one wonders whether any other aristocracy has possessed such all-embracing functions as the members of this dominant clan. Like the Brahmins of India they formed a hereditary priestly caste, but their sacerdotal prerogatives were combined with the authority of Roman senators, the intellectual prestige of the Chinese literati, and the military leadership of the Mamelukes in contemporary Egypt. The Karanga were their serfs who accepted the Rozwi as overlords; they gapingly acknowledged them to be a magic people and the elect of Mwari, who were

77

the intermediaries between themselves and the awful powers of nature.

There is no evidence that the Karanga ever resented the privileged position of the Rozwi. To us of the twentieth century their easy acceptance of an inferior status seems a little strange; we tend to forget that in our grandfathers' time class distinction was accepted without rancour in England, and that then Cecil Francis Alexander could hymn quite seriously the theme of 'the rich man in his castle, the poor man at his gate, God made them high and lowly, and ordered their estate'. In any case it is a Bantu trait to accept confident leadership without question, particularly if that leadership has religious undertones. In a larger context by endorsing the concept of a ruling élite the Karanga were merely resuming the submissive habits of their forefathers. The reimposition of a paramount chief's authority must have seemed a return

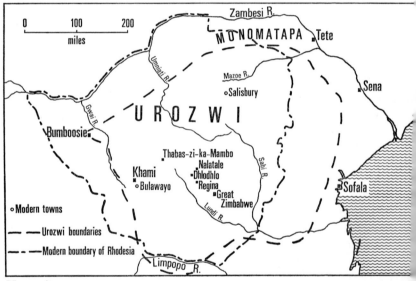

Urozwi, *c.* A.D. 1700

to normality after the brief interruption when an alien people had exerted a political influence out of all proportion to their numbers, and one has the feeling that if the Karanga had not again been subjected to outside pressures, they would have never changed their attitudes.

The Mambo himself lived amid pompous state in a 'palace' on the hill at Great Zimbabwe, just above the arched cave whence the disembodied voice of Mwari could be heard speaking at intervals. Like another Dalai Lama the Mambo was kept hidden from the common people, but would give audience to his office bearers in a large terraced enclosure on the hilltop bounded by huge granite rocks and dry stone walling which can still be seen. The Mambo's 'Great Wife' similarly held court and received tribute in the oval palace below, whose tremendous walls are the most impressive medieval relic in Rhodesia. His vassals would bring tribute of building stones here to enlarge his palace, or gold to be used as ornaments or hammered in thin sheets on to wooden plaques and utensils. The Mambo reigned until such time as his sexual powers began to fail or he suffered some other infirmity, such as the loss of a tooth, when the wretched man would be subjected to ritual murder, usually at the hands of his most junior wife.

The power of the Mambo and the Rozwi clan was maintained by a curious blend of prestige, intimidation, and fraud. These Romans of Bantu Africa formed an *élite sans pareil*, lacking social mobility, and entrapped within their own narcissistic shell from which they had not even a desire to escape. Rozwi culture was a common inheritance for all the Karanga but they knew two ways of life: that of the aristocrats who were equipped to rule and that of the vassals born to serve. Perhaps it was inevitable that in time the Rozwi aristocrats should have become degenerate: a Portuguese account written in 1789 reports that they 'pass their whole lives in the indolence of sensuality and the activity of spoliation, hold agriculture and commerce in contempt and consider themselves superior to other races. They consider work as a degradation. . . .' Yet the Rozwi were sustained by an almost intangible prestige, and we learn from this same report that 'six or seven of these desparadoes . . . will, it is said, intimidate 600 negroes of other tribes'.

During the eighteenth century the Mambo's kingdom reminds

us of a half-grown child in a state of arrested development. The abrupt withdrawal of foreign influences had made the Karanga turn in upon themselves; they had no conception of the revolutionary changes which were sweeping through contemporary Europe or even of the tremendous events occurring nearer home in south-east Africa. They lived in a complacent mental vacuum of their own, and perhaps thought of themselves as inhabiting a small and separate universe. Although they had been happy to enjoy the luxuries looted from the Portuguese settlements while they lasted, the Rozwi nobles at the same time utterly repudiated the skills of Europe and reverted almost instinctively to the dark groping Africa of their forebears. Indeed one can instance no better example of the intrinsic atavism that characterises the Bantu than the Karanga withdrawal into the past after 1700. Reason became corroded again by ancient superstitions; initiative was blunted by the old insistence on uniformity; and institutions slipped into frozen postures which were far too brittle to withstand the changes which are always inherent in the future.

Yet by a whim of history the sybaritic decline of the Karanga during the Rozwi hegemony was accompanied by cultural advances which give an almost baroque grandeur to the period. Techniques in stone building enabled Rozwi architecture to attain the highest level ever reached in Bantu Africa. The splendid additions made to Zimbabwe, Dhlodhlo, Nalatali, Thabas-zi-ka-Mambo, Khami, and a score of other buildings provide our most revealing expressions of the Bantu soul in stone and can with confidence be ascribed to the eighteenth century: their style and lavish wall decoration may have owed something to the advice of Arab sycophants or Portuguese prisoners at court, but essentially these grand and imposing edifices are African in concept and design. The Rozwi loved display and they reflected this in stony ostentation while separate princes proclaimed their importance in chevron and chequer patterns somewhat in the manner of European heraldry. There was cultural progress in other directions: carving in soapstone, ivory, and bone became more sophisticated, and particular care was taken in fashioning the Zimbabwe birds which each represented the ancestral spirit of some dead Mambo.

We know too from the number of spindle whorls found in Rozwi ruins that cotton spinning was extensively practised. But all, or nearly all, that had been learned from the Portuguese was forgotten: no form of writing or numbering survived, while the uses of draught animals and the wheel dropped out of the communal memory.

By the first quarter of the nineteenth century the Mambo's kingdom was like a rich estate which lay basking in the sun and presenting an open invitation to any burglars who might be in the vicinity. Its owners had become far too indolent and apathetic to defend their heritage, and there was scarcely any resistance when a horde of savage fighting men calling themselves Angoni suddenly surged on to the plateau from the Sabi valley in 1831. The Rozwi state ceased to exist almost overnight: very soon all that remained of it were the ruins of the buildings where the Mambos held court and a memory of the legend they had created. But the legend was no mean heritage for Rhodesia.

* * * * *

We must for a moment pause at this point to consider the events in Zululand which had set the Angoni and other fighting tribes raging through central Africa during the second and third decades of the century. Their intrusion was the direct consequence of the sudden check which seventy years earlier had been given to the slow migration of the Bantu through the subcontinent. The black tide, after washing the Karanga on to the high plateau of Rhodesia, had continued to flow steadily southwards and presently it reached the great watershed of the Drakensberg mountains. There it divided into two separate currents: Sotho tribes streamed on to the grasslands of the high veld to the west of the mountains, while on the eastern side the related Nguni people entered the narrower corridor between the mountains and the sea which Portuguese mariners had already named Natal. Like a flood entering a narrow gorge, the Nguni division now began to run more strongly, until in 1752 it met the van of white colonists trekking up the south-east coast of Africa from their original settlement at the Cape.

It was like the breaking of a wave on an uncharted rock, and the forward surge of the Bantu tide rippled, eddied, stopped, and finally broke back. The Nguni people piled up in Natal like the waters of a damned up river. Because of the human congestion which resulted, a century of discord followed and changes, far more revolutionary than those which had evolved so gradually in Monomatapa, now utterly altered the ethos of a large section of the Bantu race.

Land, always so plentiful before in Africa, suddenly became scarce in Natal. There was competition for living space. For greater protection against predatory neighbours, the Nguni clans amalgamated into tribal units, and then into multi-tribal blocs organised on a military basis. Individual freedom was relinquished into the hands of warrior chiefs, and a people which previously had valued non-violence now continually resorted to violence. Inter-tribal wars which had been half-hearted before were now waged with ruthlessness and savagery. Natal exploded into a holocaust of fighting and soon the insanity was no longer confined to the coastal corridor: it burst over the mountains and on to the high veld; presently it reached right up to the Mambo's kingdom.

The famous Rozwi state was torn to pieces by this Bantu riptide. The Karanga from the advantageous position of hindsight afterwards recalled that they had been given ample warning of the carnage which followed the Nguni invasions: they remembered that some time before, the high priest of Mwari had unaccountably moved the sacerdotal regalia of their cult from Great Zimbabwe to a cave in the Matopos called Njelele; they recalled too that the reigning Mambo, Rupenga Chirisamaru, had been rebuked there by the disembodied voice of Mwari, and when he replied in blasphemous terms the oracle had prophesied that an invasion from the south would soon overthrow his dynasty. But apart from such occult determinants of the coming disaster, Rozwi tradition also accounts for the poor resistance made to the Angoni invasion by explaining that successive drought years and a number of highly unnecessary civil wars had already enfeebled their state.

The Nguni invasions of Karangaland completely altered the

country's destiny, and three men who happened to be born within a few years and a few miles of each other, directly or indirectly shaped its future. The oldest of the three was born in 1787: he was the unwanted son of the chief of a petty Nguni tribe called the Zulus and he was named Shaka. Three years later another boy was born to the chief of the related Kumalo clan: he became known as Mzilikazi.* And in 1792 a Boer family named Potgieter, living in the Cardock district of Cape Colony, welcomed the arrival of a son who was christened Andries Hendrik.

By the time these three boys were grown up the Nguni people in Natal had grouped themselves into two great rival confederations. One of them was ruled by Shaka the Zulu, the other by Zwide the chief of the Ndwandwe tribe. In the chaotic conditions of ninteenth-century Natal there was room for only one master, and the armies of Shaka and Zwide met in the July of 1819 to decide which of them it would be. The battle ended with a sweeping victory for Shaka and set off a series of unpredictable events. For three of Zwide's generals, by hard running, succeeded in escaping from the rout and into the history of Rhodesia. Delaying only long enough to gather up their womenfolk, these men, Soshangane, Zwangendaba, and Nxaba, fled northwards with their followers from Shaka's vengeance. They cut separate swathes of destruction through the peaceful tribes of Mocambique, but would sometimes turn from hunting down helpless victims to quarrel among themselves over some particular prize. Thirteen years and many thousand deaths later they brought their armies into the Rozwi kingdom like successive driving furies.

The full stories of the incredible fighting *odysseys* of Zwangendaba, Nxaba, and Soshangane have still to be written. Each of these remarkable men brought their impis to Rhodesia in turn from Mocambique. Internecine wars left Soshangane in firm possession of an empire† based on the upper Sabi valley, which

---

* There are at least sixteen different spellings of his name: thus the early missionaries write of him as Moselkatse. The name has been variously translated as meaning 'trail of blood', and 'a well defined track', and 'one who observes taboos'.

† It was called Gaza or sometimes (in honour of its founder) the Shangaan state. Soshangane looted Lourenço Marques in 1833, and subsequently established his kraal at Manglagazi near Mount Selinda in Rhodesia.

reached from Manica to the sea, and his runaway victories sent
Zwangendaba and Nxaba driving westwards into the heart of
the Rozwi kingdom. Zwandendaba's Angoni sacked Great
Zimbabwe in 1831, but the reigning Mambo, Chirisamaru
Changamire* succeeded in escaping to Dhlodhlo. From there he
was driven to his final stronghold, Thabas-zi-ka-Mambo beyond
Inyati. The ruins of his palace are still to be seen there perched
up on the summit of a steep kopje. It is a haunted place; today
Africans living in the Mambo Hills will tell the visitor that at
sunrise they see people walking about its ruins and smoke coming
from huts on the summit, and hear the lowing of cattle and the
bleating of sheep; but they all disappear if they climb the
kopje. Standing among the scattered stones of this stronghold
today it is not difficult to conjure up a vision of Chirisamaru's
anxious face when he heard of the final defeat his army had
suffered near Inyati, and then watched the Angoni horde coming
up the valley dragging an ancient Portuguese cannon with them.
The siege of Thabas-zi-ka-Mambo which followed is said to have
lasted three days. When the defence broke down, the Mambo
made no attempt to escape; instead he seated himself on his ivory
throne, blindfolded himself, explained 'kingship is a rock that
does not flee',† and calmly awaited his end. It is said to have
come to him cruelly: according to one tradition he was carried
away to Thabas Ikonya, the Hill of Destiny, and there flayed
alive; another legend insists that he was tortured to death inside
the ruins of his last citadel. A few Rozwi grandees managed to
hold out for some time at Khami and Nalatale before they too
were stormed and sacked by the invincible Angoni; others
escaped to Bumboosie, and were found there by Mzilikazi a few
years later.

This first nightmare of bloodshed and looting in Karangaland
lasted until 1835, when the hordes of Zwangendaba and Nxaba, in
search of richer prey, crossed the Zambesi and marched out of

* One authority gives his name as Dhlembewu.

† The Mambo's apostrophe reminds one of the Empress Theodora's exhortation
to Justinian after the disastrous Nika rebellion: '. . . for an Emperor to become a
fugitive is not a thing to be endured . . . Royalty makes a fine winding sheet'.

Rhodesian history. A timid silence then replaced the din of shouting warriors and screaming fugitives along the great Karanga plateau, and the cringing survivors of the invasion crept back to their ruined kraals and tried to pick up their broken lives. It was a short reprieve. Within three years the long shields of another Nguni people—the Matabele—came over the horizon and the slaughter began anew. There was little thought of resistance; all the will to fight had already been beaten out of the Karanga and the country fell into the strong hands of the Matabele almost, as it were, by default.

The holocaust which had overwhelmed Karangaland was only part of that larger agony of southern Africa which stemmed from Shaka's victory of 1819, and which even today is spoken of with dull awe as the *mfecane*—the crushing. For Shaka, after securing the hegemony of the Nguni people, embarked on a series of wars of conquest which set Zulu impis raging all through the sub-continent in a wild delirium of killing. Two million Africans died during the *mfecane*, and scores of tribes fled from their homelands before the Zulu impis, and like links in a hideous chain reaction fell in turn upon their neighbours. For an apocalyptic decade rabbles of starving warriors swung round Bantu Africa in a desperate search for hiding places and food—any food—even human flesh. Southern Africa was overwhelmed by the sort of chaos which beset the Congo during the nineteen-sixties, but on such a vastly more extravagant scale that the Congo affair seems in comparison like a tiff in the common room of a girls' school. The last blizzards of the *mfecane* did not blow themselves out for fifteen years and by then the sub-continent's condition is reminiscent of Petrarch's description of Italy during the black death: 'almost the whole earth was left uninhabited' he wrote then, and all that was left were 'unkempt fields, ground crowded with corpses, and everywhere a vast and dreadful silence'.

The high veld of south Africa was virtually depopulated during the *mfecane*; those who had survived it vanished into the Basuto mountains or within the huge aridity of the Kalahari. In parenthesis we must note that one group of refugees calling themselves the Makololo, rallied round a soldier named Sebituane who seemed to possess an instinct for keeping alive; he led them eventually from the desert to the grasslands of the upper Zambesi and there, on the frontiers of Rhodesia, they entered briefly into her story.

Shaka's fantastic conquests flowed from his own obsession with blood and an extraordinary ability to devise original military tactics. He merged a hundred Nguni clans into a single Zulu nation, and from it forged an army which was invincible unless opposed by firearms. Shaka tossed aside the traditional Bantu concept of mustering each clan's fighting men under the command of hereditary petty-chiefs: instead his regiments were recruited on the basis of age groupings, and the men served long enough in them to gain the character of a standing army; each impi wore distinctive dress, and was commanded by an *induna* who was nearly always a man promoted for merit rather than because of birth. This innovation was of some significance: it meant that the loyalty of each *induna* and the men he commanded was transferred from clan or tribe to the king. Shaka departed, however, from the rule of appointing commoners to command his impis in the case of one favourite general, Mzilikazi. But then Mzilikazi's position among the Zulus was exceptional: the people of his Kumalo clan had not been conquered by the Zulus; rather they had voluntarily given their allegiance to Shaka. In later years Mzilikazi often recounted the reason why they had done this: the Kumalos, he would explain, had originally been part of the Ndwandwe confederation ruled by Zwide, but one day their chief Machobane, Mzilikazi's own father, and incidentally the husband of one of Zwide's daughters, had been accused of treachery by his father-in-law and summarily executed. Mzilikazi never fully recovered from the shock of Machobane's death, and certainly he never forgave Zwide for it. As soon as the opportunity presented itself—and it came just before the decisive clash between Zwide and Shaka—he adroitly changed to the winning side.

Mzilikazi understood the implications of the new Zulu military tactics more completely than Shaka's other lieutenants, and he rocketed in the king's favour. He was rewarded with the command of a regiment recruited from his own Kumalo kinsmen, and he led them to several notable victories. The inevitable occurred when a man of his spirit began to savour the taste of military success: Mzilikazi came to regard the impi as his own private army, and in 1822, he overreached himself by refusing to send Shaka, his master, the share of cattle booty that was due to him from a raid.

Shaka presently despatched a punitive force to liquidate the

Migration of the Matabele from Zululand to Matabeleland

insubordinate Kumalo clan, and after tasting initial success Mzilikazi's impi suffered a sharp defeat: a mere three hundred of his fighting men escaped from the slaughter and headed with three or four of the chief's wives for a pass in the Drakensberg mountains and the high veld. They only drew breath at the upper waters of Oliphants river.

Here Mzilikazi's people built themselves a kraal which they somewhat prematurely named Eku-Pumuleni—the resting place —and at once proceeded to wage war on the neighbouring Sotho tribes. The results were gratifying. The Kumalos were a reckless desperate crowd of men; they wore the dress and prestige of the dreaded Zulus, and they were much more than a match for the peaceful Sotho. Kraal after kraal was sacked and burned, and instead of being a fugitive, Mzilikazi was very soon lording it over a large area of the north-eastern Transvaal.

He had absorbed Shaka's military lessons very well. Although few in numbers his soldiers had been carefully drilled in the shock tactics of the Zulus. Before battle Mzilikazi would form them up into the central 'chest', and two flanking 'horns' which were trained to race round and envelop the enemy. When more men became available, Mzilikazi formed a fourth reserve division which he called the 'loins', and its warriors were schooled to sit behind the 'chest' with their backs to the fighting until called upon to make a decisive charge.

His men fought with the Zulu short broad-bladed spear; it was designed to be used as an underhand thrusting weapon, rather in the manner of the Roman sword. They also carried two or three throwing spears and a knobkerrie together with an immense ox-hide shield which covered the entire body yet was strong enough to be used offensively as a battering ram. The warriors were ferociously disciplined, and trained to move across country hour after hour in silence, at high speed, and in perfect alignment. Their Sotho victims were like hypnotised rabbits before these ruthless killers; their fighting in the past had been conducted in a half-hearted manner with the opposing sides content to throw spears at each other until their ammunition ran out, and they had no experience at all of close-in combat. The Sotho called the terrible invaders the Matabele, which can be translated as the people of the long shields, but we should note that according to one somewhat ungallant authority the name in fact was derived from the appearance of Mzilikazi's starving and exhausted wives, and meant 'the people of the long breasts'.*

By 1825 the Matabele had so completely devastated the country round the upper Oliphants river that Mzilikazi decided to exploit the more abundant opportunities for pillage in the west, and his people moved to a new kraal whose site today is covered by the northern suburbs of Pretoria. Somewhat optimistically he named

* The more correct rendering of the tribal name is Amandabele.

it Mhlahlandhlela—the end of the road.* But Mzilikazi's road in fact was destined to take him far further, and to lead him on to the the great plateau of Rhodesia.

Mzilikazi prospered in the three years which followed his flight from Zululand, and his following grew much larger; for although his warriors butchered most of the Sotho tribesmen capable of bearing arms in the area around Eku-Pumuleni, they were careful to spare all desirable women, and they assimilated suitable youths into their own regiments, first as weapon carriers, and later as warriors. In 1832 the Matabele made still another westward move into the fertile Marico valley, and by then the original remnants of the Kumalo clan had snowballed into a nation of sixty thousand men and women. The army was the most formidable in the interior and the *amatjaha*† especially were feared for their overbearing truculence: it was as though continued success in slaughtering defenceless Sotho had made the blood run like fire through their veins. The grazing round the Marico was excellent, crops were plentiful, and the Matabele must have thought they would remain in its valley for ever. Many of the older men were now released from active service and allowed to marry, their new status being proclaimed by permission to train their hair into the extraordinary Zulu head-ring or *isidhlodhlo*; it was coiled with wax into a circle on the crown of the head, and one white observer thought it looked like a 'singular halo'. It was as unique a national head-dress as the feathered plumes of the Red Indians or a Chinaman's pigtail.‡ According to their age groups the younger warriors were drafted into new regiments, each one of which cherished its own traditions and wore distinctive 'uniforms' in the manner of their Zulu kinsmen.

Yet even on the Marico it soon became apparent that the Matabele were still not safe, for the Zulus launched three separate punitive expeditions against them during the eighteen-thirties which were only repulsed after bloody fighting. The Matabele

---

* A better translation is said to be 'to cut a path through the bush'.
† Young warriors.
‡ The Matabele *isidhlodhlo* is rarely seen now; it measured six or more inches across and many were smaller than those worn in Zululand.

now had also to face formidable raids from Griqua *banditti* parties. The Griquas, who were of mixed Hottentot and European blood, had established a semi-autonomous state in the vicinity of modern Kimberley. They were accomplished horsemen and well armed with flintlocks. Each Griqua invasion—and there were six of them within the next ten years—started off with a flourish, but every one ended in failure. For the Griquas' only concern was with the acquisition of cattle loot, and when their gangs withdrew encumbered with cattle they fell an easy prey to Matabele ambushes at night and each time the raiders were butchered in the darkness.

In 1836, however, a danger infinitely more alarming than the Zulus and Griquas began to threaten the Matabele; the Afrikaner nation was on the march, and Mzilikazi's kingdom lay directly across the line of its advance.

By that time Mzilikazi had already met several British adventurers and missionaries, and had liked them; on the advice of Robert Moffat, a missionary from Kuruman, he had even dispatched envoys to Cape Town to sign a treaty of friendship with the authorities there. He knew less about the Boers, but he had no wish to antagonise the trekkers who came riding northwards across the high veld in 1836. Indeed, the first clash between the Matabele and the Voortrekkers occurred quite fortuitously; an impi returning from a raid chanced upon a Boer hunting party where it was resting at a Vaal drift used by the Griquas during their invasions. Not unnaturally, the Matabele took the Boers for a Griqua war band, and overwhelmed them with a sudden attack. Only two little white girls were spared and carried off to Mzilikazi as trophies of war.

Once hostilities had begun between the Matabele and the Boers they had to be fought *à outrance*, and the splendid prize of the Transvaal would go to the victor. The initiative rested with Mzilikazi, and he sent an impi under the *indunas* Kalipi and Gondwana to attack one group of trekkers led by Andries Hendrik Potgieter, the third of the three men who would affect Rhodesian history. The Matabele found the trekkers laagered at Vegkop and there the handful of white men successfully beat off an attack by five thousand warriors. But Kalipi drove away the Boers' cattle herds and Potgieter wanted them back, and he believed in crowding a defeated enemy. Early in 1837 Potgieter therefore swept into Mzilikazi's chief kraal with a powerful commando, fired the town and retired with seven thousand head of looted cattle. They had killed more than four hundred Matabele during the fighting without losing a single white man. Mzilikazi was still reeling from this blow when he had to head off another fierce attack from the Zulus, and before the disastrous year of 1837 was done, Potgieter's horsemen came pounding up the Marico valley again, and devastated the Matabele settlements one after the other in a running fight which lasted nine terrible days.

For all their courage and discipline the Matabele were unable to stand up to the Boers' superior fighting power and mobility. At the end of the nine days' battle Mzilikazi's army had dissolved into a rabble of frightened men who streamed off northwards with their women and children. Potgieter's horsemen pursued them as far as the Tweedepoort range. Then mercifully the pressure eased when the Boers turned for home with more herds of Mzilikazi's cattle, and as the sound of the white men's gunfire grew fainter and finally died away the ten thousand Matabele who had survived the débâcle halted thankfully in the bush. They were whipped and knew it.

Only Mzilikazi kept his head: for the next few days he stormed about the hills rallying the regiments and using them to shepherd the fugitives into the more easily defensible passes of the Dwarsberg mountains. And there the scattered Matabele people were reunited and the nation rested.

The Matabele tell us that next morning when the cold and sullen dawn came up, Mzilikazi called his counsellors together to discuss the situation; when their historians speak today of that legendary moment it is very easy to visualise again the scene of bleak despair and pessimism—the weary faces of the warriors as they look to their weapons; the women, too cold and miserable for talk, busying themselves over their cooking pots; the children huddled together in wailing groups; and Mzilikazi, erect and full of confidence still, looking back across the grey-brown veld to the distant pillars of smoke which mark his smouldering kraals. For some time he stands there motionless; then suddenly he turns and points to the north. There is an authority in him that revives the flagging spirits of the defeated people who are watching, and they listen quietly when he tells them he will lead them across the Limpopo river to the fertile green grasslands which his raiding impis have told him stretch in a great arc nearly to the Zambesi itself. 'We are going to the great river', he says, 'to the *Ilizwe ilike Mambo*,'* and even further if that is the only way to escape the Boers. And as he points to the north the sky is already paling with the dawn of the Matabele era in Rhodesian history.

*   *   *   *   *

Traditional memories are always apt to recall their heroes at the moments when they made the greatest impact on national imagination; and so the Matabele, when they speak of Mzilikazi, reconstruct him in admiring detail as he was that morning in the Dwarsberg in 1837. They see an impressive figure in his middle forties, robust, broad shouldered, moving with the vigour of a trained athlete, and quite undaunted by the disasters which have befallen his people. African and European accounts alike stress the regal way in which Mzilikazi held his head, and speak of the high brow, and the lively eyes which according to John Mackenzie were 'almost the largest I have seen'.

History, or at least the history written by white men, has typed Mzilikazi as a worthy pupil of the demented Shaka who wallowed in the blood of defenceless people. But Mzilikazi can be only fairly judged by the standard of his own savage environment. Although one cannot quarrel with Mackenzie when he asserts that Mzilikazi turned his nation into a 'dreadful organisation' which lived on 'pillage, outrage, and bloodshed', and 'every year multiplied the number of murdered innocents, whose blood cried to Heaven for vengeance', yet at the same time it must be accepted that if the Matabele were to survive at all in contemporary Africa, they could only do so by becoming more predatory than their

* Country of the Mambo.

neighbours. In the same way, Mzilikazi could have only maintained his personal position by setting himself up as a complete autocrat and by occupying the energies of his impis with continual fighting. Mackenzie himself recognised this and he explained the king's predicament very clearly when he wrote that 'in order to secure the continued allegiance of his men, Moselekatse had to devise work for them in which they would meet with the gratification of their savage passions'. And even if Mzilikazi's conduct sometimes strikes us as the extreme of callous barbarity, it must be remembered that by the standards of Africa a century ago it was considered to be comparatively mild.

Mzilikazi of course is a very good example of the self-made African tyrant of the nineteenth century. He could be very ruthless and very brutal, and all reports stress his unpredictability. Yet there were in him other qualities which make him stand out as one of the most interesting men ever produced in Bantu Africa. Although most Europeans who knew him well would have agreed with Robert Moffat that Mzilikazi was 'a man who feasts himself and his thousands on others' woes', all of them were also aware that his ferocity was tempered on occasion by unlooked for sensibility and gentleness. Thus Moffat himself admits that 'he was rather a pleasing soft countenance and is exceedingly affable in his manners. His voice is soft and feminine and cheerfulness predominates in him'. Thomas, who after 1859 got to know the king very well, found him 'kind in manner', and he would often speak of the day when, accompanied by his two recently orphaned children,* he paid a call on the king: Mzilikazi, he said, 'cried out in a feeling tone "Take the poor motherless ones to the wagon, for I cannot bear the sight." Turning to me, he said, "my child, I am sorry for you. She, who is no more, was lovely and beloved; we all loved her, and are sad after her. But go my son and may your journey be a pleasant and prosperous one. May you find favour in the sight of all you meet, until the day we shall welcome you back again. Do not be long!"' Even the prejudiced Mackenzie

* His colleague, Elliott believed that had Mr Thomas been able to see into the future he would have wished that they too might have 'been taken' for 'both fell victims to the pitiless spear of savages'.

93

had to admit that the king was 'possessed of kindly feelings, and keenly alive to the sufferings of others', and he goes on to relate with some bemusement that 'even his oxen Moselkatse did not permit to be lashed severely by the long whip of the wagon-driver; his men were allowed to beat them only with green wands cut from the bushes in the forest'.

It is clear then that there was an unlooked for streak of kindliness in Mzilikazi; it is less easy to appreciate that for all his air of authority and apparent self-confidence, the king fretted always under a deep sense of insecurity. His father's death seems never to have been very far from his mind and it was referred to tearfully on many occasions. He compensated for this psychological trauma and sense of deprivation with a demand for slavish obedience from his subjects, together with a rather pathetic search for some father figure to take Machobane's place. He found one in Dr Robert Moffat, and it was symptomatic of this discrepant aspect of Mzilikazi's personality that on one occasion he assured Moffat that the Mlimo had 'made for him another father in myself, and in future he would call me Machobane'. One suspects that had he been born in a later age Mzilikazi would have become an on-off psychiatric patient.

But that morning in 1837 when he made his decision to lead his people to a new homeland, there was no impairment of Mzilikazi's emotions and motivation. He was all determination and certainty. The *indunas* were told that the Matabele would march northwards in two separate contingents to facilitate foraging. Gondwana was to lead one section, which would include Kulumani, the king's heir, and most of the women, and he was ordered to direct his march towards the flat-topped hill of Dombo-re-Mambo which was known to be a landmark near the southern end of the Karanga plateau. The second more mobile column under the king's personal command, would move on a westerly course through the Kalahari, as he intended to explore the possibilities of settling beyond the Zambesi valley before turning back to rendezvous with Gondwana. The hegira of his people, the king concluded, was to begin immediately.

The route selected for Gondwana was by far the easier of the two. Once through the arid country beyond the Limpopo his people entered well-watered Karanga territory, and they met no resistance for the country had been laid waste only a few years before by the Angoni. Their march was swiftly and safely executed: after passing Gwanda and traversing the Matopo Hills, they reached the Rhodesian watershed a little east of modern Bulawayo, and at Entabenende settled down to await Mzilikazi's arrival. With strange adumbration they called the kraal they built Gibixhegu after a well-known town in Zululand. The name means 'take the old ones out' and it had been given to the original kraal after Shaka had called out all its grey heads he considered past their useful fighting lives and ordered them to be executed.

Eighteen months passed before the two sections of the Matabele were reunited. Mzilikazi had wandered with his following far into the Kalahari, and they suffered terrible privations. There were endless weeks of trudging through the desert, weeks that were only interrupted by sharp orders when they came to some unsuspecting Bechuana village, a massacre, a frantic slaking of thirst, and the gathering in of pitifully small grain crops. Then the march would begin again. Some recuperative months were spent at the Makarikari salt pans, but further north the Matabele entered tsetse country and lost most of their cattle. Soon afterwards they experienced another setback when they clashed with the Makololo in the Zambesi valley, and in the face of their resistance Mzilikazi had to abandon his intention of reconnoitring the country further north. Instead he turned back to keep his rendezvous with Gondwana. Some happier weeks were spent pillaging the Rozwi who had taken refuge from the Angoni in the Wankie area, and when their last stronghold at Bumboosie was sacked the heir to the Mambo dynasty was captured. He was reputed to have been born with two hearts and Mzilikazi was able to indulge a laudable interest in aberrant anatomy by having him killed and dissected in his presence; it is said that the king was grievously disappointed to discover that the reports were unfounded.

As they ascended the plateau, Mzilikazi's people entered more fertile country, and near Thabas Ikonya at the confluence of the Bembesi and Ingwegwesi rivers, they at last obtained news of Gondwana. That news was disturbing: believing Mzilikazi to have perished with his impi in the desert, Gondwana's *indunas* had agreed to accept his son, Kulumani, as their new king, in order that they might purify themselves at the great ceremony of the First Fruits or *Inxwala* which required certain ritual objects to be handled by a king.

This was the third crisis of Mzilikazi's career, and he needed a good deal of his proverbial luck if he was to avoid destroying himself and his people in a civil war. But neither his fortune nor his finesse deserted him now. A message was sent to Gibixhegu suggesting that the dissident *indunas* meet him at the summit of the flat-topped hill which had been arranged as their rendezvous, and celebrate the reunion with a feast. His invitation was accepted. The scene which followed has etched itself very sharply into Matabele memory, and it is discussed even now as though it happened only yesterday: a herd of fine oxen is driven up the hill, fires are lighted and great cooking pots prepared. When all the preparations are complete Mzilikazi calls the chiefs together and says to them 'you wanted another King; I will give you one', and he turns to his own followers with a peremptory order; hidden weapons suddenly appear, and the 'rebel' *indunas* are clubbed to death and their bodies flung down the slopes of the hill;* another order dispatches a servant with orders to strangle Kulumani. But at this point the celebrated story dissolves into tantalising uncertainty: his murderers afterwards spoke about Kulumani's death, but they disagreed among themselves about its manner, and we shall probably never know what truth there was in the rumours that Mzilikazi's heir in fact escaped to Natal and later played the role of the 'missing dauphin' of Matabele history.

But the fate of Kulumani seemed unimportant at the time; what did matter was that Mzilikazi had successfully reasserted his authority over his people and in a manner which caught at

* One authoritative Matabele source insists that the *Indunas* were executed some distance away from the hill and that Gondwana was taken back to Gibixhegu to be hanged.

their imagination. The Matabele named the hill where the executions had taken place Thabas Induna, and even now they claim that whenever an east wind comes up to blow away the precious rain clouds, it is conjured up by the magic spells of a single recalcitrant chief who managed to escape the slaughter.

The Matabele now entered into possession of the larger part of Rhodesia, for the military subjection of the abject Karanga who had survived Zwangendaba's onslaught a few years earlier presented very little problem. Mzilikazi is said to have apportioned out the country among his chiefs from a vantage point on the top of Thabas Induna. Settlement for a radius of about eighty miles round Bulawayo was quickly accomplished by the Matabele. This became the heartland of their new state. The tribes and clans living on its fringes submitted to Mzilikazi and paid him annual tribute. The Gwaai valley was cleared of its inhabitants and reserved for the royal cattle herds, while the Wankie district beyond was given over to wild animals and came to form the basis of the present game reserve. To the south Mzilikazi claimed dominion up to the Maklautsi river, but the strip beyond the Shashi in fact became a sort of no-man's-land to be constantly disputed with the Bechuana. To the east, direct Matabele rule extended roughly to the Umniati and Tokwe rivers, but suzerainty was claimed much further to a rough and ready boundary line mutually agreed upon with Soshangane; the inhabitants of this enormous vassal country retained a precarious independence, but were subjected to continuous raids by Mzilikazi's impis. The Matabele regarded them as victims to be killed at their pleasure, and gradually they became known as the Amaswina or Mashona—the lost ones.

Gibixhegu, Gondwana's old kraal, was abandoned after the executions on Thabas Induna, and Mzilikazi set up a new town nearby. He called it Matlokotloko.* To the great confusion of the Europeans who later came to visit the king (and even more to the future historians of the Matabele), Mzilikazi repeatedly

* It is difficult to render some Matabele names into English: in common with other Nguni tribes the Matabele had assimilated three of the five click consonants in the Bushman language. Matlokotloko when spoken is a much shorter word than it appears in writing, the repetitive 'tlo' being rendered with two rapid clicks made by the tongue against the palate.

moved the site of Matlokotloko during the remainder of his reign.*

Matabeleland was divided into four territorial divisions, and over each of them an *Induna* governed in the royal name, rather in the manner of Cromwell's Major-Generals. This was something of a departure from Shaka's centralised system; indeed it held in it the seeds of weakness since it encouraged the development of regional attachment to semi-hereditary chiefs. But that danger was to some extent mitigated by the establishment of many of Mzilikazi's three hundred queens in kraals scattered throughout the country; here they acted as hostesses during the king's constant perambulations and as royal informers about all local events and dangerous personalities.

The Matabele state was characterised by a caste system but it differed from those of Monomatapa and the Rozwi by condoning an easier movement of approved individuals into the élite. At the very apex of power stood Mzilikazi, this Bantu Moses who had a great advantage over his biblical predecessor by being able to write his own commandments. Placed below the King were the *Abazansi*—the original members of the Kumalo and kindred clans who had escaped from Zululand. Next in prestige came the *Abenhla*—those of Swazi and Sotho stock who had been incorporated into the nation during the early years of the Matabele migration. The base of the social pyramid was constituted by the *Amaholi*—those elements of indigenous Karanga stock who were found useful by the Matabele and who in time might aspire to assimilation by their conquerors and even to high office among them.

For the Matabele élite was never a closed one. Their position might be compared to that of the Normans who settled in England after 1066: they stamped their customs quite ruthlessly

---

* It was customary for the Matabele to move their kraals a few miles when the surrounding grazing, firewood, and water supplies showed signs of running out. The first Matlokotloko was built beyond Glengarry; later the king seems to have moved just east of Lobengula's later capital of Bulawayo. In 1847, Mzilikazi moved again to successive sites in the Inyati area, until, in 1863, he transferred his capital to the edge of the watershed, establishing himself first near Khami, and finally in a kraal on the verge of the Matopos which he called Mhlahlandhlela in memory of his town in the Transvaal. This time it was aptly named; near here he reached his 'end of the road'.

upon the conquered people, yet they did so in such a way that their subjects fervently wished to become indistinguishable from their masters. And in one important respect—their adoption of the Mwari-Mlimo religious cult—the Matabele assimilated an important element of the Karanga-Rozwi culture. The spell of their new country, they said, had prevailed over them, and they wanted to be 'at peace with the land'. They had a secondary reason for accepting this 'conversion': the highly developed 'secret service' of the Mwari priests was of great use to Mzilikazi and it suited him to support them. At all events the king was very soon making offerings at the shrine at Njelele and his example was followed by his people when they wanted to placate the Oracle or to ask for his assistance in making rain.

Mzilikazi's 'foreign policy' was confined to isolating Matabeleland from the outside world so far as it lay within his power: when Europe was expanding irresistibly into every corner of the globe, the Matabele king for many years succeeded in limiting the European penetration of his country to a handful of traders, hunters, and missionaries. It was to his great advantage that the borders of Rhodesia were so easily supervised and defended: the only practical access to the kingdom from the south was through the Mangwe pass, and here a sort of customs and immigration post was established.

At home the economy of the Matabele nation was based on raising cattle and pillaging the Mashona tribes living beyond the Umniati. National cohesion was maintained by the blind obedience of his people (and particularly of the army) to the king's personal authority. Mzilikazi was the only source of power in his Bantu Sparta; he claimed ownership of the national cattle herds as trustee of the nation and later he further buttressed the monarchy by assuming the monopoly of the valuable ivory trade; Moffat comments on this when he ruefully reveals that 'Moselkatse is the only one with whom barter can be effected. Every tusk of ivory is his, and no one dare dispose of one but himself. . . . He can ask what he likes.'

Our knowledge of the first fifteen years of Matabele rule in Rhodesia is owed almost entirely to African aural memory, but after 1854, when Robert Moffat first entered the country, we begin to obtain a far more sharply defined picture of conditions there. Moffat is perhaps our most lucid observer of what he called Mzilikazi's 'monstrous government' (and which he suggested 'needs an axe putting to its roots'). He was fascinated, and yet repelled, by Mzilikazi's personal power. 'The King', he tells us, 'is the centre and soul of everything', and he goes on to express with melancholy surprise that 'whatever he orders to be done, however outrageous to humanity and common sense, is received, even by those to whom he confides important matters, with expressions of the profoundest admiration.'

But whatever its faults—and there were many—the Matabele state holds a special interest for the modern world: for it was the last important Bantu nation to preserve its independence when the rest of Africa succumbed to the expanding forces of colonialism.

*   *   *   *   *

As Moffat is at pains to point out, Mzilikazi ruled his subjects by terror, and yet he was adored by them as a God.* His authority was every bit as arbitrary as that of any dictator of modern times. Death was the only punishment for misdemeanour, although the forms it took bore some relation to the crime. The methods used in execution were noted down once by a Catholic missionary in his diary. 'There are', he writes, 'three varieties of capital punishment' and he proceeds to list:

(1) The kerrie. The head of the condemned person is crushed as one would kill an animal in the slaughter-house; or else one squeezes the criminal's head in the cloven trunk of a tree and tortures him with a species of pincers until he is dead.

(2) The rope, or hanging from a near-by tree, something like lynch-law in the United States.

(3) The pillory. The patient is bound and tied to a tree and abandoned to die of starvation, or to be devoured by wild beasts. The body of the tortured man becomes the prey of hyenas and vultures.

* Moffat did not realise that the adoration sprang from Mzilikazi's special position which allowed him, the king, to appease the ancestral spirits. So far as the Matabele were concerned he was the chief intermediary between the living and the dead.

It is a gruesome list but in fact the missionary omitted two other common methods of execution. Persons suspected of witchcraft were often thrown to the crocodiles, and the pools of the Umguza river were particularly favoured for the purpose. But the most cruel of all Matabele punishments, impalement, was likewise reserved for 'witches' and for those convicted of *lèse majesté*: the victim was pulled in a sitting position down on to the top of a sharpened stake which had been firmly embedded in the ground, its point being directed up through the rectum or, in the case of women, the vagina. Moffat refers several times with horror to this torture: 'I heard this morning', he writes in August, 1857, 'that a man suspected of witchcraft and who had been seen joking with the king's wives was impaled this morning. These', he adds grimly, 'are the dark places of the earth.' On another occasion he laments that 'sometimes at night, when sleepless, . . . I think of the scenes which have passed before my eyes in the course of the day, and the gross darkness which covers the land in which I sojourn, the prostrate intellect which adores the man who is a man of blood and without whose permission they scarcely dare think. . . . When I look around me on the untutored native savage, their dwellings, their customs, their towns, I repeat, I involuntarily repeat, with all my heart, "How amiable are thy tabernacles, O Lord of Hosts."'

Another day Moffat sighs that the Matabele who are 'verily the greatest savages in South Africa . . . possess no moral impulse to check their inconsistencies. . . . They think they are made or "grow" only to eat, drink (I wish I could add dress) and live for Moselkatse', and he goes on to complain that '. . . the Christian mind can never become accustomed to their savage songs, their boasts of bloody feats, their fanatic adoration of the son of Machobane. . . .'

Poor Moffat could not overcome his repugnance at the king's baneful influence over his subjects, which, he says, makes them '. . . see the stars as they see stones, and the sun shining in his glory is to them nothing more than a thing that gives light and is sometimes very hot. To them the future is shrouded in darkness. . . . At his orders they will at any day rush into death, die for Moselkatse, the son of Machobane. This is all their glory.'

There was a great deal of truth in his appreciation: the Matabele were taught from childhood to find their only pleasures in war and the service of their king. Thomas Baines, who vies with Moffat as being the most punctilious delineator of the Matabele a century ago, assures us that they were 'a people who despise the arts of peace and reckon warlike prowess and savage cold-blooded massacre their greatest glory', and this opinion is confirmed by another source which states simply that 'The Matabele are a nation of warriors. All the men are soldiers and do nothing, and think of nothing else but war.' Moffat is at his most censorious on this subject and once described the Matabele as 'an army of whoremongers, a people taught from childhood to fear no one, to love no one, to offer thanks to no one but Mosel-katse, a nation of murderers whose hand is against every man'.

The Matabele army was the backbone of the nation. It was divided by Mzilikazi into thirty-one impis whose names are still remembered with pride in Rhodesia. Each impi numbered anything from five hundred to a thousand men* and was based on a special regimental kraal. So cherished were their traditions that until recently Matabele youths could tell you to which of these military kraals they belonged. Every impi possessed its own 'personalia', and all the barbaric truculence of the Bantu went on show when the army prepared for war. The appearance of the warriors was intended to strike terror into their enemies: certainly it startled and fascinated every European visitor to Matabeleland. Baines, after witnessing the return of a war party to the Matabele capital writes: 'they numbered probably 1,200 or 1,400 men and, with their large oval shields some black, some black and white and others red and white according to the colours of their regiments, and their large capes of black ostrich feathers and head wreaths and tall plumes of the same, they looked as formidable a body as one could wish to meet'.

Some idea of the ferocity of the younger warriors—the *Amatjaha* —is revealed in this description of one of their peace-time divertissements at the king's kraal:

* This is the largest number of men that can be effectively controlled by a man on foot.

A young bull was turned loose among the soldiers, and the king ordered them to put down their weapons, and without any other help than their hands and teeth to catch and eat the bull alive. The order was at once obeyed and executed, the young soldiers displaying their fierceness and thirst for blood by at once springing on the animal like a pack of wolves, so that in a short time nothing remained except the horns.

But however bloodthirsty the *Amatjaha* may have been, it is clear that their discipline and drill were above reproach. One visitor refers with admiration to their having performed 'a military tattoo . . . as good as anything I have ever seen either in Europe or British India', while another narrator tells us that an impi which had displeased the king was made to perform a war dance for four days and nights without stopping.

When they were not decked out in their war apparel, the Matabele preferred to be clad with only a Bantu variant of the classical fig-leaf. Baines, having been an interested observer of the care taken in collecting some specially shaped leaves, 'was instructed that these strips were for the purpose of the *um'nwato*, the only article of dress absolutely necessary to the Matabele, a hollow cone, about 6 inches long, covering the scar of the circumcision and swinging loose and pendant from the member to which it is attached',* but he hastened to add that 'Generally a short kilt is worn, or rather a few bits of skin forming a fringe of about a finger's length. . . .'

If the European visitor to Mzilikazi's court viewed his soldiers with grudging admiration, they were far less charitable about the appearance of the Matabele women. One feels that with an effort they had been able to overcome their Victorian scruples about nudity in men, but that they were quite unprepared to accept nakedness in women, especially if the women were stout. Moffat has a good deal to say about this:

'The men are in general good-looking here', he informs his wife, 'but the women are sorry objects. If fat and plumpness constitute African beauties, as I have heard, then they may come

* The white men who first came to Matabeleland jokingly called this small article of apparel 'a K.C.B.'.

in for a share, but most of the women, *lintombies*,* large fat women with large hanging daries,† and a mere shadow of a covering about their loins, looked disgusting in the extreme.' He returns to the subject with something of an air of shrillness on another occasion, writing, 'The women are really coarse-looking figures. Not a bit of ornament on their persons, not even in their ears, and a bit of rag not even enough to cover their hips—and some even without that, only a small rag before—made them disgusting objects,' and while on the subject he bids Mrs Moffat to 'think only of a great belly with a navel so thoroughly surrounded with fat that a swallow with a little labour might make a comfortable nest in it'.

In yet another letter Moffat gasps '. . . some of the *lintombi* had not a shadow of anything behind, and very little before', but a later visitor to Matabeleland, Vaughan-Williams, sounds far more temperate on these matters: 'The girls', he writes, 'wore no clothes except a string of beads, usually blue and white ones, round their middles, with a little beaded apron about six inches wide by three inches deep, for decency. It is an extraordinary thing', he goes on to point out, with pained surprise, 'that, no matter how they sat or stooped, this little affair effectually hid what they wanted to hide.'

* * * * *

Once they had consolidated their position in Matabeleland Mzilikazi's impis were sent off raiding the Mashona living beyond the Umniati river. The raids were conducted in so brutal a manner that they are still spoken of in Rhodesia with horror, and even today the Matabele and Mashona maintain a deep-rooted aversion for each other.

The forays took place each winter. The target for the year was indicated at the ceremony of the First Fruits held during the rains, when the king threw a spear in a chosen direction. After being 'doctored' with all sorts of weird charms and given dagga to smoke, the warriors would then pour into Mashonaland in an orgy of looting, burning, and killing. Even now it is impossible

* Maidens.　　† Breasts.

to read about their behaviour without recoiling. It is not so much the warriors' brutality that seems so appalling, for after all that was commonplace in Bantu Africa before the colonial era, it is rather the air of cold-blooded nonchalance with which the raids were conducted that gives them their special flavour of horror.

The Matabele, we are told by one indignant observer, regarded their raids 'as an Englishman might view the annual training of a militia battalion or his yearly shoot on the moors'. For them the Mashona were mere spear fodder or moving targets to provide practice in the art of killing. The impis would move swiftly through Mashona territory and hope to surprise the selected kraals. 'The usual practice', runs one grim report, 'was to swoop down on the unaware Mashona in a part of the country which it was decided beforehand should be raided, kill all the men and old women they found, and then carry off the cattle, young women, and children. The excuse for the raid was that someone in that part had offended His Majesty. These raids were carried out with the utmost secrecy and speed. As frequently happened the alarm would be given, announced from one kraal to another. "Masweti wia" struck terror into those who heard that warning cry. Most of the Mashonas had hiding places for themselves and their stock in the rocks and caves, and if the warning came in time the chances are that they would escape as the Matabele had no time to invade the place which was difficult to take.' Another report says that after a raid 'the women were made to carry the plunder of their own villages as far as the confines of the victors' kraals, where they were collected in a circle in the centre of the Matabele army and there, amidst their yells and jeers, brutally speared by the assegais of two lads, who thus had their first opportunity of flushing their maiden spears'. A missionary's wife recorded that these captured women were even more cruelly treated on other occasions, being 'tied to a tree with dried grass around them, and burnt to death'.

It is difficult now for us to estimate the number of Mashona who were killed by the Matabele impis each year. According to one visitor, 'the whole of Mashonaland was a desolate wilderness, given over to wild beasts', while another rather lurid piece of Victorian journalism, after referring to the numbers of Africans 'sacrificed to the crimson assegai', goes on to say that 'the most competent authorities have estimated the Matabele "butcher's bill"' at some two thousand men and women and children slaughtered yearly'. This was probably a conservative figure, for a third observer writing about the way the *Amatjaha* were sent out raiding when their 'blood needed cooling', assessed the results in a different way by conjecturing that 'if the ruined villages within a radius of two hundred miles of Bulawayo were placed together they would cover an area larger than London', and he came to believe 'the Matabele kingdom to be the greatest and most cruel native power in that part of the world'.

What is the most surprising aspect of the Matabele raids is the poor resistance put up by the Mashona. 'We had only to shout as we approached', a warrior remembered later, 'and when we came all they had was ours, while the cowardly dogs whom they resembled, climbed the hills and rocks and hid themselves.' All the ancient bravery of the Karanga seemed to have evaporated. 'They are a cowardly, cringing, thankless lot of dirty beasts', noted an American who came to know them well, 'lacking even that redeeming quality possessed by many savage races—courage.' Leask, a celebrated hunter, is hardly less derogatory about the Mashona whom he speaks of as 'the fag end of *genus homus*'.

In Mashonaland the impis rarely raided beyond the Hunyani river; for many years the presence of the tsetse fly made this their 'ultima Thule' in the north-east. To the east they respected the boundaries of Soshangani's kingdom, and northwards the Makololo in the Chobe flats were too formidable to tackle, especially as the Matabele did not enjoy campaigning in swampland: 'they are no swimmers', Moffat once explained to his wife and 'were afraid of entering the water'. But the Tonga in the Zambesi valley and the Barotse beyond did not escape these Huns of central Africa: the celebrated Lewanika once described how an impi 'scourged Bo-Toka for three months, destroying property and killing many of my people in the most revolting manner. Women were ripped open and impaled, men and children made targets of and roasted alive like meat. Nothing, not a dog escaped where they passed. . . .'

For the Matabele of course the raids were wild and exciting: the forays slaked their blood lust, and like modern big-game hunting, possessed just enough element of risk to give edge to their enjoyment. From a practical point of view too they brought in a rich dividend of grain and cattle, and at the same time recruited strength for the nation in the shape of the selected young captives who could be assimilated. And the Matabele were usually shrewd enough to avoid killing the goose that laid the golden eggs for them: they tried not to wipe out the Mashona in a particular area; rather they culled them, leaving sufficient survivors to replant crops and to build up cattle herds which would warrant another raid in a few years time.

It was afterwards suggested that Rhodes and his lieutenants exaggerated the horrors of the Matabele raids to justify their intervention in the far interior. This was unfair. The missionaries working in Matabeleland, who were in the best position to know, believed the Matabele government to be an insult to the age of humanity, and positively welcomed its overthrow: 'the hateful Matabele rule is doomed', wrote Carnegie and Elliott of the London Missionary Society in their letter of congratulation to Mr Rhodes after his successful occupation of Mashonaland in 1890, and went on to say, 'we as missionaries with our thirty years history behind us, have little to bind our sympathies to the Matabele, neither can we pity the fall of their power, but we earnestly rejoice in the deliverance of the Mashona'. Nor were they less approving of the final subjection of the Matabele state three years later: 'now is the grand chance', one of them exulted, 'of Christianising the Matabele'.

At this stage, it is only fair to interject a point which is some-times forgotten: if the Matabele were abominably cruel, the Mashona, when they had the opportunity, behaved with equal barbarism, and it is quite wrong to represent them, as some Europeans did, as a mild, peace-loving people. Robert Moffat did not fall into this error: 'The Mashona', he noted in 1855, 'have again and again taken cattle from the outposts of the Matabele, and on the last occasion, having caught some women, they cut off their legs and arms and left them to perish.'

The return of the victorious impis to the Matabele royal kraal at the end of a successful campaign was always a great occasion. It began with a report of their activities being given in public to the king. Baines describing one such ceremony writes of an exultant wing of the army 'running in, two abreast, like troops coming on at the double. They turned off in succession to the right and then, facing toward the king, formed a close line, two deep, the shield of each man overlapping that of the man on his right, and the successive regiments as they came in and joined the line, forming rather more than a semi-circle, dressed with a precision that would have charmed the military eye. . . . The commander-in-chief first came forward and narrated in order the progress of the expedition. They had gone in the direction they were sent, turning out to the right of their course and sweeping the country as they went, killing 186 persons, of whom 84 were women, and capturing very close on 3,000 cattle . . . the petty chiefs were allowed to come forward and boast of their deeds and then the various men who had distinguished themselves sprang out in turn and running, leaping, crouching behind their shields, charging, retreating and stabbing in the air, gave one decisive stroke for each victim they had slain. . . .'

*　　*　　*　　*　　*

If Mashonaland presented the Matabele with golden opportunities for plunder, Mzilikazi during the first few years of his settlement in Rhodesia was always conscious that the Boers might suddenly decide to resume their vendetta with him. The memory of 1837 was very fresh. The older Matabele especially remembered Potgieter's prowess; they called him 'Endeleka' which was the nearest they could get to his second name, and to them it conjured up all their old memories of pitiless killing, galloping horsemen, and burning kraals.

They had good reason to be concerned: Potgieter was a bitter-ender who never liked to abandon a quarrel. And the hundreds of miles of arid country that separated Matabeleland from the Boer settlements in the Zoutpansberg would be unlikely to deter him if he once decided to attack his old enemies. For Potgieter had crossed the dried-up low veld once before: in 1836 he had ridden through it and far into Karangaland searching for a practical route from his fief in the northern Transvaal to the sea. He was the first white man to enter Rhodesia since the eviction of the Portuguese. Potgieter had been delighted by the docility of the Karanga who were just recovering from Zwangendaba's onslaught, and when he reached the foothills of the great plateau somewhere near West Nicholson, he was charmed by the fine grasslands that could be seen stretching far away to the north.

Potgieter never lost his interest in the country beyond the Limpopo; he listened to all he could learn about the Matabele after they settled there, and when he heard of their fat cattle herds it was only a question of time before he would ride north again to dispute the country's ownership with Mzilikazi.

The opportunity came in 1847, and it was initiated by the Boers' renewed interest in two little white girl captives who according to rumour were living as concubines at Mzilikazi's court. It is difficult now for us to know how much truth there was in the report; certainly two girls had been kidnapped ten years before when a Boer hunting party on the Vaal had been butchered by the Matabele; but we hear no more about them, as would have been expected if Mzilikazi had indeed taken them to wife. Two captive Griqua children, however, are known to have been living at Matlokotloko at the time, and this probably gave colour to the story. At all events it was so far believed that the initiation of a rescue operation had already been debated in the Transvaal Volksraad before 1847.

Yet one suspects that when he had decided that the time was ripe to attempt the conquest of Matabeleland, Potgieter seized on the story of Mzilikazi's white wives as a piece of propaganda material which would drum up support for his project. Certainly he had little difficulty in recruiting some 250* Boer horsemen for the invasion, together with more than 200 native levies.

We cannot now be certain whether Potgieter intended his expedition to be a cattle raid, a reconnaisance in force to test Matabele resistance, or whether he planned to drive Mzilikazi

* Sources differ as to the number; it varies from 238 to 283.

across the Zambesi and claim his country by right of conquest. And of course there is the possibility that he really did believe the story of the kidnapped white girls; Potgieter may have been the essence of quick temper and inflexibility who during the Great Trek had devoted a great deal of his time to fighting Africans and quarrelling with the other Boer leaders—and yet his blue eyes had an uncanny way of lighting up when he was with children, and he was always very tender to them.

Probably the nearest we can get now to Potgieter's thoughts in 1847 was that he was undecided about the way he would conduct the foray into Matabeleland until after the opening moves had been completed. As we would say today, he wanted to 'play it off the cuff', intending to exploit any openings that presented themselves and hoping for a stroke of luck which would allow him to kidnap Mzilikazi. And there seemed a very good chance that if he moved sufficiently rapidly to Matlokotloko he would be able to seize the king before any warning reached him, and hold him to ransom for his kingdom.

If this was his scheme, Potgieter was in for a disappointment: Mzilikazi had recently moved his court forty miles away from Matlokotloko to Inyati.

Whatever may have been its purpose, there is no doubt that Potgieter was undertaking a very hazardous exercise. The Boers would be facing enormous odds, and for success would have to rely very heavily on surprise, mobility, and fire power. But their morale was good and they had not forgotten the ease with which they had defeated the Matabele ten years earlier. Indeed Potgieter was so confident of the outcome, that at the very beginning of the invasion he detached half his force to ride eastwards in an attempt to realise his old dream of finding a practical route from the Transvaal to the sea.

With his numbers thus reduced to about a hundred Boers and a similar number of levies, Potgieter crossed the Limpopo just above its confluence with the Maklantsi river. Then the commando settled down impatiently while the African levies cut a broad swathe through the mopani bush beyond to drive away the tsetse fly. It was an immense task, and it is incredible that a belt a quarter of a mile wide was cleared so quickly through the scrub. Now the Boers were able to ride through the bush at night in safety, and for the first time the mopani barricades of Rhodesia had been breached by horsemen. The invasion had got off to a good start. The next task was to deal with an impi which Potgieter knew was maintained on the southern fringe of the Matopos near a hill named Thabas Manyoni. Its duty was to prevent unauthorised entry into Matabeleland, but the soldiers were of poor fighting quality, having been recruited for the most part from Karanga *holi*. Once through the tsetse country the commando accordingly moved quickly up the Shashani valley past the future site of Antelope Mine, and camped five miles from the Matabele outpost without having been detected. At first light next morning, Potgieter's horsemen galloped into the military kraal. The surprise was complete and all the more effective because the Karanga women had never seen mounted men before. Shouting 'muka dzi no bereka bana'— 'there are animals carrying their children'—they fled in a wild scramble up the hill followed, after a sharp flurry of fighting by what remained of the impi. The commando waited long enough to pick off the warriors one by one on the open slopes before riding on. Since that day Thabas Manyoni has been known as Mfabantu—the place where the people were killed.

In the diamond sunlight of Rhodesian winter Andries Hendrik Potgieter now led his commando up the Tendele valley which is spoken of today as Endeleka's Pass. It is a perfect place for ambush. Here the Boers were extremely vulnerable, and it is very easy for the modern visitor to sense something of their apprehension and excitement as they rode through this pass that seems like an entrance into a fairy domain. On either side its rocky walls swell into long ridges crinkled by hectically shaped crevices in which many trees have somehow found precarious footholds. Round every corner there are fresh views of the blue-green Matopo hills where nature's architecture has become singularly boisterous and ungovernable. These hills are heaped together in a confused mass of granite domes, and nearly all of them are surmounted by towers of balancing boulders and pinnacles in whose grotesque shapes the human eye persistently and rather pathetically attempts to find resemblances to familiar forms. It is a landscape from the story-book Africa, but one which is still uniquely Rhodesian: motionless yet permeated everywhere by unseen movement, a clean high land of steep kopjes and narrow aloe-crowded valleys, of grey rocks which are tufted sparsely with vegetation and verdigrised generously with streaks and sheets of yellow-green lichen.

By now the Boers had been observed and already messengers were hurrying through the hills to warn Mzilikazi of the danger. There were many strange things to report: they spoke of a screen of mounted scouts who probed the valleys, of the Matabele's faithful enemy Endeleka, tall, alert, and erect in the saddle, his head shaded by a well-remembered straw hat with a wide flapping brim, his gun covering a pressed guide running ahead. They spoke of two hundred mounted men, clustered together behind Potgieter, rifles in their hands, bandoliers criss-crossed over their chests—hard-riding, hard-hitting, nail-hard men, who were splendidly qualified for fighting on the veld. This cavalcade was a far more formidable fighting machine than Barreto's arquebusiers who 278 years earlier had marched in heavy armour behind the flags of Christendom to attempt the white man's first invasion of Rhodesia.

Tradition insists that it was Lobengula, one of the king's sons, who was the first messenger to reach Inyati. If true, it was his début into Rhodesian history.

After brushing aside some improvised opposition, and capturing several thousand head of cattle, the Boers left the hills near Figtree and rode on through open country to Matlokotloko. The kraal was deserted. It was a bitter disappointment. Potgieter's gamble on capturing the king by a sudden coup had not paid off, and it was only a small consolation to learn from the natives that the story of the white girl captives was untrue. Potgieter knew it would be foolhardy now to press his luck another notch. The Boers were four hundred miles from their base and the country was alive with rumours of approaching impis. Reluctantly he made the decision to retire, and driving the captured cattle ahead, the commando rode back into the foothills of the Matopos. The Boers bivouacked that night at Thabas Nyama, prudently sleeping at the summit of the hill with their horses' bridles in their hands; the native levies were left to guard the cattle at its base. They had no idea that the crack Zwangendaba regiment from the Plumtree area had been shadowing them all that afternoon; in any case Potgieter was sure that if the Matabele intended to attack the commando they would wait until they had reached the broken hill country further south.

It came then as a complete surprise when the Zwangendaba commanded by the *induna* Mbigo, fell upon the levies' camp during the night, killing every one of them and recapturing the cattle. In the darkness and confusion the Boers managed to get away; they had had a lucky escape.*

We are not certain of the route Potgieter followed back to the Transvaal. Rather than risk taking the dangerous road through the Mangwe pass he probably rode far to the west and round the Matopo hills. But it is known that the commando was harried nearly all the way to the Limpopo.

Potgieter's invasion had failed. Nothing really had been accomplished, except that the rumour about the white girls had been scotched. The Boers never made an armed attempt against the Matabele again.

Even Potgieter, that most unrelenting of enemies, now gave up his quarrel with Mzilikazi, and before he died in the Zoutspanberg six years after the failure of his invasion, the Boers signed a treaty of friendship with two of the king's envoys. It was never broken.

*   *   *   *   *

Mzilikazi's authority over Matabeleland was not directly challenged again. But a more subtle threat began to hang over his kingdom after the signing of his treaty of friendship with the Boers, for he withdrew his mandatory objection to white hunters and traders entering Matabeleland. They came on sufferance at

* The Boer version states that the white men escaped unscathed, the Matabele that they suffered some casualties.

first, but inevitably as their numbers increased they irretrievably committed the country to the modern world. Indeed from 1854 onwards, it is the Europeans who dominate the history of Rhodesia. Robert Moffat, the missionary, was one of the first to arrive and the consequences that flowed from his visit were imponderable. But it can be argued that the influence of the traders was equally significant in the end. The first land grant ever made to Europeans by Mzilikazi may have been the one given to the missionaries at Inyati, but much larger concessions were afterwards made to white traders and hunters: John Lee for instance was presented with two hundred square miles of land in the upper Mangwe valley. Then again the hunters brought a new scale of values to the country: ivory was in great demand at the time, and Mzilikazi went into commercial partnership with the white men to exploit it. The gifts they brought him and the tremendous execution of the herds of elephant made Mzilikazi a rich man during the eighteen-sixties: in three years alone it was estimated that 2,500 elephants were killed and half the profit went to the king.

In 1865, when the elephants of Matabeleland had been shot out, Mzilikazi reluctantly allowed Henry Hartley and other hunters to move into Mashonaland. It meant of course that the Matabele terror in their raiding grounds would be exposed, but no one really foresaw the other consequences that followed: beyond the Umfuli river Hartley chanced to bring down an elephant near a reef of quartz which showed visible gold, and he made a mental note that there were ancient workings in the vicinity: two years later he was back on the Umfuli with a geologist named Karl Mauch who confirmed his rediscovery of the Mashona goldfields. During the same year of 1867, diamonds were discovered for the first time in South Africa, and a white man prospecting in the Mashona bush country stumbled upon the ruins of Great Zimbabwe. All at once it seemed that the fates had decided to reveal every secret of the far interior, and their revelation made a tremendous impact on Europe. The legend of Solomon's riches which had eluded the Portuguese during the sixteenth century was revived, and when Mauch published a lyrical report on the wealth of the Mashona goldfields,* everybody wanted to know more about the country. After 1868 several books appeared with titles like *To Ophir direct* (complete with map) and *England's Eldorado in South Africa* to whet their interest, and it was only a matter of time before Matabeleland's isolation would be destroyed for ever.

But for much longer than anyone expected, Mzilikazi succeeded in exercising control over the numbers of white men entering his country. In this he was greatly assisted by the Europeans' belief that he commanded so formidable an army that only a large-scale military expedition could hope to tackle the Matabele with any prospect of success.

In fact the effectiveness of the Matabele impis was grossly exaggerated. Discipline had declined as the original *Abazansi* died off and the pure Zulu strain was lost. And Mzilikazi had entirely failed to move with the times. This apt pupil of Shaka's innovations refused to recognise the superiority of modern firearms over assegais and naked courage; nor did he appreciate the opportunity of increasing his soldiers' mobility by training them to ride the horses which the white hunters introduced into Matabeleland. These lapses were bad enough but Mzilikazi compounded them by failing to make any effort to alter the traditional Matabele military tactics. The impis continued to rely on the 'spear-crescent' rush to fight at close quarters; they were never trained in the far more effective methods of guerrilla warfare. But then, of course, it would probably have been impossible for any man to modernise the Matabele army. The Bantu by nature are conservative; tactics which had served their fathers they believed would still suit them very well. And the Matabele had a curious attitude towards guns; they distrusted them, felt that somehow their use was cowardly, and they tried to ignore their existence to a greater extent perhaps than any other contemporary Africans. Possibly, their fixation stemmed from an incident which

---

* He enthused, 'The vast extent and beauty of the fields are such that at a particular spot, I stood as it were transfixed, riveted to the place, struck with amazement and wonder at the sight, and for a few minutes was unable to use the hammer. Thousands of persons might here find ample room to work in this extensive field without interfering with one another.' Letter from K. Mauch to *Transvaal Argus*, 3.12.1867.

had taken place years before when an impi had butchered a Griqua raiding party, and which Baines has described very well: 'The Griquas', he says, 'were overtaken and massacred while they were sleeping and over-gorged with beef. The Matabele collected all their guns, hardly any of which had been discharged, so sudden and complete had been the surprise; and collecting dry wood, piled the guns, powder horns and bandoliers upon it, setting fire to the pile, and danced round it rejoicing in the destruction of these terrible and mysterious weapons, when, as the fire reached them, the guns began to explode and, lying low, shot several Matabele in the legs. Before they had time to recover from their astonishment and disperse, the occasional flashing off of the powder horns also added to their wonder and terror, and they began to say, "What witchcraft is this, and what dreadful things are these, that not only destroy in battle but also kill us even after the fight is over and their owners are dead." It appears this spontaneous explosion has done more to impress upon them the dread of firearms than any amount of slaughter in battle could have done.'

In any case, the Mzilikazi of 1854 was already very different from the man of 1838. His sharp initiative and neologism had been dulled. The sense of insecurity which had afflicted the king ever since his father's death became obsessional as he grew older, and, in a way made familiar to modern medical practitioners, he sought solace for his emotional discrepancies in alcohol. All contemporary accounts during the last fifteen years of his life, lay stress on the enormous quantities of beer the king consumed, and it was inevitable that he soon began to show signs of chronic alcoholic poisoning.

It affected his mind as well as his body. Mzilikazi the energetic soldier of fortune turns during the eighteen-fifties into a fidgety invalid; the warlord with the questing mind becomes a morose, irascible, maudlin, old man. His interests narrow down to the presents that can be extracted from his European visitors and the pots of beer which are passed to him almost continuously by a circle of obsequious queens. Now the enthusiastic tipster begins to complain of neuritis in his legs and in time they become paralysed; he grumbles about muscle cramps and the rheumy pains of gout; an incipient cirrhosis of the liver develops and leads to abdominal dropsy. He is irritable and befuddled, though, as is characteristic of any drunkard, he readily responds to the mood of those he admires—in his case the Europeans whom he believes are mysteriously talented. Yet, miraculously (as it seems to him) when one of these father figures can persuade him to abstain from beer, his symptoms are at once alleviated, the old sense of purpose replaces the bewildering lack of predictability, and the purveyor of abstemious advice is at once elevated by the grateful patient to the rank of royal physician. But the moment the sobering influence is withdrawn, the beer drinking starts again and all the symptoms return.

The stages of Mzilikazi's mental and physical decay, so typical of the chronic alcoholic, were noted by many observers. Moffat in 1854, was shocked to find 'the vigorous active nimble monarch' he had known before, 'now aged, sitting on a skin, with feet lame, unable to walk or even to stand'. In 1856 we have a reference from another source that the king is 'attacked in his big toes by gout'; next year 'the belly is dropsical', and he suffers from 'complete lameness in both legs from the knees downwards'; in 1859, he looks 'changed and really seems in his dotage', although thanks to Moffat's therapy he still manages to walk a little; in 1860, Emily Moffat notes 'the trembling hands' of this 'old half-naked porpoise of a human being'; next year the gout returns and we learn that 'His Majesty is suffering from dropsical symptoms again'; in 1862 the gout has become so bad 'as to deprive him of the use of his feet', and he has to be 'carried about in his old arm chair, like a child, by four of his wives'; 1863, finds him so severely paralysed that he can neither stand nor walk without assistance; next year he seems 'a physical wreck. His lower limbs are paralysed', while someone else notes with pity that 'he appears to have entirely lost the use of his legs'. In 1866, a hunter describes the king as 'a little, palsied, frail old man in his second childhood'. And so the crumbling away of Mzilikazi continues.

Perhaps what strikes one now as so remarkable is the fact that the king lasted for as long as he did. The end did not come until 6th September, 1868, when he was nearly eighty years old.

Mzilikazi died some miles away from Mhlahlandhlela in a small kraal to which he liked to retire for privacy. The Matabele still speak of his death with awe: 'the lightning flashed out of a clear sky' they say, and at the precise moment of his death, 'twelve people fell dead'.

His death was a matter of tremendous significance to them: the king had seemed indestructible and, like the British nation when Queen Victoria died, his people realised that his passing meant an uprooting change. A short message—'the mountain is fallen'—was whispered through the land, and a noisome 'lying-in-state' was held which had a close resemblance to that which had followed the death of Nogomo Mapunzagutu three hundred years before; it was as though the Matabele had appreciated that the mantle of the Monomatapas had fallen on Mzilikazi. For eight weeks the corpse was allowed to corrupt in a hut surrounded, Sykes tells us, by 'parties of headmen' to 'guard against hyenas', and he adds with quickening interest that 'more extraordinary still some of the Queens were lying in the hut every night with their noses plugged to prevent suffocation'.

When decomposition was complete, the 'High Priest' of the nation supervised the interment of the king's bones in a cave lying in one of the loveliest valleys of the Matopos; Mzilikazi's most treasured possessions together with 'things which he had handled such as beads, brass rings, buttons, and various articles of European manufacture' were reverently laid beside him together with the bodies of human sacrificial victims. The number of persons so sacrificed differs in our accounts of Mzilikazi's funeral: probably three slaves were buried with the king to carry his blanket, beer and snuff through the shadowy passages of the Matabele Valhalla, but one report suggests that three wives and three hundred slaves bore their king company in death. The king's favourite wagon was installed in a nearby cave for his use in later life, and the ceremony was concluded by the ritual killing of fifty black oxen.

Mzilikazi did not rest undisturbed in his sepulchre for very long. Ten years after his burial a bush fire swept through the area, and several hundred villagers whose duty it was to guard the

Soapstone bird, Zimbabwe

Mzilikazi

A Matabele warrior by Thomas Baines

tomb are reported to have been killed for their dereliction. Then in 1896 some British troopers hunting for loot ransacked the cave and gave Cecil Rhodes an opportunity to examine the king's skull which he found disappointingly small. It is only fair to add that Rhodes made every possible attempt to atone for the desecration and arranged to sacrifice black oxen to appease the king's spirit. Even today the Matabele are disinclined to show visitors the way to their first king's grave; its entrance has been blocked up with stones, but in the adjacent cave the wheels of Mzilikazi's wagon are still plainly visible: they are painted a celestial blue and their maker's name can still be read on them.

More than any other man Mzilikazi had preserved his country from the Boers and for many years this was considered to be his greatest achievement. Yet the perception of history is apt to change with time and it may well be that in the future this contribution will appear less significant. But Mzilikazi will be remembered with gratitude for another reason which has so far been ignored: it was he who protected Rhodesia from the abominations of the African slave trade; when 'this cursed trade in human flesh' was assuming its most terrible proportions north of the Zambesi, the military strength of the Matabele discouraged the slavers from raiding south of the river. And however cruel the treatment of the Mashona by the stronger Matabele may have been, it must be recorded in their favour that they never captured men and women with the intention of selling them into slavery; those victims they spared were eventually assimilated into the nation. The consequences for Rhodesia were incalculable; the country's Bantu were never degraded or corrupted by the slave trade, nor did it ever poison their relations with Europeans. The Rhodesian African of today looks on the ancient glories of Monomatapa and the Matabele hegemony with equal pride, and on the white élite which followed them with a respect which is untinged by any sense of humiliation. Such a race relationship, based on mutual consideration, is rare in Africa, and it has allowed people to hope that a plural society based not on discrimination but on merit may continue to develop in Rhodesia. If it does so, Mzilikazi must be reckoned as one of its chief architects.

THE SECOND CHRISTIAN VENTURE

If anyone were asked to suggest a day on which the modern history of Rhodesia began, the 26th January, 1857 would be as good a date as any to choose. For on that wintry day the Board of Directors of the London Missionary Society resolved to send a Christian mission to the Matabele. With that decision they set in motion a chain reaction which was eventually to establish British rule in Rhodesia.

A little earlier the L.M.S. Directors had discussed how they might best exploit the emotional surge of goodwill and missionary zeal which had seized Great Britain after the return of Dr Livingstone from his remarkable trans-African journey. Dr Livingstone, an agent of the Society, himself came to address the Board, and the Directors listened with rapt attention to his suggestion that the opportunities he had opened up for propagating the Gospel in central Africa could best be exploited by the 'planting' of two separate missions, one among the Makololo, and another in Matabeleland. Such missions, he explained, would support each other and promote peace between two traditionally hostile tribes. The Makololo, he told the Board, were the most worthy Africans he had ever encountered and he believed that they were 'ripe for evangelisation'. He then went on to say that his own influence with the tribe would ensure a cordial welcome for any missionaries sent to labour among the Makololo, and he had no doubt that the friendship of his colleague and father-in-law, Dr Robert Moffat, with Mzilikazi would likewise promote a favourable reception from the Matabele.

During the discussion which followed, Livingstone admitted that the Makololo inhabited a particularly unhealthy part of the Zambesi valley; but they did this, he said, only because they dreaded Matabele aggression, and he was certain that once this fear had been dispelled by missionary influence in the two countries, Sekeletu, the Makololo chief, would move his capital from Linyanti to the more bracing (though less easily defensible) Batoka highlands on the northern bank of the river. Before the meeting broke up Dr Livingstone also spoke to the Directors about his own plans for returning to the Zambesi, and he expressed a polite hope that once there he would be able to assist any missionaries who might in due course be sent out to labour among the Makololo.

It all sounded very simple and very plain, and the Directors can hardly be blamed for failing to appreciate that Livingstone had succumbed to an almost maudlin admiration for the Makololo which later events would show to be quite unjustified. Still less could they have been expected to foresee that circumstances (and particularly their own subsequent estrangement from the Doctor) would deflect Livingstone from his original purpose of meeting and assisting the Makololo missionaries at Linyanti. But at least the Directors were on firmer ground when they turned to consider the help Dr Robert Moffat would be able to render a mission to the Matabele, for Moffat undoubtedly had enormous influence with Mzilikazi, and they could be certain of his unswerving loyalty to their Society.

Moffat at the time rivalled his son-in-law David Livingstone as the brightest star of the missionary constellation which illumined the religious life of Britain during the first half of the nineteenth century. Ever since 1816 he had worked for the L.M.S., and more than thirty years had passed since he had established the flourishing mission station at Kuruman in the heart of Bechuanaland, a station that could provide a firm base from which the two missions suggested by Livingstone might operate. Moreover for nearly thirty years Moffat had fostered a friendship with the Matabele king which, as Livingstone had pointed out, would be bound to enhance the prospects of any mission sent to Matabeleland. And so before the Directors concluded their final meeting they accepted all Dr Livingstone's somewhat grandiose proposals, and the Society's secretary was instructed to approach Moffat with the suggestion that he journey again to Matabeleland and obtain Mzilikazi's permission for the establishment of a permanent mission there. It was somewhat vaguely assumed that Livingstone would assist the Makololo mission by performing the same service with Sekeletu, but unfortunately nothing definite was arranged with him.

The Directors' instructions to Moffat were embodied in a letter dated 4th April, 1857, and it took three months to reach Kuruman. Moffat when he read it was sixty-two and he was beginning to feel his years. In appearance he was still a most impressive figure: he was tall, robust, and moved with the portentous dignity of an evangelist who had achieved a remarkable authority over a vast area of Africa. In many ways he typified the missionary ideal of contemporary Britain. For one thing Moffat's background was exactly right: he was a Scot and boasted of having come from 'the God-fearing poor', and in fact had been employed as a gardener's apprentice before being accepted as a candidate for the South African mission field by the L.M.S. By nature Moffat was rigidly pious, marvellously self-disciplined, the soul of integrity, and a firm believer in the influence of the 'Bible and the Plough'. He was, it must be admitted, sadly lacking in a sense of humour, and there was a streak of vanity running through his character so that he was never so happy as when practising his voluble oratory before an admiring audience.

In 1857, Robert Moffat could look back on a wonderful record of missionary achievement. After his gardener's eye had seen the possibilities of the fountain of Kuruman he had made that oasis 'a veritable Eden in the desert' and a centre of Christian endeavour; there too he had undertaken the secondary but immense task of translating the Bible into Sechuana. And, what was of even more importance for the future of Rhodesia, a series of chance encounters had enabled him to forge an enduring friendship with Mzilikazi, the Matabele king.

His first meeting with the king had taken place in a haphazard sort of way in 1829, when the Matabele were still established in the Marico district of the Transvaal. Mzilikazi that year had dispatched two *indunas* to investigate the reputed wonders of Kuruman, and Moffat had treated them very kindly. Anxious about their safety during the return journey through hostile tribes, he had even insisted on escorting them back as far as the nearest Matabele outpost. Once there the *indunas* had persuaded Moffat to go on a little further and meet their king. Moffat and Mzilikazi had taken to each other at once. Both were men of domineering character, and both of them enjoyed making a display. Mzilikazi had always been stimulated by the unfamiliar, and he appreciated the company of a man who was not afraid to disagree with him; he even went so far as to 'adopt' his new friend (whom he called Moshete) as a father. For his part Moffat was fascinated by the king's absolute power over his subjects, and was flattered too by the many little attentions Mzilikazi took such obvious pleasure in showing him.

A second meeting between the two men took place in 1835. Only a little later the Matabele migrated across the Limpopo, and for nearly twenty years the friends did not see each other again. But in 1854 Moffat, weary of his self-imposed task of translating the Bible, lightheartedly undertook the seven-hundred-mile journey to Matlokotloko to renew the association. It was during this third visit that their already incongruous friendship assumed its most florid proportions.

Once within Matabeleland, Moffat's casual holiday trip took on the character of a royal progress. He was fêted everywhere, and by no one more enthusiastically than by Mzilikazi. Moffat was startled by the reception and we find him recording the king's 'odd passion' for himself with bemused wonder: he writes to his wife that Mzilikazi appeared 'to feel an unusual enjoyment to sit with me', and 'seemed at a loss to know what to do next to show me he loved me', and even appeared 'determined to be enrolled among my domestics' so that he might remain close to him. One letter even speaks of Moffat's embarrassment when the king 'laid hold of my beard and he really looked as if he intended kissing me', and when the time came for the missionary to return to Kuruman he was genuinely touched to see that this 'despot of the first order' had tears in his eyes. Mzilikazi's compulsive and emotional affection for the white man (which yet sometimes turned into suspicious jealousy) might be ascribed to a glassy-eyed manifestation of chronic alcoholism, or to his need to find a father figure who would act as a moral censor. But no such consequential explanations for Mzilikazi's 'odd passion' for himself ever entered Moffat's pious mind: he considered it to be ordained by God, or, as Mrs Moffat put it, 'there is something very remarkable in the uncommonly strong attachment of the poor savage Moselkatze to my husband . . . and we cannot help thinking that this circumstance is to be overruled for some great objective'.

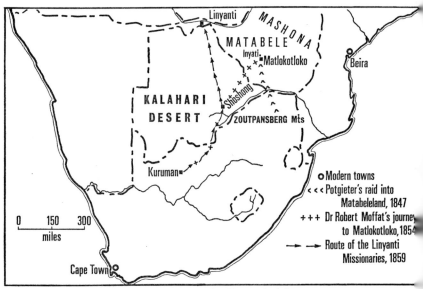

Mid 19th century European routes in Central Africa

During this visit of 1854, Moffat was asked to treat Mzilikazi's infirmities: he writes of massaging the king's swollen feet and even of giving attention to his piles. No doubt his successful therapy contributed to the king's admiration for his friend Moshete, and enabled the missionary to accomplish two of the three formidable tasks he had set himself before journeying to Matlolotloko. For not only did Moffat induce Mzilikazi to release a captured coloured girl named Gertrude, but he also obtained the king's permission to preach to the Matabele at the royal kraal. His first requests to do so had been resisted on the grounds that Moshete's revolutionary teaching might disrupt the social structure of the kingdom, but as the time for Moffat's departure approached, a desperate anxiety to please his friend overcame the king's scruples. One has only to read through Moffat's journals to realise what a joy it was for him to preach the gospel to the heathen Matabele, and we can be sure that he was listened to very carefully for instant execution was threatened to those who were inattentive. Admittedly the results of these first Christian sermons to be heard in Rhodesia since the departure of the Portuguese were slightly unpredictable: Moffat was shocked on one occasion after he had regaled the Matabele court with a description of the horrors of hell fire, by the king's anxiety to show that these afflictions could be avoided without submitting to Christian discipline—which led him to order his warriors to stamp out the faggots and embers of an immense bonfire with their bare feet.

Robert Moffat's third objective when he visited Matabeleland in 1854, was to carry provisions and mail up to David Livingstone who was exploring the Zambesi at the time. In this task Moffat was only partly successful. When he asked Mzilikazi 'for the road' north the king seemed affronted: he argued, equivocated, prevaricated, refused—even refused peremptorily—and finally consented, but only on condition that he himself accompany the missionary on his journey. And now for nineteen days the ill-assorted friends travelled together in their ox-wagons, accompanied by a noisy crowd of retainers, rolling along the bush route which fourteen years earlier had brought Mzilikazi to Matabeleland. Beyond the Nata river they entered tsetse country and were compelled to turn back. However disappointed Moffat may have been, at least he had the satisfaction of seeing his son-in-law's stores dispatched to the river by Matabele porters, and of knowing later that there Livingstone found 'they had remained from September 1854 till September 1855 in perfect safety'.

Robert Moffat's journey to Matabeleland in 1854, was a prodigious accomplishment. It is only necessary to glance at a map of Africa to appreciate the vast distance he covered on what, after all, began as a mere domestic adventure. If only for this single expedition Robert Moffat is assured of a secure place in the history of African exploration. It almost doubled the size of the white man's Africa, and opened up regions whose ultimate significance was to prove even more consequential than Livingstone's discoveries. Its political effects were profound too, for Moffat pioneered a road into the interior which the British Government decided must be kept open and so prevented subsequent Boer expansion into Bechuanaland. Yet posterity has stubbornly declined to give Moffat his proper due either as an explorer or as a moulder of central African history. Perhaps the reading public of his time had grown used to thinking of African explorers as adventurers with guns in their hands who strode through the jungle at the head of a long line of porters: somehow Moffat with his old fashioned ways and his cumbersome ox-wagon rumbling over the veld did not quite fit into this picture, and certainly he never caught at the imagination as Stanley, Burton and so many other explorers had done.

Then again, for all the spacious figure that he was, Robert Moffat's reputation was always overshadowed by that of his son-in-law. Moffat may have been Livingstone's equal in courage and fortitude, but he lacked his breadth of spirit and the power to inspire others with a new vision of redeeming Africa by carrying commerce as well as Christianity into the interior. And although Moffat was a notable recorder of African life, his observations are never so exact or so interesting as those of the younger man, and he entirely lacked Livingstone's flair for descriptive writing; Moffat's *Missionary Labours and Scenes in Southern Africa* is a classic of its kind, but its author was not blessed with the gift of formulating a memorable phrase and somehow it failed to make the impact of Livingstone's later *Missionary Travels and Researches in South Africa*. Yet most detrimental of all to the emergence of a posthumous Moffat legend was the fact that Dr Robert Moffat died peacefully in bed at the advanced age of eighty-eight, and his splendid career was denied the final heart-rending tragedy of his son-in-law.

*   *   *   *   *

It was on 6th July, 1857, that Dr Moffat received the L.M.S. Directors' letter which asked him to prepare the way for the

Matabele missionaries, and he read it without enthusiasm. He had always advocated a deliberately measured Christian advance into the far interior, and he doubted the wisdom of the sudden jump forward that was now proposed. Yet as the Society's loyal servant Moffat accepted its commission without protest and at once began making preparations for a second journey to Matabeleland. He left Kuruman before the end of July and reached Matlokotloko two months later. Somehow his welcome there seemed a shade less effusive than before. Since the last visit Mzilikazi had aged considerably and something of his old jaunty eagerness to please his friend was missing. He even taxed Moffat with an ulterior reason for his journey when the missionary conveyed a request from some Boers waiting on the Matabele borders to be allowed to hunt in the country. We know now that the king behaved as he did because of the long-term effects which the Christian teaching might have on his subjects; but in the end he reluctantly agreed to admit a missionary party, provided that Moffat's son, John Smith Moffat, was included in it and that its members were introduced to and vouched for in Matabeleland by Moshete himself. He would go no further: to his friend's anxious requests to be assigned a well-watered site for the proposed mission Mzilikazi answered with a bleak 'I know of no such fountain', a reply which to Moffat came 'like an icicle in my bosom', and in the end Moffat left Matlokotloko without having determined where the missionaries could settle. It was an omission which was later to cause him much unhappiness and mortification.

* * * * *

If Moffat in 1857 had hastened to make all possible arrangements for the establishment of the Matabele mission, the Directors of the L.M.S. had shown no similar sense of urgency. It was as though the fates were allowing them a chance to reconsider the matter: a whole year went by before six recruits for the missions to the Matabele and Makololo were selected, and another before they were all gathered under Dr Moffat's roof at Kuruman.

His six guests formed a strange little company. All of them

were utterly different in temperament, upbringing, and ability. To make matters worse they had become edgy and highly-strung since learning that the Transvaal Boers were on the warpath and had threatened to hang Dr Moffat on one of the big syringa trees in front of his house at Kuruman. The fledgling missionaries had been selected with very little regard to suitability or merit: a readiness to serve in Africa had appeared to be the only qualification the Society required, and although fully aware of the risks they would run, the Directors had decided against including a doctor in either party. Nor had any obstacle been placed in the way of the missionaries taking their wives and children into regions where malaria and dysentery were known to be prevalent and dangerous.

We are here more immediately concerned with the three men destined for Matabeleland than with their colleagues going to Makololo country, and as they were to cast such long shadows over the future history of Rhodesia, it is as well if we pause for a moment to consider the characters of Brother John Smith Moffat, Brother William Sykes, and Brother Thomas Morgan Thomas.

At first sight John Moffat appeared to be by far the most promising of the three young men. He was twenty-four, newly married, and his whole life had been spent preparing to continue his father's work in central Africa. Yet constitutionally the younger Moffat was ill-adapted to the life of a missionary. He had a drooping and reticent personality, something of which shows up in a photograph we have of him taken in 1858, where his pose is seen to be curiously wary and withdrawn. As Moffat himself once admitted, he made 'an uncomfortable colleague to those who had to labour with him'. That was his trouble: a natural pessimism made him take a deeply suspicious view of events unrolling around him, and he was inclined to become disillusioned and fall out with his associates. Although most of Moffat's life was spent in the African wilds there is a suburban flavour to his career, and no picturesque adventures ever seemed to befall him. Twice he was given the opportunity to play an immensely important role in the creation of modern Rhodesia, yet somehow one feels that he muffed his cues a little on each occasion. Cast for a hero's part, John Moffat, in short, played one of a remarkably pale hero.

Somehow it was typical of him that even before he began his work in Matabeleland, John Moffat's position in the mission was irregular and even embarrassing. This circumstance was by no means his own fault: after applying for a post in the African mission field, the L.M.S. Directors had unaccountably delayed some months before reaching a decision about his appointment. Both John Moffat and his brother-in-law, Dr Livingstone (who had just resigned from the Society following a disagreement with its Directors)* were exasperated by the procrastination. 'The conduct of the Directors is merely trifling, and it involves trifling with the affections of your wife', Livingstone snorted in one of his letters to Moffat, and he went on to persuade the young man to withdraw his application, to accept instead a subsidy of £150 a year from himself, and to serve the Makololo as an 'independent' missionary attached to the L.M.S.

Only in Cape Town did John Moffat learn of his father's promise to Mzilikazi that his son would be a member of the Matabele mission. His formidable brother-in-law, however, raised no objection to his ministering to the Matabele instead of the Makololo: 'Do whatever you think will be best for the cause of Christ', he told him, and somewhat grudgingly John Moffat agreed to change his plans and to join the Matabele party.

John Moffat was wonderfully fortunate in the character of his wife. Emily Moffat was not beautiful, but she was gay and full of spirit. She had been brought up among genteel surroundings in Sussex, and, according to her son, until 1858 'was one of the most constitutionally timid of women' whose 'chief experience in land travelling had been in the train between Brighton and London'. Yet she possessed an unsuspected store of vivacious courage, and another quality too—a smiling irony—which enabled her to make light of the hardships she met in central

* In his father's biography John Moffat explains that the reason for Livingstone's decision to resign was as follows: 'Finding that some of the supporters of the Missionary Society were a little dissatisfied at what seemed to them a disproportion between his geographical and his evangelistic work, he deemed it well to withdraw from the Society's service.'

Africa. Indeed, of all the mission party she strikes us now as displaying by far the most attractive personality.

The second member of the Matabele mission was the Rev. William Sykes. Sykes was a Yorkshireman just turned thirty who had begun life as a grocery clerk before being caught up in the atmosphere of religious idealism which swept over industrial England during the fifties of last century. His natural gloom was aggravated at Kuruman by the tragedy of losing his wife.

Sykes was to work in Matabeleland for nearly thirty years until his death in 1887, yet for all his long service there is always something a little low-toned about him. He flits through the drama of the pre-pioneering history of Rhodesia as a shadowy, unsubstantial, character who did not very much like his part. No one ever appears to have got to know Sykes very well, and his influence among the Africans was minimal. Emily Moffat found him 'quite unprepossessing' at first, although she admitted later that 'he has much improved on acquaintance'. His ineffectiveness during the trek from Kuruman was an irritation to the versatile Dr Moffat, who we find grumbling that Brother Sykes has 'not anything like a strong constitution. He always seems an invalid. He does nothing', and Moffat counted it typical that Sykes had the 'misfortune to lose his *only* spectacles, and he now wears those of his late valued wife'.

All in all the third member of the missionary party going to Matabeleland must be considered the most remarkable of the 'brethren'. Thomas Morgan Thomas was a self-assertive young Welshman on the make. He was ambitious and far more enterprising than either of his colleagues. Although thrown into the working world at the age of seven, Thomas had yet succeeded in elbowing himself up from poverty. While working as a farm labourer he educated himself and, after studying at Brecon College, was ordained and accepted for a post with the L.M.S. Thomas was quite different from his fellow-missionaries: he was flashing-eyed and self-opinionated, and there was not much sensitivity in his make-up. He alone among the brethren wanted to make a name for himself as an explorer and he did not care very much about offending them in the process. Emily Moffat was not far wrong when she sarcastically summed him up as 'a Welsh imitator of Livingstone', but Thomas in many ways reminds us much more of his compatriot and near contemporary, Sir Henry Morton Stanley. One has the feeling that the only thing that really mattered to him was the welfare of the Rev. Thomas Morgan Thomas. Unfortunately he was also very quick to take offence and became truculent when he did so. Yet one cannot help admiring his compact energy, and his genuine success in identifying his interests with those of the Africans among whom he lived in Matabeleland.

* * * * *

The scare among the brethren about the Boers' hostility soon died down and the first week of July 1859 saw immense activity at Kuruman as final preparations were made for the great adventure that was to take the Gospel to the far interior. They had decided to travel in separate groups in order to conserve water and grazing for their oxen. On the 8th the Makololo missionaries rumbled off northwards in their wagons; a week later the John Moffats and Mr and Mrs Thomas followed them; finally on 1st August, Sykes and Robert Moffat jolted off in their tracks. At Shoshong the Linyanti party began the long haul through the Kalahari towards the Zambesi while the others turned along Moffat's old route to Matlokotloko. All went well at first with the Matabele party, but on the borders of Mzilikazi's kingdom their trek-oxen went down with lung sickness. Fearful of carrying the infection to the royal herds, Moffat very correctly halted, and sent a messenger on to warn the king of the danger. Mzilikazi's response was dramatic. One hundred and sixty warriors appeared a few days later at Moffat's stand place, swarmed round the stranded party and yoked themselves to the wagons in place of the oxen. The newly recruited missionaries found being pulled along by human draught animals a startling introduction to Matabeleland. Emily Moffat thought this a 'truly awful' experience; she winced at the spectacle of the 'poor naked fellows, with eager wondering eyes staring at us and all we do' and 'turned to my wagon, wishing I could shut out such sights and sounds. I can't tell you what I felt, such a strange mingling of pity and fear, of despair and helplessness.'

Three months after leaving Kuruman the little party at last reached Mzilikazi's temporary headquarters on the banks of the river Bembesi. This was the moment which they had contemplated with such excited anticipation for a whole year. Again and again they had discussed what they thought would happen next: the king, they said, would greet his old friend Moshete with effusion, load them all with kindnesses and presents, and then lead them to some favoured site where his subjects would erect the church from which the great task of converting the heathen could begin.

It was a pleasant prospect, and it had cheered them through all the gruelling weeks of the journey. But the reality turned out to be very different from their expectations: Mzilikazi's welcome was anything but friendly. After expressing a few casual civilities he adopted an attitude of surly suspicion, and treated even Dr Moffat to a royal exhibition of bad manners. Admittedly the king accepted all the presents that they had brought for him, but he did so with little grace and plainly aspired to the missionaries' personal possessions as well. He was frugal in the food he sent to their wagons and often none came at all. He insisted on their camping near a ramshackle kraal on the river bank from which a plague of rats descended upon their tents every night. The king even forbade his guests to shoot game for the pot or to fish the river. All through November and December, both hot months of incessant rain, the missionaries were virtual prisoners. Because they had left their draught oxen behind they could not even move their wagons to another camp; their enquiries regarding a site where they could build a station were either met with patent prevarication or ignored.

It was very wearisome and very distressing, and perhaps it was worse of all for Dr Robert Moffat. All his accounts of Mzilikazi's affection for him seemed now to have been the senile fabrications of an old man, and rifts began to appear in the brethren's elaborate façade of friendship as they turned on their leader to criticise and carp at him, and complain that they had been misled.

None of them, least of all Dr Moffat, could understand Mzilikazi's apparently hostile attitude: they had no inkling that the king was preparing for the ceremony of the First Fruits and that tradition forbade him to meet strangers. And he had come to a parting of the ways. For weeks he had been a prey to doubts about the wisdom of allowing Europeans to enter his country. Many of his advisers insisted that the missionaries constituted not only a threat to the Matabele way of life (and particularly to polygamy) but were probably the 'spies and precursors of Boers', whose presence in the country would inevitably lead to growing outside pressures and ultimate European subjugation. Of course, the king's counsellors were perfectly correct: they were shrewd enough to see that in the end the first mission settlement would prove to be the thin end of the wedge of conquest. But Mzilikazi was pulled in another direction by his old affection for Moshete, and in the end the fact that he had already given his friend a promise that a mission could settle in his country proved decisive, for although inclined to prevaricate for as long as possible, Mzilikazi was not a man to go back on his word.

For two months, however, the king refused to discuss the future of the mission with Robert Moffat, and during that time he undoubtedly behaved very badly: he demanded gifts of guns and ammunition; he haggled over payment for the loan of the human 'oxen' which had been sent to pull the brethren's wagons to the Bembesi; he would disappear with his 'court' into the bush for days on end. All through these trying weeks one can sense a rising tide of chagrin and disappointment in the missionaries' journals and correspondence. Mzilikazi 'seemed inclined to make us wait' writes the mystified Dr Moffat in one of his letters, and he admits that 'this looked very like a put off'. 'Patience, patience, patience', he tells himself a few days later in his diary, 'Lord increase our faith'; another day he sighs 'we are living in painful, galling, soul-wearing-out suspense', and that 'we have been here more than six weeks. We have not been allowed to plant or sow, or build or even to shoot game.' Sykes, unburdening himself in a letter home, grumbled that the king's 'reception of us was not what I expected from Mr Moffat's published and *viva voce* representation of the man. . . . His unreasonable demands in nine cases out of ten were an insuperable barrier to success . . . my impression was, before long, that he designed to fleece us and send us about our business.' Thomas reached a similar conclusion about the king's behaviour; 'it struck me', he writes, 'that he was much more inclined to get our things than to have our company', and he notes that 'a hostile feeling against Mr Moffat was growing' for 'this rebuff was soon followed by greater insults'. According to Thomas it was only the intervention of himself and young Moffat which prevented the elder Moffat and Sykes from packing up, buying oxen, and returning to Kuruman.

Of them all, Emily Moffat alone seems to have remained cheerful. As they waited beside the Bembesi (which she spelled Impimbezi) she became entranced by the miracle of rejuvenation which comes to the parched Rhodesian veld every year with the onset of the rains. Sometimes an almost lyric quality touches her letters after she had breathed the crystalline and scented summer air, had seen the thrusting green grass about the camp, and had watched the nearby river agitated with fresh currents, and sparkling as though charged with electricity. Only she appears to have appreciated the fascination of the newly greened bush whose stillness was broken occasionally by whispers of wind in the yellow mimosa trees or the rustle of a startled buck. All the charm of the African spring veld was new to Emily Moffat, and she revelled in it. 'The country around us had wonderfully changed during the last seven weeks', runs one of her letters home. 'The foliage is now rich and luxuriant, the grasses are beautiful and the banks of the Impimbezi are so lovely. We stroll there every evening, and the sunset scenes in these tropical skies are of rare loveliness—and then their reflection in the clear, murmuring waters! Oh, it is a sweet spot! Our moonlight nights too have been bright, *bright*.'

Robert Moffat was sustained during the weeks of waiting and criticism by his faith. He was a man who always saw things in scriptural terms, a man who could genuinely believe that Mzilikazi behaved as he did because 'Satan is making a desperate effort to shut the door against the blessed Gospel'. And his faith was

Dr Robert Moffat
Rev. John Smith Moffat

Rev. Thomas Morgan Thomas
Emily Moffat

Charles Rudd

Rev. William Sykes

justified: on the 15th December an invitation was brought from Mzilikazi asking the missionaries to visit him at the royal kraal. For the king had at last reached a decision—or rather he had resolved on a compromise: he would allow the missionaries to remain in the country, but at the same time would take good care that his subjects were not influenced by their teaching

Now suddenly all was friendliness at court; the missionaries were greeted with unaccustomed courtesy, and were presently taken to a 'peaceful' valley which had been chosen for them. There followed a great stir in their camp beside the Bembesi as they packed up their boxes and set off in their wagons towards their appointed home. It lay close to Inyati, the kraal of the king's favourite wife, and there in Thomas's words they 'settled down under a wild plum tree'.

* * * * *

A pious myth has been woven round the early years of the Inyati mission. Generations of Rhodesian children have been taught about the hardships which beset the first Protestant preachers in the country; again and again they have read of their virtues, of the communal struggle to keep alive, of their illnesses, of Mzilikazi's alternating kindliness and neglect, and of their ultimate triumph, through fellowship, in creating a little oasis of content and civilisation among the heathen, an oasis which in the end provided a firm base on which was built a multiracial community modelled on Christian standards. The legend errs. It is almost as though a conspiracy was devised to gloss over the fact that, far from being the paragons of Rhodesian tradition, the first Inyati missionaries were thoroughly cantankerous men who quarrelled incessantly among themselves, and who, thirty years after the 'planting' of the mission, could count only two genuine converts to the Christian creed.

John Smith Moffat himself much later came to believe that the missionaries' evangelistic labours at Inyati had been futile and he could even conceive that the failure might in part have been due to something lacking in themselves. 'The promoters of missions', he grumbles, 'are too apt to regard a tribe or chief as interesting only in proportion as the region is difficult of access and as the conditions are unpromising', and he goes on to suggest that it would have been far wiser if the Society in 1859 had concentrated its efforts on the closer and more promising South African diamond fields instead of distant Matabeleland. When he revisited Inyati thirty years after the 'planting' of the mission, we find John Moffat wondering glumly 'what is there to show' for all their efforts, and reaching the sad conclusion that 'a few individuals may have been influenced for good, but there is no organic result, by which I mean there do not seem to be three, or even two people of the tribe who trust each other and recognise each other as Christians', and that there was 'no indication that the life of the tribe is in any way touched by the Gospel'.

But then, of course, the younger Moffat was a life-long pessi-mist. It could equally well be argued that the missionaries' mere residence in the country, which made them familiar to the Mata-bele, had justified all their discomforts and suffering a hundred times over. For this familiarity was to be of immense advantage to the white adventurers who followed them and played so large a part in developing the far interior. Certainly Mr Thomas took a more cheerful view of their own influence and he shrewdly noted that 'our work has been almost entirely of a preparatory character, and in this we have been successful. We have succeeded in doing something in emancipating the slave, teaching the ignor-ant, elevating the degraded, correcting the erroneous, clothing the naked, staying the hands of the slayer, obtaining civil and religious liberty for the subjects of a despot, opening up the country for commercial and scientific purposes and diminishing the evils from war, polygamy, and witchcraft. The language has been acquired, access to the heathen gained and commerce introduced.'

One feels that such comments show that Thomas, far more than John Moffat, had grasped the real significance of the mis-sionaries' work at Inyati. Their mere presence in Matabeleland and their endurance had laid the nation's foundation stone truly. What staggers those who study the early days of the first British mission in Rhodesia, however, is the uncharitableness which these men of God showed to each other.

In fairness to them the singularity of their circumstances at Inyati must be continually recognised and emphasised; probably more than anything else it accounted for their venomous attitudes to each other. Their predicament is easily comprehensible: these men from different backgrounds were thrown together in such peculiar intimacy that their minds often became engrossed and even obsessed, not by mission work, but with supposed rebuffs and imaginary grievances. In a way their situation can be likened to that of a group of survivors from a shipwreck cast upon an uncharted island that is populated by savages: everything there is novel and nearly everything is hostile; talents which were valuable before have become worthless and those which were previously scorned are suddenly seen to be invaluable. Just as the valet Crichton becomes the admirable Crichton in the play, so all their own criteria are suddenly turned upside down and manual dexterity counts for more than intellectual faculty. For merely to exist in central Africa a hundred years ago required unusual resilience, and all of these men and women, unused to roughing it, were confronted in Matabeleland with a physical struggle for existence. Indeed it is something of a marvel that any of the missionaries survived the first years at Inyati. Their crude huts faced onto a patch of relatively infertile veld which had never been tilled before, and they had to tame it if they were to live. That was the first essential. Moffat and Sykes had little knowledge of farming (and according to Thomas 'were small men and weaklings') and although Thomas had learned its rudiments in Wales, they were hardly applicable to Africa. For many essential foodstuffs they were dependent on the whims of the unpredictable Mzilikazi, who at best regarded them as servants to be used in mending his antiquated guns and wagons, and at worst as Boer spies and even wizards, since their arrival had coincided with poor rainy seasons.

The heavy manual work required for their survival allowed the missionaries scarcely any time to preach the Gospel, and that, after all, they regarded as their prime duty to the Matabele. Even when they did manage to gather congregations to listen to their sermons, the brethren were either baffled by their apathy or infuriated by the money demanded for attending: 'they expect *pay* for listening', fumes Emily Moffat in one of her letters. None of the newcomers had much insight into the African mind, and at the same time they had no realisation of the absurdity that they themselves, the owners of guns, wagons and other coveted articles, presented when haranguing the naked Matabele about a Gospel of self-denial which regarded property as a spiritual encumbrance. The king himself considered their sermons as opportunities to show off: once he shocked the missionaries by announcing that it was he, not God, who had made the sun. He was inclined to scoff at their homilies and to drown their scriptural revelations with loud interjections of dissent and even shouts of 'liar'. And since the Matabele were perhaps the most resistant of all Bantu tribes to scriptural teaching it was inevitable that the brethren's morale should have ebbed away as the realisation grew that their congregations had not the slightest intention of altering their pagan ways, and were unlikely to, since one African who showed some interest in their teaching was summarily executed together with his family. A lighter but still revealing incident occurred when one of the white men lectured the king on the evils of polygamy: Mzilikazi promptly retorted that 'we Matabele like many wives', and silenced further remonstrances with an additional crushing explanation that 'we Matabele love many wives'.

The missionaries' efforts to plant out the veld seemed just as futile as their attempts at proselytism; every year their crops failed, either because of drought or due to the amateur farmers' inexperience. Theirs became an existence on so low a scale that it could only have been made reasonably tolerable by true forbearance and sympathy for each other's frailties, but these were the very last qualities the brethren seemed inclined to exhibit at Inyati. 'That horned spectre, *contention*' (the words are Robert Moffat's) ruled the mission. Sometimes one feels that only Emily Moffat found any pleasure in the 'Swiss Family Robinson' sort of life they were leading in an environment which was far less favourable than that described in the book. She was helped by her sense of the ridiculous: this is best reflected in the letters where she makes fun of Mzilikazi when he was 'most shabby in his treatment', and she usually referred to him as 'Catsey', or with even less respect.

But even Emily Moffat's brave front could not long be maintained in the face of continual illness, frequent child-bearing, and heart-rending withdrawal from her civilised world; for these trials seemed utterly unjustified by results. She literally ached with loneliness: 'This is isolation with a vengeance', she writes despairingly to her father before she had been at Inyati six months, and it was symptomatic of her distress that all through her correspondence there runs the theme of her exaggerated longing for letters from the outside world, and of her delight on the widely spaced occasions when they arrived.

*   *   *   *   *

However disagreeable the hardships that the Matabele missionaries had to face, at least they were spared the horrors which overwhelmed the sister mission to the Makololo. Even now the sinister tragedy of Linyanti seems more like a fragment from some medieval legend of persecuted Christians than an event which took place during the age of enlightenment. For the story of the Makololo mission is set in idiom unlike that of any other evangelical ventures undertaken by the British church a century ago, and its harrowing details make scarcely bearable reading. Although the historical context of its tragedy is Rhodesian, by a second curious chance the martyrdom of the Linyanti missionaries, like that of Gonçales three hundred years earlier, took place just outside Rhodesia's boundaries. It was as though the country was determined to preserve its soil from infamy.

The L.M.S. had recruited three men for the Makololo mission. Its leader was Holloway Helmore, a saintly veteran who had spent more years in the African mission field than Livingstone himself, and was the head of a particularly united family.* His

---

* Bessie Moffat described the Helmores at the time as 'that loving family. . . . They are all love and that is their greatest fault . . . there's no seeing each others faults among them. . . . But each is perfect in the other's eyes.'

intended companions were two pastors in their twenties, John Mackenzie and Roger Price. Both of them were married, and both their wives were pregnant in 1859 when the expedition to Linyanti was ready to trek away from Kuruman. At the very last moment, however, Mackenzie decided to stay on there until after his wife's confinement.

On the 8th July, a week ahead of the party for Matabeleland, Helmore and Price took the road to Shoshong and the north. Even without the Mackenzies they still made an imposing cavalcade. They had bought four wagons, and in them travelled the Helmores with their four small children, Mr and Mrs Price and two African evangelists. With them they also had a dozen Bechuana mission boys to drive the oxen. Their route after Shoshong took them into arid country bordering on the Kalahari, and the Prices were depressed by the dismal desert landscapes which were quite unlike anything they had expected. They had an appalling time: 'just sand—sand—sand', runs one dejected entry in Mrs Price's diary before they had been on the road a week, and it was typical of many others which followed. As they trekked further north conditions grew worse, but the travellers all got on very well together, and every now and then they took heart when the desert gave way to fine savannah country where progress became much easier. By September the rhythm of the trek routine had taken hold of them, and with familiarity their discomforts became a little easier to bear. Their world had contracted to the 'scofs' their wagons could accomplish in a day and the sand horizons around them; their thoughts were confined to their fellowship, the intolerable heat, and a crushing anxiety about reaching the next water-hole alive. In the last week of the month they halted at Lotlokani where they found an open pan of good water, and there Isabella Price was safely delivered of a baby girl. Increasingly hard going followed right through October, and Mrs Price felt particularly wretched for as she tells us she 'suffered most intensely' from 'a gathered breast'. At the Zouga river, which they reached in the third week of October, the little party had its first experience of malaria, but it was not until November, after they had entered the trackless wastes of the Chobe desert that their real troubles began. Water—or rather, the lack of water—now dominated their lives; for the next 250 miles they either went thirsty or depended on the foul liquid that some stray bushmen sucked from a hollow tree and which, according to Mrs Price, tasted 'like water from a dunghill'.

At the end of the month they were delighted to come upon a depression containing rainwater, and there they stopped long enough to baptise the Price baby. But beyond conditions became worse than anything they had known before, and to keep the party alive, Helmore was obliged to walk distances up to thirty miles each night to collect sufficient water for the next day's journey. The grazing was poor and the oxen were losing condition and all the known water points they came to were dry. To go on seemed suicidal, and one desperate day the wagons were turned about and the little party moved back slowly to the 'Baby pool' where Eliza Price had been christened.

There the missionaries spent a miserable fortnight in temperatures that varied between 107° and 110° in the shade, and all the time their precious supply of water was dwindling away before their eyes. Because his four children were 'almost mad with thirst' Mr Helmore walked thirty-eight miles one night searching for the water that would enable them to survive; he returned next day with only a small quantity of muddy liquid, but it saved their lives. They passed a depressing Christmas at the 'Baby pool', then somehow found the strength again to move on through the desert toward Linyanti. One imagines that they were led on only by the prospect of the friendly welcome they expected from Dr Livingstone and Sekeletu, the Makololo chief. On the 11th February, they came to the Chobe river, and now were freed from all the terrors of thirst. Three days later their wagons rumbled into Linyanti, Sekeletu's capital. The journey from Kuruman had taken them more than seven months.

A dreadful disappointment awaited them: there was no sign, nor even news, of Dr Livingstone and, of more immediate concern, Sekeletu's attitude to them was utterly different from anything the missionaries had been led to expect from Livingstone's reports. Sekeletu turned out to be even more unfriendly to the

Helmore party than Mzilikazi had been to the Matabele mission-aries. We know now that there were several reasons for his behaviour: one was his disappointment that no member of the Moffat family had been included in the mission party, for Sekeletu had come to believe that the presence at Linyanti of any relation of Moshete's would be a kind of insurance against further Matabele aggression. Indeed his earlier hospitality to Livingstone had been entirely due to the doctor being Moffat's son-in-law. Another reason for Sekeletu's hostility was that he had recently been selling slaves to half-caste Portuguese, and was concerned lest the missionaries discovered and reported this to the authorities in the south. Finally, the chief was suffering from leprosy: not only was he sensitive about his appearance but the dementia which is often a feature of the disease seems to have been causing all sorts of odd notions to run through his mind, and Mrs Price perhaps gives us a clue to one of them when she noted in her diary that 'Sekeletu seems quite jealous of me'.

The missionaries had to wait three days at Linyanti before Sekeletu would see them. They were told that he had gone out hunting, but in fact he was busy consulting the oracles in a nearby hut. When he at last condescended to meet Helmore, he was brusque and refused point-blank to allow the missionaries to move on into the healthy country beyond the Zambesi: he insisted instead that they remained at Linyanti. But on the next three successive Sundays Helmore or Price were permitted to preach in the town; the rest of the time they spent building huts for the accommodation of their families. Then a terrible lethal thing descended on them out of the sky: February and March are the most unhealthy months of the year in this swamp country, and now, one by one, the members of Helmore's party went down with fever. They had no knowledge of medicine, they had brought very few drugs with them, and they were tragically unaware that only a hundred yards away bottles of life-saving quinine were lying in a wagon Livingstone had left in Sekeletu's care seven years before.

On 2nd March, Price's wagon driver died. Four days later little Henry Helmore was found lying dead in one of the wagons, and his parents themselves were so ill by then that they seemed scarcely concerned. On the 9th March baby Eliza Price was suddenly taken ill, and one of its most harrowing passages now appears in her mother's diary: 'Ah! Providence, how mysteriously art thou dealing with us', wrote Mrs Price that evening, 'my own sweet little one has today taken her flight from us. I saw a change in her countenance this morning and determined to keep her in my arms altogether; she took no food yesterday and this morning refused the breast—wine, however, she took well. Roger suffered much this morning from oppression of the chest and just before midday wished for a cold sheet. I refused help at first as I saw my precious one was dying, but on finding it really needed I laid her on the mattress for a few minutes while I served Roger. She turned her head and gave me a look, then to the other side and gave papa a look. I seized her to my bosom and gave her a press. Then laying her on my lap I found her eyes were fixed and and she ceased to breathe. I immediately washed her and dressed her in that dear little nightgown which Mama gave me and in which we always liked to see her. Then I wrapped her in two pretty karosses given her, one by Mrs Hughes, and the other by Mrs Thomas, sheepskins beautifully dressed, and the precious little bundle was laid in the grave by the side of little Henry. Ah! I do feel lonely tonight. My little darling was pretty, very pretty and her disposition very sweet. She was much beloved and noticed by all the people. When I think of her sweet little face beaming with smiles upon me, I feel it hard to part with my precious and yet she is now a little angel saved from all the evils of life. I do not murmur. I feel I can say: "Thy will be done". But my heart bleeds at the parting. My heart's desire now is that I may become more holy and devoted to the service of my master.'

Of such quality was the faith of the missionaries who attempted the conversion of the Makololo.

Nobody in 1860 had definitely associated malaria with mosquitoes, and the missionaries had no conception of the nature of the illness which was afflicting them. In any case they were by now all too weak to spare much thought for anything except their own misery. On the 11th March, two days after Baby Price, Selina

Helmore died; that evening we find Mrs Price bravely wondering in her journal 'who will be the next?' and going on to add 'That passage in the Scripture "be still and know that I am God" has much calmed me today.'

The next one was Mrs Helmore; she died the following day. 'Poor Mr Helmore seems wonderfully calm', runs Mrs Price's diary that day, 'but there is a sort of indifference to everything manifested by most in this fever. They just lie and sleep and sleep, except when extreme restlessness prevents them; they seem too wretched to think of anything but their own suffering.'

On the 14th March, Roger Price in turn became 'seriously ill, delirious and rambling'. His wife was sure he too was going to die, but even now she was sustained by her faith, and was able to write: 'I am quite alone and have no one to whom I can unburden my feelings; but my heavenly Father is very precious and lifts me up on the light of His countenance.' It came as a tremendous relief when the crisis passed and Mr Price improved, but the disease continued to take a terrible toll among the servants who had come up from Kuruman.

Then Mrs Price went down with the mysterious fever. But suddenly the clouds lifted when her illness burned itself out, and the five white survivors began to rally and grow stronger. It was a short respite; on the 21st April, Mr Helmore suddenly sank into a coma and died. The Prices were now placed in a terrible predicament: they were newcomers to Africa; physically both of them were extremely weak; and they were dreadfully concerned about the health of the two little Helmore orphans. Worse: the ugliest part of their ordeal still remained to be faced. For the Makololo who had ignored them before, now swarmed round their stricken camp, plundering it of everything that caught their fancy. May was a terrible month. 'Then began our real trials', Price recalled later, 'the reins of barbarism were let go and we became the victims of the most horrid provocation and cruelty.' Even Mrs Price neared breaking point. The last entry she was able to make in her diary recorded 'we have been robbed most fearfully. . . . I am so thin that I am obliged to plaster my poor bones and have lost the use of my legs.'

In such circumstances the Prices decided it would be preferable to attempt the thousand-mile desert journey back to Kuruman than to perish miserably at Linyanti. After long argument they persuaded Sekeletu to give them permission to go. It still took Price another month to pack his wagon; he was so weak that the slightest exertion prostrated him, and he had to be carried to each box in turn by the few servants who remained alive. Sekeletu, meanwhile, was behaving abominably. He deliberately stole two of the wagons, and then insisted on the helpless Price delaying his departure until he had broken in a team of oxen to draw them. One day when Helmore's valuable collection of books was looted, something snapped in Price's mind and the bleak acceptance of persecution which so far had marked the missionaries' behaviour was temporarily abandoned. He seems to have been more mortified at seeing the Makololo tear out the books' pages to adorn their heads than by anything else that had occurred. 'I am not soon cast down by events', he wrote later, 'but on that occasion I went and called upon the Lord for support'; he then loosed off his pistol over the looters' heads.

Unknown to the Prices, help was already on its way to them from two separate directions. On 16th May, 1860, Dr Livingstone had at last set out from Tete on the six-hundred-miles journey to Linyanti, while only nine days afterwards the Mackenzies started off from Kuruman to join their brethren in Sekeletu's country. But on 19th June long before either party arrived there Price succeeded in getting away from Linyanti. A heavy toll was exacted from him by Sekeletu at both rivers lying south of the town, and he was even made to pay an extortionate fee for the grass his oxen ate while waiting to cross. Price could not resist the blackmail: as he pointed out his position was 'like a lamb in a lion's mouth'. All he could do was remonstrate that he could hardly survive such robbery, and his distress was not lightened when Sekeletu replied that he 'might as well die here as anywhere else' and anyway was leaving on his own responsibility.

Eventually, 'after a good deal of pleading' the Prices shook off the Makololo while they still possessed two wagons, sufficient oxen to pull them and a bare minimum of clothing. For the next few days they felt happy and stimulated at being on their own again, and the desert air seemed to recruit their health. But, on 5th July, the worst blow of all fell. For the events of that terrible day we cannot do better than quote Roger Price's own words: 'My dear wife had been for a long time utterly helpless', he wrote. 'In the morning I found her breathing very hard. I spoke to her and tried to wake her; but it was too late. I watched her all morning; she became worse and worse and a little after midday her spirit took flight to God who gave it. I buried her the same evening under a tree, the only tree on the whole of the immense plain of the Mababe.' How easy it is even now to imagine his despair and crushing sense of loneliness as he read the burial service very slowly over the grave he had scooped out of the desert, while beside him in the light of one of those red impossible Kalahari sunsets two forlorn and emaciated little children watched him listlessly and without understanding.

Roger Price's misery was heightened a few days later when he learned that his wife had not been suffered to lie in peace for long. A group of Makololo were still following Price's wagon tracks like vultures anticipating a carrion meal: they came upon the poor grave in the desert, dug up the corpse, cut off its face, and carried it back to Sekeletu for public exhibition at Linyanti.

Dreading another ordeal in the thirstland of the Chobe desert, Price now struck westward from Mababe and headed towards Lake Ngami. We are not told a great deal about this part of his journey: Price himself seems to have got through it in a sort of trance, and only thanks to a great deal of luck. For some stray Bushmen guided him—on Makololo orders, according to Price—into fly country, and 41 of his 44 trek oxen perished there. Price and the frightened Helmore children were now marooned in the wilds, and they prepared for death. But by some miracle he was found and befriended by a party of Bechuanas, and they led him to their chief, Lechulatebe, who treated the despairing man kindly. Price was too debilitated to go any further: all he could do was remain in Lechulatebe's country and hope that eventually someone would come looking for him. He knew that this might take months or even years. But by another miracle on 8th September,

1860, Mackenzie discovered him, reduced to a mere 'shadow' and suffering from amnesia. Mackenzie coming north through the desert to rejoin his colleagues had strayed so far from his course that he had entered Lechulatebe's country and was taken (or in Robert Moffat's pious opinion was 'divinely directed') to where Price was living. With him Mackenzie carried ample supplies and medicines, and the health of Price and the children very quickly improved. By the 20th September he was strong enough to take the long road south again with Mackenzie. There was a delay for some weeks during December to allow the confinement of Mrs Mackenzie, but by the middle of February, 1861, Price and the two surviving Helmore children were safely back at Kuruman. They were all that had survived of the party which had set off so confidently from that station eighteen terrible months before.

To the end of his days, Robert Price was convinced that Sekeletu had murdered the missionaries at Linyanti with poison introduced into meat and beer he had sent them, yet he admitted he found it difficult to understand why the chief had spared himself and the two children to survive as witnesses to the crime. Livingstone for his part, scornfully dismissed Price's poisoning theory: the missionaries, he was certain, had died from malaria, and in any case, as he pointed out of the Makololo, 'the spear, not poison, is their weapon'.

Yet a nagging doubt remains that malaria could not have been the real cause of the tragic deaths at Linyanti: the missionaries' symptoms simply do not fit in with the diagnosis. Price, for instance, refers to the intolerable spasms of pain in the loins suffered by the patients during the terminal stages of their illnesses, and loin pain is not a usual manifestation of malaria. Price himself was well aware of this, and used it to support his theory of poisoning: 'in African fever I have not seen so much pain suffered', he writes, 'but some of my friends suffered pain of the most excruciating character'.

There seems little doubt now that in fact the Helmores died from a complication of malaria—blackwater fever. That disease unaccountably tends to affect groups of people residing in the same compound. It is characterised by a rapid haemolysis (or dissolution) of the red blood cells, whose resulting products block up the kidneys, and cause intense pain in the loins. Blackwater fever had been recently recognised on the west coast of Africa when the Helmores died, and only the year before had been reported in America and Madagascar. The Makololo missionaries, it appears, had the melancholy distinction of being the first known victims of this mysterious disease in central Africa. Very soon, however, and for the next eighty years, it was to be one of the far interior's most dangerous hazards.

If we are nowadays more sure of the nature of the disease which killed the Helmores, it is still necessary to keep an open mind regarding the other controversial issue raised by their deaths— how far was Livingstone responsible for their deaths? Without doubt both Helmore and Price fully expected to find Livingstone waiting for them at Linyanti, and it was a terrible blow when they discovered he was not there. Livingstone was still six hundred miles away at the time, having been deflected from his original plan of proceeding up river to Linyanti by difficulties encountered at the Kebrabasa rapids on the lower Zambesi. Indeed all through 1859 he had become so engrossed with exploring the newly discovered country round Lake Nyasa, that he gave little thought to the mission party approaching Sekeletu's country, and it was not until the May of 1860, that he at last set out on the long march up the Zambesi to meet them. He reached Linyanti in August, long after Price had left.

Price accounted Livingstone's failure to meet him at Linyanti a breach of faith and he did not disguise his feelings; he insisted too that the doctor had misled him about the Makololo in general and about Sekeletu's character in particular. In consequence a coolness developed between the two men which became all the more embarrassing when Price, for his second wife, took another of the Moffat family, Livingstone's sister-in-law, Bessie.

Price was not alone in believing Livingstone had broken faith with the Makololo missionaries: some of the Directors of the L.M.S. thought so too, and allowed Moffat to know it. News of their scarcely veiled opinions soon got back to the doctor. 'Their agent, Mr Farebrother', he wrote indignantly, 'goes about the country telling at public meetings that I am morally responsible for the loss of the missionaries at Linyanti.' These imputations were not altogether fair. Although Livingstone may have suggested sending the mission to Sekeletu, there is little evidence that he *promised* to meet the missionaries at Linyanti; all he had done was to say that he *hoped* to do so. His plans were changed primarily because of physical difficulties he had encountered on the lower Zambesi but one suspects that the ill-feeling engendered during 1857, when Livingstone resigned from the L.M.S., may have also had something to do with his attitude of bland unconcern for the Society's Makololo mission, and the delay in travelling to their assistance. But even so, the Directors of the London Missionary Society must bear much of the responsibility for his indifference. After his resignation they never approached Livingstone for the advice which would almost certainly have prevented Helmore's tragedy, nor did the Makololo brethren themselves bother to get in touch with the experienced doctor before setting out for Linyanti. 'Helmore', wrote Livingstone when answering his critics, 'did not write me even.' The snub was deliberate: when the Secretary of the L.M.S. was asked why he had made no effort to inform Livingstone of Helmore's movements, he shrugged off the question with a bleak, 'I have no official connection with Dr Livingstone.'

If it is thus possible to understand why Dr Livingstone gave precedence to his own plans rather than concern himself with the Linyanti missionaries, it is less easy to excuse his lack of charity towards them. But to Livingstone, of course, failure was the most heinous of crimes, and Helmore's mission undoubtedly was a disastrous failure. When he did at last reach Linyanti, the doctor coldly wrote that he felt 'rather sorrowful at finding Helmore dead and Price retired'. But he tended the Helmores' graves, and finding no stones in the vicinity, heaped animal horns over them as bizarre memorials. Yet he took Sekeletu's side when the chief was reproached for his treatment of the missionaries: Price, Livingstone said, had brought the chief's hostility upon himself with his provocative arrogance. What he really felt about the Makololo missionaries comes out most clearly in a letter Livingstone sent to John Moffat in which he writes, 'I think they wanted to do it all themselves, and have it to say they did not require any aid from me'; then in a spasm of irritation he added 'a precious mull they made of it'.

Looking back on it now we can see that the Directors of the L.M.S. not only merited criticism for allowing their prickly dignity to prevent them seeking the advice of the most accomplished African explorer of the time, but even more for their Himalayan optimism and utter lack of foresight. No doctor accompanied the mission to Makolololand although it was well known that Linyanti was wretchedly unhealthy; only an absurdly inadequate supply of drugs was provided, and no one in the party had been taught their usage; no effort was even made at Kuruman to provide them with means of carrying an adequate reserve water supply, and they were not even given a horse with which to reconnoitre the water-holes on the road ahead.

Sekeletu did not long survive the missionaries of Linyanti. He died from leprosy in 1864. Within a few years his Makololo tribe, too, was virtually annihilated by the subject Barotse in a bloody rebellion, and even its name ceased to exist. A lesser spirit than that of Isabella Price might have found some satisfaction in the unpleasant end which overwhelmed her persecutors so soon after her death, but neither she nor the other members of the Helmore party were the sort of people who would have enjoyed revenge. Instead one feels that they must have applauded Roger Price when he exacted a truly Christian vengeance and decided, even after his ordeal, that Africa was still worth saving. During the remainder of his long life he laboured as a missionary among the tribesmen on Rhodesia's western borders, and to this day he is remembered there as the 'Great Lion of Bechuanaland'.

*   *   *   *   *

If the missionaries at Inyati were spared the horrors which overwhelmed their colleagues in Makolololand, they did not avoid misfortune of quite another kind—domestic quarrels of their own making. Nothing is more remarkable (or farcical) in the history of modern Rhodesia than the way the country's three earliest pioneers made each other's lives miserable.

The first rifts in the brethren's friendship were noticeable even before they reached Inyati, and surprisingly enough they appeared in the closely-knit Moffat family. John and his wife Emily were immensely critical of the way Dr Robert Moffat reinforced his influence over Mzilikazi with presents as well as with assistance in mending his guns and selling his ivory. They maintained that these actions amounted to trading for profit and even bribery, and they determined to have nothing to do with them. As early as August, 1859, we find Emily Moffat reflecting her husband's opinions by complaining to her father that 'while Grandpapa has opened the way, he has also opened up difficulties for his successors', and she added with emphatic underlining that 'I can't believe *in bribing*'. Although it was perhaps a little unbecoming and even presumptuous for the young couple (John was twenty-four at the time, and Emily twenty-eight) to criticise the veteran missionary in this way, they had some justification in doing so. For it is hard to distinguish some of Dr Moffat's transactions from outright trading, and they certainly ran counter to mission policy: 'The rules of the Society', the Directors had laid down, 'entirely prohibit the missionaries from carrying on any kind of trade with the natives with a view to pecuniary profit.'

Young Moffat's disapproval of his father's activities was not discussed in public, but privately it was never far from the minds of the Matabele missionaries. During the six months Dr Moffat remained at Inyati, assisting in the establishment of the station, his son complained that he had been subjected to 'bitter and almost daily provocations', and Emily confided in a letter home that 'the establishment has just been trading in ivory', that 'there is much that pains us' at the station, and that 'our dissatisfaction with Grandpapa's doings has made all writing unpleasant'. It took a long time for Emily to forgive her father-in-law: two years later she could still write that 'my blood boiled again' when she remembered his conduct. Only late in 1863 did John Moffat conceive that his originally rigid attitude might after all have been wrong. 'I have taken to gun-mending', he admits, and goes on to explain that 'my ideas of missionary work are very different from what they were; perhaps I have come down a peg. Be it so. . . .' Twenty-five years later his opinion of how to run a mission had undergone an even more radical change. 'The course which it appears to me ought to be adopted', he wrote in 1888, was that 'a missionary ought to live here, with the Chief, be within daily call, and making himself useful to the Chief in carrying on trade'.

The trouble was that the dissension among the Moffats during the early days at Inyati soon affected Sykes and Thomas, and made them take sides in the dispute. From the start Sykes wholeheartedly condemned Dr Moffat's actions, while Thomas equally emphatically supported them. Thomas, the materialist, asserted that it was only fair that he himself be allowed to follow Dr Moffat's example and undertake a little trading on his own account since his salary was considerably less than the subsidy allowed John Moffat by Dr Livingstone, and here of course he immediately touched upon a sore point. The controversy came to a head in May of 1860, when Sykes went off on leave to look for a new wife in the Cape. Mzilikazi chose to regard his departure as an opportunity to sell some 'elephant teeth' down south, which set Emily Moffat indignantly recording that 'with threats he tried to force Sykes to take ivory to the Colony to trade for him'. Sykes point blank refused, and in the end, according to Mrs Moffat, he 'gained his point; though not entirely to our satisfaction for he and we wanted *a united* expression to the king of our trading views and of our object in being here'. Clearly Thomas had made it plain that he did not share the views held by Sykes and Moffat about missionaries who traded. Perhaps his attitude was the right one: his son clarified it later when he explained, 'The interchange of presents was an inborn custom of natives. The king often sent gifts to the white people and of course expected presents in return. The king's presents were either slaughtered animals or cows. The white men gave in return coffee, sugar, beads, calico, and so on. Sykes and Moffat disapproved of the custom, holding it was a form of trading. Thomas argued that it was the best means of establishing friendly relations with the people. He spent his substance in doctoring and helping them in every way, and considered it only fair to himself to accept their gifts as some compensation for the personal expense he incurred in helping them.'

After Dr Robert Moffat's departure in the June of 1860, only the Moffat and Thomas families were left at Inyati. The two men went about their duties without much friction but it is clear that their relations were still a trifle strained. Improving conversation is apt to flag after a few months and soon Emily was confessing to her father she had found 'the Welsh are narrow-minded', and that 'no true friendship' had developed between the families, while her husband sniffed that the Thomases were 'no company, having about as much notion of English home life as I have of Cochin Chinese'. The Moffats were also annoyed because they discovered that Thomas was privately making arrangements to abandon his mission work for a few months and make a journey of exploration to the Zambesi. They were vexed too by their colleague's attempts to preach in the vernacular before he had mastered it, and John Moffat pointed out with some justification, 'It seems to me the climax of absurdity to attempt a long statement of abstruse truth to such benighted beings when we cannot even tell them how to cook a leg of mutton.'

In July, 1861, Mr Sykes came back safely to Inyati with his bride, and almost at once the brethren again began indulging their natural aptitudes for finding fault with each other. The rains had failed that year; there was famine in Matabeleland and the near-starvation of their 'parishioners' seemed all the harder for the missionaries to bear because of the vast herds of game they could see grazing the surrounding veld. Many of the Matabele had guns, but they were shocking marksmen and in any case the guns were usually out of order. After examining their consciences, both John Moffat and Sykes made up their minds that they could not assist the Matabele through the crisis either by hunting or by mending their firearms, for as they pointed out that if they put their guns in order there was nothing to prevent the Matabele using them later to hunt down more unfortunate Mashona.

Thomas, predictably, took a different view of the situation. In the autobiography he wrote ten years later, he speaks of 'the unusual course I adopted in labouring among the heathen. It was a time of famine in consequence of the scarcity of rain. Many were suffering from hunger, and some contracted diseases which resulted in death from eating improper food. I then first became convinced it was my duty to use the gun, in order to feed the hungry. Many were the applications for help the poor starving people made to us. . . . Accordingly, I went out often and shot, from time to time, some hundreds of antelopes and other game, in order to satisfy their hunger; and I employed dozens of men and women, not so much for their work's sake as for the sake of feeding them, and teaching them good habits and the work of God.'

It is of course easy to see both sides of the missionaries' argument. Sykes and Moffat believed that their duty was confined to preaching the Gospel; to give the starving Matabele more practical help would, they believed, only result in their conversion to what they called 'rice Christians' and the massacre of a few dozen more Mashona. Thomas on the other hand declared that 'a good missionary must be a *man* in the best sense of the word— must show those among whom he labours that he has all their interests—temporal as well as spiritual—at heart'.* Whichever opinion may have been the more ethically correct, there was no doubt about the Africans' reaction: they were grateful to Thomas for the food he provided and he immediately acquired an influence in Matabeleland which he never lost. But this of course only deepened the rift between the missionaries: according to Thomas, his new authority infuriated Sykes, who from now on was consumed by a 'burning jealousy' for his Welsh colleague, while Moffat became his 'greatest opponent'.

Soon afterwards, and to the further disgust of the other

---

* It is interesting to compare this with the views expressed by Father Depelchin, one of the Catholic missionaries who entered Matabeleland twenty years later: 'One of the best ways of entering into the minds of these barbarous tribes', he wrote on 10th September, 1879, 'is to teach them . . . the elements of the arts which are useful in life . . . we must teach them in a practical manner . . . it will, therefore, be necessary to provide first the material needs in order to lead them subsequently little by little towards the life of the spirit, towards the sublime virtues of Christian morality.'

brethren, Thomas's prestige rocketed still higher when Mzilikazi made him the royal physician. In African eyes he had replaced Moshete's son as head of the Inyati mission, and he promptly took advantage of his new eminence to expand his trading activities.

At the same time Thomas's increasing influence in Matabeleland began to cause John Moffat a good deal of heart searching as well as annoyance. 'Are we justified as missionaries in mending firearms and using ammunition for purposes of barter?' he enquires anxiously early in 1862, and he goes on to explain that 'there is no means of gaining influence so potent in South Africa as gun-mending. A good gunsmith at once takes rank, and can obtain what no one else can. I shut myself out from gaining an influence over those who are the most influential men and sometimes at a great sacrifice of feeling to myself, when some very decent fellow comes and entreats me to mend his gun, which very likely will be a great assistance to him in obtaining game to feed himself and his family. I often wish I could know what others would think of the question. I believe it is one upon which there would be no unanimity among the constituents of the L.M.S., any more than there is among its agents.'

Realising that they must work better together, the Inyati missionaries met during the April of 1862 to discuss their differences and they ended up by agreeing to accept a majority decision among themselves in all future matters of contention. The atmosphere at the mission improved still more when John Moffat travelled south on a prolonged spell of sick leave, for it is always much harder for two men to quarrel than for three. In any case, Sykes was drawn closer to his difficult colleague after Thomas had lost his wife and baby from fever within a few days of each other, and we even find Sykes referring to him as 'our beloved friend and fellow-labourer' when he wrote home about Thomas's sad surrender to the temptation of trading with the Matabele.

The rapprochement lasted only until the Moffats returned from leave a year later. They were accompanied by John Mackenzie who after rescuing Price from the Makololo had accepted an appointment at Inyati. The newcomer was an intolerant man and Thomas now found himself very much in the minority at the station. Moffat, Sykes, and Mackenzie united in accusing him openly 'of receiving ivory and feathers from the natives in exchange for ammunition, beads, etc., and for mending their guns', and it was clear that a fresh storm was brewing.

It did not develop at once since Thomas was too busy preparing to go on leave to take the accusations very much to heart. He left Inyati in September 1863, carrying with him the manuscripts of a hymnal—the first book ever to be written in Sindebele (the Matabele language) which was to be printed at Kuruman. There had been a great deal of argument about the spelling of many of the words used by Sykes and Thomas but in the end they had come to a reluctant agreement on the matter. Once at Kuruman, however, Thomas's natural contrariness gained the upper hand and quite arbitrarily he decided to use the spellings he himself favoured.

Peace reigned at Inyati while Thomas was away, but it was otherwise in London. The Directors of the L.M.S. had by now received their first intimation that all was not well at the station in the far interior of which they were so proud. It came in the form of a particularly depressing letter from John Moffat: 'Hitherto', he informed them, 'our agency here as missionaries has been of so passive a nature as to make one feel more inclined to hide one's head in the thicket than look in the face those at home who expected such great things of us four or five years ago. The spirit of the Lord', he goes on to explain, 'has not been with us in this mission . . . in this gloomy realm of sin and violence.' The Directors were quite nonplussed by his despondency.

Young Moffat became even more dejected when Mackenzie, evidently anxious to get out of the hornet's nest in which he found himself, announced that he was leaving the station. Within a fortnight Moffat himself decided to quit Inyati too, and he wrote to inform the Directors of his decision.

Then something quite unexpected happened: John Moffat received a letter from Dr Livingstone telling him that the British Government had recalled his Zambesi expedition and that he would not be able to subsidise him much longer as an independent missionary. Moffat had now no option but to swallow his pride and ask the L.M.S. for an official appointment. In due course he was accepted and posted to Inyati. His changed status meant, of course, that he was no longer an 'outsider' at Inyati, but a fully-fledged member of the mission, and that in every dispute there would now be three official opinions. 'I cannot see', sighed Moffat in gloomy anticipation, 'but that my relations with the brethren will be more difficult to maintain for my insular position at present enables [me] to choose my own ground, whereas I shall be involved, *nolens volens*, in much which jars the heart.'

He was perfectly correct; only a little later Inyati learned that Mr Thomas had arranged for *his* spelling to be used in the newly printed Sindebele books. There was uproar at the station; all previous quarrels faded into insignificance compared with this one. When tempers had cooled down a little, however, the brethren made a feeble attempt to compose their differences about the hymnal and decided to make a fresh start by agreeing 'that they each select, compose, or obtain in any other way twelve setebele [*sic*] hymns during the month of April'. But when they met again to consider the results, Thomas's hymns were again found to be written in the 'heretical' spelling. The absurd vendetta which for so long had been the leading theme of the missionary repertory at Inyati was at once resumed *cum brio*, and Sykes and Moffat, after angry consultation, informed their 'dear brother' that since, 'a sound represented according to the alphabet by "hl" was written by you "ll" ' they had decided never to use the offending hymns at the Inyati services.

Thomas would have been less than human (and a great deal less than Thomas Morgan Thomas) had he taken the snub lying down, and he promptly launched a countercharge which was littered with a wealth of local topographical detail: during his absence on leave, he wrote (for from now on written notes were the favoured medium of communication at Inyati), the mission church had been 'built right away from our house but near yours' although as he pointed out the brethren had previously agreed to the church being 'erected on a spot equally near to all parties'.

Thomas must have gibbered with rage when he received a broadside in return from his colleagues a week later: 'We think we may be excused', they told him, 'if we express our contempt for such an imputation', and although a good deal more followed in similar vein, their letter was still soothingly signed with the customary, 'we are, dear brother, yours sincerely, John Smith Moffat, William Sykes.' Thomas lost no time in getting off an answer which, though hastily scribbled, was not lacking in emphasis: 'I must tell you candidly', he wrote, 'that some of your letters to me are most offensive and insulting', and he went on, 'I shall consider it my duty to cast any and every communication from you on one side and take no notice of it.' Five days later Moffat and Sykes poured oil on the Inyati flames by suggesting that Thomas had misappropriated some Society funds to purchase a 'smith's bellows' and a 'school bell'. Thomas retorted that he found this suggestion 'very impertinent', and he informed his colleagues 'that I cannot meet with you for common deliberation or united prayer any more for I deem such a meeting unscriptural'; he ended the note with an unfraternal 'yours faithfully'.

It was all very childish and all very petty; it also promised to be disastrous to the future of the mission. By the July of 1865, the brethren at Inyati were no longer on speaking terms; all communication between houses standing only a few yards apart in the wilds of Matabeleland were effected by written messages that were faithfully copied to the Directors of the Society in London. The Directors must have sometimes wondered whether their brethren at Inyati were living in reality or in a confused dream-world brought on by the African climate. Thomas, to his credit, made one attempt at reconciliation when he was threatened with the exposure of their recent communications, and, appearing in the unusual role of peacemaker, he suggested that they kept their quarrels to themselves and that his colleagues should 'consider me the only sinner and forgive me' in order 'to prevent the spread of our imperfections to the four winds'. All he got back in reply was a curt intimation that Moffat and Sykes did not find his suggestion 'satisfactory to us'.

The strain of living and quarrelling at Inyati told first on the

Moffats: by this time John was drooping in the unhappy atmosphere and his wife's gaiety was quite extinguished. Wearily they decided to quit 'poor benighted Inyati' for good, and took themselves off to the more felicitous air of Kuruman. After a short truce the two remaining missionaries resumed their long duel when Sykes accused his colleague of monopolising the mission work and then raked up the old grievances about trading. There was always a delightful abandon about Thomas's written replies, and now he turned the tables with the totally irrelevant domestic charge that the Sykes's laundry was soiling the common water supply and 'thus filling our fountain with soap and dirt'. Then, having exhausted all possible *casa belli* Thomas withdrew with dignity from his mission duties to the pleasanter (but still, to Sykes, reprehensible) task of pioneering a route to the Zambesi.

By now the Directors of the L.M.S. were only too well aware of the way things were going at their Inyati mission station. Their files were bulging with the accumulated copies of the missionaries' acrimonious correspondence, and they had learned to dread the sight of another batch being piled upon their desks. It was not only the contents of the letters which bothered them: they also had difficulty in deciphering them. Thomas's writing happened to be the most legible of the three and the exquisitely deferential aplomb of his prose was by far the most convincing, and the Directors' sympathy on what they termed 'this discreditable contest between the brethren at Inyati' was inclined to rest with him. They agreed among themselves that Thomas might well have indulged in trading, but they were suspicious that his colleague was sinning in this way too, and they crushed the blameless Sykes with their opinion that he 'has laid himself open to the same charge and, therefore, does not enter the lists as accuser with perfectly clean hands'. The letter ended with a tactfully phrased suggestion that Sykes should withdraw from Inyati.

This was unjust; whatever may have been his failings, Sykes had been uncompromising in his opposition to trading with the Africans, and it was not surprising that towards the end of 1868, he took his injured feelings off to Kuruman to lay the whole matter before Dr Moffat and the missionary brethren who had gathered there for the occasion from seven widely scattered L.M.S. stations in Bechuanaland.

Sykes conducted his case with an unnatural warmth and eloquence made all the more effective by Thomas's absence. Each successive affront was conscientiously reconstructed, delivered with loving detail to his colleagues, and devoured by them with relish. After this Thomas was roundly denounced in a flurry of condemnations: the deep notes of Dr Moffat's indignation were joined by his son's shriller imprecations and punctuated by Mackenzie's bursts of anger that went off like a minute gun. In the matter of trading, the meeting exculpated Sykes by informing the Directors (in a deliberate parody of their words) that they considered his 'hands to be thoroughly clean'. As for Mr Thomas, they reported that he 'had very seriously compromised his character as a Christian man, especially by repeated, wilful and malicious departures from the truth'. The brethren concluded by recommending his dismissal from Inyati.

This was turning the tables with a vengeance, and consternation reigned at L.M.S. Headquarters in London when the Kuruman mail came in. The Directors were bound to take notice of the Bechuana missionaries' advice, even though they had judged their erring colleague unheard. They wrote back that they found the brethren's 'condemnation . . . very severe', but at the same time Sykes was exonerated from any guilt in trading and told that he could stay on at Inyati. But even at this stage the Directors still seem to have retained a good deal of sympathy for Thomas, although they were more confused than ever by the vast volume of charges and counter charges that continued to rain down on them. Then suddenly Mr Thomas quite dramatically settled their doubts by putting himself irretrievably in the wrong. Mzilikazi had died shortly before Sykes left Inyati to attend the Kuruman 'inquisition' into his colleague's behaviour and scenting increased power for himself, Thomas took advantage of the political vacuum by getting himself elevated first to the rank of *induna* and then to the unofficial post of Prime Minister to the Matabele Regent. The achievement may have been a striking tribute to his personal influence among the Africans, but in the Directors' opinion it was also 'meddling in politics', and this they believed was just about the most dreadful crime a missionary could commit. Their disapproval became positively vitriolic when it transpired that Brother Thomas had not only set himself up as the supreme civil authority in the country, but had gone so far as to inform his colleague the Governor of Cape Colony, that in future 'all Englishmen entering the Matabele country must have passes signed by himself and pay him, on behalf of the Government, all local custom-house fees', and had received the proceeds of his *diktat* on the verandah of the mission house at Inyati.

By this time the old isolation of Matabeleland was disappearing as increasing numbers of prospectors and concession seekers entered the country, and there seems no doubt that Thomas now began to overplay his hand. He was dazzled by the title and social position of one of the newcomers, Commander Sir John Swinburn, Bart., R.N., and an unkind suggestion reached the Directors' ears that he had not been above accepting remuneration for his services when he obliged Sir John by ordering all his rivals out of the country.

This for them was going much too far. In the July of 1870, a stern letter from L.M.S. Headquarters recalled Thomas to London to face charges of interfering in political affairs, and (surprisingly) of countenancing a 'strange mingling of barbarous ceremonies and Bible-reading'* at their mission station of Inyati. And in due course at the end of a very painful interview in London Brother Thomas was dismissed from the London Missionary Society.

It is difficult for us now to realise what a terrible disgrace this was. Nothing quite like it had ever happened in missionary circles before, and Thomas predictably did not easily bow to the Directors' condemnation. His unwearied pen ran fresh explanation and protests, all of which succeeded in portraying him so effectively in the alternating roles of crusader and damsel in

* This was a reference to Thomas's assistance in the pagan rites which attended Lobengula's 'coronation'.

distress that the unhappy Directors began again to waver in their attitude towards their *enfant terrible*. And Mr Thomas was able to emphasise the telling point that if he had not taken over the leadership of the Matabele after Mzilikazi's death the country would have drifted into a bloody civil war; this he supported with several testimonials. One of them had been personally dictated by Lobengula, the new king, and in it he made it clear where his sympathies lay: 'I have no cause for complaint against him', he wrote of Thomas, 'in this country he has done no wrong. The Amatabele love and respect him . . . I know no evil of Mr Thomas . . . Mr Sykes is the quarrelsome one, let him go rather than Mr Thomas—no one will cry after him.'

It was all very confusing for the Directors and in the end they fell back on the traditional English solution of appointing a Commission of Enquiry to go into the full details of the Inyati scandal. They did something else, too, which should have been done years before; they collected all the letters exchanged between Thomas, Sykes, and John Moffat and printed them. The whole scrawly correspondence added up to a fair-sized book of over 80,000 words, and for the first time the Directors were able to wade through it without being distracted by a maze of scarcely legible handwriting. The case for Thomas was now sadly altered. Rendered into cold and factual print, his sins took on a new enormity, and the Directors now felt able to inform the delinquent that his letters 'condemn you out of your own mouth' and entirely justified his dismissal without having to go to the expense of an official enquiry.

Their judgement was supported by a strongly-worded memorandum which summed up their opinion of the whole incredible dispute. It began by declaring that the Inyati mission had been 'placed in circumstances peculiarly unfavourable to its spiritual usefulness', and went on to say that it 'contained within itself an element of disunion which must have destroyed all its strength. For seven years the two missionaries who were its principal members lived in constant collision with each other . . . they never worked together, preached together or prayed together.' The memorandum then charged the missionaries with having given the Africans 'a wrong impression of the Gospel' and roundly condemned Thomas as being 'wholly unfit to be a missionary of the Society' since he was 'greatly wanting in consideration for the judgements, and feelings and the plans of the brethren. His spirit was unloving; his temper hasty; and at one time he entirely withdrew from communion with them; and his sarcasms and insinuations must have kept the brethren concerned in constant irritation.' Thomas, the Directors concluded, was 'an unloving colleague with whom it was very hard if not impossible to work'.

This was not quite the end of the Society's *cause célèbre* at Inyati. There was an unseemly wrangle about some arrears of pay claimed by Thomas, and he refused to vacate the house built by mission funds at Inyati. Then he confounded the Directors by writing a book about the early struggles at the Matabele mission, which, although studiously discreet, left no doubt about the identity of its real hero. The book was first written in its author's native language and bore the unpromising title of *Un Mylneddar Ddeg yn Dehuol Africa*, but subsequent editions appeared in English, and they still make good reading. It was copiously embellished with illustrations of its author triumphing in the face of peril from lions, rhinoceros, and snakes (twice) and 'preaching to a thousand natives' together with some bad copies of Thomas Baines paintings. The book became a best seller. 'There are two books', the gratified author was told a little later, 'that would be found in practically every home in Wales, the Bible and Thomas's book', and it nearly split the London Missionary Society in two, for its Welsh supporters took up the side of their compatriot with tremendous gusto.

But in the end they failed to have Thomas reinstated, and Inyati saw him no more. With Lobengula's approval* Thomas set himself up as a missionary-trader at a place named Shiloh some twenty miles away. But like an incident from a recurrent bad dream, the L.M.S. Directors were still occasionally treated to fresh incriminations written in almost tearful terms from their

* The concession was confirmed by Thomas making a present to the king of 'a box of superior shirts, and Mrs Thomas gave him a case of cutlery'.

'unloving colleague', and it seemed almost like old times when they received a copy in familiar writing of a letter addressed to a new missionary at Inyati informing him (with a snort which nearly penetrated its pages) that Mr Thomas was 'much concerned at the conviction forced upon me . . . that you are very regardless of what the truth is'.

But as the years went on, comfortably (and increasingly profitably) installed with his large family in the tea-kettle warmth of Shiloh,* Thomas grew more mellow,† and the last communication the long-suffering foreign secretary of the L.M.S. received from him was an admonition (in clear copperplate writing, so very different from the angry script of earlier years) to 'cheer up, therefore, my dear Sir', since the Matabele after all were 'not wanting in spiritual sensibility'. The final entry in Thomas's diary was made on 6th November, 1883, when he recorded 'two more baptisms'. Towards the beginning of 1884, the old warrior died of enteric at Shiloh; Sykes continued to labour on at Inyati for three more years until his own death.

Thereafter a curtain came down on the mission's troubled infancy; the drab years of acrimony were forgotten as the spirits of both Thomas and Sykes were reverently installed in the mental pantheon of Rhodesian history, where they were misrepresented as pious and dedicated colleagues who created a thriving mission and paved the way for Christian government in the country.

Even now it is not easy to decide exactly where our sympathies lie in the absurd rivalry which divided the two men and nearly ruined their work. Perhaps, given their exceptional circumstances and personalities, the quarrels were inevitable. But of one thing we can be certain: the influence of Thomas was greater in Matabeleland and far more lasting than that of Sykes, and his success in preventing chaos after the old king's death may well have been the most valuable service the first missionaries were ever able to render Matabeleland.

---

* The second Mrs Thomas bore eleven children in seventeen years.

† Thomas for instance in 1879 welcomed the Jesuit missionaries whereas Sykes actively tried to prevent their entry into Matabeleland.

6

MR RHODES

In that first week of September, 1868, when Mzilikazi died at Ingama kraal in the Matopos, Matabeleland stood on the brink of tremendous changes. For the era of exploration was over, and the 'scramble for Africa' was about to begin. Interest in Mzilikazi's kingdom had been kindled the year before by Karl Mauch's announcement of his rediscovery of gold reefs in Mashonaland, and now George Black had found gold at Tati on the Matabele border and had proclaimed the territory to be British. The President of the Transvaal Republic had caught the prevailing gold fever and had threatened to cut off British enterprise from the far interior by proclaiming his intention of annexing Bechuanaland. The diamonds that would provide the funds to conquer Matabeleland had been found that very year on the banks of the Vaal river; Richard Gatling was perfecting the machine-gun which would destroy Mzilikazi's cherished impis, and Alfred Nobel had just stumbled on the invention of dynamite that would rip the wealth out of his kingdom.

And in 1868 two boys of fifteen were growing up in England. Leander Starr Jameson (the names embarrassed him and he preferred to be known as Lanner) was a promising pupil at Hammersmith School, while not far away at Bishop's Stortford the son of its vicar, the Rev. Francis William Rhodes, was preparing to enter university; he wanted, he said, to become a barrister, or failing that, a clergyman.

But none of these events which were going to alter their lives so significantly were known to the Matabele as they sorrowfully interred their dead king in a natural sepulchre among the Matopo Hills which must be considered one of the grandest tombs in the world.

Mzilikazi's death had thrown the whole of Matabeleland into confusion over his successor. The legitimate heir was Kulumani, but there was doubt as to whether he was still alive; some of the *indunas* maintained that he had escaped execution in 1840 at Thabas Induna and had got away to Natal. Mangwana, the heir presumptive had recently dropped out of the running after being detected in *flagrante delicto* with one of the dead king's wives, but other sons of Mzilikazi were undoubtedly alive in 1868: the trouble was that none of them were anxious to be considered as candidates for the throne in case Kulumani reappeared; indeed one of them, Jandu, had gone so far as to disappear from view inside the Rev. Thomas's hospitable house at Inyati.

For a whole year Matabeleland was without a king, and a regent, Nombate, assisted by the Rev. Thomas Morgan Thomas, ruled the country. During that time the Matabele were treated to an incredible display of African power politics which Mr Theophilus Shepstone sparked off when he announced that no less a person than his own garden boy (who was variously known as April and Kanda) was in fact Kulumani, the 'missing dauphin' of Matabele history. There seemed little to support April's claim except that like the real Kulumani, he had lost an eye, and one suspects that Shepstone's real motives here were concerned more with the hope of spreading his influence into the far interior than by a strict revelation of the truth. April's claims failed to impress Nombate, and in the July of 1869, after long consultations with the *indunas*, the Regent announced that Jandu was the legal successor of the dead king.

Jandu was seriously disturbed at being precipitated into a dangerous and explosive situation. He was thirty-three at the time, the son of Mzilikazi by a Swazi wife, and therefore not acceptable as king by many of the true-blue Kumalos; he had been brought up without any thought of ever succeeding his father and he had never been made familiar with the punctilio which governed the Matabele court. Many legends grew up later about Jandu's childhood: he is said to have escaped the massacre at Thabas Induna by being smuggled into the Matopo Hills by Sarah Liebenberg, one of the white girls allegedly taken as a wife by Mzilikazi, and there was protected by the Mlimo. Two other stories have been handed down about Jandu's early days: they say that he carried the news of Potgieter's raid to Mzilikazi at Inyati, and was wounded as a young man during a fight with the Bechuanas (a wound which, his enemies whispered, had occurred not in battle but while fiddling with a gun). Jandu had inherited very little of his father's belligerent nature: if one word could be used to describe him it would be genial. The missionaries at Inyati, whom he had always been careful to cultivate, speak in their accounts of his being a good rifle shot and fond of hunting, which again provoked criticism from some of 'the real nation'.

But after anxious consultation with his white friends and the Mlimo, Jandu agreed to accept the crown and early in 1870 he went through an accession ceremony which was witnessed by ten thousand Matabele as well as several Europeans. Mbigo's Zwangendaba and several other Matabele regiments, however, refused to accept his succession until it could be proved that Kulumani was dead. The Zwangendaba according to Baines 'reckoned itself the flower of Matabelean Chivalry', and it was probably the most formidable fighting force in the country. Certainly Jandu, essentially a man of peace, had no wish to begin his reign by fighting a civil war, and there seems little reason to doubt his account that one morning he rode to Mbigo's fortified kraal hoping to parley with him; he was followed, he says, by a mob of his own supporters carrying hunting weapons. Baines tells us that his peace offering was contemptuously repulsed with 'gross and indecent gestures', and we learn from another source that the women in Mbigo's kraal ran out, turned their backs on the king, and lifted up their skirts. Jandu's people could not be restrained after this affront, and he himself seems to have used his gun as they stormed the village, killing more than three hundred of Mbigo's men. He showed an unusual moderation when he afterwards refused to countenance a massacre of the Zwan-gendaba women; this leniency was not forgotten and for the remainder of his reign some of his subjects were critical of the king's moderation which they equated with cowardice. According to one version of Matabele history, Jandu after his victory was given the praise name of Lobengula—the scatterer; other sources, however, insist that this name was bestowed on him much earlier as an allusion to his ill health during childhood.* As was the custom with Nguni chiefs, Lobengula established a new capital soon after his accession, and mindful of the threats to his life by the Zwangendaba he called it Bulawayo, which can be best translated as 'the place of he who has been badly treated, or hunted down to be killed'.

In many ways Lobengula's reign for the next few years seems now to have been a mere pendant to that of his father's: the names in the Matabele story may change but the life of the people flows on unaltered for twenty years after 1870; the missionaries continue to preach unfruitfully to the same little congregations, and the impis go off raiding into Mashonaland every year just as they had done before; the witch-doctors keep on preparing their rain-making potions and smelling out the king's enemies, and every year the nation gathers for the 'Great Dance' and is purified by its traditional ceremony. Nothing much appears to have changed. But all this time Europe is on the march in Africa, and for all his twenty thousand warriors Lobengula never really has a chance of resisting its progress. The only uncertainty is whether the independence of the Matabele will be destroyed by Germans, Boers, Portuguese, or British. As it was, the fate of the far interior was about to be determined by the young man from Bishop's Stortford who had not become a barrister or a clergyman after all; even while Lobengula fought for his succession at Mbigo's kraal, Cecil Rhodes was preparing to sail from England to join his brother cotton-planting in Natal. For by 1870 he had decided to make his career in Africa, and in a few more years his broad shadow would begin to fall across Matabeleland.

*   *   *   *   *

Few men during their lifetime can have been the subject of so much admiration and so much vituperation as Cecil John Rhodes. Even now, although he died more than sixty years ago, it still remains difficult for us to approach this man without prejudice: our personal assessment of his character depends very largely on whether we consider that the European nations (and

* Gula means 'to be ill'.

Great Britain in particular) were or were not justified in the belief that they had a civilising mission to discharge among those unfortunates whom they chose to call 'the backward peoples of the world'. Rhodes himself never had any doubts on this score: he had the very highest opinion of the British character and of its influence: 'I contend that we are the first race in the world', he once said, 'and that the more we inhabit [of the world] the better it is for the human race'; those words summed up as well as any others could have done one of the two themes which ran consistently through his life.

The details of Cecil Rhodes's career have of course been recorded in the most trivial detail. Its salient points are familiar to us all but they can be conveniently set down again here. He was born at Bishop's Stortford in 1853, the year in which Mzilikazi and Potgieter affirmed their friendship by a treaty which seemingly ensured eventual Boer domination of Matabeleland. Young Rhodes grew up in a Hertfordshire vicarage, the fifth child in a boisterous family of eleven children. Too delicate to go to a public school like his brothers, he attended a local grammar school and now, when he is only sixteen, we get the first indication of the second theme which was to dominate his life—his struggle against ill health.

Rhodes's biographers have usually ascribed his boyhood illness to consumption and their diagnosis seems to be confirmed when we note that Cecil Rhodes a year later was sent out to Africa for the sake of his health, a reason which he later disputed, insisting typically that in fact he left England to get away from 'the eternal cold mutton'.

On 1st October 1870, Rhodes landed at Durban and found all Natal suffering from diamond fever; he succumbed to it like his brother, and towards the end of 1871 turned his back on the cotton country and trekked four hundred miles to Kimberley, the centre of the fabulous new diamond industry. And now a strange transformation comes over the mild-mannered, lanky adolescent: he matures into a forceful thickset man of the world; Rhodes finds it possible to live with tough 'diggers' on equal terms and yet at the same time he becomes an addict of wealth;

his mind fills with new visions and within a year he begins to talk about ways of effecting imperial expansion: that concept was to be a siren song strumming in his ears for the rest of his life.

It is difficult to explain just why these changes came over Cecil Rhodes at Kimberley: perhaps it was the realisation of the sudden wealth which might fall into his lap during those first exciting years of the diamond rush; possibly the competition he was experiencing had forced him into his true metier. Physicians, on the other hand, would suggest that the high altitude of Kimberley suited the young man's constitution, and in some way made him feel physically and mentally fit for the first time in his life. At all events as the torrent of new ideas and designs began to surge through the young man's brain, the direction in which they are leading him is suggested by a will which he draws up leaving his entire wealth (which has not even yet materialised) to the Colonial Secretary with instructions that it be used for the extension of the British Empire.

By a combination of hard work and good luck Rhodes very quickly made a vast fortune in the diamond fields, and yet, incredibly, he found time to keep terms at Oriel College, Oxford, and to take an interest in local politics. And in 1881, only a few weeks after Great Britain's humiliating surrender to the Transvaal following the defeat of Majuba Hill, Rhodes entered the Cape Parliament.

He was only twenty eight at the time but already people were beginning to speak of him as 'the old man', and our image of him even at this early stage of his career is of a shrewd middle-aged manipulator of power. The ideas which would grow until they brought about the conquest of the Matabele kingdom were even then beginning to take root in his mind, and we know that he travelled to his first parliamentary session promising himself that 'I will go and take the north'. From now on 'the north' is his *idée fixe* but he does not think of it only in terms of territorial expansion: 'if we get Mashonaland', he would tell his friends, 'we shall get the balance of Africa', and he meant that the occupation of Mashonaland would reassert Great Britain's paramountcy in southern Africa by tipping the scales of power in her favour at the expense of Kruger's Transvaal Republic. If the British could encircle the Transvaal by occupying the land north of the Limpopo, he said in spirit if not in words, Kruger would eventually be obliged to federate with the remainder of South Africa and join a powerful dominion under the Union Jack.

But to 'get Mashonaland' he would first have to 'get Bechuanaland'. He had strong views about that arid country; it was not, he protested a useless desert; it was, instead, of immense strategical importance, and in parliament and out of parliament he went on repeating that Bechuanaland was 'the neck of the bottle' and 'the Suez canal of the interior'. It was in fact largely due to Rhodes's efforts that a British protectorate was proclaimed over northern Bechuanaland in 1885 while the southern part was annexed to Cape Colony.

This was Rhodes's first success as an empire builder; he found it heady stuff: and now as his eyes lifted to the lands beyond the Limpopo, it seemed that the man and the moment had met. For these were the years when Africa was being partitioned between the European powers, and here he was winning political control of the Cape, the firmest base in the whole continent. British statesmen were thinking on lines parallel to his own: the sedate epoch of material improvement, bright-eyed spiritual enlightenment, and good intentions which had characterised the first half of Queen Victoria's reign (and which had been reflected in the penny postage, the foundation of the Salvation Army, and the passing of the Factory Inspection Act) had been replaced during the 1880's by a livelier era: suddenly the clerks in Whitehall (like those in the Quai d'Orsay and Wilhelmstrasse) found themselves engaged in phrasing démarches or announcing new spheres of interest. The tempo was infectious: Kipling was moved by the success of *Soldiers Three* to try his hand at more rousingly imperialistic verse in *Barrack-Room Ballads*, while the British public instead of discovering merit in earnest gentlemen arranging extensive slum clearances, suddenly found it had developed a taste for officers in khaki and slouch hats leading a charge against the Queen's enemies or rallying a broken square as the fuzziewuzzie attack came in. One is inclined to think of this jingoistic mood as a brand-new phase in British national thinking, but the imperialism of the late nineteenth century was really no more than a manifestation in changing times of Great Britain's traditional concern with the safety of the sea route to India. That concern made Queen Victoria's statesmen anxious to secure their country's strategic position in both Egypt and South Africa, and almost as an accidental consequence it turned the British people into brazen imperialists who were prepared to die for tokens no more tangible than the notes of a patriotic song, or the unfurling of a flag above a lonely fort on the North-West Frontier. And somewhat to his surprise it also elevated Cecil Rhodes into a new hierarchy of national heroes which included figures like Gordon of Khartoum and Roberts of Kandahar.

By 1887 Rhodes had gained what he described as 'the whip hand' in the diamond industry. He had become Chairman of De Beers Company whose articles (or trust deeds) allowed it to undertake almost any commercial or political task, and he was presently engaged in acquiring a second fortune on the Witwatersrand where gold had been discovered in fantastic quantities the year before. It has been estimated that Rhodes's income at this time was more than a million pounds a year, and it was still growing. He regarded wealth in an unusual way: he used it, not to provide opulent comfort, but to gain the power he needed to wrest 'the north' from Lobengula. To that task, he wrote 'I shall bring both my private fortune and my Trust Deeds with twenty millions behind it.'

If he was to succeed in winning the far interior for the crown, it was clear in 1887 that he would have to move fast. For the condition of the Matabele kingdom at this time might be likened to that of a patient lying anaesthetised on an operating table waiting for a radical amputation, and surrounded by a cluster of surgeons all jostling each other in their efforts to pick up the scalpel and make the first incision. The Kaiser was one of the 'surgeons', having already proclaimed a protectorate over South-West Africa, and he seemed to be on the point of extending its boundaries to the Karanga plateau; the Portuguese Cortes (following some eager research in the national archives) was

172

reviving the old Monomatapan claims to the interior; and President Kruger at Pretoria had moved even more adroitly by establishing a Consul Grobler as his permanent representative at Bulawayo and by concluding an agreement with Lobengula which virtually established Transvaal paramountcy over his kingdom. Kruger, so far as Rhodes was concerned, was his most serious rival in winning control of the far interior; but the immediate danger subsided when an obscure mêlée (which Kruger did not hesitate to say had been arranged by Rhodes) in the no-man's-land lying between the Shashi and Maklautsi rivers, permanently withdrew Consul Grobler from the scene. It was a fortunate breathing space, and while Pretoria, Berlin, and Lisbon hesitated before making any more forward moves, Rhodes shrewdly induced John Smith Moffat to travel to Lobengula's court and to act there on his behalf.

He had made an astute choice. Moffat, by now well into his fifties, was something of a legend to the Matabele. More than twenty years had passed since he had left their country, and to them he seemed a living link with the great days of Mzilikazi's reign; and the intervention of this somewhat indecisive man in Matabele domestic affairs in the December of 1887 speedily turned out to be decisive. For Moffat, after playing skilfully on Lobengula's fears of Kruger's chauvinism succeeded in impressing him with the superior virtues and power of Britain's Great White Queen. Lobengula was persuaded to repudiate the Grobler convention, and he signed instead a treaty of friendship with Great Britain which pledged him to cede none of his territory to another power without British consent.

As Rhodes was quick to point out in his queer speculator's jargon, the Moffat treaty had effectively 'warned off' Germany, Portugal, and the Transvaal from Matabeleland and it gave the British 'an option' on Lobengula's kingdom.

*   *   *   *   *

Thanks to Moffat, Rhodes, to pursue our previous metaphor, was now the only surgeon remaining in the operating theatre, and he moved at once to grasp the amputation knife and proceeded to use it with exquisite skill and speed. Within seven years he had made himself undisputed master of the African far interior.

We should pause at this point to take a good look at this astonishing man whose mind at the age of thirty-five was filled with visions as grandiose as those of the Caesars, and whose personality so completely bestrode his chosen sphere of southern Africa that people were already beginning (with an aptness that is still pleasing) to call him 'the Colossus of Rhodes'.

Yet no one ever felt that they really knew Rhodes or understood him fully and even now when his personal life and political activities have been so minutely scrutinised, his true character still remains remarkably elusive to us. Almost unconsciously we shrink from studying Rhodes in any more detail, and perhaps it is because we are afraid of turning up some new and unsuspected shabbiness. He is ambivalence epitomised; there seems to be too much good and too much bad in this single man to be comprehensible; he is seen to be the classical example of a public figure whose dynamic abilities are matched by unbelievably grievous shortcomings. There was never any middle ground in the way people thought about Cecil Rhodes. To many he was the homespun Bayard of Victorian imperialism who once, when asked by the queen what he had been doing lately, replied without a trace of affectation, 'I have added two provinces to Your Majesty's dominions'; to others, however, Rhodes was no more than an unscrupulous speculator, whom a man of Labouchere's calibre could dismiss contemptuously as 'an empire jerry builder', and 'the head of a gang of shady financiers'.

It must be admitted that as time goes on, Rhodes is coming to be viewed in an increasingly critical light, and it is more and more difficult for us to assess his character objectively. For all Rhodes's undoubted virtues are balanced by their antitheses: he is a dreamer and a schemer too, a statesman as well as a share pusher, a philanthropist with a sharp knowledge of double-entry bookkeeping, a hero and a fraud, an inspired guesser who often guessed wrong, a visionary whose greatest quality according to Kipling was imagination and at the same time the cynic who once said

'Tell me a man's ambitions and I will tell you how to square him'. Rhodes always 'thought big' and yet he was notoriously small-minded when dealing with those whose usefulness to him he considered over. And, most puzzling of all, Rhodes is the humanist who could say with conviction that he preferred 'peace and gold' to 'blood and iron' and yet in the end adopted Bismarck's maxim as his own, fought a succession of private wars for his own aggrandisement and was able to inspire such abhorrence in his acquaintances that even his dying words were venomously parodied into 'so many done, so few to do'.*

Rhodes has always been so controversial a figure that one looks around for an explanation of all the contradictions in his dual personality. One might of course say that Rhodes's faults were those of his age, but this seems scarcely valid for they shocked and were condemned by his contemporaries. And as the search is made for a key that might unlock the enigma of his mental paradoxes, one comes to look for it, as with so many other enigmatical historical figures, in the record of his physical health.

It has been generally accepted that Cecil Rhodes developed tuberculosis of the lungs as a boy and was accordingly sent to Africa in the hope that its climate would improve his health. But this is another of those misconceptions which are the imps of history: there is not the slightest evidence that Rhodes in fact ever suffered from pulmonary tuberculosis; his recorded symptoms simply do not accord with that disease, and no sign of any tubercular lesion was discovered when he came to autopsy.

Yet ill health was Rhodes's constant companion. If tuberculosis was not responsible, we must search for another cause, and with a fair degree of certitude we can now diagnose it as a congenital cardiac defect or (in laymen's terms) a 'hole in the heart'. Consider the evidence: at sixteen we learn of Cecil Rhodes, the schoolboy at Bishop's Stortford, that 'Fatigue no longer blanched his lips— it turned them livid, and exertion was followed by alarming

---

* He puzzled his contemporaries in little things too; one example will serve to demonstrate this: 'from one with such a presence you would have looked for a firm hand grip', wrote one of his young assistants, 'instead you got a limp touch—hardly a clasp from two fingers, the other two being tucked into his palm'.

faintness. .... At last, one day in search of some decision as to the future, Louie (his mother) took him to the doctor who had watched him from infancy; the doctor sent him for a brisk walk up Wind Hill, where stood the parish church, and on his return, panting and exhausted, advised rest, a change of air, a sea voyage, and continued medical supervision and nursing for six months or more. "The lungs are sound", he said, "but the heart, though not actually diseased, was seriously overtaxed, labouring quite inadequately to meet the demands of his rapid growth." ' Young Rhodes, then, during his early teens, experienced alternating bouts of intense pallor and livid cyanosis, and the pattern once established continues. In 1871 a friend remarks on the way the youth turns livid on occasion, and at nineteen he has the first of those heart attacks which eventually were to prove fatal. There is another heart attack in 1872 and the following year he consults Sir Morell Mackenzie who tells him he has only six months to live. There is another serious heart attack in 1877, and more follow next year.

Yet now this man suffering from what we would have expected to be a crippling malady begins to accomplish feats of physical endurance which would have taxed the powers of an athlete. During the struggle to secure Bechuanaland for Great Britain he spends days of hard riding in the veld followed by nights of furious arguments and negotiation. At the end of these endeavours he turns with a single mindedness and vigour scarcely matched in history to conquer the far interior of Africa for his company, while at the same time he continues to manage the immense commercial empire of De Beers and to govern Cape Colony as its Prime Minister. During these same years of power he finances and wages private wars against the Portuguese and the Matabele, and even makes an attempt to fight another one against the Transvaal. And at the end of all these prodigious exertions Rhodes comes back to the country which he has created from the wilds, and during the great rebellions of 1896 wears out his younger companions by his energy and vitality. Yet all this time the heart attacks continue, and at forty-eight he dies in cardiac failure.

This combination of dynamic energy interrupted by prostrating heart attacks may seem puzzling to the layman, but the symptom complex is well known in medicine: the syndrome is typical of a form of congenital heart disease where a defect exists in the wall separating the two upper chambers of the heart. In medical terms the condition is called an auricular septal defect, and before modern surgery devised its cure the expectation of life in this condition was given as forty-nine years.

In the normal individual unoxygenated venous blood passes from the right auricle of the heart into the right ventricle and then goes to the lungs for oxygenation; from the lungs it returns to the left auricle and left ventricle whence it is pumped round the body carrying oxygen to all its organs. In the congenital abnormality we are discussing, whenever the pressure in the right auricle exceeds that of the left auricle, some stale blood, instead of passing by the right ventricle to the lungs, passes instead through the defect in the wall separating the upper heart chambers and enters the left auricle where it mixes with aerated blood. In other words, when this 'shunt' occurs, blue unoxygenated blood is pumped in the arterial system all round the body and gives it a characteristic cyanotic or livid tinge. Of more consequence is the fact that insufficient oxygen is fed to the body's tissues including the brain and the muscle of the heart itself. Yet when the pressure in the left auricle reverts to its ordinary higher level no 'shunting' of blood occurs, the subject is normal in all respects and can undertake physical activities without discomfort.

One result then, of having a 'hole in the heart' is to limit the body's efficiency at certain times, and to cause heart attacks. The effects on the human mind of this syndrome are less well recognised: when the 'shunt' is in action the brain of course is being supplied with stale unoxygenated blood and it seems logical to believe that all higher flights of cerebration remain grounded, and their place is taken by more basic and pedestrian thoughts. The alternation of dynamism and phlegm and all the other contrary phases of Rhodes's psyche, can in theory then at least be accounted for by the changing oxygenation of his brain: for when the relative blood pressures on the two sides of his heart were reversed the charismatic visions of this extraordinary man would contract into those of an unextraordinary mortal. It is an attractive hypothesis to explain the inexplicable; but it leaves us rather sadly reflecting on what Cecil Rhodes might have accomplished for England and Rhodesia had he been born a century later when his heart defect could have been remedied by surgery.

Before we move on from the consequences of Rhodes's cardiac defect, it is important for us to appreciate that the condition had another, more predictable, effect after 1885 when the heart attacks became more numerous and a growing awareness of the short time left to him made Rhodes increasingly anxious to hasten events. He began to gamble and look for short cuts. After Mashonaland he takes Manicaland, and after Manicaland he conquers Matabeleland. Then in 1895 he reaches out again to win the Transvaal and Dr Jameson sets out with his raiders for Johannesburg. Political disaster follows. Yet it is not complete disaster. For Rhodes, cut off from the exercise of a sovereign's power, turns his remaining energy into the service of the country which bears his name and which is the only outlet now left open for him to give substance to his dreams. And these last years are not wasted; during them he earns an affection and respect which has been given to few men, and which is still alive in Rhodesia to this day.

Although to do so anticipates the sequence of events, it is convenient here to give an account of Rhodes's death. It comes in a manner which must evoke pity even among those who are most conscious of Rhodes's defects of character. Rhodes had said, 'I, with my heart and everything, shall just go off pop without any warning', but his last illness turned out to be a lingering one. The descriptions of these days of suffocating agony in the little cottage by the sea at Muizenberg make grim reading. He is irritated almost beyond measure by the ghastly incriminations of a Princess Radziwill whose absurd machinations seem to belong more to the fiction of another Anthony Hope than to real life in the present century. He can breathe easily only when sitting up. According to his friends 'he was always asking us for more fresh air'. To cheer him they bring a kind written message from the Kaiser, together with a newspaper in which has been inserted a faked optimistic bulletin about his progress. Painful tubes are used to drain fluid from his swollen ankles and belly, oxygen is fed to him through a funnel, and the walls of his bedroom are hacked about to admit more air. The agony comes to its end at 6.30 on the morning of 26th March, 1902. At autopsy no signs are found of the suspected consumption or of the aneurysm which had also been so confidently diagnosed in life that even his recent biographers insist that it was proved *post mortem*. A slovenly, inky-fingered autopsy report is composed and written out by three different physicians with such 'erasures, and corrections, mis-spellings and some confusion of times and dates', that, as Dr Charles Shee has pertinently commented, 'it suggests the strong emotional strain under which the participants laboured, and possibly suitable fortification for the occasion'.

And so ends the life of this remarkable man, and it somehow seems inevitable that it should have finished on one of those notes which had characterised his whole career—a note of nobility spoilt at the end by shabbiness. We are left knowing only one thing about Rhodes that is indisputable, and which posterity may yet consider outweighs all the other less admirable facets of his character: his patriotism. For Cecil Rhodes never deviated from a genuine love for southern Africa which yet encompassed undeviating loyalty to Great Britain. His vision saw them, England, Cape Colony, and Rhodesia, all as constituent parts of a giant commonwealth which he was certain would serve to keep the peace throughout the world. His enduring loyalty at bottom was to his own British stock and the Crown. 'Do you know', he once told Lord Grey, 'you have drawn a big prize in the lottery of life—you were born an Englishman', and on another occasion he said: 'Take away my flag and what have I left? If you take away my flag you take everything.' There are worse allegiances.

*   *   *   *   *

Cecil Rhodes still had fourteen years to live when John Smith Moffat signed his treaty with Lobengula at Bulawayo on 11th February, 1888. Provided it was not repudiated, the Matabele kingdom from now on was closed to all but British enterprise; in diplomatic terms it had been brought within the British 'sphere of interest'. Rhodes was determined that his company should monopolise the 'option' on the far interior, and he moved fast. Concession hunters had been thronging into Matabeleland for several years now, and in 1888 nearly thirty of them were camping round the king's private kraal at Umvutcha, six miles from Bulawayo. 'They were a queer jealous lot of men that came and went to and from Lobengula's country in those days', one of these adventurers recalled afterwards, 'all trying to get something out of Lobengula, and afraid someone else would get what they wanted.' When they were not pestering the king for mining rights these concessionaires were quarrelling among themselves. To the irreverent they were known as 'Lobengula's Foreign Legion', and 'the white sharks', and they were by no means averse to using bribery to gain some advantage over their rivals. Moffat complained that 'a perfect avalanche of present giving' was going on to obtain the favour of the king and his more influential *indunas,* while Leask gravely noted, 'The chief is being much beset with applications. I have reason to believe that during the two months I have spent there just now, at least five hundred pounds in gold has been given to him by different parties, in order merely to pave the way for concessions.'

Rhodes started off his campaign by sending one of his employees, John Fry, to Bulawayo early in 1888 with instructions to gain a mineral concession from Lobengula. It was an unfortunate choice; Fry was in poor health (poorer than he knew—he was to die of cancer within a few weeks) and he was obliged to return to Kimberley almost at once without having accomplished anything but the annoyance of Rhodes. 'How true it is', Rhodes noted unfeelingly after this setback, 'never to have anything to do with a failure.' He then turned to choosing more suitable emissaries to take poor Fry's place, and in the end he selected three men who set off from Kimberley on 15th August, 1888, armed with an introductory letter from the British High Commissioner at the Cape which described them rather unctuously to Lobengula as 'highly respectable gentlemen who were visiting your country.' Their leader was Charles Rudd, a serious man who looks out from his portrait with the melancholy good-tempered look of one of Landseer's dogs. This appearance did not belie the man: Rudd's two noticeable qualities were loyalty to Cecil Rhodes and a depressing lack of imagination.

The second member of the mission was 'Matabele' Thompson, who has been described as 'a biggish thick-set man, with a rather swarthy complexion'. Thompson seemed an excellent person to choose: he was able to get along in several native languages, and was generally considered to be something of an expert on the Matabele and on friendly terms with Lobengula. Very few people knew about the one unfortunate flaw in young Thompson's character: as a boy he had seen his father mutilated and killed by a gang of natives (and had himself only narrowly escaped from an agonising death at their hands) and not unnaturally he was afterwards apt to lose his nerve and become jittery when trouble threatened with Africans. Indeed it must be accounted as showing high courage that Thompson even ventured into Matabeleland at a time when Lobengula was under great pressure from the *amatjaha* to order the massacre of all the Europeans in the country.

The third member of the party, Rochfort Maguire, was the oddest choice of all. Maguire was an Oxford don, a dreamy, detached, and unpractical man who was utterly unsuited to rough life in the bush. Rhodes had some queer notion that Maguire would be able to frame the anticipated concession in legal language, and would help pass the time on the journey by coaching Thompson in the classics. In fact Maguire and Thompson were poles apart; nothing more was heard about Latin tutorials once the trio had left Kimberley, and right from the start we find Thompson grumbling that Maguire was a nuisance who could not even use a tin opener and 'who came with us to Matabeleland for want of something better to do'. We get the impression that Thompson had a mean streak in him: thus he seemed delighted to watch poor Maguire's difficulties with the unaccustomed native food, and he describes with relish how 'the mealies stuck in his throat, and he suffered from acute indigestion. The dilettante member of parliament, ex attaché, Fellow of All

Souls, was completely out of his element and he suffered accordingly'.

Rhodes saw the three men off from Kimberley with a cheerful exhortation that 'if you can get Lobengula's seal to a concession, I'll go nap'. Five weeks later they reached Umvutcha and joined the other white concessionaires already hanging about the royal kraal. Rudd sweetened the wary king with a present of a hundred golden sovereigns at their first audience, and at once began to press him to come to terms with Rhodes. The other Europeans, however, slandered the new arrivals at every opportunity and the events of the next few weeks are a confused story of clandestine negotiations, bribery, deals that never came off, intrigues, and denigration of other concessionaires. Day after day Lobengula sat down with Rhodes's envoys, listening patiently to their solicitations, and we can imagine how delighted he must have been as Rudd went on raising his offer always a little higher.

Rudd had undoubtedly the most to offer of the concession hunters, and he was not without influential allies at the Matabele court. The Rev. Charles Helm, a missionary who was trusted by the king, was on his side, and so was Lotje, one of Lobengula's senior *indunas*. Assistance came too from no less a man than Sir Sidney Shippard, Her Majesty's Administrator of British Bechuanaland, who now appeared unexpectedly in Bulawayo complete with black frock coat, grey gloves, malacca cane, the star of the K.C.M.G., and an escort of sixteen troopers of the Bechuanaland Border Police. Sir Sidney was a pompous man who made everybody snicker at his efforts to play the English milord even when eating 'raw lumps of fat beef with his fingers' in the Umvutcha goat kraal, but so far as Lobengula was concerned Shippard was the representative of the Great White Queen, and he was most impressed too by his escorts' mounted drill. So when Sir Sidney put in a word or two for his friend Mr Rhodes, the king decided that after all it might be wise to grant Rudd his concession; at least to do so would get rid of all the other troublesome concessionaires.

On the 30th October Lobengula accordingly put his mark to a document which granted Rhodes's company 'the complete and

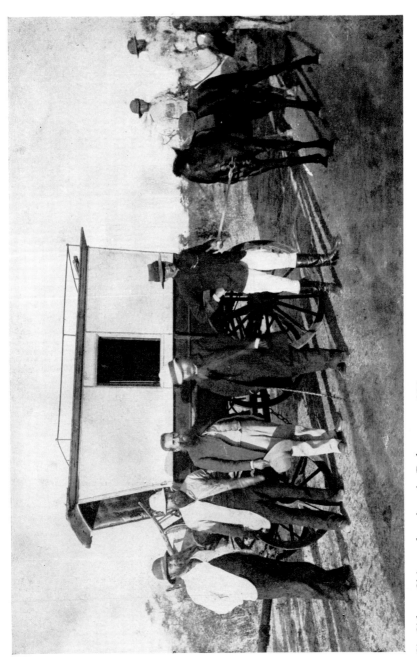

Sir Sidney Shippard arrives in Bulawayo, 1888

Cecil Rhodes and Dr Jameson

exclusive charge over all metals and minerals contained in my kingdom . . . together with full power to do all the things that they may deem necessary to win and procure the same'. In return Rudd promised to pay Lobengula £100 a month, supply him with 1,000 modern rifles and 100,000 rounds of ammunition, as well as (a happy inspiration on Rhodes's part) a gun-boat on the Zambesi.

As Lobengula made his clumsy cross at the bottom of the document, and Rudd scribbled his signature below it, both men were congratulating themselves on having completed a clever piece of work. Lobengula believed that a mere handful of white men would come and dig a hole in some out-of-the-way place in his kingdom, and that the other concessionaires would leave him alone; moreover the document he had signed had shrewdly pandered to his self-importance by suggesting that Lobengula's suzerainty extended far beyond his *de facto* boundaries, he knew that the arming of his impis with modern rifles would increase his military power, while the gun-boat would enable his impis to cross the Zambesi where the rich raiding grounds of Barotseland could be expected to compensate for those lost in Mashonaland. Rudd on the other hand recognised that Lobengula had opened up the Matabele kingdom to exploitation by a commercial company on a scale which he did not appreciate, and that he had in fact signed something which could be interpreted as giving land rights to Rhodes's company.

Within a few hours of the completion of the little ceremony in the goat kraal at Umvutcha, Rudd was riding south with the precious concession in his pocket. He very nearly lost his life on the journey, but eventually he reached Kimberley, to be met by Rhodes, returning again to the jargon of his card-playing days, with a delighted exclamation that now 'I can go nap, double nap, Blücher or anything.' The great man confided to another friend that the concession was 'so gigantic that it is like giving a man the whole of Australia'. Clearly Lobengula had given far more away at Umvutcha than he had imagined.

Maguire and Thompson remained in Bulawayo with orders to 'keep Lobengula sweet' and to prevent the rival concessionaires (who were still dancing their minuet of malice and backbiting round the king) from persuading him to abrogate the Rudd concession. What seems remarkable now is that Rhodes's agents failed in each of these objectives.

At first all went well; the bookish Maguire became a firm friend of the king and was even sent off with an impi to turn away some unauthorised white visitors from the border, but both he and Thompson were becoming terribly bored. There was very little for them to do at Umvutcha Kraal: 'no one can conceive the weariness of the ensuing days', wrote Thompson afterwards, adding that 'they had spent most of the time playing backgammon or reading' in a stuffy tent near the king's compound. It was a frightening time too; they were well aware that the hot blooded *amatjaha* only needed a word from the king to kill all the Europeans in Matabeleland. Things got worse when Maguire was accused of witchcraft after he had been seen cleaning his false teeth with pink toothpase in the Umgusa river, and he slipped away unobtrusively when Dr Jameson returned to Kimberley after paying the two men a short visit to raise their morale. The nervous Thompson was now left to hold the fort by himself at Umvutcha. He was becoming more highly strung every day, for Lobengula bowing at last to the entreaties and threats of his almost mutinous young warriors, repudiated the concession he had signed with Rudd, and (in a way which reminds us of Charles I's treatment of Strafford) ordered the execution of Lotje, the *induna* who had advised him to sign it, together with more than three hundred of his household.

Thompson's nerves finally failed him as he sat in his hut that night listening in terror to the killing of Lotje's people outside: 'each dull thud of the execution stick', he remembered later, was 'followed by a shrill cry of "ay yi yi"'. In the morning he bolted.

Not one of Rhodes's agents now remained in Bulawayo, and his concession had been repudiated by the king. It seemed that after all he had lost the game.

Rhodes had just returned from London where he had been negotiating a Royal Charter to exploit his concession when he heard the news. A political vacuum, he said now existed in

Bulawayo, and it had to be filled at once. As usual he reacted swiftly to the crisis: he sent his friend Dr Leander Starr Jameson, up to Bulawayo with instructions to use all his charm and everything else he could think of to persuade Lobengula to recognise the Rudd concession again.

*   *   *   *   *

Most people would have thought that Dr Jim (one falls at once into the slang of the period) was just about as unsuitable a man to win over the king of the Matabele as it would be possible to imagine; in fact, Mr Rhodes had made one of his most inspired choices in selecting him for the task. Jameson had unusual assets for coping with the situation at Bulawayo: for one thing he was carrying syringes and morphia with him on his journey, and Lobengula was a martyr to gout; then again his charm really could become irresistible. Most important of all the doctor was a man of extraordinary versatility and possessed a rare strain of ebullient courage. Nothing really ever daunted him. For Jameson was a born gambler: life to him was like a game of whist; he regarded the Rudd concession as a trump card to be played for no other reason but to win a rubber, and it was typical of Dr Jameson that, in his explanatory letters to his brother and his sister, he wrote that 'there may be some finessing to be done with the Chief', and that he hoped 'my affairs will turn up trumps'.

There is a faintly raffish and free-wheeling air about Jameson: one has the feeling that he would have felt very much at home in Regency London. Nobody could help liking him, if only because he was always so vividly and brassily alive. Although, in most respects, he was the exact antithesis to Rhodes, this made him his perfect foil, and one observer hit it off when he wrote that Jameson was a 'wonderful lieutenant to the Colossus because he possessed certain characteristics that are wanting in Rhodes'.

By 1888 Jameson was well on his way to becoming Cecil Rhodes's greatest friend. Rhodes usually preferred the company of young and rather dull men, but his friendship with Dr Jim, who was very sharp and highly intelligent, was an exception.

Both of them were confirmed bachelors, but while Jameson enjoyed feminine company and was known as 'the gay Lothario' in Kimberley, Rhodes all through his life was shy with women, and once somewhat archly confessed that the only time he had ever kissed one was when he had bent over Queen Victoria's hand. Although all the evidence denies that Rhodes was a homosexual, he was inclined to strike up vehement friendships with other men; as an example one can quote his highly emotional relationship with Neville Pickering to whom, in 1882, he left his entire fortune after changing his will for the third time. Rhodes was distraught when young Pickering died, but slowly he transferred his friendship to Dr Jameson, a man of his own age who at the time was very profitably engaged in private practice in Kimberley.

The two men were as different in appearance as they were in character, and both of them (like the Nazi leaders of Germany) were unlike the Aryan type of manhood whom their political philosophies idealised. Whereas Rhodes was heavily built and slow moving, Jameson was a small and darting figure, a quicksilver man of nerve and intuition. Rhodes's dreamy grey eyes and crop of blond hair were utterly different from his friend's urgent expression and the dark hair which was already balding, and the general air of hubris. Rhodes's slow deliberation and the drowsy dignity which always made people refer to him as *Mr* Rhodes were in exact contrast to Dr Jim's computer-quick decisions, his hail-fellow-well-met manner, and the curious lapses in taste which were remarked upon by many of his acquaintances. Clothes hung on Mr Rhodes and they seemed to mutter 'he put us on when he was thinking of something quite different' and his habits inclined to be unostentatious ('I think', Colquhoun wrote disapprovingly 'he was the worst dressed man I have ever seen! His old felt hat was battered and dirty, his trousers bagged at the knees, and his coats at the pockets. Later on, when he was in London, friends got hold of him and took him to a good tailor, so that his things were well cut at all events, but I should think he was quite capable of buying them ready made!'); Jameson on the other hand was something of a dandy, and even in the bush liked to do himself well. Finally, Rhodes is always the imperialist; never for a moment does he cease to be the manipulator of events and men who thinks only in terms of power. Jameson, on the other hand, is his instrument, a strange combination of *beau sabreur* and Hawkins of the veld, a man who became an empire builder at second hand.

Yet the two men's minds worked in such uncanny rapport that it was said they could communicate to each other by telepathy. And their friendship was enduring. When his dreams of absolute power in the sub-continent crumbled after the Jameson raid, Rhodes did not take refuge in recriminations; his concern for Dr Jameson far outweighed the crushing disappointment of his dreams.

*　*　*　*　*

Lobengula and Jameson had met briefly in the April of 1889 when the doctor had thrown aside the responsibilities of a busy practitioner's life to pay a flying visit to Matabeleland to steady the nerves of Maguire and Thompson during their long wait at Umvutcha after Rudd had gone south with his concession. Now, within a month of Thompson's panic-stricken flight following Lotje's execution, Jameson was back in Bulawayo, and this time he stayed four months. It was a difficult, risky time to be there: the king was angry with Thompson for running away and even more at having been tricked, as he maintained, into signing the concession. He was drinking heavily too and his temper was not improved by gout. The *amatjaha* were more truculent than ever, and Jameson's letters to Rhodes about the situation were despondent; he was very doubtful, he said, if he would ever succeed in persuading the king to re-ratify the concession which had been so angrily repudiated. Such was his pessimism that it drove Rhodes to prepare a desperate *coup* to seize control of Matabeleland, but fortunately for his reputation it was never put into effect. For presently Dr Jameson's charm and his hypodermic syringe began to work their magic. He flattered the king with the tactful assurance 'that his gout came from up above and it was specially sent to the great kings in Europe and was the result of over brain work and too little exercise'. An attempt by the Portuguese to extend their influence in Mashonaland allowed him to play skilfully on Lobengula's fears and when a friendly letter arrived in Bulawayo from Queen Victoria addressed to Lobengula the doctor adroitly edited it before handing it to the king. Something else played into Jameson's hands: some preposterous notion in Whitehall had caused the royal letter to be escorted to Matabeleland by four Horseguards in full-dress uniform, and when Bulawayo found itself treated to the curious spectacle of these resplendent figures strolling among their kraal huts in helmets, shining cuirasses, and polished jackboots (and only slightly hampered by their spurs), Dr Jim's prestige rose higher in their reflected glory. The king was vastly intrigued and we read that he asked the Guards 'to go through the sword exercise, and, in inviting them to attend the "Great Dance" . . . made a point of their appearing in full panoply'. Things were clearly now going the doctor's way—the king made him an *induna*, and Jameson one day made a rather ludicrous appearance in all the glory of an ostrich feather cape and ox-tail garters. His slightly odd methods of diplomacy were undoubtedly beginning to pay off: in December the king grudgingly gave him permission to dig for gold at Tati in the southern end of his kingdom, and in a tipsy and unguarded moment added that if no gold was found there, his new friend might prospect for it in Mashonaland. That promise was just what the doctor wanted: he spent a few days at Tati superintending the digging of a large hole; then he was back in Bulawayo with the news that there was no gold to be found in it, and reminded the king of his promise to allow him to seek it in Mashonaland. Lobengula weakly assented, and he was so carried away that he even discussed a route the company's miners might take into Mashonaland which would avoid the Matabele heartland and not provoke the *amatjaha*. The king then accepted delivery of an instalment of the rifles and ammunition promised to him by Rudd, and, in effect, renewed the concession. It had been a neat performance on Dr Jameson's part, and in the middle of February 1890 he set off again to Kimberley with the good news that Lobengula would permit the

passage of the company's miners and prospectors into Mashonaland. He had carefully avoided telling the king that instead of a
mere handful they would come in their hundreds, or that so far
as he was concerned permission 'to dig' in Mashonaland sanctioned
the occupation of the country.

* * * * *

Rhodes meanwhile had been fighting another kind of battle
in England: he had gone there to petition Her Majesty's
Government to grant him a Royal Charter to exploit Lobengula's
dominions. This everyone knew would throw a mantle of legality
over the Rudd concession. As usual he got his way, but this time
only after a great deal of political manœuvring. Admittedly he
could list plenty of precedents for the granting of such a charter,
but as his critics pointed out, it would vest Rhodes with all the
functions of Government from the levying of taxation to carrying
out private wars. For Rhodes sought unlimited powers to
promote mining in Lobengula's dominions: powers to dispose
of its land, to recruit an army of his own, to make treaties, and to
promulgate laws. It had needed all Rhodes's appeals to imperial
sentiment and his masterful lobbying to prevail against the sting-
ing barbs of Labouchere's invective which joined with the more
semantic protestations of Mr Joseph Chamberlain at Westminster
in denouncing these almost sovereign powers that were being
sought. But if Rhodes had earned the strong disapproval of the
group he nicknamed 'the negrophilists of Exeter Hall' and of the
Aborigines Protection Society, and had set the leader-writers
in the liberal press shaking stern editorial fingers at his machinations, at the same time his exhausting but very plausible mas-
querade as a mirror of altruistic propriety had captivated Society,
and the queen clearly approved of him. Moreover, the City,
which was confident that a torrent of wealth would soon flow
from the Mashona goldfields, backed his newly formed British
South Africa Company, and Rhodes had tactfully persuaded the
Prince of Wales's brother-in-law (together with several other
noble personages) to serve on his board of directors. And so,

towards the end of October, 1889, when Jameson was engaging his professional talents over Lobengula's gout, Rhodes secured his Charter. With it the British South Africa Company had been turned from a wild speculation into a Chartered Company possessing a monopoly to exploit the far interior; now in London excited brokers lent, borrowed, promoted, intrigued, and sold their interests in a desperate attempt to get on the Chartered Company's bandwagon, and the financial means to secure Rhodesia for white settlement was over-subscribed. In its own way Mr Rhodes's performance in London had been every bit as neat as Dr Jameson's at Umvutcha.

7

THE PIONEERS

A curious air of unreality hangs over the story of the British expedition which occupied Mashonaland in 1890. It seems hardly possible that such a gigantic enterprise could have been initiated and sustained by the vision and energy of a single man; it seems scarcely credible that the warlike Matabele allowed Europeans to occupy so large a part of their dominions without a fight. The legendary march of Rhodes's pioneers began at the Maklautsi river on 26th June, 1890, less than a year after the Royal Charter had been granted to the British South Africa Company. It ended twelve weeks later at Salisbury. A thousand men took part in the venture, and not a single life was lost during its course. One feels that Norris-Newman was not entirely exaggerating when he described it as 'one of the most magnificent marches ever made in modern or ancient history'.

If Rhodes was the driving force behind the expedition, a great deal of the credit for its success must go to a young man with a loud voice, furtive eyes, and a big jaw named Frank Johnson, who one morning impulsively entered into a contract with Rhodes to effect the occupation of the far interior on his behalf for £40,000 down and £50,000 to be paid in instalments.

One cannot help being somewhat bemused by Frank Johnson: his career seems more suited to an imaginative film scenario than to real life. Here we are concerned only with its earlier part. When he was sixteen years old Johnson left Norfolk to make his living in South Africa. He saw service during the British occupation of Bechuanaland, and in 1887 after coming across some natives from Mashonaland carrying vulture quills filled with gold he went off prospecting beyond the Limpopo, and afterwards journeyed to Lisbon to claim mining rights there under the impression that the Portuguese still controlled the Mashona country. In 1889 he was back in the Mazoe valley just north of modern Salisbury, joined Selous in partnership, and obtained an important concession from a chief who claimed with some justification to be independent of Matabele control. Perhaps it was because of such *lèse majesté* that Johnson was soon afterwards accused by Lobengula of being a spy, and he was only allowed to leave the country after paying a fine of £100. Thereafter Frank Johnson nourished a grudge against the king. He also succeeded in antagonising Mr Rhodes by asserting that at least some parts of Mashonaland were not included in Lobengula's dominions, and therefore were not covered by the terms of the Rudd concession. But in the event things turned out very well for Johnson: Rhodes bought his silence with a suitable bribe, and the small amount of gold he had panned in Mashonaland proved sufficient to be used to make a wedding ring when he married. It was towards the end of 1889 that this youthful adventurer tells us he turned *entrepreneur*, and entered into his famous contract to hand over Mashonaland 'fit for civil government' to Rhodes by 1st October, 1890. It was an astonishing agreement and one finds it difficult to know whether to be more surprised by young Johnson's confidence in himself or by Rhodes's rash agreement to confide the execution of his cherished plans to a youth of twenty-three whom he hardly knew.

Johnson in his autobiography has left an engaging description of the events which led up to this 'conquest by contract', and in considering them we cannot do better than follow his published account:

'Early in the morning of December 22, 1889' he begins, 'I arrived in Kimberley by the post-cart from the "interior" . . . I breakfasted at the Kimberley Club. Outside the summer heat lay heavy on the town. A few minutes later Rhodes entered the room. He looked vaguely at me, and then, suddenly recollecting me, silently sat down at my table. He gave an order for bacon and eggs, and then in his downright, direct, inimitable way, he plunged without preamble into the story of his troubles and asked for my opinion. Up to this time he had been unable to find any practical way of taking possession of the country for which he held the Charter.' Rhodes according to Johnson then went on to say that having considered hiring regular British troops for the task, he had turned for advice to General Carrington, a professional soldier commanding in Bechuanaland at the time. Carrington had depressed him with his opinion that two thousand five hundred men would be required. Rhodes confessed he was aghast at this figure for he calculated that the maintenance of such an army would cost him a million pounds. Having explained all this to his companion the great man sank into a depressed silence over the breakfast table. Frank Johnson tells us he could not help feeling very sorry for the dejected man, and he takes up his story again at this point: 'Purely from a desire to cheer Rhodes up', he writes, 'I suddenly broke in:

"Two thousand five hundred men is absurd."

'Then wishing to emphasise my statement, I added rashly: "Why! With two hundred and fifty men I would walk through the country!"'

According to Johnson's book another strained silence followed as both men began to tackle their eggs and bacon. Rhodes one imagines was considering the youth's unexpected suggestion, while we can be certain that Johnson was wishing he had never made it, for as he admits 'I might just as easily have said twenty-five men as two hundred and fifty. I had merely blurted out the first divisible of Carrington's figure that came into my head.' But brashness was natural to Johnson and when Rhodes suddenly exclaimed 'Do you mean that?', he continues his account with an explanation that as 'I was not going to plead guilty to having said something I did not mean I answered at once:

' "Of course I do."'

'Another long, characteristic pause, while he rapidly calculated —and then came out the practical business man.

'"How much will it cost?" he asked.

'"I have not the slightest idea," I replied. "But give me the use of a room and plenty of paper, and by lunch-time I will let you know."

'"Right", was Rhodes's laconic decision.'

Johnson tells us that he then retired with a sheaf of writing paper and got down to work. In a good deal less than the specified four hours he was back to inform Rhodes that he could get a column of pioneers to the vicinity of Mount Hampden and effect the occupation of Mashonaland for £87,500. 'Good', replied Rhodes, 'I accept your offer.' In fact, Johnson says, it took another five days before all the details of the contract had been discussed and final agreement reached,* after which he suggested that a lawyer should be asked to draft its terms. Rhodes characteristically demurred: 'If you are capable of handing over my country to me', he said, 'you are capable of drawing up an agreement.' And on this note according to Frank Johnson, the arrangements for the occupation of Mashonaland were settled.

Johnson's account leaves the reader with the impression that the whole affair was arranged in this casual sort of way in Kimberley Club by two men who hardly knew each other; indeed the story of the comparative strangers arranging for the conquest of the far interior over bacon and eggs has passed into legend. The true facts, however, are different.

To begin with, Mr Rhodes and Frank Johnson were anything but strangers at the time: they had come to know each other very well long before the famous breakfast at Kimberley Club. Several months earlier Rhodes had paid Johnson handsomely to keep to himself his opinion that the Mazoe chiefs were independent of Lobengula, and only six weeks prior to the date which Johnson gives for the Kimberley Club agreement they had become involved in a very different sort of scheme which, fortunately for their reputations, was never put into effect. It was not one of those episodes on which Rhodes's admirers chose to dwell, and probably it is impossible now to extract the full truth about the two men's earlier plot to effect the occupation of the far interior. But it is certain that in December, 1889, when Jameson's gloomy messages from Bulawayo were speaking of Lobengula's obstinate reluctance to implement the Rudd concession, Johnson and Rhodes decided to capture the Matabele king in an armed coup

---

* Johnson is said to have made £20,000 from the contract. He may very well have considered this to be inadequate since he was reported a little earlier to have offered his services to the Portuguese for four million pounds.

which bears a remarkable resemblance to that attempted by Potgieter forty-two years earlier.

Johnson, it will be remembered, loathed Lobengula: 'I may as well admit', he wrote in a moment of candour, 'that I wished to be revenged on old Lo Bengula for the way he had treated me during my visit to his country', and for some time he had been looking round for an opportunity of 'getting his own back'. In Rhodes's ambitions he saw that opportunity, and here again he is refreshingly candid about his motives for wanting him to occupy the king's country: 'I frankly confess', he writes, 'that I was activated more by the wrongful spirit of vengeance than by any desire to stop the eastward expansion of the Germans or northward of the Boer republic, or to further British dominion in South Africa.' First of all Johnson persuaded Rhodes to organise a filibustering expedition against Matabeleland led by Johnson himself; then, getting down to details, Johnson drew up an agreement in his own hand which stated that for the sum of £50,000 and the allocation of 100,000 acres of conquered territory, he would raise 500 mounted men and 'carry by sudden assault all the principal strongholds of the Matabele nation and generally to so break up the power of the Amandebele as to render their raids on surrounding tribes impossible, to effect the emancipation of all their slaves and further to reduce the country to such a condition as to enable the prospecting, mining, and commercial staff of the British South Africa Company to conduct their operation in Matabeleland in peace and safety'. In other words, without suggesting any such nicety as a declaration of war, Johnson pressed an agreement on Rhodes which envisaged taking forcible possession of Lobengula's kingdom, although he was careful to excuse the aggression with the somewhat distasteful hypocrisy that it was carrying out a civilising mission. Johnson confesses that he was a little upset when Rhodes, before agreeing to his terms, pointed out that the contract would become void if its author were killed during the coup 'and demanded an alternative'; this difficulty was overcome when Maurice Heany agreed to act as the required proxy for his partner Johnson, and the discussion next went on to consider ways of manufacturing an 'incident' on the Bechuana border to justify the aggression, very much in the manner made so familiar to us fifty years later by Nazi diplomats. Everyone concerned was delighted when it was agreed that at the right moment an announcement would be made that a big force of Matabele had attacked a defenceless herd post in Bechuanaland without warning; and on this note the contract was signed.

Johnson schemed to concentrate a private army at a hideout on the Shashi river ready to pounce on Bulawayo when the time was ripe. 'I was to make the spring on a moonlight night with four hundred men', he wrote later, and he goes on to admit, 'I had an open mind as to the procedure after securing the king and his entourage. . . . We might make a complete job of it by killing Lobengula and smashing each military kraal before they had time to concentrate or—and this I favoured most—I might dig in at Gubulawayo with Lobengula and his entourage as hostages. Then I could open negotiations with the regiments for their peaceful surrender, while they acknowledged my administration on behalf of the Chartered Company.'

One is hard put to it to decide, as so often where Frank Johnson is concerned, whether the extreme daring or the improbity of this plan is the more extraordinary. Subsequently, it was pulled about to fit different circumstances when Jameson raided the Transvaal six years later, and although Johnson believed that 'the coup could have succeeded, but alas it had to be dropped like a hot potato' it would almost certainly have suffered the same fate as the raid of 1895. It was dropped when the filibusters were already on the Shashi because as Johnson sadly admits having 'so many smart men around' caused suspicion and because his partner, Heany, 'unfortunately had a failing for drink' and talked in his cups. Rumours of what was going on ultimately reached Sir Sidney Shippard, who quite correctly informed his superior, Sir Henry Loch, about them. When taxed about the matter Rhodes blandly denied all knowledge of it, but the venture now had to be hurriedly abandoned.

Johnson admits (with a tinge of new respect) in the first draft of his autobiography that afterwards 'I had a bad half hour with

Rhodes whose anger was as violent as his command of language was surprising while he told me what he thought of men who drink too much.' It was at this stage that Rhodes turned to General Carrington for advice; but very soon afterwards, on 21st December, 1889, his way was suddenly made clear when word reached Kimberley from Jameson that Lobengula had at last assented to his company prospecting in his dominions. There would be no need now for Rhodes to fight for his 'north': as one of the witnesses to the earlier piratical contract puts it, 'this sudden change of front of Lobengula's made us pause and during the pause a second plan, an alternative one, suggested itself to Mr Rhodes'. He returned to discuss the situation again with Frank Johnson and together they evolved the plan for the peaceful occupation of Mashonaland by a body of pioneers. They may even have reached agreement over breakfast in the Kimberley Club on that occasion as Johnson has suggested.

* * * * *

Even if the methods actually used to secure the far interior for the Chartered Company were a good deal less dramatic than the coup contemplated at first, the march of the pioneers into Mashonaland still remains one of the great epics of modern adventure. After considering, and then rejecting, Barreto's old Zambesi route into the interior, Jameson and Selous (who was now the company's 'intelligence officer') advised Rhodes that the column could best enter Mashonaland along a road to be made from the Maklautsi and which would avoid the Matabele settlements. The proposed route admittedly would traverse many miles of unhealthy mopani bush, but there was a very good chance that if it were used the march would not be contested by the king. In the end Rhodes accepted their suggestion, and while Frank Johnson went to work organising the column, Dr Jameson rode up to Bulawayo again with instructions to pacify 'the old buster', Lobengula, and obtain his permission for the pioneers to cut the 'Selous road' through the low veld.

Johnson was no time waster. Rather more than two hundred

men were quickly recruited for the column, armed, fitted out with uniforms, and given rudimentary military training. He next turned to the immense task of equipping the expedition: he worked on a lavish scale, and with a speed and foresight which still seems enormously impressive. The details are hard to grapple with. A hundred wagons and two thousand trek oxen formed only one of the items which he had to purchase. He went a little wild in some of his arrangements: thus he had a queer notion of buying a captive balloon which he hoped would deter the superstitious Matabele from contemplating an attack on the column; in the end, however, the idea of a balloon was discarded in favour of a naval searchlight (complete with an enormous steam engine) which could be turned on at night during the march in a dramatic demonstration of the white man's magic. Four field-guns, two rocket tubes and a variety of Maxim and Gatling guns, were also acquired and placed under the command of a burly officer named Burnet who is best remembered now for the surprise he caused by appearing on parade in size twelve boots.

The authorities at the Cape were beginning to take a sharper interest in the expedition to Mashonaland by now, and they ruffled Rhodes by insisting that the pioneers be protected during the march by seasoned troops. This would cost the company money but Sir Henry Loch was adamant and four hundred troopers of the Bechuanaland police were accordingly seconded to the column; they were to form the nucleus of the British South Africa Police, a fine unit which has since served Rhodesia with singular devotion. Finally, Johnson enrolled more than two hundred Africans as labourers to assist in cutting the road.

Frank Johnson had no difficulty in recruiting the pioneers: more than two thousand men applied for the two hundred vacancies. Young fit men, preferably unmarried, were chosen for this land voyage of the Rhodesian *Mayflower*; one pioneer who had reached the advanced age of forty-four was universally known as 'Daddy'. The men were picked from every trade and profession, and they formed a cross-section of the contemporary South African community. 'They were', Jameson's biographer tells us with a faintly patronising air, 'such men as Rhodes loved, of

ameson, Harrison, Selous and Colquhoun having tea on the way to
Jmtasa's Kraal
urvivors of the Alice Mine and Mazoe Patrols

The Pioneer Column crossing a river

British blood in the main, of all classes, artisans and working miners rubbing shoulders with cadets of good families—some famous English cricketers among them—with a sprinkling of likely young Dutchmen—in a springtime of youth, and fired by the great adventure.' Marshall Hole, one of Rhodesia's first historians, has maintained with good cause that 'no finer *corps d'élite* than the British South Africa Company's Police and the Mashonaland Pioneers have ever been raised'. Selous put things rather differently when he described the pioneers as 'a rough, hardy lot of men who some have called heroes and others filibusters', and he goes on to soliloquise that such a description would have been 'equally applicable to the followers of Drake and Clive'. It was Sir Robert Morier's son who unexpectedly turns out to have a more critical insight into the pioneers' character: 'they were', he says, 'on the whole an excellent body of men', but admits that 'neither the Police nor the Pioneers are quite all we heard from the enthusiasts in London . . . the privates are exactly the same class of men as our troopers, i.e. chiefly miners, etc., thrown out of employment by the smash of the Johannesburg goldfields, a sprinkling of army and navy deserters, clerks, etc.' Another observer was astonished by their incongruous backgrounds: 'such a mixed lot I never saw in my life', he wrote, 'all sorts and conditions from the aristocratic down to the street arab, peers and waifs of humanity mingling together'. Labouchere as might be expected was far more vitriolic about Rhodes's golden young men whom he described as 'border ruffians of Hebraic extraction'.

But Labouchere was an exception: on the whole Rhodes's enterprise commended itself to the British nation. An earlier generation might have admired men like Moffat and Livingstone; but by 1890 the public had lost its taste for figures moving on so high a moral plane and now the pioneers seemed just right, particularly as not only were they adding another province to the queen's dominions but were apparently thwarting the impertinent designs of Germans, Portuguese, and Boers alike. Certainly their subsequent progress through central Africa was followed in the English papers with the same sort of attention that today would be accorded to a cricket team touring Australia, and Labouchere's invective was lost amidst the applause that accompanied the march.

It must be admitted, however, that gold was the chief lure which led the pioneers into the far interior. The old legend of Ophir exerted its spell as strongly in the nineteenth as it did in the sixteenth century. And like the Portuguese before them every member of the 1890 column expected to gain sumptuous wealth in Mashonaland. But they had other motives too. This was an age whose laureate was Kipling, an era when Lord Lugard could implore young men in England to emulate the Romans who had brought civilisation to their own barbarous island; and hidden away behind the pioneers' pose of nonchalance and cynicism was a steadfast belief in the benefits that British rule would bring to the far interior.

While Johnson was fitting out the pioneer column at Mafeking, Dr Jameson was having a remarkably difficult time in Bulawayo. The king had changed his mind and for weeks he persisted in his refusal to allow the white men to make a road through the low veld to Mashonaland; they must come, he said, through Bulawayo. By the end of April the doctor was nearing the end of his patience, but he made a final plea to the king before returning to Kimberley and he buttressed it with a threat: at the last audience with the king he said, 'well, King, as you will not confirm your promise and give me the road, I shall bring my white impi, and if necessary shall fight.' Lobengula seems to have mumbled something in reply which Jameson tells us he took to be an assent,* and he rode away with the full intention of getting the pioneers moving into Mashonaland even if they were opposed. He took the precaution, however, of leaving a conciliatory subordinate to represent him at Bulawayo, fortified with characteristic instructions to 'continue talking piffle to the king'.

By this time the preparations at Mafeking for the venture were being completed. The pioneer column moved up to the Maklautsi

---

* 'Fairly satisfactory interview with Loben', he wrote later, 'ending in an admission of all he had promised me before.' It must be conceded, however, that Lobengula's version of this conversation differs from Jameson's.

river in June and now they had only to wait for General Lord Methuen to pronounce himself satisfied with their defensive arrangements to begin the march proper. A great deal had been accomplished in a remarkably short time. Much of Johnson's planning of necessity had been improvised and although they happened to dovetail into each other very well, those of us who have known something of the intricate planning required for the launching of even a minor operation during the Second World War will find them absurdly amateur and feckless. We catch their flavour best, not from Johnson's written orders but rather in Colquhoun's preparations for the journey* and from Lord Methuen's parting message to the pioneer column after his inspection: 'Well, gentlemen,' he said, 'your destination is Mount Hampden. You go to a place called Siboutsi. I do not know whether Siboutsi is a man or a mountain. Mr Selous, I understand, is of the opinion that it is a man; but we will pass that by. Then you get to Mount Hampden. Mr Selous is of the opinion that Mount Hampden is placed ten miles too far to the west. You had better correct that; but perhaps on second thoughts, better not. Because you might possibly be placing it ten miles too far to the east. Now good-morning gentlemen.' And as the parade came smartly to attention he turned on his heel and walked briskly to the mess tent.

There was even some doubt as to who was really in charge of the column. Frank Johnson assumed such airs that the pioneers christened him 'Napoleon Buonaparte Johnson', and one diarist recorded that he 'laughed behind his hands at Johnson's stentorian "the-column-will-advance-by-fours-from-the-right"' every morning; but Johnson for all his swagger was only 'the contractor' to Rhodes and not the column commander. Colonel Pennefather was indubitably the senior military officer among the pioneers but Mr Archibald Ross Colquhoun, the explorer of Yannan, had been appointed to the civilian post of Administrator-designate of the new colony and not without justification had pretensions to a higher authority; Selous was the company official who determined the column's route, but with him rode Dr Jameson,

* His luggage included thirty cases of whisky and sixty cases of champagne.

who regarded himself as Rhodes *alter ego*, and he never failed to show an awkward tendency to take charge whenever he thought fit while the men accepted him as their leader. Perhaps in the circumstances it was fortunate that the march of the pioneers was never disputed.

On the 27th June, 1890 the wagons jolted slowly forward across the Maklautsi into Matabeleland with a great cracking of whips over the straining backs of the trek oxen. At Tuli the

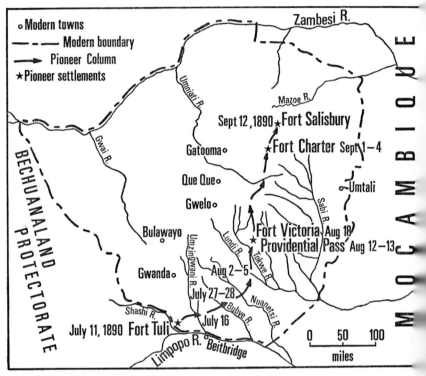

Route of the Pioneer Column, 1890

pioneer column stopped long enough to build a fort and there Frank Johnson was startled to receive an order from Lobengula to halt the march if he wished to avoid being skinned alive by the Matabele at a later date.

'Immediately on the force leaving Fort Tuli', Johnson writes, 'we found ourselves in possible enemy country', and the picnic atmosphere was abandoned as the pioneers moved slowly east- wards along a track which was laboriously hacked out for them from the bush. Undoubtedly the column was now in extreme danger. Twenty thousand Matabele were believed to be hanging on to its flanks, and it was passing through country which was perfectly suited to ambushes. Everyone was aware that in Bula- wayo Lobengula was being subjected to almost intolerable pressure from his 'turbulent young soldiers' to attack the column; only eleven years earlier eight hundred British regular soldiers had been overwhelmed by a Zulu impi in similar circumstances at Isandhlwana, and a serious Matabele attack through the mopani veld could scarcely fail to be successful. The sheer physical difficulties of the march were stupendous too: Selous's route was intersected by a series of rivers like the Nuanetsi and Lundi, and although it was the dry season each crossing was a very serious obstacle to heavy wagons. At the Umfuli on 6th September, we learn from one of the pioneers that 'the oxen had now become so weak that in fording rivers where the beds were sandy and the banks steep . . . the men actually placed the yokes on their necks and thus pulled as though they were cattle.' The crossings divided the column for hours and even days on end and during these times it was particularly vulnerable to attack. But the men were very tough and the risk only seemed to stimulate their excitement. All through the march they were effectively supported by their comradeship, a sense of accepted destiny, and the realis- ation that hardly ever before in history had there been anything quite like the march of four hundred miles they were making through uncharted Africa.

During July and the first weeks of August the column averaged about ten miles a day; Selous led it first eastwards through the thick bush, determining the route with compass and sextant as though he were navigating a course at sea; then he inclined increasingly to the north, and pointed it towards the high veld.

Somehow Lobengula restrained the *amatjaha* from attacking the pioneers in the low veld, and on the 17th August they came to the step-like granite scarp of the great Rhodesian plateau; they found a practical way to it up a long valley which they thankfully named Providential Pass. At the top they built a stockade and named it Fort Victoria in honour of the queen, and from there pressed on into open park-like country. The danger of a Matabele attack was now diminished, the obstacles were less, and they could move ahead much faster. On the 12th September the pioneers halted near 'a good sized kopje' within sight of Mount Hampden. The ground seemed suitable for settlement,* and the next day the Union Jack was run up on the site of modern Salisbury. No one paid much attention to Lobengula's claim to the sovereignty of Mashonaland, and possession of the country was taken in the name of the queen. The occupation had been effected without the loss of a single life; the 'great adventure' was over and the golden age of Rhodesian anecdotage had begun.

And Mr Rhodes had secured his foothold in the far interior. That was the important point, and if his methods could be criticised for their chicanery it must in all fairness be admitted that he had been certain that he was acting for the best: sooner or later this favoured part of Africa, Rhodes said, was bound to fall into European hands, and he genuinely believed that it would be best for all concerned if those hands were British. Yet at the same time one feels a great deal of sympathy for Lobengula: he had been outmanœuvred at every turn by a much shrewder man; certainly he had never expected that so much could have been read into the Rudd concession he had signed at Umvutcha kraal or that Rhodes would now claim ownership of the land his pioneers had occupied. It was only natural that in the November of 1891 he attempted to play Rhodes off against a rival concessionaire, and granted a Mr Lippert land rights in Mashonaland which were far more comprehensive than those he had conceded to Rudd. But the king's action was that of an animal struggling in a noose; and all it did was to tighten the noose around his neck, for Rhodes by prior arrangement with Lippert now bought up this second concession, and his position in Mashonaland was

* Later malice claimed that the column halted one day's march short of its destination because a wagon load of whisky caught it up at the Makabusi crossing.

thereby strengthened and given an aura of legality. Lobengula had always said that he felt like a fly being stalked by a chameleon, but this last sweep of the chameleon's tongue proved too much for John Moffat who had been so useful in the past to the Chartered Company: 'I feel bound to tell you', he wrote indignantly to Rhodes, 'that I look on the whole plan as detestable, whether viewed in the light of policy or morality. . . . When Lobengula finds it all out, as he is sure to do sooner or later, what faith will he have in you?' But this was a question that now did not worry Mr Rhodes unduly. His dream for the 'north' had acquired form and substance, and he was certain it was only a matter of time before the remainder of Lobengula's dominions would fall to him.

The 'Selous road' up which the pioneers marched into Mashonaland served them for three years until the conquest of Matabeleland opened up the shorter and more convenient route from the south through Bulawayo. Thereafter, the old pioneer road slowly reverted to the African bush. Today its course can be followed only with difficulty, and in places all traces of it would have been lost were it not for the graves scattered along it of the policemen and transport riders who kept it open during the first vital years of the Chartered Company's rule.

* * * * *

'Men are ruled by their foibles', Lord Milner once informed a friend when discussing Mr Rhodes, and then went on to explain that 'Rhodes's foible is size'. He was perfectly right of course; Rhodes was never a man to be content with his winnings; he would always attempt to use them to play again for higher stakes. And so, even before the pioneer march to Mashonaland began, he was considering how he might add Manicaland (and if possible a wedge of Moçambique as far as the sea) to the immense country he was going to occupy under the terms of the Royal Charter.

Nature has cast Manica in a different mould from the rest of Rhodesia; its charms are entirely separate things from those of the central plateau or bushveld. Its deeply gorged mountain ranges rising from rolling grasslands that awake memories of the

Berkshire downs, possess a far more obvious appeal, and one feels that Rhodesia without Manicaland would be no less bereft than an England lacking Wales.

The Manica highlands* have always been isolated from the main stream of Rhodesian history. Its climate was too forbidding to make much appeal to primitive men or to the Bantu, and it was never heavily settled during peaceful times. These uplands did, however, offer a haven to refugees during the Zimba incursions, and many Karanga clans—Celt like—fled to the eastern hills and erected a complex of buildings covering three thousand square miles of country. There the visitor sees the remnants of well-planned water furrows, and line after line of terracing which held back the soil along the steeper slopes. Here too among the Inyanga mountains are to be found numerous circular stone pit-buildings that credulous tourists are still assured were once used to corral slaves. The ancient gold workings which Homen's men-at-arms investigated so hopefully in 1575 abound in Manica, and it was partly his knowledge of them that made Rhodes covet the province. But Manica also had another, and even more imperious attraction for Mr Rhodes—its annexation would be the first step to winning an outlet to the sea for his new country. And so it was that even before the pioneer corps was being enrolled he was making plans to appropriate the legendary land of the Manicas as well.

The trouble was that the Portuguese claimed the province too, and the British Government seemed prepared to uphold their pretensions. Undoubtedly Manica lay well outside the range of the Matabele impis, and Lobengula could scarcely say it was part of his dominions; the Portuguese on the other hand could assert with some degree of truth that they had 'effectively occupied' Manicaland from 1575 until 1832, and that in 1876 had recovered their old position when Umtasa, the paramount chief of the Manicas, acknowledged Portuguese suzerainty in traditional form by presenting an elephant tusk filled with earth to a Portuguese official.

* In the context of this book the area is taken to include the mountain country round Inyanga as well as Melsetter.

One must note here that on several later occasions Umtasa vehemently denied that he had ever accepted Portuguese suzerainty. But he was an unpleasant and crafty character who had succeeded to the Manica chieftainship after stabbing his predecessor—an uncle named Vumba—to death in 1870, and we shall never know now how much truth there was in these assertions. Certainly since his accession Umtasa had behaved as an independent chief, playing off his formidable neighbours against each other with considerable skill—his neighbours being Lobengula's Matabele, the Gazas, and a Goanese adventurer rejoicing in the *nom de guerre* of Gouveia who had carved out a fief for himself round Gorongosa mountain and on whom the Portuguese had conferred the title of Captain-General.

The Portuguese of Mocambique had been seriously alarmed when they learned that Charles Rudd had extracted a concession from Lobengula and that Mr Rhodes had been granted a Royal Charter to exploit it; they reacted by dispatching flag-raising missions from Zumbo and the fort at Macequece* to kraals in Manicaland and northern Mashonaland; even Lomagundi, whose territory included the old Monomatapan heartland of the Dande and who for years had paid annual tribute to Lobengula, was induced to accept Portuguese sovereignty. (It was a mistake that cost him his life: in 1891 a Matabele impi swooped upon Lomagundi's kraal and put him to death.) As a final gesture to emphasise their claims the Portuguese then built a fort at the junction of the Umniati and Nyabosa rivers.

This was too much even for Whitehall. Lord Salisbury maintained that although in 1817 and 1847 Great Britain had acknowledged Portuguese occupation of the east African coast, she had never recognised any claims to the enormous territory lying between Angola and Mocambique, whose occupation would cut off all hope of British expansion in central Africa; his Lordship in the past had even dismissed their description of the 'fairs' they had established in the far interior during Monomatapan times as mere 'archaeological arguments'. In 1886, however, his

* Usually spelled Massi Kessi by the Rhodesian pioneers, now renamed Villa de Manica.

position had been weakened when both France and Germany recognised Lisbon's sovereignty of the disputed territory and in the end he had been obliged to accept a compromise: on 22nd August, 1890, when the march of Rhodes's pioneers was actually in progress, representatives of Portugal and Great Britain initialled a convention which among other things agreed that their respective spheres of interest in south-east Africa should be divided by the Macheke and Sabi rivers. This agreement virtually handed over Manicaland to Portugal and it only required ratification by the *Cortes* in Lisbon for the settlement to be finalised and Mr Rhodes's aspirations were thwarted.

By this time, however, the northward march of the Rhodesian pioneers had brought them very close to Manicaland and Rhodes was always a firm believer in the dictum that possession is nine points of the law. He had forseen the situation that was developing and as early as 13th May, 1890 he had instructed Colquhoun that 'as soon as practicable after entering Mashonaland you will . . . visit the chief of the Manica country, and obtain from him on behalf of the Company, a treaty and concessions for the mineral and other rights in his territory'. To these orders Rhodes had added the significant rider: 'you will endeavour to secure the right of communication with the sea board'.

By 3rd September, 1890, when the pioneer column had established its second embryo settlement on the high veld at Fort Charter a few days march north of Fort Victoria, Colquhoun decided it was time to visit Manicaland and extract the required concession from Umtasa. Although aware that this might conflict with Lord Salisbury's intention of leaving Manica within the Portuguese sphere of interest, it is less certain that he knew the British Government had actually come to an agreement with Lisbon on the matter only two weeks earlier and he can have had no inkling of its effect on the Portuguese. For when the terms of the convention were published the *Cortes* indignantly refused to ratify them on the grounds that they were not generous enough, and in a burst of patriotic exuberance declared it would be satisfied with nothing less than the whole of the central African interior. Whitehall would be certain to oppose this, and towards the end of 1890 there was just a chance that Rhodes's gamble for Manicaland might pay off. Lord Salisbury had been galled by the brusque rejection of the convention's terms, and since his hand had recently been strengthened by Bismarck's agreeing to accommodate British aspirations in the region in return for concession elsewhere, he was quite prepared to raise his terms for a settlement with the Portuguese in Africa.

During his journey to Umtasa's kraal Colquhoun was escorted by a handful of mounted police and accompanied by Harrison his secretary, Dr Jameson, and Selous. We have a photograph of these three men sitting with Colquhoun in their mess tent during one of their halts. Colquhoun lounges heavily in his chair on one side; he is a thickset man, looking rather like Edward VII without his beard, and somehow he seems a little out of place on the veld. The appearance does not belie him: Colquhoun emerges from all the pioneers' accounts as a paper-bound fusspot who utterly lacked flair as an executive and leader. He had taken a job with the Chartered Company simply because he was unemployed at the time following a classical *faux pas*: his promising career in Burma had ended abruptly when he wrote a scathing report for Whitehall about his superiors and then inadvertently put it in an envelope addressed to them. Colquhoun radiated pomposity and it is not difficult for us to imagine the jokes that must have enlivened the pioneers' messes when they stumbled deliberately over his name, which unaccountably to them was pronounced to rhyme with balloon. Selous appears in our photograph holding a gun in one hand and a cup of tea in the other, but has moved his head and his face is blurred. Harrison poses a little stiffly by him. Jameson sits nearest the camera; his legs are crossed and his expression is pugnacious and set, and one can see at once why his friends so often compared him to a fox terrier. There had been some friction between the three men just before the photograph was taken when Colquhoun had learned with chagrin that Jameson would have much preferred to deal with Umtasa by himself, but they had got over this slight unpleasantness and the atmosphere in the party was beginning to relax. It seemed to them all that they were embarked on an enchanted journey which, with fortune, would add another province to the empire. All the ingredients of high adventure accompanied them as Colquhoun, Jameson, and Selous rode through the sparkling, lion-coloured landscape, whose tall swaying grass gave it the appearance of an endless undifferenced field of corn. They were travelling across one of the most lovely parts of the great Rhodesian plateau, and during the best season of the year; it reminded an American trooper in the escort of 'the undulating prairies of Kansas and Iowa, with here and there a few trees', and he noted that 'spring seemed to be approaching for most of the trees, having shed their last year's foliage a few weeks before were budding out with small delicate leaves, some pale green others yellowish green; but the predominating colours were pink and reddish'. This was a welcoming country, an easy land to live in. Nearly everywhere its broad smooth sweep filled all there was to be seen except the sky; only to the east was the arched horizon broken by the blue jagged line of the Manica mountains which grew larger with every hour of the ride. Even the prosaic Colquhoun was affected by its beauty: 'We passed through some of the most charming scenery imaginable', he writes in his autobiography, 'crossing numerous streams of clear, swiftly flowing water over rocky beds, winding their way amongst perfect wooded mountain scenery, of which one could find the exact counterpart in favoured portions of either Scotland or Wales.'

In this adventure within an adventure, Selous usually rode in the lead; he alone of them had seen this countryside before; its quality of expansiveness had fastened itself on to his imagination long before, and every time he returned its grasp grew stronger until now he could never shake it off. Frederick Courtenay Selous was a slight and solitary man. He was already famous in 1890; for nearly twenty years he had hunted through the country between the Zambesi and the Limpopo, and it was very largely due to the publication of his *A hunter's wanderings in Africa* that British interest had been aroused in this part of central Africa. For Selous's first book is one of the best that was written about the far interior prior to the occupation, and it still makes exciting reading. It had turned its author into a legend: people in England were beginning to think of him more as a fictional character invented by Rider Haggard than as a figure of reality. Yet there was a business-like streak in Selous which few people suspected. Only the year before, he had joined Frank Johnson in obtaining important mining concessions from 'independent chiefs' in the Mazoe district of Mashonaland; and then after £2,000 had changed hands he surrendered his rights in what he called 'the richest little piece of country in all Africa' to Mr Rhodes, and had been taken on his pay roll like his partner Johnson.

By the fourth day out of Fort Charter Jameson was beginning to find it difficult to get along with Colquhoun whom he thought 'rather an ass', but before their relationship could deteriorate any further he was obliged to withdraw from the expedition; for a wager he lightheartedly jumped his horse over a fallen tree, took a heavy toss, and trailed off dejectedly with two broken ribs to recuperate at Mount Wedza.

Umtasa and his court jester received Colquhoun and Selous on 14th September. In his autobiography Colquhoun, fresh from a visit to the Zimbabwe ruins, tells us with ponderous humour that the chief was dressed 'in a naval cocked hat, a tunic (evidently of Portuguese origin but of ancient date and forming perhaps some of the "ancient remains" to which the attention of the world had been so pathetically drawn), a leopard skin slung over his back, the whole toilette being completed by a pair of trousers that had evidently passed through many hands, or rather covered many legs, before assisting to complete the court uniform of the "roitelet Mutassa" as the Portuguese termed him'. On being questioned Umtasa explained that he owed no allegiance to the Portuguese, although he admitted he was terrified of their Captain-General Gouveia, whose lands bordered on his, and was extremely anxious to avoid upsetting him. But he cheerfully signed an agreement which granted his country's trading and mineral rights to the Chartered Company. Six days later Colquhoun rode back to join the pioneer column at Salisbury well pleased with himself for acquiring Manicaland, the fairest province of Rhodesia. Conscious, however, that his concessions might be challenged by the Portuguese, he took the precaution of sending Captain Patrick Forbes with sixteen troopers back to a camp near Umtasa's kraal with instructions to keep an eye on the chief and prevent him being intimidated into repudiating the concession.

Umtasa meanwhile had been spending some uneasy weeks wondering whether he had done the right thing by allying himself to the British. The consequences soon overtook him, for on 5th November, a small Portuguese army marched up into his hill-top kraal some twenty miles north of modern Umtali. The force was jointly commanded by a Colonel Joachim Paiva d'Andrada and the abominable Gouvcia. D'Andrada had a fine administrative record, but no one could say he cut an impressive military figure: an officer who met him a little later describes him as 'very swarthy and slight in appearance, not unlike a dark-skinned dancing master'. Yet d'Andrada without doubt was a cultured and fastidious man, and he must have felt embarrassed to be associated in this new Portuguese effort at empire-building with a colleague of Gouveia's reputation. For Gouveia was a savage and bloodthirsty monster. Born Manuel Antonio de Sousa in Goa, he had inherited an estate between the Zambesi and Revue rivers and he had built it up into a prosperous slave-hunting principality based on Gorongosa. Gouveia boasted that he could put ten thousand armed men into the field, and every year he sent out slaving parties to ransack the countryside. He had a well-founded reputation for terror in Manica which he deliberately enhanced by a remarkable piece of personalia: while on campaign Gouveia had his prisoners' throats cut ceremoniously over a great war drum after which the proceedings were concluded by vigorously beating the blood-stained drum.* An Englishman who came to know Gouveia described him as an 'awful cut-throat and scoundrel who ought to be strung up on account of the atrocities he has committed', and it comes as something of an anticlimax to learn that only a few days after marching into Umtasa's kraal the monster of Gorongosa was found to be

* The drum is still said to exist as a battle trophy standing beside the grave of a Matoko chief who captured it in battle. Gouveia has another claim to distinction; the Mashona call venereal disease by his name presumably because it was introduced to them by his levies.

dressed 'in a striped sleeping suit of various colours, and appeared to be a rather retiring mild mannered, old half-caste gentleman—a thoroughbred Goanese', when he submitted to capture by a small number of pioneers.

Forbes wisely lay low when Andrada marched up to Umtasa's, tore down the Union Jack and replaced it with the Portuguese flag; Andrada then summoned all the local chiefs and headmen to a ceremony to be held at the kraal on 15th November where they were to be required to acknowledge Portugal's sovereignty over Manicaland. But before this date Forbes had been reinforced by twenty-six men, bringing his strength up to forty-two, and he decided to use them in reasserting British control over the province. He planned to arrest Andrada and Gouveia and to disperse their askaris; considering the odds against him this was perhaps the most daring of all the chances taken by the pioneers during their occupation of the far interior, especially as no one knew how Umtasa himself would react at the critical moment. To recapture the flavour of his exploit we cannot do better than follow the account left by one member of Forbes's force, Corporal Victor Morier: Colonel d'Andrada and Gouveia, he tells us 'were comfortably installed up in Umtasa's kraal, holding *indabas* (talkytalkies) with him, and threatening him with extermination for having made treaties with us. Their band of armed bearers, 200,* luckily for us were encamped at the bottom of the hill. As it afterwards turned out, they had ordered Umtasa to attack us if we made any move against them, and this he had promised to do. But we were too smart and sudden for them. Ten of us made a sudden raid up into the kraal, whilst the remainder disarmed the bearers at the bottom of the hill. We had an awful climb. It was two o'clock, with a blazing sun, and the kraal about 300 feet up, perched on perpendicular rocks. Of course it was *au pas de charge* with loaded rifles. The niggers couldn't make out what we were after, and luckily were too surprised to barricade the narrow little gates in the stockade, through which one had to creep on all fours. We seized the Portuguese, pulled down their flag, which was gaily floating in the middle of the kraal, and

* The official British estimate of the Portuguese strength was 370 armed men.

proceeded to clear out as fast as we could go. But things looked monstrous bad. The niggers had all flown to arms the moment they had recovered from their astonishment, and were dancing round us, shouting furiously and waving their assegais and brandishing their guns. There must have been over a thousand. I will never forget it. It was one of the most extraordinary and distinctly unpleasant sights I ever wish to see. I am convinced that had we not got straight away, in another two minutes we would have been massacred. . . . I can assure you I was considerably relieved when I had crept through the narrow hole and was outside the d——d kraal. We took our prisoners down to our camp and dispatched Andrada and Manuel Antonio off to Fort Salisbury next day.'

Andrada was infuriated by his arrest, but he behaved with dignity. Gouveia on the other hand folded up: he grovelled to Forbes, whining for mercy. No one of course had any intention of harming him; Forbes merely wanted the two men out of the way. They were sent off to Cape Town and put on board a ship bound for Lisbon, their injured feelings being soothed to some extent by Jameson's having arranged for them to be received aboard with diplomatic honours; their ship was dressed overall, and they walked up its gangplank to the strains of the Portuguese national anthem.

After turning the Portuguese out of Umtasa's, Forbes's men occupied the fort at Macequece (where his little force sustained their first casualty when Trooper Black swallowed a lethal dose of 'liberated' vino tinto) and on 22nd November Forbes with six troopers set off for the coast intending to crown his accomplishments with the capture of Beira. 'We shall secure the north bank of the Pungwe', he wrote back excitedly, 'all the country between the Pungwe and Busi, and all the necessary seaboard.' Clearly Rhodes's foible of 'thinking big' was spreading to his lieutenants.

The sheer physical hardships of the journey which followed were incredible, but by now Forbes had the bit between his teeth, and he moved quickly. Morier takes up his account again on 13th December, 1890: 'We have had an awful forced march', he wrote, 'eighty miles on horseback; we then left our horses owing to tsetse fly (too late I am afraid), then 110 miles foot march, twenty-five to thirty miles a day in the tropical sun; I almost barefoot, my back raw from the sun owing to the holes in my shirt. Nothing to eat most of the way till we got into the game region, but Kaffir corn. . . . We saw several lions and, unfortunately, lost one of our party, Mr Banman,* *The Times* correspondent, through them.'

One feels that Forbes's men deserved to have gained more than they did from their brave attempt to secure a port for Rhodesia. But the time when events were controlled by individuals had suddenly passed, and when Forbes was only two days' march from Beira he was recalled by a peremptory message from Colquhoun. Colquhoun knew that Lord Salisbury recognised Portuguese sovereignty of the coast and he had suddenly become apprehensive of exceeding his powers, but Rhodes never forgave him for his caution while Dr Jameson when he heard the news that the Administrator had halted Forbes exploded with 'Damn the fellow; I got him his job'.

If Rhodes had failed to secure the coast, the removal of the two Portuguese 'generals' from the scene at least allowed the pioneers to effect the occupation of Manicaland. But the arrests plunged all Portugal into hysterical rage. The press thundered against the insult to the national flag; mobs in Lisbon smashed the windows of the British embassy and the statue of Camões was wreathed in black crepe; posters in Oporto exhorted the rabble to set fire to British property and English-speaking civilians were manhandled in the streets of Lourenço Marques; a subscripton list to purchase a battleship was opened in Portugal and university students thronged to enlist in the volunteer battalion which was being recruited to revenge the outrage. Mr Rhodes at the beginning of 1891 discovered that he had a war on his hands.

February saw the students' battalion encamped on the coastal plain near Beira. Tempers were riding higher than ever in Mocambique after a steamer chartered by Rhodes had made an

* The name of this journalist who enjoyed the melancholy distinction of being the first war correspondent to be eaten by a lion was in fact Baumann.

attempt to force a passage up the Limpopo river and run guns to the king of the Gazas in payment of yet another concession which violated Portuguese sovereignty. But in March, when the Portuguese troops moved up country to Sarmento with orders to drive the Chartered Company troops from Manica they were beginning to suffer from fever. One must remember that the association of malaria with mosquitoes was still unrecognised at this time, and the warlike students of 1891 were just about as vulnerable to the disease as Barreto's men had been in 1569. Like them they died off at a terrifying rate. By April when they moved forward again, the command of the expedition had descended to Major Xavier and Captain Bettencourt, and their army was no more than a mob of half-trained askaris who could be depended on to bolt at the first serious check and a collection of highly-strung white youths, all groggy with fever.

A Captain Heyman of the British South Africa Company's police had by now taken over at Macequece from Forbes who had been promoted to the post of Resident Magistrate in Salisbury. Heyman's men were scarcely in a better condition than the Portuguese: according to Morier they numbered 'seventy wretched fever-stricken men (of whom only thirty-eight were fit for duty owing to the others having no boots)'. And so in April, when the Portuguese taskforce came forward again, Heyman discreetly retired to Umtali. A few days later Xavier marched into Macequece with drums beating and flags flying.

Some rather farcical parleys now followed between the two commanders. Heyman on one occasion submitted to being blind-folded and taken into Macequece, where he learned from the Portuguese officer, that 'martial law was proclaimed in Manica and he would drive us out when he thought fit'. Heyman had no intention of allowing this to happen: only a few days before he had received a message from Rhodes warning him about the Portuguese troops in Macequece which had ended with a stern 'you must turn them out', and it was clear that the outbreak of local hostilities could not be delayed much longer. The danger was that it might grow into a full-scale Anglo-Portuguese conflict. There was a pause for several days before Xavier put in his attack, and Heyman made good use of the time: he advanced his small force of fifty policemen and at the end of 'three days and nights of killing work' had them well dug in along the Chua hills only two miles from Macequece. He also succeeded in hauling an ancient seven-pounder gun up to his position; fortunately he camouflaged it so well with a tarpaulin that a Portuguese officer who came up one day carrying a further ultimatum was satisfied with the explanation that it was a new kind of tent.

At midday on 11th May, 1891, the British were disturbed at lunch by reports that the Portuguese were advancing from Macequece in two columns. They certainly outnumbered Heyman's policemen but it is difficult now to be certain of Xavier's strength. The highest British figure gives it as 600 men, but a Portuguese officer reported it to be 250 Europeans and 500 Africans, while the official figure in the British Blue Book estimated the little army at '150 whites and 300 blacks'. Xavier deployed his soldiers some 700 yards from the British positions, and with mounting concern watched Heyman making ostentatious flag signals to non-existent reinforcements in the rear. A gun was then fired, sharp bugle calls sounded the advance, and the Portuguese officers, anxious to observe the niceties of war, courteously raised their hats to the enemy before leading their men forward. One of the troopers with Heyman, entranced by the sight of the white uniforms extended as if on manœuvres in front of him, thought the scene must be 'the last of old time battle-pictures'.

Xavier's plan, such as it was, bordered on military lunacy. He had been so impressed by Heyman's bogus signals which suggested reserves coming up that he gave up all idea of out-flanking the entrenched British position; he simply ordered his men into a frontal attack. It was doomed from the start but nothing could have been more gallant than the way the Portuguese officers tried to lead their askaris forward in the face of heavy fire. 'Though their officers behaved really splendidly,' Morier tells us, 'exposing themselves freely to a heavy fire, they could not get their men to face the open', and one account speaks of their encouragement being given with the flats of their swords.

Heyman himself served the seven-pounder with excellent effect; he fired twenty-three rounds which one of his men thought was 'pretty good going for a muzzle-loader under fire when you think of all the sponging and ramming and priming that has to take place'. Heyman was blessed with a stroke of luck when his last shell exploded in Macequece fort itself. This seems to have been the final shock for the Portuguese and they nervously withdrew, officers not omitting to raise their hats in salute when leaving the field, although Xavier so far forgot himself that he then shook his fist at the British before disappearing from view.

During the two-hour fight not a single company man was hit. Estimates of Portuguese losses varied: Heyman himself put them at thirty killed; another observer speaks of finding 'forty-seven bodies in the long grass', while Morier made a note that 'the Portuguese lost between forty and sixty killed and wounded'. The British took two prisoners, one of whom 'put up his hands for mercy saying he was a Delagoa Bay policeman', to which Tulloch tells us 'Sergeant Paxton (patting his head) replied "you're a long way off your beat"'.

Next day, after a patrol discovered that the Portuguese had vanished in the direction of Sarmento, Heyman triumphantly reoccupied Macequece and gathered in the spoils of victory. 'All the stores were left', we are told, 'and nine machine guns, seven Hotchkiss, and two Nordenfelts, with thousands of rounds of ammunition.' Plenty of looted wine was also available to celebrate the end of a remarkably successful campaign.

Heyman reported his victory to Salisbury in a message scribbled on a visiting card he had found in the fort and he ended it with a proud 'The English force entered Massikessi next morning and took possession, burning the fort. Casualties on the English side nil.' This, however, turned out to be a shade premature: Trooper Green, like Trooper Black on a similar occasion before him, succeeded in drinking enough wine to cause his death a few days later from acute alcoholic poisoning.

News of the engagement at Macequece reached London and Lisbon in somewhat different forms. Dr Jameson diplomatically gave the impression that the fighting had not only taken place a good seventeen miles from Macequece and well inside the company's frontier line, but he said it had been caused by the aggressive Portuguese, who 'elated at finding Massi Kessi evacuated, proceeded westwards in the direction of Fort Salisbury', and came into collision with a body of the company's police. The Portuguese account was scarcely more accurate: after reporting Xavier's reoccupation of Macequece it continued: 'next morning without the slightest provocation, the Company's police attacked Massi Kessi, defeating the Portuguese with a loss of seven killed and several wounded.'

But it did not seem to matter very much by this time. Although a year earlier the Portuguese would have reacted feverishly to a humiliation of this sort they were now mourning too many sons dead of malaria even to bluster: it was as though sadness had drained out all their venom and bitterness. The *Cortes* in Lisbon meekly agreed to withdraw from Manica, and Rhodes's gamble had gained him his eastern province after all. But, as always, he wanted to double up on his winnings, and he promptly got off a typical message to Heyman reading, 'Take all you can get and ask me afterwards.' So now, stimulated by his success and in a curious reprise of Forbes's earlier attempt, Heyman dispatched a handful of men to find parts missing from the captured machine guns and make another attempt on Beira. The tortured remnants of the Portuguese army either fled before them or surrendered, and for a moment it again seemed that Rhodesia might have a seaport. But this was too much for the long suffering Lord Salisbury: he had never felt any doubts about Portuguese rights to the coast, and on his instructions Sir Henry Loch, the British High Commissioner at Cape Town had already hurried his military secretary, a Major Sapte, off to Beira with urgent orders to intercept any of the company's police making an attempt on the port and to order them out of Macequece. Sapte, unfortunately for Mr Rhodes, was a man of resource and energy. Loch wrote in his report to Whitehall a little later that 'Major Sapte pushed on through this country at times wading to his waist, and on the 29th May arrived at the Portuguese station of Chimoio where he was hospitably received. Starting early in the following morning he came within a short distance upon an advanced party of the British South Africa Company's police which were making arrangements to surprise and destroy the Portuguese camp.' The police could hardly ignore Sapte's official instruction, especially when they learned that three British men-of-war were cruising off Beira with instructions to hang any filibusters who pushed through to the coast, and they reluctantly gave up this last bid for the glittering prize of a Rhodesian seaboard. Rhodes was incensed at the second disappointment; he expected his subordinates to take no notice of orders that conflicted with his own plans: 'Why didn't you put Sapte in irons?' he signalled furiously to Heyman, 'and say he was drunk?'

If he was denied Beira, Rhodes (whom the Portuguese now not unnaturally referred to as the *homen horivel*) had nevertheless gained a great deal. When agreement on the disputed border was finalised on 11th June, 1891, although Macequece was left in Portuguese hands, nearly all Umtasa's country was ceded to the Chartered Company, and Manicaland had become part of Rhodes's empire. His first private war had ended with a qualified but still exhilarating success. Now he would have to wait nearly three years before he could begin his second war.

* * * * *

We must go back here to consider the situation in Mashonaland after the pioneer's march. They had been having a very rough time. Once the country had been officially declared 'occupied' their terms of service allowed each of them to take up fifteen mining claims and a farm of three thousand acres, and towards the end of September, 1890, the majority of the pioneers had hurried off into the surrounding country which Jameson so glowingly described as 'a happy combination of Canaan, Ophir and the black country'.*

The Mashona who watched these white men feverishly 'pegging out' mining claims, or 'riding off' farms, or stocking up

---

* One must note here that the missionaries in Matabeleland has welcomed their intervention in Mashonaland since it meant that 'the hateful Matabele rule is doomed'.

improvised trading stores had not the slightest comprehension of the meaning of Rudd's concession. They fully expected the pioneers to leave the country once they had taken all the gold they wanted; it astounded them when they learned that these white strangers not only intended to stay for good, but claimed the right to levy work and taxes from them. Their reaction was predictable.

They made trouble: they simply could not accept the settlers' assertion to own the country. Yet looking back on it now their opposition at first seems strangely muted. For although many Mashona clans in the past had bleakly accepted harassment from the Matabele impis, others had lived beyond the range of their spears and had retained their independence. But at the same time the Mashona in 1890 had no sense of unity, and thoughts of armed insurrection took time to mature; and in any case there was no paramount chief among their headmen to whom they could look for leadership, since each kraal was economically self-sufficient.

Interclan vendettas and the lifting of neighbours' cattle had been a part of the Mashonas' lives and it came as another shock when the white men announced that in the interests of peace and security neither clan-fighting nor thieving from European farms would be tolerated. But it was one thing to lay down laws of this kind and another to enforce them, and undoubtedly pilfering from the newcomers went on. This was something the new administration could not countenance, and it decided to make an example of one particularly truculent headman. But when the offender was summoned to stand trial in Salisbury he proved 'very impertinent', and a small punitive expedition commanded by a Captain Lendy (whom we shall meet again) was dispatched from Salisbury to take 'summary measures' against him. According to the official account Lendy's little force was met by gunfire when it approached the recalcitrant kraal, and in the skirmish which followed twenty-three tribesmen were killed. Given the situation, incidents of this sort were probably unavoidable, and indeed one is surprised that so few occurred when the Mashona first found themselves committed to European rule. But news of Lendy's exploit was seized upon with grave misgiving in Britain, and it received a good deal of publicity. From what later became known of Lendy one has to concede that he may indeed have acted with undue harshness, and the best that can be said now for the manner in which he executed his commission is that it served as a dramatic and effective assertion of the white man's new authority; and for nearly six more years the Mashona lay low and sulked.

The pioneers had other troubles to contend with in Mashonaland during their first year: one was the rainy season which turned out to be one of the wettest on record. Transport came to a virtual standstill; imported goods including drugs were difficult to obtain and very expensive; the settlers suffered badly from malaria and they were reduced to a near-starvation diet. They were terribly disappointed too with the gold prospects of the country. How they reacted comes out in Colquhoun's autobiography where he writes that the prospectors 'who expected to find gold in chunks ready to be picked up, squatted in their wagons and waited for the liquor to arrive'.

Colquhoun was having an unhappy time himself, and one cannot help feeling a good deal of sympathy for him. After negotiating his concession with Umtasa he took up his appointment as Administrator at Salisbury and discovered that, without authority from him, Dr Jameson had set off with Frank Johnson to pioneer a new Pungwe route into Mashonaland from the sea. Colquhoun always stood tip-toe on his dignity and in any case he had no wish to provoke the Portuguese, but Jameson scornfully ignored an order to return, and then compounded his insubordination by triumphantly completing an incredible journey to the sea which must take its place among the most daring epics of exploration. Colonel Pennefather, commanding the police, turned out to be a scarcely less awkward colleague: he point-blank refused to allow his men to be employed on manual labour even though the sanitation of the little settlement at Salisbury was causing some alarm, and the Administrator had no money to pay native workers. This was only the beginning: the contemptuous defiance of Jameson and Pennefather was infectious and soon it was clear that although Colquhoun was nominally the ruler of Mashonaland, hardly anyone seemed inclined to accept his authority: 'Johnson would never have dreamt of acting as he had done', the distracted Administrator wailed to Mr Rhodes, 'but for Jameson, who, instead of acting with me as a colleague and friend, has worked all the mischief which his ingenious and busy brain can devise.' But Rhodes took Jameson's side in his 'tiff' with Colquhoun when he turned up at Cape Town at the end of his remarkable Pungwe adventure, and very soon afterwards the doctor was reigning in Salisbury while Colquhoun took his drab acrimony back to England leaving a vague impression among readers of Rhodesian history that he had been no more than a misprint. Colquhoun had been well meaning but his tidy mind had proved a liability in the confused Mashonaland of 1890; Jameson's administrative methods of course were quite different—someone even described them as 'Government by crony'—but they appeared to work surprisingly well.

The new Administrator was not only faced with the pioneers' problems, he also had to maintain peace with the Matabele. His 'foreign policy' was largely concerned with Lobengula's insistence that the Mashona tribesmen were still his subjects, a viewpoint which the company could hardly accept if it was to maintain its own position in Mashonaland. Jameson was genuinely anxious to find a way round the difficulty and had no intention of allowing it to lead to war. Indeed it is a little ironic that this man, whose name in 1895 was to become the epitome for unwarranted aggression, should have earlier been branded as the instigator of the Matabele war which he had tried so hard to avoid.

For British Liberal circles were soon suggesting that by 1893 when the wealth of the Mashona goldfields was proving disappointing, Rhodes had abandoned his policy of 'peace and gold' for one of 'blood and war', and that Jameson obediently provoked war with the Matabele. Thus Henry Labouchere assured the readers of 'Truth' that 'The Mashonaland bubble having burst, a war was forced by the Company on Lobengula in order to get hold of Matabeleland', and he went on to charge that 'when the train had been laid, a quarrel was picked with the Matabele'.* This was by no means fair: from the day the flag went up in Salisbury until the middle of 1893, Jameson did all he could to consolidate what had been gained and to keep the peace. He tried hard to avoid irritating the king: thus although he welcomed any Matabele entering Mashonaland to work, the doctor refused to allow white men to violate a frontier along the Tokwe and Umniati which had been agreed upon with Lobengula. Nor does a man who intends to launch a war cut down his police force to a bare minimum as Jameson did. On only one issue did he oppose Lobengula: the new Administrator made it clear he could not accept the king's contention that his impis still had the right to raid over the company's side of the border and to 'wash their spears' in Mashona blood. Only when they continued to do so in the July of 1893, did Jameson decide that he had to fight the Matabele and that he must do so before the seasonal rains set in. His decision was welcomed by the missionaries: 'the sword alone' they had told Lendy earlier that year 'will christianise the natives'.

Lobengula bears at least some of the responsibility for drifting into a war which could and should have been avoided. The king was a great deal more than an ignorant savage: he was a very shrewd and a very calculating man. Yet sometimes he fumbled badly in dealing with his problems: his attitude to the company's occupation of Mashonaland for instance seems now to have been the extreme of naïvety: his best course, one can see, would have been to accept the *fait accompli* (plus his salary) and continue to rule Matabeleland under British protection. But Lobengula came to cherish a notion that 'not having attacked him they (the settlers) were afraid of him', and believed he still held the whip hand. He refused therefore to restrain his regiments from raiding into the company's territory, and this meant of course that sooner or later the settlers in Mashonaland would have to fight him. Rhodes himself summed up the true position very well in a speech

---

* 'Labby' also printed the words of the 'Pioneers' hymn' whose first verse went:
Onward, Chartered Soldiers, on to heathen lands,
Prayer books in your pockets, rifles in your hands,
Take the glorious tidings where trade can be done;
Spread the peaceful Gospel—with a maxim gun.

made in Bulawayo a little later at the end of the triumphant Matabele war: 'the reason you came here', he told the victorious settlers, 'was that you knew your property in Mashonaland was worthless unless the Matabele were crushed'.

The real key to the situation was held by Sir Henry Loch, the British High Commissioner at Cape Town, for he could use his influence to restrain both Jameson and Lobengula from going to war. Loch was a prickly man whom Jameson with some justification once stigmatised as 'possessed of egotism and vainglory'. Certainly his actions in 1893 strike us now as being both devious and hypocritical. Loch had never relished the way the queen's boundaries had been expanded beyond the Limpopo by a commercial company: he firmly believed that this prerogative belonged to the imperial Government; accordingly he made up his mind that if war with Lobengula became inevitable it would be fought and won by imperial troops, so that he, not Jameson, would dictate peace terms in Bulawayo. And so when the war clouds gathered and Jameson recruited volunteers in Salisbury and Fort Victoria, Loch set to work reinforcing and equipping the Bechuanaland Border Police—an imperial unit—for the campaign.

The flash-point in an already tense situation was reached on 9th July, 1893, when a large impi began hunting down defenceless Mashona outside Fort Victoria; several white men's servants were killed in their masters' presence and crowds of refugees flocked into the European settlement. The Matabele *indunas* then demanded that the fugitives be handed over to them for slaughter although they considerately announced that they would kill them where there was no risk of contaminating the town's water supply.

How all this appeared to an Englishman recently arrived in Fort Victoria is disclosed in a letter which was 'reproduced in nearly every journal in the Kingdom and was made the subject of a stirring picture in the *Graphic*': 'you have, of course, heard', he writes, 'of the trouble we have had with our beloved next-door neighbour, Lobengula. Not content with the stipend the Chartered Company have been paying him for some years past, he must needs kick up his heels, and allow his warriors to approach our very towns in pursuit of the helpless, and likewise worthless Mashonas. An Englishman can, and does, stand a lot of cheek from a nigger, but when it comes to killing our own native servants in the precincts of the town—even we, who take our pleasures sadly, and our cheek soberly had to rise in our wrath, and chastise our dusky brethren. Of course, according to the gospels of "St Labby" and Exeter Hall we should not have done this . . . and then they would have swooped down in their tens of thousands and butchered man, woman and child.'

Yet when he first heard of the killings outside Fort Victoria Dr Jameson's instinct was still to parley with the Matabele. The settlers there he said 'had got the jumps' and there was no need at all for alarm; but when he drove down to the township on 17th July, the doctor was badly shaken by seeing the dead bodies lying on its outskirts. Early next morning he held an *indaba* with the commanders of the Matabele impi, and was much less inclined to be conciliatory. After an angry altercation which only ended at 12.30 p.m. Jameson ordered the *indunas* to withdraw their soldiers from company territory and he added something to the effect that if they were not out of sight by sundown he would 'drive them across' the Tokwe. He then sat down and notified the company that if necessary he would 'send out Lendy with fifty mounted men to fire into them'. Two hours later he instructed Captain Lendy to take a patrol of thirty-seven men to shepherd the Matabele towards the border and he went on to say that 'if they resist and attack you, shoot them'.

Jameson, in discussing the events which followed said that Lendy returned that evening and 'reported to me, then and there, that on the edge of the commonage he had come across about three hundred of the Matabele . . . that Sergeant Fitzgerald had been fired upon by them, but had not been hit; that he had then ordered his men to charge and then fire; that about thirty natives were killed; and that he had then ordered the retire, as it was getting towards sundown'. Naturally the doctor accepted the substance of this report, and next day he assured London that 'the Matabele fired first'.

This account of the ultimatum by Jameson, the apparent

acquiescence of the *indunas*, and their treacherous attack a little later on a small European patrol for a long time remained the accredited version of the incident which sparked off the Matabele war and no one took very much notice of Lobengula when he announced that Lendy had in fact been the aggressor and the first to open fire. But as Professor Glass has pointed out Lobengula's interpretation of the incident was probably more correct than Jameson's and there is good reason to believe that Lendy was stretching the truth when he said the Matabele had started the shooting. But it is only fair to note that at least some of the Matabele had not followed the doctor's instructions to move towards the border but had sacked another kraal only four miles from Victoria and were burdened with loot when Lendy encountered them.

One would very much like to put the clock back and discover exactly what did happen outside Fort Victoria on that afternoon of 18th July, but the consequences are clear enough. Three days later the settlers in the township presented the doctor with a petition which said 'unless active measures are promptly taken to effect an immediate and final settlement you must assuredly anticipate a certain number of people now here returning to the [Cape] Colony or Europe'. Jameson could hardly ignore this threat by Rhodes's pioneers to abandon the country: he would have to deal with the Matabele and he prepared for war. Fighting men were recruited in Salisbury, Victoria, and Tuli, with the company offering them each twenty mining claims and six thousand acres of farmland in the conquered territory at the end of the campaign. Major Patrick Forbes of the Inniskilling Dragoons assumed command of the combined Victoria and Salisbury forces while Goold-Adams concentrated his regulars at Tuli in the south and there he was joined by a soldier of fortune named Peter Raaff who had enlisted additional volunteers in Johannesburg (and so according to a reporter with a taste for puns had 'purged the town of its riff raff'). Jameson then began to spread reports of Matabele impis waiting on the Mashonaland border ready to pounce on the white settlements, while another company man, Johann Colenbrander, raised a similar scare on the Bechuana frontier. Rhodes for his part was anxious to avoid becoming publicly embroiled in what might turn out to be an unsavoury business, but behind the scenes he encouraged Jameson's efforts at warmongering and when appealed to for advice replied with a telegraphed 'read Luke XIV 31'. Jameson was fretting to go by the end of September, but he still had to obtain Loch's approval before beginning the invasion of Matabeleland, and Loch was disinclined to provide this *imprimatur* until he judged Goold-Adams and his imperial troops were in a position to get to Bulawayo first. And so he airily ignored Jameson's report of a border incident on 30th September, and only on 5th October, when Goold-Adams announced he was ready to move, did Loch seize upon another 'incident' this time in Bechuanaland, and give official permission for both columns to commence hostilities.

In the saga of modern Rhodesian history one comes across many unlikely events, and high on the list of them is the success which crowned Dr Jameson's advance on Bulawayo. By any standards his chances of defeating the Matabele were pretty low. He had mustered only six hundred and seventy horsemen for the campaign which was far less than the minimum number estimated to be safe by professional soldiers. Although some Matabele regiments would be drawn off by the troops under Goold-Adams and Raaff coming up from the south he could still expect to be opposed by anything up to ten thousand warriors who had never really known defeat. Yet no one in Mashonaland that October ever seems to have had any doubt about the outcome of the invasion. But then of course there never had been an army quite like Jameson's. It was essentially an amateur force, but it was commanded by regular soldiers and it was composed of extremely tough men; their morale was high, and they really loved the piratical little doctor who had turned soldier and, despite Forbes's official position, was directing the campaign. And Jameson was powerfully helped by several other circumstances. One was the way the Matabele fought: they preferred all-out assaults in the traditional manner to the far more effective guerrilla tactics, and each one they mounted was shot to bits by rifle and machine-gun fire. Nor were the warriors experienced in dealing with the white men's weapons: several accounts tell us that they would shoot at shrapnel bursts believing them to be devils. Moreover Lobengula seemed half-hearted about fighting and declined to lead his army in person. Finally, one of Lobengula's cousins who cherished a grudge against the king was engaged to lead the column to Bulawayo, and his advice about the tactics and dispositions of the impis proved to be of crucial importance.

The Matabele contested Jameson's advance first near the Shangani river close to the spot where Lobengula had executed a famous Mashona spirit medium who before his death was said to have prophesied 'at this spot where you kill me they [the white strangers] will conquer you. They will rule over you.' The revelation was fulfilled when the Matabele charged at a run into a killing fire of musketry; their attack was bound to fail and it failed very quickly. They made another assault on Jameson near the Bembesi river, 'I must say the enemy faced the machine-gun fire better than one could imagine', wrote one NCO with the column, but again Lobengula's crack impis were torn to bits by concentrated small-arms fire. This action was decisive. On 4th November, at the end of a remarkable cavalry *blitzkrieg*, Jameson's column marched triumphantly into the Matabele capital. He had got there eleven full days before the imperial troops from the south and the war was over; Goold-Adams with a far shorter distance to cover had been confused and delayed by the misleading advice of a 'liaison officer' thoughtfully attached to his staff by Dr Jameson, and Loch's hopes of the Imperial Government dictating peace to the Matabele were disappointed.

Amid the resounding applause that greeted Jameson's dazzling accomplishment the shrill denunciations of the Liberal press were hardly audible; but Olive Shreiner did focus some criticism on the Chartered Company's policy with a highly allegorical novel and William Blunt denounced the war as 'slaughter for trade'. Labouchere again drew on his rich store of invective and thundered about atrocities committed against wounded Matabele, but this fell rather flat after it had been shown that Jameson himself had attended them professionally, and even flatter when a highly respected L.M.S. missionary came out with comfortable assurances that 'no campaign has ever been carried out against natives with more humanity or consideration'. And while Sir Henry Loch found some outlet for his disappointment in repeated recriminations concerning Goold-Adams's lack of initiative, Whitehall had to make the best of the situation and reluctantly acquiesced in the Chartered Company taking over Matabeleland.

Dr Jameson after all had turned out to be right and the professional soldiers wrong and he was beginning to think of himself as an African Clausewitz. Mr Rhodes had won his second war and doubled the size of his country at a bargain price which, he allowed, was 'a mere nothing—about £100,000'. The two men that first week in November could hardly be blamed for beginning to think a trifle extravagantly of their capabilities. But they were both going to be disillusioned exactly a month after Jameson's victorious entry into the Matabele capital which Lobengula, in a Rhodesian version of the Great Fire of Moscow, had ordered to be burnt to the ground. The blow fell on the banks of the Shangani river.

THE SHANGANI PATROL

About a hundred miles above its confluence with the Zambesi, the Shangani river runs through a region of sombre mopani forest. These forests possess an odd quality of timelessness, and one feels they can have hardly changed since the first days of the Creation. In winter the forests' colours are the infinitely graded browns and greys of Rembrandt's paintings, shot through with thin shafts of sunlight like those which pierce the gloom of a Gothic cathedral. The thin straight trees are then quite bare of leaves, and stand out stark and separate from each other, looking rather like the shell-torn trunks seen in photographs from the First World War. Their summer foliage is green enough, however, to remind a northerner of beech woods but it throws very little shade, for in the heat of day the leaves fold themselves together like the wings of arboreal butterflies. An immense silence posseses the mopani forest, and very little there is seen to move. Human life comes rarely to these thicketed woodlands: the sandy soil supports little vegetation apart from the trees and some stunted grass, and tsetse fly flourish there. But innumerable game trails are threaded through the trees, and along them antelope come quietly every day to browse on the shrivelled foliage followed by the animals of prey which stalk them. An occasional clearing only seems to emphasise the monotony of the forest; all are about the size of tennis courts and seemingly identical— except for one near the Pupu spruit some four miles north of the Shangani river. This glade seems a thing apart. In it one is conscious of great solitude and the silence is strangely brooding there. Yet once for six mortal hours it was crowded with fighting men and filled with the din of battle. In it occurred the most heroic episode of modern Rhodesian history—the last stand of the Shangani patrol.

From dawn until noon on the 4th December, 1893, thirty-four

white men fought three thousand Matabele in this clearing. Not one of the thirty-four men in the patrol survived. Their story is treasured by Rhodesians rather in the way that the memories of Custer's last stand, and the Alamo are cherished in America. But the Europeans did not monopolise the courage shown that morning: here the Matabele, who had been humbled at the Shangani and Bembesi, found their temper again.

When Dr Jameson led his column into the royal kraal of Bulawayo to the jaunty sound of bagpipes in the November of 1893, it seemed that the Matabele war was over. It had been a charmed campaign which had lasted less than a month, and all of his hard-riding colonials were heady with their success. But the triumph could not be considered complete until Lobengula came in to surrender with the remnants of his impis.

But there was much more fight left in the Matabele than Dr Jameson or anyone else with him believed; the Ihlati and Isisba regiments were still intact, while the Insukumeni and Imbesu, although badly mauled, were of pure Zulu stock and their morale was good; and the young warriors of the Ingubu and Bambeni, although admittedly of inferior fighting quality, were rallying to the king.

While Jameson was taking stock of the situation in the smoking ruins of Bulawayo, Lobengula was only thirty miles away, camped out in the bush beyond Shiloh Mission. Magwegwe, his chief *induna*, several of the queens, his brother Ingubugobo, and a considerable retinue were with him. Five ox-drawn wagons had been used to bring up the king's possessions and treasure from Umvutcha, and he had refused to be parted from a cherished bath-chair which Rhodes had presented to him in happier days. And significantly several thousand warriors were concentrating between Shiloh and Bulawayo to protect their king.

Mtjaan, their commander, was a man in his middle fifties, a wizened veteran of many battles, but still a dogged, head-down fighter. He had just seen how the royal impis had twice been shattered by the white men's fire power and superior mobility, and he was determined that if he had to fight again to prevent the king's capture he would do so in broken country where his enemies could be ambushed. But there was a very good chance that Mtjaan might not have to fight after all, for Dr Jameson was genuinely anxious to avoid more bloodshed as well as the expense of a drawn-out guerrilla war. As soon as he had settled down in Bulawayo, Jameson therefore attempted to get in touch with Lobengula and negotiate his surrender. On the 7th November, his emissary, a Fingo tribesman named John Grootboom (whom Burnham was later to eulogise as 'one of the pluckiest negroes I have ever seen') succeeded in making contact with the king, and he presented a written message to him asking Lobengula to 'come in' to Bulawayo within two days and surrender. The request was stiffened with the threat that if he failed to do so, Jameson would 'send after him'. The king replied at once that he would indeed 'come in' and rather touchingly added 'where will I get a house for me as all my houses is burn down'.

But probably the king's reply was little more than a gesture which might gain time: by now Lobengula was not unnaturally extremely suspicious of British good faith; he had no intention of surrendering without proper safeguards; and his position was not nearly so desperate as Jameson thought. Admittedly the king had been bewildered by the failure of his crack regiments in battle, and physically he was in a bad way—he was so swollen with dropsy that he could scarcely walk. But increasing numbers of warriors were rallying to him, and an intact impi had been recalled from the Zambesi. Moreover, the rains were due to break at any moment and this would be certain to hinder the white men's pursuit if the king's entourage moved further north and sought refuge in one of the Angoni kingdoms beyond the Zambesi.

Only on the 14th November, when there was no sign of Lobengula actually coming in to surrender, did Jameson decide it was time to 'send after him'. All the information Jameson could get was that Mtjaan's army lay at Inyati, while the king himself was nearby, at Thabas Ikonya. A strong force of mounted men, commanded by Major Patrick Forbes, was therefore sent hurrying up the 'Hunter's Road' to disperse the impi and attempt the capture of the king. Forbes's men were drawn from the Tuli,

Victoria, and Salisbury columns, and none of them were very pleased to go. The rush down to Bulawayo had been exciting enough, but they would now have much preferred to return home, or to spend their time dividing up the campaign's loot or prospecting the ancient gold workings round Bulawayo. The troops in consequence were in a bad humour as they rode north, although they were comforted to see that the Matabele they passed seemed thoroughly demoralised. Inyati was occupied without a fight. No impi was found there, but some old women reported that Lobengula had headed further north.

Forbes believed that there was a good chance of intercepting the king before he got very far, and after garrisoning Inyati he took the remainder of his troops off on a forced march up the Bubi river to cut him off. Almost at once he ran into unexpected trouble: his men's confidence in him was drying up: they resented being placed on short rations and also showed very clearly that they disapproved of their commander's brusque attempts to improve discipline. 'Forbes called "C" troop men scoundrels because they collar sheep', runs a typical entry in the diary of one of the troopers after an angry altercation, and next day he notes that the 'men wanted to ask Forbes where they would get rations —what they were to do when a comrade was wounded, etc.— Forbes had general parade and finds that most are not disposed to follow him.' Here the trooper is referring to the inglorious occasion when Forbes called on those 'who are not satisfied with the rations and the way we are going on' to step one pace forward;— and he was then badly shaken to see that all except six of the men complied.* But he succeeded in turning the tables on the grousers for the time being by announcing that he still intended to continue the pursuit, if necessary with only the six volunteers, and in the end the whole column moved on. It was not so much that the soldiers objected to the danger of their situation, as Forbes chose to believe—it was rather they disliked their commanding officer's behaviour; Captain Spreckley made this clear later on when he said that 'the whole of the dissatisfaction was due to the way the men were bullied when they really were doing well'. But at the

* According to Forbes the number remaining in line was seventeen.

same time it must be admitted that the soldiers were becoming somewhat uneasy about the military situation too: the rains had begun, the mud was slowing them down, and now they were moving among large numbers of armed Matabele who were openly hostile. Commandant Raaff, a veteran officer with the column, became particularly anxious when he learned from some of these warriors that they were 'guarding the king's trail'; morale was not improved when he allowed it to be known 'that in his opinion the expedition was in a dangerous position' and ought to fall back, and several men were so shaken by his pessimism that they had to be sent to Inyati suffering from 'funk fever'. An older and more experienced man than Forbes might have handled the situation better than he did and put fresh heart into the soldiers; but he never seems to have realised that these irregulars were men who could be led but not driven. In the end however, he unbent and discussed the situation as coolly as he could with Raaff: he was emphatic that he had no intention of abandoning the pursuit, but admitted in reply to Raaff's expostulations that 'if we find that we are too hard pushed we can retire'. Raaff flared up at this and shouted 'For God's sake do not make use of the word retire. You do not know what it means. I do. I have been in it before. It will mean a panic and we will be cut up to a man.' It was strong language to use to a commanding officer, but perhaps Raaff's outburst can be excused when we remember that he was an old campaigner while Forbes was only thirty-two, militarily inexperienced, and also lamentably lacking in tact. But the bad relations that were thus established were indirectly responsible for the annihilation of the Shangani patrol, and the story of that disaster must be read in the light of the two men's antipathy for each other. In the end Raaff this time had his way: after some delay on the Bubi, Forbes reluctantly gave orders to withdraw and he brought his force safely back to Inyati. Only later did he learn that he had given up the chase three miles short of Lobengula's wagons.

New orders were awaiting Forbes at Inyati. He was to march to Shiloh, pick up fresh rations, and resume the pursuit.

At Shiloh many of the Salisbury men announced that they had

no intention of going on, and since they were volunteers, Forbes had to send them home. He drew rations for the remaining three hundred men, rode north again, and soon picked up the king's wagon 'spoor' in the bush. It was raining continuously now and when the wagons became badly bogged down Forbes decided to send them back to base together with some more dissatisfied troopers. His command had now shrunk to one hundred and sixty horsemen with two maxim guns mounted on 'galloping carriages'. He moved forward again after sending a message back to Jameson to say that if no contact had been made with the king by the time the column reached the Shangani river, he would march up the river bank to the 'Hunter's Road' north of Inyati, where he would expect to be re-rationed.

Forbes's flying column was still composed of men from all three of the original contingents; it lacked homogeneity and by now it was bedevilled by petty jealousy. Most of the men were volunteers: only the enlisted troopers of the Bechuana Border Police were under proper military orders. The Victoria contingent was furious that Forbes rather than their Major Wilson had been given overall command of the taskforce, while Captain Lendy and the men from Tuli were even more resentful of the way the old campaigner, Commandant Peter Raaff, had been passed over in favour of a comparatively inexperienced man like Forbes. Then there was the matter of the rations and ammunition that Forbes was carrying: 'I consider it a criminal mistake on the part of the OC', Raaff, who felt strongly about this, said later, 'to force men into country of which we had inaccurate knowledge', and on such a low ration scale, 'that the men were insufficiently fed.'

But the column, once lightened, moved now at a faster pace, and although the grumbling and a certain amount of straggling continued, the excitement of the chase began to possess them all: after the Bubi river was crossed on the 1st December, everyone was encouraged by increasing signs of Matabele demoralisation: large numbers of warriors were still drifting southwards, and to all enquiries they replied that they were making for Bulawayo to surrender. On the Gwampa, Lobengula's bath-chair was found, burnt out and abandoned, and now everyone was sure that they were close to the king. One of the scouts with Forbes actually seems to have ridden into a kraal where Lobengula was sheltering, and perhaps it was this narrow escape which made the king send an emissary to Forbes with a thousand sovereigns in a white bag and the message 'take this and go back. I am conquered.' Even now we cannot be quite certain whether this peace offering was genuine or merely another ruse to gain time by persuading Forbes to call off the pursuit. Either way it failed: the king's envoy was intercepted by two troopers who quietly pocketed the cash without saying a word to anyone. Their dishonesty was to condemn over four hundred men to death.

Beyond the Gwampa the chase was pressed even more vigorously. On 3rd December, the column passed many more armed Matabele moving south 'who bluffed us' a trooper admitted later, and he goes on to explain, 'little did we dream that their orders were that we were to be allowed to cross the Shangani river and then none of us were to be allowed to return'. But Forbes seems to have gained a foggy insight into the Matabele plans: he hurried his men forward in skirmishing order as they approached the river, although according to Lendy he wasted valuable time by calling a halt 'to allow one or two to have a shot at some buck'. About 3 p.m. on the 3rd, the column at last broke out from the bush into a narrow valley opening on to 'a wide open flat' that led down to the Shangani some five miles away. Forbes formed his men into a square for the final advance to the river just as skirmishers scouting ahead brought in a cattle herder they had captured near the river bank. By an evil chance they hauled him off for questioning to Raaff instead of Forbes. The cattle herder was quite prepared to talk: Lobengula, he said, had been delayed by his wagons and was only a mile or so away and probably still on the southern bank of the river; he then pointed to some shelters ahead, and said he had seen the king there that very afternoon. Raaff at once hurried the boy off to repeat this information to Major Forbes.

It was a most unfortunate moment to approach him. Forbes was still smarting from another unpleasant altercation with Raaff.

There had been angry words exchanged between the two men only a little earlier when Raaff had ostentatiously mounted guard over a large number of starving Matabele women and children who had come up to the column and asked for food. The implication was plain enough: for several days Raaff and his friend Captain Lendy had been loudly denouncing Forbes for failing to deal firmly with one of his troopers who had been accused of rape, and now they had exhibited their disapprobation again for the whole column to see. Forbes reacted by stigmatising Lendy as 'a nervous man . . . who invariably took the worst possible view' and by making a show of ignoring Raaff.

And so when Raaff came up to him with the cattle herder Forbes called over Colenbrander, his interpreter, and brusquely dismissed Raaff.

The herder repeated his story to Forbes and now he added that Lobengula was practically unprotected, had no wish to fight and was anxious to surrender. Colenbrander admits he was puzzled by the information: the reports of the number of men with the king, he said later 'were so contradictory, I did not believe anything'; and now he bluntly told Forbes, 'this native is lying to you'.

Forbes was not so sure, and to verify at least part of the herder's story he rode down to the huts where the boy had said Lobengula spent the night. Clearly it had only just been vacated, for he found 'fires were still alight and a number of cooking pots were lying around'; Forbes doubts were settled when a small boy discovered sleeping in the camp confirmed the herder's account that Lobengula had rested there the day before.

Forbes rejoined the column a little after 4.30 p.m., just as it was approaching the river bank. He was certain now that he would be able to capture the king next day, and after giving orders to set up a laager, he called a conference of his two senior officers. Wilson and Raaff joined him at once, and at 5 p.m. on that afternoon of 3rd December, the three men stood together for a few moments on the southern bank of the Shangani river.

Even now, after all these intervening years, it is still not difficult to see them again in the mind's eye. Forbes is hiding his excitement and is very much on his dignity; Raaff is frantic with suppressed rage; Wilson is quiet and restrained but wondering all the time if it would not be possible to do the others 'a shot in the eye' and capture Lobengula himself. Wilson had only twenty hours to live, Raaff would die in mysterious circumstances within the month, and Forbes would pass the remainder of his life regretting the decisions that were made that day.

They were an ill-matched trio. Forbes stood a little apart from the others. He was a fresh-complexioned man, thickset, and handsome—a typical product of Sandhurst. Undoubtedly he possessed many of the virtues of his class, and he had managed things very competently in the border dispute with the Portuguese three years before, as well as during the recent march on Bulawayo. But his peace-time service with the Inniskilling Dragoons had made Forbes an implicit believer in 'spit and polish' discipline and even his admiring biographer, while saluting his 'bulldog tenacity of purpose', had to admit that his hero sometimes exhibited 'a certain bluntness and simplicity of speech and manner'. It was this 'bluntness' which had infuriated his men during the last few days: one of them later confided to a reporter in Bulawayo that they were all 'agreed that Major Forbes showed himself fidgety, bad-tempered, abusive in his language and utterly lacking in tact and courtesy, jealous of advice or interference and forgetful of the fact that most of the men under him were pure volunteers, of equal status, of greater age and experience, and with large commercial interests in the country'.

The second member of the little group on the river bank, Commandant Peter Raaff, was just about as different from Forbes as it was possible for a man to be. Raaff was full of his own importance, talkative, and, according to Forbes, indiscreet. A butcher by trade, Raaff had nevertheless fought in many African campaigns: indeed he boasted of having survived the same number of Kaffir battles as his weight in pounds, which was one hundred and twenty. He was a man of paradoxes. Although of Boer descent, Raaff had yet succumbed to an almost maudlin admiration for the British way of life and he liked to believe that he had been assimilated into the tight caste of the 'establishment' in southern Africa. He had anglicised his first names, and during the Zulu war, had raised a unit which had won some renown as Raaff's Rangers. A year later he had even sided with the British during the First Boer War. Yet at the same time Peter Raaff had perversely developed an odd contempt for all regular soldiers: his attitude towards them came out in a letter written to his wife just before joining the column pursuing Lobengula, where he grumbled about 'The obstinacy, the asinine stupidity of the imperial army officers'—and Forbes to his mind epitomised all their faults. What is more surprising in Raaff's personality was the streak of vanity that ran through it: during the Matabele campaign, for instance, he surrounded himself with a group of sycophants who treated him with exaggerated respect; Forbes during the pursuit to the Shangani sarcastically referred to them as Raaff's 'staff', and they in return made him their especial target for contemptuous criticism. Raaff's conceit showed up in another odd way: after gaining a well-earned decoration for his services during the Zulu war, he never failed to add its magic letters to his signature, and even went so far as to paint over his butchery a sign which announced that its proprietor was 'P. E. Raaff, C.M.G.' Now, on the afternoon of the 3rd December, 1893, Raaff's preposterous *amour propre* had been badly wounded. When he joined Forbes and Wilson on the river bank he was feeling deeply humiliated at the way he had been spoken to only a short time before by his commanding officer, and when Forbes began the discussion with a recapitulation of the story given by the captured herder, Raaff tells us 'that as I already had that information, and in view of his [Forbes's] previous insolence, I turned my back on him and went away'.

But it was the third man on the river bank who would have particularly caught the attention of anyone watching them— Major Allan Wilson.* He towered over Forbes and Raaff, twirling great piratical moustachios, and fidgeting with irritation at the time that was being wasted in talk when the king was only a mile or two away. Wilson could have been the prototype for

* There is a curious confusion about the spelling of his first name; it often appears incorrectly as Allen, Alan, and even Alen.

one of Kipling's incomparable young Paladins of empire; no other white man in Rhodesian history has ever quite measured up to him. He was one of those very tough men who yet are the soul of good nature; none of his contemporaries ever have a bad word to say about him, and those who served under him and knew him best are especially effusive in their admiration. But for all his toughness Allan Wilson was nevertheless a little different from the usual pattern of Rhodesian pioneers: for one thing he was abstemious and drank nothing stronger than ginger ale; he was at his best with children; and he exhibited a remarkable consideration for other people's feelings. Indeed, one feels that if Wilson possessed a single fault it was a tendency to over-indulge his particular friends; all through the Matabele campaign he was determined that if there were any laurels to be gained from it the men from Fort Victoria would be the ones to wear them.

After Commandant Raaff had stalked off, Forbes and Wilson agreed it was just possible that the king could be seized before nightfall and after some cajoling Forbes gave Wilson permission to take twelve men across the river immediately and try to locate Lobengula's camp. Forbes's orders to him were rather loosely defined. If Wilson found the king, he was to attempt his capture, put him on a horse, and bring him back to the laager; should this for some reason or other prove impractical an attempt was to be made to keep the king under observation until the main column came up; at the same time (and this might well seem to contradict the previous instruction) Forbes gave Wilson a direct order to return to the laager before nightfall. On this last matter Forbes was subsequently quite definite, and all the evidence supports him: 'they all understood they were to be back that night' he wrote afterwards, and we know that when Wilson's patrol rode away one of its officers shouted to a friend to keep his supper hot for him.

It took only a few moments for Wilson to select twelve men from the Victoria contingent for the patrol. Men would later recall the chance incidents which had determined his choice of those who were to go with him and those who would remain behind in the laager; most of the horses were worked out by now and in general the best mounted men were chosen. As they saddled up and hurriedly checked their ammunition, five of Wilson's personal friends—all officers—went up to Forbes and asked for permission to accompany the patrol. Forbes acquiesced casually, and as their hands went up to their big hats in awkward salutes, he turned as an afterthought to shout out for Burnham and Ingram, who were both skilled trackers, to go along with them too. Raaff, standing apart with his 'staff' watched with dismay as the small party of nineteen mounted men filed into line and followed Wilson on his big white horse. Each of them was silhouetted in turn for a moment against the evening sky as they walked their horses down the river bank and rode on into the haze of legend. After they had gone Raaff turned to one of his officers: 'they will never come back', he muttered, and of course he turned out to be perfectly right.

It never crossed the minds of either Forbes, or Wilson, or of anyone else but Raaff, that by this time the initiative had passed out of their hands and had been firmly seized by the other chief actor in the coming drama—Mtjaan. Yet for the next few days it was he who dictated the actions of its entire cast. By 3rd December he had already hatched out the rudiments of a scheme to destroy the British column, and although it was not particularly well co-ordinated, the plan had the virtue of being loose enough to be pulled apart when the circumstances changed and then tied together again to fit them. In essence, Mtjaan had decided to use the king as a decoy, and although Lobengula had in fact been hustled away from the Shangani on 2nd December —the day before Forbes's column rode up to the river—his wagons were ostentatiously left in his last camp at Malenku, a few miles beyond. Mtjaan was confident that they would act as a bait to the white men. The cattle herder, who had told Forbes that the king was encamped nearby, was well aware that Lobengula was in fact a day's march further north; he had been merely carrying out instructions to mislead the soldiers if he got the opportunity, when he poured out his story to Forbes.

Mtjaan hoped that the wagons left in plain view at Malenku would entice all the white men over the Shangani; he then intended to cut off their retreat by seizing the crossing place with a strong force which had been shadowing Forbes for some time and to attack the column from the front and rear. Leaving half his force at Malenku, Mtjaan had already led the Ingubu, Ihlati, Isiziba regiments southwards past Forbes's column, and although this movement had been noted, the white men were quite satisfied that the warriors were merely 'demoralised Matabele' making their way back to Bulawayo to surrender. Mtjaan had got his impis close behind the pursuit column when it came up to the Shangani on 3rd December, and he was disappointed to see it halt for the night without crossing the river. The advance of Wilson's small patrol over the Shangani a little later disturbed him too: it meant that it would probably reconnoitre Malenku that evening and discover that the king had pushed on north again.

But Mtjaan also saw that he might be able to take advantage of this division of Forbes's taskforce, and he determined to overwhelm each section in detail. He directed the Ingubu to march downstream, cross the river before dark, and get between the patrol and Forbes's laager. He next sent runners forward to warn the Bambeni, Insukumeni, and Imbesu regiments, still concentrated in front of Malenku, to allow Wilson's patrol to pass through them as far as the king's wagons. Finally, the Ihlati and Isiziba were ordered to remain on the south bank of the Shangani during the night and to attack the British main column in the morning. Satisfied at last with his dispositions, Mtjaan himself then followed the Ingubu across the river to Malenku.

Meanwhile Wilson had led his patrol down stream for nearly two miles before coming to the place where the king's wagon spoor indicated that he had crossed the river. The Shangani here is nearly two hundred yards wide and its banks are high and steep. But there was only a little water running across the drift that evening and the patrol spattered through it without difficulty. Climbing the further bank the men bunched up into a tight little group and trotted off into the mopani bush. Although they were very much on their own now, every one of them was in fine fettle and perfectly sure that before very long they would pull off a coup which would be flatteringly compared with Hodson's dramatic capture of the king of Delhi during the Indian Mutiny thirty-five years before. And there was good reason for their confidence; thus far the campaign against the Matabele had been a walk-over, and there seemed to be very little fight left in the warriors whom presently they began to pass in the mopani; indeed the Matabele obligingly stood aside to let them ride by, and one of them even agreed to lead Wilson to the king's camp.

Back at the laager, Forbes was likewise indulging in some pleasant daydreams. He believed that although Wilson might locate the king that evening, he would be unlikely to seize him with the force at his disposal before nightfall. That triumph, Forbes mused, anyway rightly belonged to himself, and he resolved next morning to leave Raaff and Wilson in charge of the laager and lead a sortie of fifty men to effect the capture of the king. Having settled all this in his mind Forbes turned dutifully to the further questioning of the cattle herder, whose previous information had proved so useful.

He was appalled by what he now heard. For by this time the boy's resolution had broken down and he began to speak the truth: an impi of several thousand men, he told Forbes was shadowing his column and only waiting for a favourable opportunity to attack it. Quite suddenly Forbes realised that the hunters had become the hunted—and at once dropped all idea of carrying out his sortie in the morning. Unfortunately, he made no attempt to warn Wilson of the real situation but in fairness it must be remembered that he expected the advanced patrol to return by nightfall.

In any case, it was now probably too late; Wilson by this time had ridden several miles into the mopani. He was passing increasing numbers of armed Matabele, and Captain Napier, who had recognised their regiment was calling out 'don't shoot Bambeni', and assuring them that the war was over and that his commander merely wanted to speak to the king. But Wilson grew increasingly concerned as he rode on: instead of finding the king's camp just beyond the river as he had expected, he learned from the guide that it was still several miles ahead; his men's horses were beginning to knock up, and two of them—those ridden by Troopers Ebbage and Judge—were close to foundering. Coming to a sudden decision, Wilson ordered them to walk their horses back to the laager—and so two men were fortuitously saved from the slaughter which followed.

As the last light drained from the sky distant thunder could be heard and the wind was becoming gusty. It was quite dark when the patrol clattered out from the mopani at last and entered a wide vlei at the far end of which they could see some canvas wagon sails inside a low stockade. The patrol had reached Malenku. Mtjaan's trap was sprung.

Kicking his big white horse into a canter, Wilson led across the vlei, reined in at the stockade, and shouted in his great voice for Lobengula to come out and surrender. There was no reply, but he heard a soft voice inside whispering 'Father, shall I shoot now': and a quiet answer of 'not yet'. There was a moment's hesitation as Wilson's men peered through the darkness and the horses pawed the ground: then lightning flashes suddenly revealed dark forms and guns being levelled at them, and Napier turned with a warning shout of 'Major, they are going to attack us'. Wilson hesitated for a long moment: then he wheeled his horse round and rapped out an order to retire. The rain swept down as the patrol urged their tired horses into a gallop and followed Wilson back across the vlei and into the comparative safety of the forest. Not a shot had been fired. It seemed that the Matabele were still hesitant about starting a fight. Wilson dismounted beside an ant-heap to take stock of the situation and to confer with his officers. His orders of course were to return to the laager before dark and it was well past nightfall by now—yet he had also been told to keep the king under observation if possible and he was certain that Lobengula was inside the stockade. To return tamely to the laager would of course risk the king getting away during the night, and almost inevitably Wilson succumbed to an impulse which was nevertheless close to lunacy. He told his officers that he intended to spend the night in the mopani bush and rush the king's stockade in the morning. There was a short discussion and Wilson agreed that this might perhaps be construed as disobeying orders, but he pointed out that they could get a message back to the laager during the night and no doubt when Major Forbes understood the situation he would bring the whole column up to Malenku before dawn. And so it was settled among them without another word of dissent. The men dismounted and huddled together in the dripping forest and they hardly looked up to watch Napier and two troopers cantering back down the wagon trail with Wilson's message. There is some dispute as to its exact terms; Napier says that he was told to ask Forbes 'to be here very early in the morning with the rest of the column and the maxim gun' and Forbes in his account confirms that this was the message he received. But according to Raaff, Wilson merely 'asked him for a maxim gun and some more men'.

Wilson's men spent an uncomfortable night: it rained continuously and everyone was anxious about a sudden rush of Matabele through the darkness. They were concerned too about three troopers who had lost touch with the patrol during the hurried withdrawal from the king's wagons, and several hours went by before they turned up. Some of the soldiers managed to snatch some sleep while one or two sentries kept watch: presently the wakeful Wilson heard something which disturbed him—the faint sound of many feet squelching through the mud nearby. The implication was obvious: a large impi was moving into position between Malenku and the river: it seemed that Forbes might have a fight on his hands if he marched through the bush that night to reinforce the patrol.

But Forbes had not left his laager on the river bank. He too was spending an uneasy night. He had been fretting about Wilson's safety and was not at all comforted when Judge and Ebbage walked their horses into camp at 9 p.m. and told him that the patrol had ridden much further into the forest than he had ever intended. This was the first shock Forbes received that night: a worse one was to follow; Napier rode in through the driving rain two or three hours later and reported that Wilson had no intention of returning to the laager, but expected the main force to march and join him at once; he added that he had

Hoisting the flag at Fort Salisbury
Wilson's last stand, from a painting by J. P. McDougal

Nyanda and Kagubi shortly before their execution

experienced some difficulty in getting across the Shangani which was now beginning to rise.

Forbes found it difficult to control his indignation at Wilson's message. He burst out with 'Major Wilson is playing the fool', and, when he had simmered down, asked plaintively, 'why does Major Wilson not come back with his party . . . knowing that my orders were only to patrol for a short distance?' He had every right to feel resentful: he had now to make a most difficult decision and he knew very well that whatever he did would be seized upon by one or other of his critics. His first inclination was to send a curt message to Wilson ordering him back to the laager at once, and in this for once he had Raaff's support. Then the unhappy Forbes hesitated, for he realised that Wilson's withdrawal might well throw away the last chance of capturing the king (and what was worse might lay himself open to charges of timidity); in any case Napier was insistent that Wilson did not consider himself to be in any particular danger and kept pointing out that he had just ridden back six miles through the bush without being fired on.

And so Forbes next considered marching the column to the patrol's support after all just as Wilson had suggested. But all his regular army training, and every instinct in his body told him that to do so would be militarily unsound. Wilson, he explained to his officers, had not heard the cattle herder's revised story and it had put an entirely different complexion on the situation; 'we are surrounded', he went on wearily when Lendy protested, 'and it would be very dangerous to cross the river through deep sand and in the dark'. Tactically, Forbes of course was perfectly correct: the machine-guns would be out of action during the crossing and his column terribly vulnerable to a night attack; in Forbes's view it was much wiser to risk losing the patrol than to endanger the whole force. From the advantageous position of hindsight, however, we can see now that when he dispatched Wilson to hunt the king that afternoon Forbes should have moved his laager across to the north bank of the river in case the forward patrol needed support. It can also be argued that even if he had still pushed across the river that night towards Malenku he would probably have got his men to the other bank safely and have rescued the patrol; this, however, we cannot be certain of but it certainly would have saved Forbes from the censure that presently overwhelmed him.

But after spending two fatuous hours seeking and dismissing advice and then retiring to commune with himself, two hours during which he was watched all the time by the unadmiring eyes of Raaff and his other officers, Forbes at last decided on a third course, and it was just about the worst one he could have thought out: he chose to sit tight where he was until morning and only then take the whole column across the Shangani to Wilson's relief. Yet when someone pointed out that this would leave the patrol in grave danger for many hours, Forbes compromised by ordering Captain Borrow to march that night with a small reinforcement of twenty men and a maxim gun to Wilson's bivouac. This caused another explosion from Raaff. 'I remonstrated', he reported later, saying, 'Do you consider it right that we should break up a small force. We are too small as we are.' At this Forbes, according to Raaff, equivocated once more and replied, 'I shall send the men and not the gun.'

As Lendy says, this seemed 'a great piece of folly', and one cannot help agreeing with him. For one thing it meant that Forbes was asking twenty men to face a risk he considered unsafe for a hundred and twenty. And the addition of their few rifles to Wilson's force could hardly be considered an adequate reinforcement; it might even be an embarrassment if it came to a hurried withdrawal. 'This is the commencement of the end', Raaff remarked in his usual pessimistic vein when, at a little after one o'clock that night, Borrow and his men groped their way down the wagon spoor and across the swollen river to their deaths.

It took four hours for Borrow to make contact with the doomed patrol. Dawn was already streaking the sky when the watchful Wilson heard the sounds of approaching horsemen. It seemed like a wonderful deliverance at first; but Wilson's relief changed to concern when only twenty men emerged from the trees and Borrow told him that they made up his entire reinforcement and that he had not even brought a maxim gun. It was a grim moment, but in fact the situation was not yet absolutely desperate; the Matabele would probably not fight if no further attempt was made to capture the king, and it only needed a hard gallop to get the patrol back to the safety of the laager: Borrow, after all, like Napier, had come through an impi without a shot being fired, and the river might even now be low enough to cross. But Wilson's madness was still upon him: he determined to try his luck another notch. For what occurred next we can do no better than follow the account written by Burnham, one of the American scouts with the patrol: 'It had stopped raining,' he says, 'Captains Judd, Kirton, Fitzgerald, Greenfield, and Borrow gathered round Wilson. The first three were experienced colonials and Wilson asked each what he thought to be the best move. Kirton with a bitter smile said "there is no best move". Fitzgerald said, "we are in a hell of a fix—there is only one thing to do—cut our way out". Judd said, "this is our end". Borrow said, "We came in through a big regiment. Let's do as Fitzgerald says though none of us will get through." When they had all finished Wilson said . . . "let's ride on Lobengula".'

By any reasoning Wilson's decision was rash to the point of lunacy. The Matabele surrounding the patrol would almost certainly resist another attempt to rush the king's wagons. But such was Wilson's ascendancy over his men that all of them fell in at once with his suggestion that they 'hit the king hard', and use him as a hostage to assure their own safety. There seemed a thin chance that Wilson might be right (although considered dispassionately it was no chance at all) and in the raw wet dawn they cheerfully mounted their horses, pulled them into ragged line and went back across the vlei at a slow trot to Malenku.

The Imbesu and the Ingugu regiments were waiting for them at the wagons, while from the rear the Bambeni and Insukumeni were closing in for the kill. At the stockade Wilson shouted again for the king to come out and surrender. He was answered this time with menacing shouts of 'we are here to fight', and 'we will see if the white men are afraid to die'. For a long moment those words hung in the dawn air as the men of Wilson's patrol reined in their horses and stood immobilised in front of the stockade

like figures in a Western film which has unaccountably stopped;
then the spell broke and the actors all suddenly came to life;
an *induna*'s peremptory voice could be heard shouting and a
flurry of firing began from the Matabele hidden in the stockade
and the surrounding forest.*

The shooting was grossly inaccurate: only one trooper and two
horses were hit. Returning the fire from the saddle (and not
omitting to retrieve the ammunition wallets from the fallen
horses) the patrol withdrew in good order and regained the cover
of the forest without further loss. There Major Wilson rallied
the men, leaping on to the top of an ant-hill to direct them into a
defensive circle. Almost at once the Matabele came at them in a
rush—and their charge was shot to bits. Then the warriors fell
back through the trees and opened up a desultory rifle fire on the
patrol from close range.

The white men had very little cover; the position was plainly
untenable and Wilson now decided to attempt a fighting withdrawal to the laager. At a signal the soldiers formed up in a
rough square with the wounded and dismounted men in its
centre, and they moved slowly down the wagon trail. During
the next half hour they covered about a mile, suffering casualties
all the time, and it became clear that no one in the patrol would
reach the river alive unless the wounded were abandoned. That
suggestion was unthinkable: as Ingram said later, 'some of those
with the best horses might have got away, but they were not the
sort of men to leave their chums'. All they could do now was to
go on through the forest until they came on a reasonably good
defensive position and fight it out there with the Matabele hoping
that Forbes might still come up. That was the only hope, and
according to Burnham, Wilson now asked him if he would ride
through to the laager and impress Forbes with the importance of
hurrying up to their support. Burnham says he agreed to try,
asking only that two well-mounted men might accompany him.

* This is the generally accepted version about the beginning of the fighting on
the Shangani, but it is only fair to note that according to one Matabele account
Wilson's patrol entered the stockade, looted the king's wagons, and opened fire on
some warriors who remonstrated with them.

As they galloped off, Burnham turned for a last look at the thirty-four men left in the patrol; they were moving slowly down the track again with hunched up shoulders, firing as they walked, Wilson in the lead: the patrol was approaching a clearing close to the banks of the Pupu spruit. Only a few moments later Wilson threw up his hand and the patrol halted. Immediately in front, on the further edge of the glade, they could see a solid mass of Matabele. Mtjaan had formed up the Ingubu and elements from the other regiments in traditional 'chest' and 'horns' formation; now the 'chest' stood waiting in silence for the white men while on both flanks warriors were running through the trees to surround the patrol. After each side had watched the other for almost a minute in silence Wilson resumed the march. But now, as though concerned with ending their saga in a manner befitting his men's courage, he changed direction slightly to the right, and headed straight towards the *induna* commanding the Matabele 'chest'. The silence continued: those moments when Wilson turned the patrol's retreat into an advance might have been expertly stage-managed for their effect.

The Matabele 'chest' stood firm. In the centre of the glade the patrol halted, the horses were pulled in to form a rough circle, and the firing began. The last fight between the thirty-four white men and three thousand Matabele had begun.

Burnham and his two companions could hear the rifle-fire as they zigzagged their horses through the mopani towards the river. It was nearly 9 a.m. when they reached it. By now the Shangani was running in full spate and they had difficulty in swimming their horses across. On the southern bank they found the main column hotly engaged with the Matabele and Burnham realised at once that there was no hope at all of it ever moving to Wilson's assistance.

Forbes, Burnham learned when he galloped in, had broken up his laager early that morning and prepared to march towards the river crossing and Malenku. Yet even now it seemed he could do nothing right: there was some delay in getting the men moving and Lendy bluntly insisted later that 'we might have moved an hour earlier'. But probably the time wasted would not have affected the slow doom gathering around Wilson's patrol, for the Ihlati and Isiziba were waiting now to attack the main column and after advancing only half a mile it came under fire from the left flank. There was just time for the white men to form square and unlimber the maxims before the warriors came swarming down upon them from a wooded ridge. Machine-gun fire drove them off without much difficulty, and Forbes only lost five men wounded; but if they had done him no particular harm the Matabele had jolted him so badly that he at once abandoned all idea of continuing the march to Wilson's relief. For nearly three hours the column remained immobile in the open, and by now it does not come as any surprise for us to learn from one of Raaff's staff that 'although splendid cover for men and horses existed within twenty yards under the river bank . . . it was not moved until Commandant Raaff had remonstrated three times'. Forbes then pulled his men back to a better defensive position, close to the previous night's laager, dug rifle pits, and waited anxiously for the next assault which developed just as Burnham whipped in his lathered horse and whispered to Forbes 'it's all over, we are the last of the party'.

The Matabele delivered several more attacks on the column during the morning of the 4th and, although each one was beaten off, they prevented Forbes's men from sparing much thought for the lost patrol. Afterwards some of them recalled having heard rifle-fire across the river which continued until midday; it was followed they said by some scattered revolver shots and then silence.

As soon as it was dark Forbes sent Ingram riding hard for Bulawayo with a verbal situation report. On Raaff's advice nothing had been committed to writing lest the message fell into Matabele hands: Ingram was instructed to tell Jameson that the column had already expended half its ammunition, that Wilson's patrol must be presumed lost, and that Forbes intended to withdraw as arranged up the Shangani to the 'Hunter's Road' where he hoped rations and other assistance would be waiting for him. But as it turned out several of Raaff's officers persuaded Ingram to carry scribbled messages to their families, and all of them implied that Forbes was entirely responsible for Wilson's loss.

And Forbes had another piece of bad luck: when he reached Bulawayo Ingram was so overcome by his ordeal or his bad conscience, that he did little to refute the impression that Forbes had lost his head and had virtually sentenced Wilson's patrol to death.

*   *   *   *   *

Meanwhile, by the Pupu spruit the battle between the thirty-four men of Wilson's patrol and Mtjaan's impis had been fought and lost, and the last white man was dead. Four hundred Matabele had died too that morning. By any standards it had been an epic fight. The patrol was made of splendid fighting material; its men were of the type who, one imagines, in the Second World War would have all enlisted in the Commandos. They had come to this clearing in the mopani forest from the strangest places in the world and from widely different backgrounds. Of the thirty-four men, eight were officers. Three of the six NCO's were graduates of Oxford or Cambridge. Of the twenty troopers with Wilson, several were of Boer stock, one was a New Zealander, three came from British India, while another was the son of a well-known professor of music. But they all looked and acted alike, and all of them were very tough; they were a typical cross-section of the pioneers who had brought western civilisation to Rhodesia.

They were outnumbered by a fantastic margin, and it was a margin that increased with every minute as Mtjaan threw more Matabele into the fight. The story of this white men's last stand seems to be written more in the idiom of antiquity than that of modern times, for all the ingredients of heroic Greek legend are ingrained in it: the valour, the unflinching devotion, the feeling that nothing matters except their loyalty to each other, and death, and the seeking of it in a way that would become them. Wilson dominates and charges the atmosphere of this battlefield with his courage; throughout the fearful morning every single man in the patrol leans always on his resolution. His character for months had influenced and moulded them: now it supported each one in their last ordeal. Only once do some of these young men falter, but not for a moment does their leader fail them. Mtjaan himself has recorded the incident: early in the battle, he tells us, 'some of the white men ran to their horses to mount, but a tall *induna* with a big hat in his hand shouted to them and pointed to the men who were bleeding. They all got off and tied their horses in a ring head to head.'

We do not know the course of the battle in any precise detail, and what knowledge we do have is owed to Matabele accounts. There seems to have been a frenzied charge of warriors across the clearing at the beginning of the fight, but the attack withered away under accurate rifle-fire and throughout the remainder of the action the Matabele were content to destroy the patrol with long range sniping. According to one *induna* the struggle lasted 'from sunrise to midday' and this is confirmed by another chief who stated that it ended only 'when the sun was right overhead'. Although the Matabele rifle-fire was erratic, it caused casualties all the time and the white men's circle slowly contracted, and after Lobengula's elephant hunters—the best marksmen among them—came up, the end was hastened. The Matabele were amazed by the white men's stamina; 'they took a lot of killing' one *induna* said later, 'not like natives'. Even the wounded were seen to go on fighting: 'they lay', according to another report, 'on their backs and held rifles between their feet and fired', or they acted as loaders for their uninjured comrades. 'Shortly before the end', we learn from a different source, 'Major Wilson was seen with blood pouring from a wound and still fighting, and another wounded man loading for him.' Another witness remembered watching 'one white man with arms dropping and bleeding. He carried a belt of cartridges in his teeth from one who was dead to another who was still fighting.' And according to the Matabele 'the white men frequently called upon them to come closer and fight it out, but they replied "No, we have got you today and we are going to take our time on this job."'

Towards eleven o'clock there seems to have been a lull, and Mtjaan took the opportunity of calling on the patrol's survivors to throw down their weapons. They 'would have been spared if they had surrendered', he explained later, 'even if one man had stepped forward we would have let him go'. But there was no

thought of submission among the white men. Instead they seem
to have used the respite to scribble notes to their loved ones on
scraps of paper, and one feels sad that these last words never
reached their destinations. Then the Matabele heard the leader of
the white men say to the others. 'let us thank God who will
receive us today', and one of the warriors who was familiar with
European ways reports that now 'The white *induna* took off his
hat and the others stood with bared heads. They sang a chant and
some put their hands this way (clasping or crossing them) just as
they do in Victoria when the white man prays to his God for
strong medicine. We watched but did not fight.' Probably
Wilson's men sang a few verses from a hymn, but legend insists
that they sang the National Anthem.

Firing was now resumed by the patrol and it went on for
another hour; then it slowly died away and silence resumed its
possession of the smoke-filled glade. It was broken only when the
Matabele cautiously approached the circle of men and horses
sprawled out on the sand. The soldiers were not all dead and the
survivors, too weak to grasp their rifles, held off the warriors for
a little longer with revolvers before submitting to the final
killing. 'They did not die like Mashonas', one respectful Matabele
account continues. 'They never cry or groan . . . they are men . . .
they are not afraid to die', and we know from another particularly
poignant passage that when their time came the wounded men
lying silent and helpless on the ground 'covered their eyes with
their hands' as the assegais flashed down. According to one
account Major Wilson was killed by a warrior named Mdilizeiwa
Fuyana who thrust his assegai with such force into his forehead
that he was unable to pull it out.

One cannot be certain now which of the white men was the
last to die although there is some evidence that it was Borrow;
an enquirer learned that 'this man was so hard to kill that they
were going to leave him alone because he was a wizard'; but we
do know that before the end he found the strength to climb on
top of a nearby ant-heap and defended himself a little longer
before a shot brought him crashing down. Even then he struggled
to his feet to meet death. 'He was bleeding all over and had no

cartridges to shoot', Burnham was told later, 'so a young warrior rushed up to him with an assegai in his hand. The white man stood still and looked straight at him, so the warrior put down his spear; then he raised it again and plunged it into the *induna*'s chest and drew it out dripping with blood. The *induna* staggered towards him, and he threw the spear again leaving it sticking in the *induna*'s chest. The *induna* fell forward, dead. He could not raise his hands to pull out the spear.'

When it was all over the Matabele dragged their own dead into the encircling mopani. Then they came back to strip the white men's corpses and to pile them together in a bloody heap. Later, anxious to ingratiate themselves with the victorious Europeans, Mtjaan's *indunas* assured them that there had been no mutilation of the corpses; but neglect to do so would have been at variance with Matabele tradition, and other accounts speak of the customary ripping open of bellies to allow the escape of the dead men's spirits. After a struggle to withdraw the assegai which killed him, Wilson's body seems to have been untouched and was left lying a little separate from the others. There was a feeling among the Matabele that something magnificent had ended, and before they slipped away from the clearing an unusual tribute was paid to the dead: the warriors stood for a moment with arms raised in salute while Mtjaan intoned words which are still remembered with pride in Rhodesia: 'they were men of men', he said, 'and their fathers were men before them'. It was an epitaph which the Shangani patrol would have appreciated.

When all the Matabele had left the clearing a cooling breeze came up and set the grey gun-smoke drifting away through the scarred mopani trees, and presently a soft rain fell upon the dead men as though nature itself was mourning all the young lives which had been lost that day. Then the night settled down over the forest and the immemorial silence in the glade became once more complete.

*   *   *   *   *

Four miles away that night uneasy sentries went pacing round Forbes's laager, while their comrades tried to snatch some sleep.

They could hear the Matabele all about them, shouting and clearly 'very much elated', and everyone expected another attack at dawn. They were all greatly concerned about their safety, and Raaff so far lost his nerve that he suggested clearing out of the area that very night. Forbes, to his credit, insisted on holding their ground until daylight in case any of Wilson's men had survived and were able to make their way back to the laager. But in the morning he bleakly agreed to begin the withdrawal up the river bank.

'Forbes's retreat lasted fifteen days', a young soldier jotted down in his diary later that month in Bulawayo—'were attacked six times—lost almost all their horses . . . rain saved them from being annihilated. No news from Wilson's party—Forbes in disgrace—Raaff practically running the show.' These laconic remarks summed up the column's experiences during the retreat very well. When they eventually reached the safety of Inyati the men were close to the end of their tether and they had divested Forbes of his authority.

It is difficult to account for the way the column's morale fell to such a desperately low ebb during the retreat that Sir Henry Loch, the British High Commissioner at Cape Town, could write in a blistering report of 'the demoralisation of the force' which, as he pointed out had cracked up 'in the face of an enemy which there is nothing to show exceeded in numbers the patrol under Major Forbes's command'. One reason may have been the men's complete loss of confidence in their commanding officer; they had been very badly shaken too by Wilson's loss, as well as by the way they themselves had been checked by a single Matabele attack when they began marching to his assistance. Then again they went through a dreadful time during their retreat to Inyati: they were drenched with incessant rain and reduced to eating horseflesh; their boots were so worn out that many of them had to make do with ammunition wallets as substitutes; sniping from the impi which hung on to their flanks and rear continually harassed them, and they were constantly having to fight off attempts to overwhelm them. Ammunition ran low, and casualties slowly mounted. Worst of all, everyone was driven nearly out of his mind with fatigue and a glum smouldering anger. All their resentment slowly became focused on the unhappy figure of Major Forbes. This was unfair: their predicament was due just as much to his subordinates' misconduct as to Forbes's poor leadership, and Loch made this point very plain when he wrote that if the commanding officer 'failed to command the confidence of his officers many of the officers for their part failed in loyalty to their commanding officer.' But it is impossible not to feel a good deal of sympathy for the men's attitude. For Forbes put up a remarkably uninspired show during the retreat: his judgment and confidence seemed to have ebbed out of him. He was miserably aware that his soldiers wanted to replace him with Raaff; and the army convention which required officers to support their commander in all circumstances did not apply, he discovered, to irregular forces. Soon Forbes found himself being treated by Raaff's 'staff' and the other officers with the derisory respect shown by pupils for a schoolmaster who cannot keep order in class. Indeed, at every fresh crisis, they turned more and more for advice to his second-in-command, and Raaff seemed to have no compunction about dispensing it very generously.

The situation came to a head on the sixth day of the retreat. A particularly violent storm had compelled the column to halt in a bad defensive position and there it had been nearly overrun by a surprise attack. That night the men were near to breaking point. They 'felt very anxious', Forbes wrote later, 'and their anxiety was increased by two who could understand what the natives were saying', for the Matabele surrounding them in the bush were loudly discussing the final annihilating attack which was being prepared for the morning.

'The real responsibility of command and the safety of our column' Burnham conceded, by now 'depended more and more' on Raaff's 'judgment', and Raaff in this new crisis was convinced that there only hope was to abandon all but the strongest horses and the gun carriages, and to slip away in the darkness through the line of encircling Matabele. Forbes did not agree, for, as he wrote later, he 'was very averse to leaving the carriages as I did not want to do anything which would make the natives think they had got the better of us', but he goes on to say that after being 'convinced . . . of the extreme gravity of the situation' he acquiesced in Raaff taking over the command. Forbes in fact folded up, and allowed his responsibility to pass to a junior officer. Perhaps he had little alternative: the men by now were openly mutinous and would have accepted nothing else. Raaff took up the command with a flourish; he called the men around him to announce his plans, and according to one trooper, 'addressed us to the effect that it was a case of "devil take the hindermost" '. Their only course he announced bluntly lay in making a bolt for it during the night.

Forbes's humiliating 'demotion' has been tactfully glossed over in nearly all the written accounts of the retreat: Raaff died before he could give his own version of the mutiny, while Forbes covered up his chagrin by representing Raaff's assumption of command to be a mere exhibition of bad manners by an oafish colonial. 'I then saw Captain Raaff', he wrote later (reducing his successor, whether by accident or by design, in rank), 'standing on a rock and he began to address everybody; he began by saying we were in a tight fix and had to get out of it as best we could, and then went on to say what had been arranged. I said in a chaffing way to Captain Napier that the little man looked as if he'd taken charge, but did not stop him, as although he was wrong in doing it I thought it was only done in ignorance of etiquette, and that he meant it for the best.' Finch, one of Forbes's staff officers, similarly attributed Raaff's behaviour to sheer gaucherie when he wrote that after the decision had been made to get away in the darkness 'Raaff immediately jumped up and shouted "order men order" and gave out his orders. It struck me as a curious thing to do.'

Raaff from now on was indisputably in command, while, as one of his officers put it, Forbes was 'apparently content that it should appear that he (Raaff) was responsible for the well-being of the column'. Without question Raaff rose to the occasion very well: he rigged up dummies in the camp to resemble sleeping men, mounted logs on maxim carriages to look like guns, and lighted fires round the perimeter. To avoid noise during the flight, he ordered the throats cut of the seven dogs which had accompanied the column and he had the hooves of the horses he was taking with him wrapped in blankets. When all was ready he gathered the tattered force together, impressed them with the importance of moving silently, and led them cautiously through the Matabele lines. By dawn he had put twelve miles between them and the enemy.

After this nocturnal escape, everything seemed to go surprisingly well. For by now the danger was nearly over. On the 11th December, Lobengula called off his impis and soon afterwards the retreating men approached 'Hunter's Road', and made contact with Jameson's relief force. They had undoubtedly been very lucky; in view of their poor morale it is something of a marvel that any of them survived the retreat. The column had lost only one man killed and seven wounded, and surprisingly the war was over. The Matabele made no more use of the initiative they had regained: they had been so impressed by the way thirty-four men had fought that they hesitated to follow up their victory at Malenku with an attack on the much larger force in Bulawayo. In any case the warriors soon afterwards lost all their spirit when they learned that Lobengula was dead, and they came flocking in to surrender. It seemed to the white men of Rhodesia that Wilson's death had not been wasted after all, and the very manner of his death deflected all criticism from the Nelsonian disobedience which more than anything else had been responsible for the disaster. But the unhappy Forbes was still alive, and almost inevitably he continued to be loaded with all the blame. His reception by Rhodes and Jameson, who both came up with the relief force, was chilly in the extreme. 'How are you, Mr Rhodes?' Forbes exclaimed on meeting the column, but the great man, we learn, 'ignored that outstretched hand and turned away without speaking. . . . Presently, however, he greeted Peter Raaff with great cordiality.' Another observer who watched this same encounter could not help feeling embarrassed by it, for he tells us that 'Rhodes walked away from Forbes and the Doctor spoke to Forbes for some time. I think no one knows what he said. Was he (Forbes) accused, or was he blamed that Wilson's party lost their lives? But when Commandant Raaff . . . came, three hearty cheers went up for Raaff. This must have been very humiliating for Forbes—there were no cheers for him. Did he (Forbes) not also go through all the dangers, hardships, hunger, etc.? He was also in rags. I for my part felt very sorry for him.'

It was worse at Bulawayo. Raaff, we read, got 'a splendid reception for his plucky, well-timed and successful effort to extricate the pursuit column', but Forbes was greeted with hints that he had erred in judgment, and with veiled accusations of cowardly irresolution. It was a wretched end to the campaign for him.

Rhodes, of course, was quite prepared to capitalise on the valour shown by Wilson, Borrow, and their patrols: the story spelled out by these brave men exactly met his need for a legend to give colour to the new country he had founded. But at the same time any suggestion of failure on the part of the golden pioneers of Rhodesia was embarrassing and he was anxious to suppress all criticism of the way the pursuit of Lobengula had been handled. Unfortunately the demand for an inquest into the loss of the Shangani patrol was too strong to be resisted, and on 20th December, 1893, within a week of Forbes's column coming in, a Court of Inquiry assembled at Bulawayo. The court consisted of three members, with Goold-Adams presiding. His terms of reference were somewhat vague: Goold-Adams later explained that his real object was 'to show the friends and relatives of the poor fellows killed that some steps were being taken to ascertain whether anyone was to blame for their deaths', but at bottom the inquiry was intended to be a public extension of the quarrel between Forbes and his staff on the one hand, and Raaff, Lendy, and their friends on the other. If he was unable to prevent the court from sitting, Rhodes at least was able to hide all the evidence and disclosures presented to it behind a smoke-screen of censorship. But everyone in Bulawayo at the time knew a certain amount of what was going on, and there were plenty of rumours afloat to discuss and embroider. Norris-Newman, a well-known newspaper correspondent who had just arrived in Matabeleland to cover Jameson's campaign, tells us that in Bulawayo 'the principal subjects of discussion were the results of the Court of Inquiry into Major Forbes's conduct of the pursuit column, held in consequence of certain charges being made against him by Commandant Raaff and Captain Lendy', and he continues, 'From all I could gather it certainly seems a very unfortunate thing for Major Forbes that he alienated all his best friends by his dictatorial conduct during the campaign; and it is a fact that it needed all the administrator's well-known tact to keep matters from coming to an open outbreak between the commanding officer and Commandant Raaff, Major Wilson, and Captain Lendy.'

The court called for evidence from most of the officers who had survived the pursuit to the Shangani. Their accusations and counter-accusations, in laborious handwriting and yellowing with age, make strange reading today. Forbes in his account made no bones about feeling that Wilson had wilfully disobeyed his orders, and he was quite straightforward about his own position: 'Though I consider that the entire responsibility of Major Wilson's remaining out with his fifteen men contrary to my orders rests entirely with him', he wrote, he went on to say that 'I take all responsibility for sending on Captain Borrow and his twenty men', but added that he considered that 'responsibility at an end when as has already been shown they reported themselves to Major Wilson.'

Raaff's evidence was of course vital to the proper assessment of events by the court, and it was a little awkward when it turned out that he was too ill that Christmas week to write it down himself. However, he roused himself sufficiently to dictate his account of the Shangani patrol to a clerk in the presence of a staff officer. All through Boxing Day Raaff recited his evidence, and despite increasing weakness he got as far as his reaction to Forbes's decision to send Borrow across the Shangani late at night on the 3rd December: he then managed to dictate 'I remarked to Captains Lendy and Francis "this is the commencement of the end"', and added, 'Both these officers and myself saw the serious position we were placed in and did everything in their power for the welfare of the column for . . .' Then Raaff said he felt too faint to go on. This was the end of the Commandant's evidence: he died that same day.

Sir Charles Coghlan and the first Rhodesian cabinet

The Eastern Highlands

The cause of Raaff's death was given as 'inflammation of the bowels supervening from Bright's disease of the kidneys and a liver complaint, both of many years standing'. This diagnosis seems scarcely valid in view of the fact that Raaff had just withstood the rigours of a difficult campaign with nothing more serious than a pair of sore feet. 'Bright's disease . . . of many years standing', on the other hand is characterised by a slowly progressive kidney failure and lingering malaise rather than by sudden death, and it was no wonder that dark whisperings were soon heard in Bulawayo that Raaff had been got out of the way to avoid what Jameson referred to as 'washing some dirty linen in public'. The gossip that Raaff had 'died by the insidious hand of another' increased when less than three weeks later, Lendy, Forbes's other accuser, also died of inflammation of the bowel 'in consequence of a strain brought about while pursuing his hobby of "Putting the shot".'* This seemed an even more implausible diagnosis than the one given for Raaff's fatal illness, but on this strange note the inquiry into the loss of the Shangani patrol ended so far as the public were concerned.

We know now that the proceedings of the Court of Inquiry were sent down to Loch in Cape Town with a request that he suppress the evidence, and only publish the opinion of the senior military officer in the Cape as to whether Forbes had in fact been 'wanting in qualities of good leadership and had underestimated the enemy'. Loch forthrightly refused to do any such thing: Forbes's behaviour, he said, was the company's concern. But we learn Loch's views on the matter from a private memorandum written on 12th March, 1894: he exonerated Forbes to some extent from blame by finding that he had given clear instructions to Wilson on the afternoon on 3rd December to rejoin the column with his patrol before sundown, and that 'Major Wilson knowingly disobeyed this order', and Loch justified Forbes's refusal to cross the Shangani during the night after he had

* Mr P. Fletcher's diary notes that Lendy's death occurred in Bulawayo on 14th January, 1894, and refutes the generally accepted account that Lendy died later in the month while on his way to stand trial in England for the killing of a Mashona chief.

received Napier's report of Wilson's predicament. At the same time he was highly critical of the commanding officer's failure to laager on the north bank of the river in the first place. As to the replacement of Forbes by Raaff during the retreat, Loch refused to be drawn: he tartly commented that 'the manner in which the retreat was conducted cannot be said to reflect credit on whoever was in command', and he added a scathing note that 'the retreat degenerated into a complete rout'. His comments in short were a very blunt but scrupulously fair summing up of the causes of the Shangani disaster.

Very few people, however, saw Loch's memorandum. But although there was some suspicion that the truth about the loss of the Shangani patrol had been suppressed, the legend of its last fight grew with the years and added, as Rhodes had hoped, a new dimension to Rhodesian life. The legend lasted long after its remaining actors slipped away from the stage. Lobengula died only a few weeks after Wilson. He had travelled northwards during the fight at Pupu and was joined by Mtjaan in Pashu's country, beyond Kamativi. With him too was Magwegwe, the 'mouth-piece of the king' and several other faithful *indunas*. Lobengula was ill and depressed, and one day, probably on the 22nd January, 1894, he reminded Magwegwe of his promise given long before that 'when you die so shall I die'; the two old men then took poison together. Mtjaan buried the king with royal honours in a cave near the Malindi river and carried the news through the land that 'the sun has set in Pashu's kraal'. Mtjaan did not join the rebellion in 1896, and died as late as 1907; he is buried on the outskirts of Bulawayo beside the romantic road which leads into the Matopo Hills.

And Forbes? Forbes remained an embarrassment to Mr Rhodes, who arranged to remove him from the scene by sending him off on leave to England. Forbes left Rhodesia on 4th February, 1894, just two months after the massacre of Wilson's patrol. In London he was summoned to the War Office where his wounds were reopened by an intimation that because he had served in Rhodesia with irregular troops it was plainly impossible to give him any recognition or reward for the part he had played in adding Matabeleland to the queen's dominions. Forbes could never see where he had gone wrong during the pursuit of Lobengula: he defended his actions to the last, but people had no wish to be reminded of failures and possible injustices, and he never got a proper hearing. For a few years he served obscurely in Northern Rhodesia before being invalided home. He died in 1923.

As for Lobengula's impis, if they had been impressed by European valour, their victory by the Pupu creek had also exorcised them of their feeling of military inferiority, and less than three years later they engaged themselves in another trial of strength with the white men. They failed, and history has called their failure the Matabele rebellion; if they had succeeded, their rising would no doubt have been known today as the Matabele war of liberation.

9

REBELLION

On the evening of 20th March, 1896, a small party of the Chartered Company's African policemen, and their blanket carriers, were sitting round a camp fire at Umgorslwini Kraal in the hills above Essexvale. Presently a number of armed Matabele came out of the darkness and began a war-dance in the firelight; they were clearly in a provocative mood; after the tempo of their dance had quickened one of them ran up to the policemen screaming 'you are killing us; you are killing us; why don't you cut our throats and make an end to it?'

According to the police sergeant's report a *mêlée* followed during which one of the dancers and two of the blanket bearers were shot. The policemen themselves got away to Essexvale in safety, but one of their comrades at an adjoining kraal was not so fortunate: the dancing warriors had smelled blood and that night they caught and assegaied him to death. This obscure scuffle at Umgorslwini turned out to be the priming flash which set off the Matabele and Mashona rebellions of 1896; before they ended it was going to be uncommonly rough on both black and white Rhodesians.

The rebellion caught the European settlers by surprise: one pioneer with an inclination for metaphors wrote later that the outbreak 'came with the suddenness of a signal rocket from an unexpected quarter on a dark night'. Admittedly the settlers had been hearing occasional mutterings about Matabele grievances for some time—but had ignored them. They had never got round to realising that although they had conquered the Matabele in 1893, their victory had never really been stamped down. Nor, two years later, had they the slightest conception that for months past a web of conspiracy had been spun through Matabeleland with the declared objective of murdering every European living there. The rising had been planned to start when the moon was full on the night of 28th March, but with the blood-letting at Umgorslwini all the pent up fury of the Matabele was released and they lashed out at every white man, woman, and child they could reach. Three months later the insurrection spread to Mashonaland, and before it was extinguished more than ten per cent of the Europeans in Rhodesia were dead—a high loss for any rebellion, a loss which far exceeds those of the French colonials in the Algerian revolt or of the British during the Mau Mau rising; the best that can be said for it is that the casualties would have been very much heavier had the insurrection not begun prematurely with the *mêlée* at Umgorslwini.

The Rhodesian rebellion was at bottom a violent protest by old Africa against the encroachments of Europe. But unlike other nationalistic movements which have disfigured the history of sub-Saharan Africa it did not centre round an educated or Christianised figurehead but was fomented and organised by a representative of the ancient Karanga religion and traditions—a priestly personage named Mkwati. By 1896 he had come to symbolise many aspects of Bantu history to the Rhodesian Africans and each one of them was going to add up to a great deal of trouble for their conquerors.

Even now we know tantalisingly little about Mkwati; from first to last during the rebellion he remained a shadowy unknown quantity so far as the Europeans were concerned. Yet to the Africans he seemed the repository of all their history, and, what was of more practical importance, he was able to mould the grievances of the Matabele, Mashona, and Rozwi alike into a single offensive weapon. The story goes that Mkwati, a member of the Lewa tribe living in the Zambesi valley, was captured when a boy by Matabele raiders and grew up a slave at Bambeni near the Koce river; he served later as a soldier in the great military kraal at Jingen, and eventually joined the Mwari priesthood, becoming an official at a shrine near Inyati. Mkwati's reputation as a prophet gradually spread and his prestige was further enhanced when he made an advantageous marriage with the daughter of an important Rozwi chief. In 1893, after Jameson's whirlwind conquest of Matabeleland, Mkwati withdrew into the Matopo Hills, and later to the celebrated Mwari shrine at Thabas-zi-ka-Mambo where he was promoted in the priestly hierarchy to become the mouthpiece of its oracle. To some extent he was now able to fill the political vacuum left in Matabeleland by Lobengula's death, and certainly from now on the unrest among the Rhodesian Bantu began to crystallise round the figure of this single man. Profound currents had been moving among the Africans ever since the European occupation, but the burning grievances of the Matabele, Mashona, and Rozwi were only fused together when Mkwati decided to use them all in evicting the white men from the country. He went about his task very shrewdly and very diplomatically. One after the other he exploited Matabele hopes for the restoration of the Kumalo monarchy, the religious influences of the children of Mwari and of the Mashona spirit mediums, and even the prestige of the Rozwi chiefs, and he added all of them to the rancid hatred felt by the ordinary Africans for the Europeans who had seized their land and cattle. The rising accordingly was supra-tribal and supra-linguistic.

Our accounts of the Rhodesian rebellion have nearly all come from European pens, and they depict the rebel leaders as scheming witch-doctors who preached a creed of terror and savage massacre, so that today it is still easy to see them as monstrous voodoo figures. But Mkwati and the other oracles were a great deal more than that: they were highly respected representatives of the Karanga religion, who symbolised to their people the continuum of Bantu life and tradition. And however difficult it is for us to understand them in western terms, one must in fairness believe that they regarded themselves as the agents appointed to deliver the Matabele and Karanga from bondage.

Mkwati established his battle headquarters at Thabas-zi-ka-Mambo near the ruined stronghold of the last Rozwi Mambo in a maze of granite hills which are a replica on a small scale of the more celebrated Matopos. His shrine—the home of the oracle—can be seen there close to the Nsangu river and it is still marvellously unchanged: it consists of two caves connected by a very narrow cleft; supplicants gathered in the larger cave to communicate their requests through this cleft to the smaller chamber which 'the Mlimo' could enter unseen from the other side of the hill. Even today the cavernous shrine seems an evil, forbidding, place filled with old currents of superstition and sorcery, and it is not difficult to imagine the awe of the petitioners who came there or the sinister figure of Mkwati squatting in the further cave like a solitary *garu* and spinning the web of political intrigue which so very nearly altered the course of Rhodesian history. There is hardly enough room to stand up in his cave, but during Mkwati's occupation we know that it was screened off with a grass curtain and later made comfortable with furniture looted from the homes of murdered Europeans. Mkwati would summon Matabele *indunas*, Mashona chiefs, and descendants of the Rozwi Mambos to the larger cave, and hammer out with them the tactics of rebellion. The shrine formed a pulpit too, from which he addressed great gatherings of tribesmen who came to stand below and listen to the voice of the Mlimo issuing from a rock. They heard a different Mlimo in 1896 from the god of peace they had known before, for now day after day the disembodied voice could be heard ordaining them at a given signal to murder every European living in the country.

One must pause here briefly to consider the different elements of the Rhodesian past which Mkwati exploited when he inspired the Rhodesian rebellion from his shrine in the Mambo hills.

From a purely military point of view the eagerness of the Matabele to restore their monarchy was by far the most important. Their national life and ritual depended on a fountainhead of Kingship, and they were 'longing' they told a missionary about this time 'for a fire at which to warm themselves'. Yet there was no unanimity about who was to become the next king. Lobengula's two sons born during his reign were the legitimate heirs, but both of them had been sent to school in the Cape by Mr Rhodes. The younger warriors supported the claims of Nyamanda, another of Lobengula's sons who, however, had been born before his father's accession, while the tribal elders favoured those of a fourth son named Umfeleza. In the end some sort of a compromise was reached when a senior *induna*, Umlugulu, was recognised as the nation's regent. Selous in his book tells us that Umlugulu was 'the high priest of the ceremonies at the annual religious dance of the *inxwala*', and he was by far the best possible man to choose: apart from having a fine record as a military commander, ever since the disasters of 1893 Umlugulu had taken great care to keep a corporate sense of unity alive among the Matabele impis. He lived near Essexvale close to Selous who thought Umlugulu 'a very gentle mannered savage, always courteous and polite', and until the rebellion actually broke out the famous white hunter had not the slightest idea that he was one of the mainsprings of a national resistance movement.

By 1896 the Matabele had become consumed with bitter resentment: they were infuriated by the new administration's taxes, and the periods of forced labour it exacted from them; they hated the truculent and overbearing native police recruited by the company, and one chief was speaking for all his people when he later complained that these 'young men left their kraals, enlisted, and came back the masters of their fathers and their *indunas*, outraged the women, stole the cattle, and lashed their betters without rhyme or reason'; it became embedded in Matabele thinking that the rinderpest had been brought into the country by the white men, and they blamed them too for successive years of drought. There were many other grievances and from them all came tragedy.

Umlugulu had taken careful note of the way Jameson had denuded Matabeleland of most of its fighting men in the October of 1895 to take part in his lunatic raid into the Transvaal, and when they surrendered to the Boers at the end of the year, the old man decided that the time was ripe for rebellion. It was now that he allied himself to Mkwati and discussed with him how they could kill or drive away the white men. Long range, their biggest problem was to gain support for a Matabele rising from the Karanga *Holi* in the country, and this Mkwati was able to accomplish when he preached a holy war against all Europeans.

The next decision of the conspirators at Thabas-zi-ka-Mambo concerned the co-ordination of the outbreak: it was eventually agreed that the Matabele should be summoned to a Great Dance when the moon was full on the night of 28th March, 1896, and that there, as a sign of revolt to both the Matabele and Karanga, Umlugulu would proclaim Umfeleza king. According to some accounts it was also decided to infiltrate groups of warriors into Bulawayo on the previous day to join servants in the little town in killing all the Europeans when the moon came up.

Mkwati was only one of several Mlimo oracles preaching rebellion in Matabeleland during those first hot months of 1896, but it was he who played on the Africans' community of religious spirit and drove the Karanga and Matabele into a temporary alliance; it was he who gave wild form and growing dimensions to their grievances and who danced an exciting vision before their eyes of driving the Europeans out of the country once for all and resuming the old savage ways they had known before. Only in one region of Matabeleland was his millenarian preaching unsuccessful, but that failure was to prove of decisive importance: the Mlimo oracle living among the vassal Karanga in the Mangwe and Figtree area, moved perhaps by jealousy for the growing influence of the rival shrine at Thabas-zi-ka-Mambo, advised his people not to join the rising, and throughout its course they remained loyal to the white government. Their defection allowed the European settlers to keep the vital road to Mangwe open, and to bring up military help and essential supplies from the south. It must then be considered a supremely ironical footnote to the rebellion that the authorities in Bulawayo having persuaded themselves that this road had been deliberately left open to facilitate their departure, agreed a few months later to Burnham's suggestion that he seek out and kill the Figtree Mlimo, who was, although they had not grasped it, their only real African ally. After a cloak and dagger affair which was boisterously applauded at the time, Burnham claimed he had succeeded in shooting the oracle and was certain this would play a large part in ending the rebellion: this exploit was to become one of the Victorian's favourite tales of derring-do; but in fact this *geste* very nearly brought the Figtree Karanga into the rising against the white men; to make it now seem even more absurd the weight of evidence that has since come to light suggests that Burnham and his friend Armstrong 'faked' the whole affair for self-glorification and that the man they killed was an inoffensive peasant.

Once the Africans in Matabeleland had gone off on a rampage of murder after the Umgorslwini scuffle, Mkwati was quite unable to restrain them, and by the 23rd March the rising had become general. His plan to stage a simultaneous outbreak all over the country had become unstitched; the rebels had lost their chief weapon, surprise, but they still presented a very serious threat to the European settlers. They enjoyed a tremendous numerical superiority over the white men, being able to put fifteen thousand warriors into the field and of them at least two thousand were armed with modern breech-loading rifles, while many of the others possessed less sophisticated fire-arms. The rebels' morale was high, for their leaders had assured them that the Mlimo's magic would blind the white men or turn their bullets into water. Mkwati moreover had very rightly insisted that his warriors abandon the traditional spear-crescent assault across open country, and in 1896 the impis preferred to fight defensive battles from behind cover. 'The Matabele', one European volunteer lamented with gloomy insight on 8th April, 'are ever so much better than before, and we will have a great deal of trouble with them.' But if their tactics were good their military strategy defies rational analysis. Mkwati and his lieutenants never seem to have appreciated the vulnerability of their enemy's lines of communications, and they never put enough emphasis on guerrilla warfare.

Reading their accounts of the Matabele rebellion, one is struck by the European's bewildered surprise when it began. It does not seem to have occurred to them that the Matabele might not be content to remain peaceful second-class citizens in their own country. The handful of officials at Bulawayo may have spent two years sitting at rough tables in mud-hut offices, busying themselves over the appropriation of the Matabele cattle herds, the enforcement of a wage economy on their new subjects, or the patient explanation that two reserves on the Shangani and Gwaai had been allocated to those who did not want to work on European farms, but they had gained little rapport with their

subjects. And the settlers who scattered with such confidence
through the countryside, putting up trading stores or prospecting
or pegging out farms in the alienated territory had even less
insight into the way the African mind was working than the
company representatives.

The news of many murders among the Europeans in the
country districts came then as an appalling shock to Bulawayo
on 23rd March. The reports reaching the acting Administrator
with the grim regularity of hammer blows soon began to take on
a near hysterical tone: seven Europeans, he learns from breathless horsemen, have been killed and mutilated at Edkin's store;
nearly forty men and women are defending themselves in a
corrugated iron store at Insiza; the native police are deserting
to the rebels with their rifles; eight members of the Cunningham
family are lying dead at Claremont, and seven whites have been
killed nearby on the Tekwe. And still the reports kept coming in.
Nerves reached snapping point on the second night of the
rising when a drunken horseman galloped through the town
bellowing 'the Matabele are coming', and a crowd of women and
children poured into the Club, previously sacrosanct to men,
clamouring for protection. As rumour piled on rumour, hastily
organised patrols of brave men rode out of Bulawayo to make
contact with the rebels and gauge the extent and severity of the
insurrection. Selous was in one of them: he speaks of finding
'eight bodies lying on the ground about twenty yards from the
homestead at Insiza', and then with increasing shrillness of
coming on many other horrors. These patrols were small and
generally had to fight their way back into laager; they usually
arrived too late to do more than give decent burial to their friends,
but occasionally they brought in some settlers who had survived
the first few days of terror in improvised laagers. More than one
hundred and fifty Europeans were killed in that last week of
March as the Africans became caught up in a blind unthinking
savagery. Typical of this illogical blood lust was the explanation
given by one of the murderers of a party of whites killed
in a ferocious little operation on Mkwati's home-ground at
Thabas-zi-ka-Mambo; the warrior sounded genuinely puzzled

by his behaviour when he explained later 'we had no grievance against these white people', but that although 'these white people were our friends . . . we decided to get rid of all the white men in the country'.

The separate scenes of murder round Bulawayo in the March of 1896 are ghastly beyond description, and somehow seem all the more monstrous because of the way the victims were often approached with a pretended message or request for help to be followed by a sudden blow from a knobkerrie or the thrust of an assegai. The rebels' very success against unarmed men, women, and children fed their savagery, and the whole countryside reeled into a crescendo of atrocity which only ceased when there were no more whites left to kill. It is easy to sympathise with the survivors' overpowering wish for revenge; it found one expression in a piece of doggerel which ended with

'Tis not of blood he wants the spilling, he fights just for the killing,
'venging those poor souls unburied in the veld;
The black fiends never cared so why should one of them be spared?
First raise up the dead; *then* ask our hearts to melt.

Bulawayo, the key rebel objective, scampered into laager amid considerable confusion. Rifles were available for only four hundred volunteers, and horses for a hundred; many men armed themselves with an assortment of sporting guns, and they had to fight as infantry. For weeks on end the little town repeatedly touched the edge of disaster as the reconstituted Matabele impis closed in. Its people lived in a cloud of rumour and conjecture and every report tended to become distorted and exaggerated. The Europeans reaction was badly co-ordinated to begin with. No one was quite sure at first who was commanding the makeshift units which were raised; there seemed to be more colonels in uniform than privates, and inevitably there was a good deal of pushing and tugging in different directions. During the first week or two of investment Selous was sure that a determined attack by the rebels would have overwhelmed the town. For

Mkwati to wait was to lose but if the opportunity of decisive victory existed he was incapable of exploiting it; as days and then weeks went by without assault confidence slowly returned to the town; news reached it that during the first week in April the British Government had bowed to public opinion and decided to give armed help to the settlers, and when, towards the end of May Colonel Plumer led up a relief column from Mafeking and a hundred and fifty volunteers from Salisbury clattered into Bulawayo, it seemed that the rebels in Matabeleland had lost the initiative.

Not quite. Early in June Mkwati rallied them for another attempt to storm Bulawayo, and on the fifth of the month they were encamped in force on the Umguza river only six miles from the town. It was the throw of a gambler, and it failed. Next morning a force of two hundred and fifty European horsemen lashed out at the impi and scattered it with heavy casualties. From then on the tide turned in Matabeleland.

Mkwati's original design had been spoiled by its premature take-off and now it ended with the separation of his fighting men into two separate groups: Umlugulu's impis withdrew into the almost impregnable fastness of the Matopo Hills, while a hard core of *Holi* and Rozwi fell back on Thabas-zi-ka-Mambo. But the rebel position was by no means desperate. In the middle of June Mkwati triggered off a second rising in Mashonaland: weeks earlier he had summoned the more dissatisfied of the Mashona chiefs to his headquarters, assured them that most of the Europeans living in Matabeleland had been killed, and persuaded them that this was their opportunity to clear their own country of the hated whites; and to make sure they followed his advice a Matabele impi accompanied the chiefs when they returned to their kraals.

*   *   *   *   *

It seems scarcely credible that three months after the Matabele insurrection had begun the settlers in Mashonaland should still have been taken by surprise when the Mashona broke into rebellion in their turn: but they were even more adrift in complacency than the white men further south; they cherished a blind arrogant assumption that they had earned the Mashonas' gratitude by freeing them from the annual Matabele raids. They also despised the Mashona as a cowardly people who lacked any corporate sense of community: 'you only need a sjambok and a box of matches', the settlers would assure each other over their drinks, to 'take any Mashona kraal'.

The pioneers had admittedly been received in 1890 by the Mashonas without hostility, but when these *vasina mabvi** alienated land, demanded taxes, and were heavy handed in their dealings with those who did not pay them, the Africans' original complacency turned into enmity. As one old man later explained: 'We saw you come with your wagons and horses and rifles, and we said to each other, they have come to buy gold, or it may be to hunt elephant. They will go again', but he went on to say that 'when we saw that you continued to remain in the country and were troubling us with your laws we began to talk and plot.'

Isolated acts of cruelty by company officials and locally enlisted police kindled the resentment: Pollard, the Native Commissioner at Mazoe, was one of those particularly hated for their harshness. Although officially prohibited from inflicting corporal punishment, Pollard and other administrative officials often flogged the bewildered Mashona for misdemeanours which they did not understand; 'I was told', one settler wrote at this time, 'that if a boy will not work or tries to run away, the usual thing is to take him to the Native Commissioner and have him given twenty-five, and I found that the word "twenty-five" said in English to any of the boys was sufficient to make them grin in a sickly way—they quite understood what it meant.' A modern African historian has even gone so far as to assert, that 'the most important and immediate cause of the Mashona rebellion was no doubt flogging'.

And so in the middle of 1896 Mashonaland was waiting only for a spark to make it flare up into conflagration. Mkwati, who represented the old Rozwi élite and the great days of Monomatapa to the Mashona, provided that spark: he won two remarkable personages in Mashonaland over to his side, Kagubi and Nyanda,

* 'the people with no knees', one of the names given to the Europeans because of the trousers they wore.

both well-known spirit mediums, and persuaded them to incite a general insurrection. The first flames were kindled when two white miners were attacked and killed without warning at Beatrice; only a few hours later the Native Commissioner of Hartley was murdered at the nearby kraal* of a chief named Mashiangombe, while two prospectors caught by the Umfuli river were thrown to the crocodiles. Bernard Mizeki, an African evangelist, was dragged from his hut near Marandellas, and killed because the Mashona believed he was attempting to convert their children into white people. Within the week all Mashonaland had been abandoned to the rebels except for a few white laagers, the Dande, and the tribal areas of Mtoko and Umtasa (who mindful perhaps of the events of 1891 refused to join the rebellion). The story of murder and atrocity which followed in Mashonaland reads like a ghastly reprise of the events in Matabeleland: in one week a hundred and thirty white men and women were hacked to death by the Mashona who for the first time since the days of Monomatapa were tasting the strange flavour of military success.

Kagubi—'the lion claw'†—the organiser of rebellion in the Hartley district, was a tall, cadaverous looking 'man of about forty years of age', who had previously specialised in providing 'medicine' to ensure success in hunting; now he preached war to the death. We read of scenes at Mashiangombe's, his headquarters, which must have been as eerie as any of those dramatised for a Mau Mau film scenario: 'Kagubi and Dakwende', an eyewitness told a court later, 'arrayed themselves in striking feather caps and fastened horns upon their heads. . . . These two worthies would then rush into the centre of the people. . . . Then falling into a trance, Kagubi pretended to be "possessed" and gave out his orders as though coming from the ancestors whom they all revered.' Another rebel was at pains to explain after his capture

---

* Mashiangombe's kraal lay on the left bank of the Umfuli some thirty-six miles south-west of Norton. Kagubi had married one of the chief's daughters.

† The man's real name was Gumporeshumba; he was believed to be 'possessed' by the ancient Kagubi spirit, by which name he was usually called by his friends and enemies alike. Similarly, Nyanda was strictly the name of an ancestral spirit bestowed on its living medium.

that the tribesmen 'were all frightened of him', and added that 'he said every white man must be killed'.

Nyanda, Mkwati's other important lieutenant in Mashonaland, was a plump woman in her middle thirties who was 'a witch of great repute in the Mazoe district'. During his lifetime Lobengula himself had respected her as a powerful 'rain-goddess'. In the May and June of 1896, she prepared the tribesmen of Mazoe for the rebellion with rites even more bizarre than those practised by Kagubi. The people would be called at night to a bush clearing: while they danced themselves into a frenzy Nyanda prepared 'bullet-proof medicine' from such ingredients as zebra tails, grass, and animal fats: the warriors would then line up to place their hands in her concoction after which while muttering weird incantations she used it to mark their foreheads. Thus 'armoured' against the white men's bullets and sternly warned against looting (for efforts were made throughout the rebellion to prevent warriors becoming distracted by loot—which in any case was considered to be the perquisite of Mkwati, Kagubi, and Nyanda and the other leaders) they would march off confidently to begin the killing of Europeans.

Nyanda's first concern was to humiliate Pollard, the District Native Commissioner: it is said that, after being caught, he was compelled to act as her servant for some time; his hands and feet were then cut off; after that he was put to death and his body thrown into the bush 'some way off', for as Nyanda explained, 'it will stink'. Her next purpose was to overwhelm the Chartered Company's little administrative centre of Mazoe.

Few events of the rebellion have quite the same drama and breathless excitement as the fight for Mazoe which resulted and however often the story is told the escape of its white people still seems far beyond the range of human luck and endurance. The siege and relief of Mazoe also epitomises the blend of courage and misjudgment on both sides which was a recurrent theme in the Rhodesian rebellion, and this justifies our considering it at some length.

The Mazoe valley today has a haunted air about it that is a carthartic to imagination: in the east it is closed in by a forbidding line of brown mountains called the Iron Mask Range; on the other side the wooded confining hills are lower, and they seem a little less grim and inhospitable. Portuguese men-at-arms had once come trudging up the Mazoe valley seeking gold and they established a settlement at Dambarare where the valley opens out into a fertile plain which is now an immense citrus plantation. The Europeans in Dambarare had been overwhelmed by the Karanga in 1693, and now two hundred years later it seemed that history was going to repeat itself.

In 1896 the infant administrative centre of Mazoe was connected to Salisbury, twenty-seven miles away, by a rough road running up the valley through very broken country, passing numerous dongas, thick bush, and long grass; for the most part it followed the course of the Tatoguru river which it crossed by a drift eight miles out of Mazoe. This village at the time of the rebellion was made up of a cluster of pole-and-dagga buildings: near Pollard's hut stood a telegraph office run by an operator named Thomas Routledge, and the office of Mr Dickenson the Mining Commissioner; on the slopes of a hill to the south was a hotel and general store managed by a Mr Burton, and a cottage in which lived Mr Spreckley, the Mining Commissioner's assistant.

Above these buildings and rather more than a mile from Mazoe a few shanties had been set up round the Alice Mine on another stony hill. The mine was managed by Mr John Salthouse who lived in a comfortable cottage there with his wife. It had been one of the first mines to be opened after the occupation and it was worked by a gang of Africans under the supervision of a Cape coloured man named George. There happened to be four other white men—Faull, Fairburn, Pascoe, and Stoddard—living on the claim at the time, engaged in setting up a new mill.

Other Europeans lived nearby, but we need only concern ourselves with those who escaped being caught and killed on the first day of violence. Two miles up the valley a prospector with the rather splendid name of James Johnson ffolliott Darling was camped out at the Vesuvius Mine; and six miles further along the Salisbury road Captain and Mrs Cass of the Salvation Army and Mr and Mrs Dickenson had houses on adjoining farms. In addition an itinerant trader named Charles Annesty lived near Mazoe, but on this particular week he had gone off to the Darwin area with a load of merchandise strapped on to a pack donkey.

News of the first killings at Beatrice and Norton reached Salisbury on the 16th June, and that same day Dan Judson, an official of the Chartered Company's telegraph department, got through on the line to Salthouse at Mazoe and warned him of the outbreak; he also advised him to get the women at Mazoe into Salisbury for safety—advice which Salthouse chose to ignore.

An African policeman in Salisbury named Masvi heard the news of the rising about the same time, and he made a far more accurate appraisal of its significance than John Salthouse: Masvi deserted at once with his rifle and ran through the night to the Mazoe valley, and passed the news on to Nyanda. Early next morning Nyanda rewarded him with the command of all the prospective rebels living in the district.

General Alderson speaks with respect of Masvi's ability and says he was 'a short but sturdy young nigger', and there is no doubt that he had unusual energy and initiative. On the very day he took up his new command he began mustering a force which soon numbered more than a thousand men, many of whom were armed with modern rifles, while forty possessed horses. He provided them with a short course of elementary weapon training, and that same afternoon sent off several parties to hunt down Pollard, then on patrol and other isolated Europeans living in the district. Next day, on the morning of Thursday, 18th June, he led the remainder of his men towards the little European settlement at Mazoe.

On the Wednesday, while Masvi was drilling his recruits, Salthouse had at last awakened to his danger, and in the absence of the Native Commissioner assumed responsibility for the Europeans living in the Mazoe valley. After dispatching messengers asking them to rally at the Alice Mine, he telegraphed Salisbury with a request that the authorities send out a wagonette as he wanted to get three ladies living in the district into town. Then, assisted by Fairburn, Salthouse feverishly began to construct a rough fort at the top of one of the kopjes adjoining the mine. It was a makeshift affair which provided no shade from the sun, until according to Fairburn, they 'closed the top in as best we could with fallen timbers and rocks'. Although commanded on three sides by higher hills, the boulders which formed the perimeter offered fair protection against rifle-fire, and probably Salthouse did the best that was possible in the circumstances. But when the other Mazoe residents saw it they were full of criticisms and Darling tried hard to persuade them all to take refuge instead in a cave two miles away. Their attitude seemed a poor return for all Salthouse's hard work; in the end, however, they decided to make the best of it and by nightfall on Wednesday eleven white men, three women, and George the coloured man were all gathered inside his fort. After two sentries had been posted, the remainder settled down to get some sleep cheered up by a wire which had just come in to say that a wagonette was on its way from Salisbury.

Soon after daybreak on Thursday, when Masvi's assault force was already moving along the road to attack the laager, the wagonette drawn by six mules drove up to the fort. From it stepped John Blakiston, a young telegraph mechanic, Harold Zimmerman a store-keeper who had been told off to accompany him, and a coloured policeman named Hendrick. They had driven through the night without incident; they 'informed us', Salthouse wrote later, 'that they had seen nothing on the road out, but deemed it advisable to start back as soon as possible'.

While the new arrivals settled down to a good breakfast of 'ham and eggs and a tin of sardines each', everyone else began arguing about whether they should follow this advice: eventually they agreed that if the authorities confirmed by telegraph that the Salisbury road was still open the whole party would leave Mazoe at noon.

When breakfast was finished, Blakiston, Zimmerman, and Darling accordingly walked down to the telegraph office where Routledge was on duty. There was some delay in making contact with Salisbury and the advice they received was confusing: the journey to town they learned might by now be risky, and they were told that 'if we stuck together, we would be safe where we were.'

But by this time an unreasoning panic seems to have gripped six of the men left in the laager, and they had come to an extraordinary decision. 'Without waiting until word had come from the telegraph office', Salthouse reported later, 'Messrs Dickenson, Cass, Faull, Pascoe, Fairburn, and Stoddard started for Salisbury taking a donkey cart with them to carry their provisions', and he added bleakly that 'after they had left I sent a note to Blakiston at the telegraph office asking him to come up at once as I was alone with the women'.

No one has ever given a really satisfactory explanation as to why Cass and the other five men suddenly decided to clear off on their own. Perhaps they simply lost their nerve and made a bolt for safety, yet it still seems strange that two of them should have so lightly abandoned their wives. A more plausible explanation may be that they had become tired of the continual bickering over their plans, had made up their minds that further delay would be dangerous and decided to force a decision, and that they regarded themselves as an advance party going off to discover whether the road was open. But if this is the correct interpretation of their actions one is still left wondering why they did not travel together: for while Dickenson and Cass quickly took the lead, the other four men, delayed by the donkey cart and fourteen porters carrying their possessions, lagged a good quarter of a mile behind.

On receiving Salthouse's scribbled message in the telegraph office Blakiston, Zimmerman, and Darling left Routledge there and hurried back to the laager. They found Salthouse badly shaken by the six men's desertion. More hurried discussions following and it was decided that Salisbury should be informed of the changed circumstances, after which, since there was now little hope of holding the laager against a determined attack, that they would all go into town. Salthouse hastily saddled his horse and rode down to join Routledge in the office: contact was quickly made and this time Judson agreed that Salthouse should get the women out of Mazoe with the least possible delay.

Thoroughly alarmed by now Salthouse rode back to the fort and found that the remaining men had got into another heated argument about a suggestion that instead of going to Salisbury they should laager up in a better position at the Holton Store where food would be available. It was only after Routledge had joined them that they all agreed their best policy after all would be to keep together and leave Mazoe with the ladies. Now all their hesitation and despondency changed into a breezy confidence as brisk preparations were made for the journey; according to Darling 'the women were laughing and joking', as mules were harnessed into the wagonette, and they were helped inside. Then Hendrick jumped on to the driving seat, whipped up the mules and set off down the hill, followed by Spreckley, Darling, and Blakiston on foot. Salthouse and Routledge went off in the opposite direction intending to send off yet another telegram to say they had started, before catching the others up.

And so now at half-past eleven in the morning when Masvi's men were only a few miles away on the Salisbury road, the Alice Mine laager was abandoned and its tiny garrison had split into five separate groups which were all in imminent danger of being overwhelmed piecemeal. The six men who had left first had drifted into two parties a mile or two down the road; the wagonette was rapidly overhauling them; some way behind trudged three more men; while Salthouse and Routledge were crouching over the telegraph attempting to get in touch with Salisbury. But however absurd this dispersion may seem, we must remember that up to this time there had been no sign of any rebels in Mazoe and everyone was still expecting to get into Salisbury without trouble.

The inevitable clash with the rebels and disillusionment came a few minutes later. Dickenson and Cass were shot at once; then the rebels opened up on the men with the donkey cart and Faull was killed. By some miracle the other three were not hit and they raced off on foot towards the laager hotly pursued by the rebels; Hendrick on the driving seat of the wagonette saw them coming in time to wrench round his mules and whip them back along the road giving the alarm as he passed to the three men following him. All of them were saved when the rebels delayed to loot the donkey cart, and they got back safely to the Alice Mine. Someone scribbled a note reading 'Come at once, we are surrounded by Matabele, wire Salisbury for relief' and Hendrick ran down with it to warn the two men still in the telegraph office. He met them outside preparing to follow the others to town. Salthouse and Routledge did not wait to send anything more to Salisbury: they came back up the hill in a rush as the rebels' firing grew heavy.

It was now 1.30 p.m., and 'the savages', Darling tells us were 'approaching leisurely in open order, about one thousand yards from us', on three sides: only the road to Mazoe still remained open, and clearly the rebels would reach it soon. The Europeans watched them anxiously, crouching behind the meagre cover of their little fort. The sun was beating down on the iron-stone rocks which were unbearably hot by now, and the recriminations began all over again. They knew very well that their only hope now was to get a wire through to Salisbury describing their plight, and Routledge was the only one trained to do it. We cannot do better than follow Darling's account of the scene which followed: 'We told Routledge he must take the horse and go with the message', he writes, 'but he said he could not ride, and would not go without an escort. We told him it was ridiculous to talk of an escort when there were only seven men to look after the women, and that if he hurried he would get along all right, as there were still no niggers on that side. After some delay Blakiston said to Routledge: "Will you go if I go with you?" He said he would; so off they started. All this time the savages were coming on, and we were keeping up a vigorous fire on them. At first they advanced quite confidently. . . .' By now Blakiston and Routledge had reached the telegraph office safely and now as the women strained their eyes to see them reappear round the corner at the bottom of the hill, Darling continues, 'I was guarding on my right and too busy to look around when Mrs Cass said "there they come . . . one on horseback and one on foot". In the meantime some niggers had gone over to the store which lay in the path of the telegraph office, and presently Mrs Cass said, "Oh, they are firing on them—the horse is shot— he is down—no he's not, he's up again—the man is shot; they're down—no, the man is up, he's running, he's running hard. Oh, he's down, he's dead, he's dead!' All this time I could not turn my head, but was banging away on my right. I asked about the other man. "He's running towards the bush", she replied, "and they are firing at him." He disappeared and some more shots were heard, and we knew that he was killed. We were awfully sorry for them especially Blakiston who had willingly risked his life to save the rest of us.'

The little garrison by now had been reduced from twelve fighting men to seven, and they had no idea whether Routledge had got his S.O.S. through to Salisbury.

In fact he had: it read: 'We are surrounded. Send us help. This is our only chance. Goodbye.'* Dan Judson reacted to it at once. He hurried round to the office of Judge Vintcent, the senior official in Salisbury, and wrung from him reluctant permission to make an attempt to get through to Mazoe with four well-mounted men under cover of darkness. The tiny patrol rode out of the town at 3.30 that afternoon.

By then the rebels had closed all escape routes from the Alice Mine and had settled down to a savage fire fight at close quarters. Their shooting may have been wild, but no one could deny it was spirited, and they had plenty of ammunition thanks to the deserting police. Masvi himself took up a commanding position on a nearby kopje: 'he was behind a rock about 500 yards above us', Salthouse reported later, 'and was using his rifle with great skill and judgment. We could only see his head when he was shooting.' Darling also has something to say about Masvi's marksmanship, and after telling us that he was narrowly missed on several occasions, his account continues, 'as we seemed to be in an exposed corner, I told the three women to get further down under the rock. They behaved very well, and kept our bandoliers filled with cartridges. . . . There were seven of us firing, and we were put to the pin of our collar to keep the beasts away.' Darling tells us too that the rebels 'got into a patch of thick bush and long grass within one hundred yards of our positions, and one of them crept into a hut near us', and Salthouse admits 'things

---

* The original has been lost; another version reads: 'We are surrounded Dickenson Cass Faull killed for God's sake . . .'.

were looking horribly serious'. There seems little doubt that one solid attack now would have overwhelmed the laager, but for all his efforts, Masvi could not get his men to risk the final rush.

Even so it is a marvel that no one in the fort was hit by the heavy fusillade which lasted all through the afternoon. Darkness brought some relief: 'as night came on', Darling says, 'the firing slackened and finally died out, with the exception of an occasional shot'. But 'the night', he continues, 'was one long nightmare . . . of course, we expected a rush in the night, for the natives knew very well how few we were. . . . They were confident that they had us in a trap.' Salthouse occupied himself usefully by making grenades out of dynamite and tossing them at intervals outside the fort, but there was little for the others to do and the garrison's depression was not improved when some distant shots were heard and they knew that Charles Annesty had been caught and killed while trying to reach the precarious safety of their fort. And all the time the dreadful uncertainty about whether Routledge had got his message through to Salisbury was torturing their minds.

But spirits rose in the laager when the sun came up on Friday the 19th June, and only desultory fire was opened upon them. The reason seemed clear a little later when some of the rebels were seen looting the liquor in the store below; what the garrison did not know was that many of Masvi's men had moved up the valley to intercept any reinforcements that might be coming to their relief and that a large detachment of rebels was already waiting at the Tatoguru drift.

Early that afternoon, there was a new development: Masvi could be heard calling on his men for an all-out assault and then, amid 'great shouting' from the rebels, Darling tells us 'a small body of mounted men came into view . . . and up galloped five horsemen, two of them each carrying a man behind him'. It was Dan Judson's patrol and although its arrival reduced the immediate danger to the laager, Darling goes on to admit that 'we were very much disappointed at the size of the party, which was too small to allow us to get out, though, of course, it was of great assistance'.

Judson had an exciting story to relate. Having picked up seven additional men as he rode through the streaky moonlit night, he had rested his horses near Mount Hampden until daybreak on Friday. A good deal of time was wasted when Judson took the Lomagundi road by mistake, and by the time he had cut across country to the Mazoe road the horses were so badly knocked up that four men had to go back to Salisbury. About ten o'clock that morning the seven remaining men reached the Salvation Army farm at the head of the Mazoe valley; they had a breather there and then rode on in single file. There was 'a strange quietness pervading everywhere', one of the patrol remembered afterwards as Judson halted briefly at the Tatoguru valley which he 'pointed out might prove to be a veritable valley of death', and he suggested that any of the men who wished could still turn back. But all seven men went on. 'After going about a mile', one of them reported later, they 'had to enter a long stretch of very tall grass terminating in a perfect jungle in low-lying ground. It was a nasty looking place and Judson gave the order to gallop.'

They had ridden into the ambush which Masvi had set up at a defile known very aptly as 'the place of death', and they were met by a tremendous fire. But it was wildly inaccurate: only two of the patrol's horses were hit, and their riders got through by clambering up behind two of their friends. This was the worst Judson had to face and although the gauntlet of fire continued for the next six miles, he was able to halt long enough further along the road to make a hurried inspection of the corpses of the three Europeans who, as he later reported drily to Judge Vintcent, had earlier 'attempted to get into Salisbury, refusing to await the promised advice from you'; it was noted that 'the body of Cass had been carefully covered with grass and bushes', and this they presumed was intended as a mark of respect 'because he was a missionary'. A few minutes later the patrol galloped through heavy rifle-fire into the Alice Mine laager to be welcomed by wild cheers from its tiny garrison.

The story of the ordeal at the Alice Mine sometimes reminds one of another siege of Lucknow on a diminutive scale: there is the same confusion and wrangling at the beginning of an insurrection, the bungling attempt by the garrison to lift the investment, the attempt at escape which is checked, the first relief by an inadequate force, the second relief, and finally the successful breakout. And now Judson was playing the part of Havelock: his arrival had improved the situation, but he had brought in no provisions and hardly any ammunition, and the addition of seven men to the garrison was hardly sufficient to allow it to fight its way up the valley encumbered by three women. Nothing less than an additional reinforcement of forty men and a maxim gun, they considered, would enable them to break out, and once again their problem was reduced to finding a way of getting another plea for help through to Salisbury. There was no question of attempting to telegraph again, but that night, when the moon went down, Hendrick, Blakiston's coloured driver (with the promise of £100 if he got through), took a horse down the hill with a written message for Judge Vintcent.

In fact reinforcements were already on the way down the valley, although nothing like so many as had been requested. The men Judson had sent back with foundered horses had ridden into Salisbury on Friday afternoon with the news that the remaining seven troopers were going on to Mazoe, and on the way they had met Captain Nesbitt of the Mashonaland Mounted Police out on patrol with twelve mounted men. Without hesitation Nesbitt set off to Judson's support. He very soon met Hendrick and received a first-hand appreciation of the situation at the mine, together with Judson's estimate of the number of men required for its relief, but his patrol nevertheless rode on followed (to his great credit) by Hendrick. The night was pitch black but tocsin fires were burning all along the hills on both sides of the valley, warning the rebels of their approach. They galloped through 'the place of death' with only one man wounded and a horse killed and dawn was breaking when at last Nesbitt's patrol rode into the Alice Mine laager 'amid cheers repeated again and again'.

There were now thirty fighting men and three women in the little fort, and it was agreed they must attempt to break out when the horses had been rested. Salthouse was anxious to wait until nightfall but for some reason he was overruled; everyone, however, was delighted when, with a flash of inspiration, he decided to 'armour' Blakiston's wagonette by fitting iron sheets on to its sides. When he had finished six of the troopers' horses were inspanned to it; as Salthouse points out 'these animals had never been used in harness before, but after a little preliminary jibbing we started off'. The three women and the wounded trooper were helped inside the wagonette and the invaluable Hendrick again took the reins. The twelve mounted men formed themselves up in front and behind it, while the footmen marched on either side. It was midday on Saturday, 20th June, 1896, when they left the Alice Mine: they had twenty-seven miles to go and could expect to meet opposition most of the way.

For two miles all went well, but then at a donga they came under 'terrific fire', and their ordeal began.

Masvi had watched the little convoy moving off and decided it must be intercepted in force at the 'nasty looking' defile a little north of the Tatoguru drift where he had ambushed Judson. In 1896 we are told that here there was 'a swamp to the east, a small stream and a bushy hill to the west' and the rebels had made the passage still more hazardous by digging a trench right across the road. Today its appearance has altered: the road has been moved; the bush cleared, the grass cut down and the marshes drained. But it still remains an evil place; a heavy silence hangs over 'the place of death' and it takes very little imagination to set the horsemen and the wagonette coming down the slope on the far side of the drift and spattering through it again with bullets whiplashing past them.

Darling tells us that their ragged column approached the drift at 'a brisk walking pace', with the rebels harassing it with fire from the rear, and increasing in numbers all the time: Dan Judson said later that he estimated the enemy at a thousand and that about fifty of them were mounted; Nesbitt puts the number even higher, at one thousand five hundred. The Europeans now were near the point of complete exhaustion; they had marched for two hours under unremitting fire; their heads were aching with the constant din and their shoulders were badly bruised from fouled rifles. They were hungry and parched with a thirst which they had not dared to quench by stopping even for a moment at a rivulet they had passed, but one of the troopers tells us that he trailed his hat in the water as he went through and sucked the brim for the rest of the march. But so far only one man had been killed, and the rebels still could not bring themselves to rush the little party: some of them explained later that they had been vastly impressed by the way the dead man's rifle and bandolier had been at once retrieved, and even more by the way one of the women, Mrs Cass, was using a gun with good effect from the wagonette. Pascoe had distinguished himself too by clambering up on top of the wagonette and he was 'doing good work with his rifle'. Now at 'the place of death' they came under very heavy fire and several of the men and horses were hit. Even so the price they paid was marvellously low, and as the wagonette pulled painfully up the slope from the Tatoguru the survivors could hardly believe they were still alive. Indeed two of the advance guard, certain that all those marching behind had been killed, rode on by themselves into Salisbury. Three other mounted men kept their heads and a little later, after a brisk gallop, secured some vital high ground commanding the road ahead before the rebels reached it.

All things considered Nesbitt's column had got off lightly: only three men were dead and five wounded when they reached more open country beyond the Salvation Army farm. And the worst of their ordeal was over; there was even time at the Gwebi river to slake their raging thirst and to replace the wounded horses harnessed to the wagonette.

Night came down when they were still twelve miles from Salisbury and although the immediate danger was over now, Mrs Salthouse later remembered the next three hours as the worst time of all. No one had come out to meet them, and she says she 'began to fear that Salisbury was in the hands of the Mashonas and that the inhabitants had been wiped out'.

It was nearly ten o'clock at night when at last the survivors of the Mazoe patrols and garrison reached town and while two of them disappeared into the nearest bar, the remainder went on to receive a welcome 'as men and women returned from the dead'. Darling was by no means exaggerating when he concluded a letter to his father a few days later with 'it was the concentrated essence of several miracles that any of us came out of it alive'.

*   *   *   *   *

When the Mashona rebellion broke out, the settlers' situation in Matabeleland was becoming much easier. A little army of two thousand white men and several hundred 'Cape boys' and 'Friendlies' were concentrated now in Bulawayo, and General Sir Frederick Carrington had arrived to take overall command. Carrington was a heavily built, rather pompous man and, we are gently told, 'was now possibly somewhat past his prime'. He was a veteran of many minor African campaigns and in the past had gained a reputation as a bold cavalry leader. He also had the unusual attribute (in a soldier) of getting on well with Mr Rhodes, but he was ageing now; in contemporary photographs his eyes are hooded and behind the fabulous moustache one can see a pair of sagging cheeks. Certainly by 1896 he was disinclined to take undue military risks and this of course meant that he was also disinclined to take advantage of any mistakes the enemy might make, and he was not really the man to tackle the Matabele once they had gone over to the defensive. Indeed, after one or two setbacks Carrington was content to occupy himself with 'planning' and learning to ride a bicycle in Bulawayo, and he left the operational command of his little army in the more energetic hands of Colonels Plumer and Baden-Powell.

Plumer, after a discouraging foray up the Gwaai valley, decided that Mkwati's stronghold at Thabas-zi-ka-Mambo, where the Rozwi sixty years before had made their last stand against the Angoni, should be his next objective. It was stormed after heavy fighting in the July of 1896, and much of the loot taken by the rebels during the early days of the rebellion was recovered. Although Mkwati himself escaped capture, the loss of Thabas-zi-ka-Mambo was a serious blow; many of the *Holi* dispersed or surrendered, and conscious now that his designs for Matabeleland had folded up, Mkwati withdrew to Mashonaland where the rebels still held the initiative.

Plumer and Baden-Powell were now supremely confident that their scrambling victory in the Mambo Hills was but the first step in an easy campaign, and they immediately turned to deal with the Matabele impis holding out in the Matopos. All available troops were deployed on the fringe of the hills by mid-July and scouting parties (usually led by Baden-Powell) reconnoitred the rebel positions. But the imperial officers were shocked to discover what ideal defensive country they were entering. The Matopo Hills are not particularly high—all of them can be climbed comfortably within the hour—but they reach up very sharply and they possess an odd aura which seems to give them added stature. Many people who see the Matopo Hills for the first time refer to them without thinking as mountains, and it was typical that during the rebellion Weston Jarvis, an experienced traveller and competent military observer, perfectly seriously compared them to a more formidable barrier when he wrote that they 'rise suddenly from the plain, very much as the Rocky Mountains rise from the prairies of America'. The hills present extraordinary difficulties to assaulting troops; they are riddled with caves, and their slopes and dome-shaped summits are littered with enormous, grotesquely-balanced boulders; the hills are separated from each other by an infinite number of steeply walled ravines and crevasses which run in every direction and are packed thickly with gesticulating trees, stunted bush, and thorny creepers. As one officer reported glumly, this was 'most difficult and dangerous country'.

In the hands of a determined enemy the Matopos are practically impregnable. Baden-Powell was very soon lamenting 'what an impossible country it was for working in', and again that it formed 'a brutal country for military operations, but a splendid one from the rebels' point of view'. The Matabele moreover had no intention of becoming involved in any set battles but were content to fight on the defensive in the hope of wearing down the European troops. They very nearly succeeded: Carrington was so depressed after only a fortnight's inconclusive fighting that he seriously suggested pulling his little army back into Bulawayo until reinforcements could bring its numbers up to five thousand men.

The disadvantages of fighting in the Matopos were, however,

unknown when the imperial troops set up their base camp on the
fringe of the hills and assaulted the stronghold of Babyaan's impi
on the 19th July. The manner in which this blow was parried was
to be repeated so often during the next few weeks that the details
of each succeeding little battle hardly vary and can be conveniently
summarised here: there is the night approach led by Baden-
Powell who had spent the previous days reconnoitring the chosen
objective, the halt until first light near the enemy position with
the men huddled together for warmth, the brisk bugling which
alerted every rebel for miles, the constricting fear during the
exhausting rush up the side of a steep kopje with guns going off
from behind every boulder, the momentary exhilaration as the
enemy retired to the next line of hills, the sickening silent wait
which follows as a few more rough graves are dug, the wearisome
march back to camp, and the frustration of the troops because
nothing really has been accomplished.

Although to those of us who have lived through two world
wars (and the slaughters on gigantic scales at Passchendaele and
Stalingrad) the casualty lists of Carrington's troops in the Matopos
seem absurdly small, in 1896 they were taken very seriously not
only by the local commanders but also by the British public at
home. An attack on the rebels at Inungu hill, intended to syn-
chronise with the drive by Plumer against Babyaan's impi,
withered away when the assault column was ambushed at a place
referred to afterwards as 'Laing's graveyard', and a second
attempt on Inungu four days later was abandoned after the troops
had sustained casualties from severe cross-fire. On 5th August,
Plumer led eight hundred men against three thousand rebels at
Sikombo's and only succeeded in driving the enemy back half a
mile to another line of kopjes at a price which was considered
unacceptable. Three days later a night approach to Umlugulu's
stronghold across 'villainous ground' was so badly handled that
several sections of the taskforce went astray and it seemed to one
observer that 'a terrible disaster would inevitably have occurred'
if the rebel commander had not lost his nerve and fumbled at the
critical moment. Very soon hardly anyone among Plumer's
troops seemed to be enjoying the campaign in the Matopo Hills,

which was becoming a bloody stalemate, except his Chief-of-Staff, Colonel Robert Baden-Powell. Our image of 'B.-P.' has today been so obscured by the adulation lavished on him during his later years, that it is a little curious to observe him when he was an unknown but extremely ambitious soldier, and when the siege of Mafeking still lay three years ahead. Yet the Matopos campaign in a sense made Baden-Powell: it brought him military distinction, and nourished his talents for scouting which were later so rewardingly developed for more peaceful purposes. But already in 1896 Baden-Powell did not conform to the accepted pattern of the British officer. There was an odd theatricality about this spry balding man who savoured every new contingency with the assiduity of the chairman of a woman's vigilante committee. Somehow it was typical of Baden-Powell that after capturing Mkwati's staff he used it as a blackboard pointer when lecturing on the campaign and it may even have inspired the Boy Scout's staff.* His African troops somewhat irreverently called their commander 'Colonel Baking Powder', and this perhaps summed up his ebullience at the time as well as anything could have done. For he adopted that casual jaunty pose in the face of danger which was only to reach its full maturity at Mafeking. In camp he was for ever organising sports days and amateur theatricals, but the 'life and soul of the party' manner would be put aside when his audience went to bed and he would then spend the remainder of the night creeping through the hills (with remarkable agility and undoubted intrepidity) studying the Matabele dispositions.

Judging by his diaries in all these forays he only narrowly avoided being cut off by a band of rebels whose guns at the critical moment fortunately never failed to mis-fire. People were inclined to be sceptical about these escapades for 'Sherlock Holmes' was not the most popular of the imperial officers serving in Matabeleland, perhaps because he was inclined to startle his brother officers and men with novel pieces of advice about how to conduct themselves in the field: they were usually of the 'doff hat, don night-cap, and

*It was also typical of 'B.-P.' that during the siege of Mafeking, he produced 'Siege-stamps' showing his head, an act of *lèse majesté* which greatly displeased Queen Victoria.

loosen your shoes before sleeping' or 'never forget to dig a hip-hole' variety, but they were to be immortalised in print and assiduously followed by whole generations of Boy Scouts. On top of everything else B.-P. was a talented sketcher as well as a faithful diarist and correspondent: after the rebellion he worked up his papers into a highly entertaining and anecdotal book which sold so well that even today most people derive their knowledge of the Matabele campaign from it; and because of the book Baden-Powell within a few months so far outshone Carrington and Plumer that he was well on his way to becoming one of the best known men in England. But if his diary of 1896 paints a revealing portrait of its author at the time, sometimes one feels that the portrait is almost too good to be true. He is always the virtuoso ready to make sage comments on any situation or to put people right, and he takes enormous pleasure in the *nom de guerre* of 'Mpeesa'*—'the beast who never sleeps but sneaks about at night'—which he said had been bestowed on him by the enemy he outwitted so many times. According to the discreetly edited book he never makes a mistake: the unpleasantness when a court martial was threatened after he had ordered the execution of a rebel leader is studiously ignored, nor is a word said about the unfortunate occasion when 'the beast who never sleeps, but sneaks about at night' failed to live up to his name and succeeded in 'bushing' Plumer's column when he was leading it to attack Umlugulu's stronghold, a lapse which nearly led to its annihilation. Instead a devil-may-care insouciance sparkles from every page recounting this the 'best adventure of my life', but sometimes it seems just a trifle forced, and the sense of humour is often callow enough to be irritating: we find its author writing 'it was very funny to note the effect of shelling' (which he refers to as 'giving them snuff'), and that 'it's laughable to watch a Cape Boy prying into a cave with his long bayonet, as if to pick some human form of winkle from his shell, suddenly he fires into the smoke which spurts from the cave before him too late: he falls, and then tries to rise—his leg is shattered'. When not occupied with military operations, Plumer's energetic Staff Officer could still spare

* He was careful to avoid mentioning that its more faithful translation is 'hyena.'

time to concern himself with events in Bulawayo. 'Cannot a detective be set to work on the ammunition and prostitute question' he asks from camp in the Matopos, and goes on to add the characteristic pleasantry that this might be the subject for a cartoon entitled 'the whore and the cartridge'.

If the somewhat 'dated' Colonel Baden-Powell of 1896 is only dimly recognisable as the 'B.-P.' of later years, Cecil Rhodes presents himself at his best during the Matabele campaign. When the rising began he was at the very nadir of his fortunes: his reputation for integrity and infallibility had been irreparably tarnished by the failure of the Jameson Raid, and it had obliged him to resign the Premiership of Cape Colony and his seat on the board of the Chartered Company. Yet he emerges from his 'fall' more poised, more focused than before, and untouched now by fear because all that he was afraid of had happened to him. He was left now with only his 'north' and early in 1896 he travelled back to Rhodesia to be met there by the news that the infant colony was on the point of being overwhelmed by rebellion.

The country and its crisis seemed to give him new purpose: 'Since I have been in the country', he assured a friend, 'I have been a happy man', and Earl Grey noted, 'I have never seen him so well, or in such good spirits'. One can perhaps guess how his mind was working: his career after all might not be finished; another tremendous task could still lie ahead; the country which had been named after him would perhaps be saved through his efforts. In a strangely ebullient mood Rhodes hurried to Salisbury and threw himself into recruiting a relief column to march to Bulawayo; his exhilaration was undampened by the series of depressing reports that reached him about the alarming military situation in Matabeleland or the distasteful inquiry into the Raid which was followed by the convictions and imprisonment of Dr Jameson and other friends. Rhodes promoted himself on his own dubious authority to the rank of Colonel and although above everything he had previously dreaded physical mutilation he seemed now to take a delight in exposing himself to enemy fire. His new recklessness surprised his friends and set them speculating as to whether his fall from power had freed him from some subconscious bondage, or if he had taken seriously a recent somewhat flippant telegram from his brother which read 'You must do something to rehabilitate yourself in the eyes of the world, even if it is only a wound in the bottom.'

Rhodes accompanied Plumer's column when it attacked Mkwati's citadel at Thabas-zi-ka-Mambo, and from a newspaper correspondent's dispatch we catch a glimpse of him there 'unarmed, switch in hand, leading the hunt' at the beginning of the engagement. But when Rhodes with a few friends was trapped during the fight by a party of the enemy, he was the only one to keep his head: 'Don't get excited', he told them in his high falsetto voice, 'we must put on our considering caps and see what is best to be done', and a little later he led them all to safety. We see him in a different mood, however, when the fight is over and he gravely watched eighteen of Plumer's men being wrapped in ox-hides before burial: he seemed genuinely affected by the killings and by the sufferings of the wounded, and that night we read, he 'sat over the fire, his shoulders again hunched up behind him. He was not restless. He was thinking, gazing into the coals— the little flickering flames—silent. It was then that there came to him the idea of meeting the Matabele themselves, learning what they fought for, and trying to bring about peace.'

But for the time being Rhodes could do nothing to explore the possibilities of peace. Carrington and Plumer at this time could think only of the way they would finish off the war by sweeping the impis out of the Matopos. With increasing concern Rhodes during the next few weeks, watched them groping about the hills and regularly failing to defeat the elusive rebels. He soon realised that the imperial officers had only a foggy insight into the fact that they were fighting a landscape rather than men; he would listen carefully to Grootboom as the famous native scout told him what he thought was wrong about Plumer's tactics: 'the column', Grootboom explained, 'would march into the hills and have a fight, and then at night go back to camp. That is no way to fight the Matabele. You must sleep in the hills after the battle and keep on following the enemy from one kopje to another, and kill so many that you break his heart.' Rhodes was becoming increasingly convinced that Plumer's tactics were not the way to break any Matabele hearts. Although thanks to the ingenious use of the English language the war correspondents could point in their dispatches to a victory or two each week, he knew very well that all of them were victories which could not be used; the bulletins from the Matopos might exult that the rebels were losing ten men to every British soldier killed, but Rhodes realised that if the attrition were to continue on even such favourable terms, Carrington's army would cease to exist long before the last rebel was dead. In any case he was still—and always would be—that odd blend of business man and visionary, and he had to consider the effect of a prolonged campaign on the value of Chartered shares and the prosperity of Rhodesia, both of which were subjects very near to his heart, and more especially so since the outbreak of the Mashona rising.

And so on the night of 5th August, 1896, when Colonel Plumer returned from his unsuccessful attack on Sikombo's impi, particularly disconsolate because his friend Major Kershaw had been among the killed, the purposeful amateur took over the initiative from the irresolute professional and Rhodes prepared to open negotiations with the rebels 'on the personal'. He would need all his magic and courage if he were to succeed, but, as so often before, he was assisted by a fortuitous piece of good luck: on 7th August, Rhodes met one of Mzilikazi's widows, an aged woman named Nyamabezana. She was a person of some importance. More than fifty years before she had acted as Regent to a Swazi tribe which had fled across the Limpopo during the *Mfecane*. She had led it to the Inyati region and there made submission to Mzilikazi who not only accepted it but took her to wife. She was also the mother of Nyanda Kumalo, one of the most influential of the rebel *indunas*, and he saw at once that she would do very well as the intermediary he was looking for.

There have been several somewhat discrepant accounts of the circumstances which had led to the capture and use of Nyamabezana as a peace envoy: Weston Jarvis, Colenbrander, Baden-Powell, and several other men have all claimed the credit which more rightly belonged to J. P. Richardson. But however the meeting was initiated, it was undoubtedly Mr Rhodes who saw the opportunity it presented and exploited it.

Nyamabezana was a strange peace emissary: one of the troopers with Plumer's force has described her as a decrepit old crone who 'gazed upon us with lack lustre eye forcibly recalling to our minds Rider Haggard's description of the old hag Gagool in *King Solomon's Mines*'. Nyamabezana may have been as unprepossessing as he says but Rhodes always remembered her afterwards with gratitude and her photograph hung in his bedroom until his death.

With some difficulty Rhodes persuaded Nyamabezana to return to the rebel lines with a message inviting the *indunas* to bring their grievances to him and discuss ways of ending the fighting. A few days later the rebels signalled their agreement, and after the invaluable Grootboom had made the necessary arrangements, on 21st August Rhodes rode unarmed into the Matopo Hills to hold an *indaba* with the enemy. The three white men who accompanied him to this first *indaba* have all left their own somewhat dramatic accounts of the occasion, so that today it has an oddly spotlighted quality, and stands out sharply from the sombre background of the Matopos campaign. All are full of admiration for their leader: 'never was Rhodes finer than in his marvellous patience and determination to risk his own life rather than miss this great chance', commented one of them, although he agrees that the manner in which the parleys were conducted would have given the military men back at the fort and especially Carrington a severe attack of the vapours, while another diarist drily noted that 'Rhodes had strong arguments with old Freddie who didn't believe in these amateur methods'. But these 'amateur methods' worked and an armistice was arranged. Although negotiations with the Matabele bitterenders dragged on for some weeks (and were jeopardised on 19th September by the 'indiscreet action of a drunken trooper, and by some of the "friendlies" firing on several of Sikombo's men'), honourable terms for the impis' surrender of arms were eventually arranged and peace returned to Matabeleland. It had all been Rhodes's work: 'his patience', Sir Richard Martin wrote, 'was colossal'. In the end his self-control and courage had earned him the nickname given years before for very different qualities.

The Matabele campaign of 1896 had ended in 'a draw'; there had been no decisive victory. Yet this perhaps was the best solution possible, for as one European observer put it 'the natives think that it was not they, but we, who asked that hostilities should cease. Their pride has not been humbled. . . .' And both sides thereafter scrupulously respected the peace.

*　　*　　*　　*　　*

But rebellion was still raging in Mashonaland and it continued to do so for another year. From a military point of view the situation there was even more complex and difficult than the one which had faced Carrington in Matabeleland. To begin with, so far as the Europeans were aware, there was no supreme authority among the Mashona rebels with whom negotiations might be opened. Each chief had to be dealt with in separate and costly engagements. The Mashonas' experience of warfare had been derived from Matabele raids and it served them very well against contemporary European tactics: after the first ferocious wave of murders had expended itself, the rebels simply withdrew into fortified kraals and caves which had been stocked up with water, grain, and cattle. The task of evicting them was difficult in the extreme, expecially after the Europeans' transport was immobilised during the rainy season.

At the same time the settlers enjoyed many advantages over the rebels. They were much better armed and they possessed the old British virtues of fortitude in hardship and a will to win whatever the odds. They were certain that the tide of history was flowing their way and had no sense of moral isolation: the missionaries in the country without exception supported their cause, and the priests of Chishawasha Mission outside Salisbury even went so far as to regard the conflict as a war between Christianity and paganism. Above all, in this crisis the white settlers knew that they could rely on the Government of Great Britain to back them to the hilt.

That support came in tangible form when a splendid body of men recruited in Britain entered the country and engaged the rebels; it was organised on lines which were later developed in the Commandos during the Second World War, and with its arrival the issue of the fighting was no longer in dispute.

Some of the recorded details of the Mashona campaign of 1896/7 make gruesome reading, and it is not pleasant to think of the sheer misery experienced during those years in Rhodesia. One rebel stronghold after another was stormed, sometimes after dynamite had been used to blow up the mouths of the caves in which the Mashona had taken refuge. The troops by now had been hardened by the rebels' atrocities and no doubt the campaign called for hardness if it was to be won—just how hard is revealed for instance in such diary entries as 'there can be no mercy after this', and 'God, its awful; revenge we must have', and it is illuminating to note that the views of one minister of religion set the Administrator writing that this man of God, 'in spite of his success in creating finished choristers out of raw Mashona children, is so convinced of the hopelessness of regenerating the Mashonas whom he regards as the most hopeless of mankind owing to the irredeemable depths of bestial immorality into which they have sunk that he states the only chance for the future of their race is to exterminate the whole people both male and female over the age of 14'. Needless to say Earl Grey did not endorse so irrevocable a 'final solution'.

By the end of 1896, the authorities had at last recognised the importance of the 'spirit mediums' to the rebel cause. 'Kagubi', explained Grey in a letter to his wife, 'is the witch-doctor who is preventing the Mashonas from surrendering', while the Native Commissioner at Salisbury, wrote with assurance that 'If we capture Kagubi the war is over.' From now on the military began to exert increasing pressure on Mashiangombe's area where Kagubi and Mkwati had set up their headquarters, but both men escaped when, after three attempts, the stockaded kraal was stormed. They took refuge in the Mazoe valley with Nyanda.

Early in 1897 Mkwati, however, touched another chord of Bantu resistance when he made a last bid to win the war by appealing to the ancient glories of the Rozwi. The legitimate heir of the Mambos was Mudsinganyama Jiri Mteveri, and he still possessed prestige among the Rhodesian Africans. Jiri was induced to lead his followers into rebellion with a promise to revive the old Rozwi paramountcy, and he responded by putting out a good deal of propaganda among the tribes on the lower Sabi in which he said his ancestors would come to life again and join the fight. But Mkwati's hope of a Rozwi revival vanished when the now alerted authorities arrested the new 'Mambo'. Although after this setback Kagubi was able to remain at large for a few months longer, Mkwati was soon afterwards put to death by his own people at Umvukwes in order, they said, to avoid further fighting: one of his followers revealed later (in words that evoke the fate of other prophets) that 'they killed him in a curious way. They cut him to pieces while he was alive with choppers. They said if he was the man who was sent by the Mlimo they had better make sure he would not come to life again and make more trouble.'

It was a sad end to Mkwati, the 'Mlimo's mouthpiece', the man who had conceived allying the aspirations for a restored Matabele monarchy to the new militancy of the Mwari cult and the revival of Rozwi glory.

As the last embers of rebellion flickered out Kagubi made for the Mount Darwin district, accompanied we are told by 'dancing girls, eight sons, seven daughters and about twelve donkeys'. He was captured on 27th December, 1897, and brought in to Salisbury for trial.

Nyanda in the Mazoe valley would probably have remained at large for a good deal longer if Masvi, who all those months before had led the attack on the Alice Mine, had not succeeded in escaping to Mazoe from prison and concentrated European attention on her operational area. Somehow Nyanda made her way to the Dande, the skill she showed in avoiding capture contributing to her hardly diminished prestige. It came as the final blow to the rebel cause when she gave herself up, purportedly to save the lives of her followers, and was taken to join Kagubi and eleven other ringleaders of the Mashona rebellion in Salisbury gaol.

Nyanda, Boadicea-like, defiantly refused to plead at her trial, and somehow in prison she took on a new quality—dignity. It seems to have affected her gaolers: the wife of one prison official on the 29th December, 1897, wrote with sympathy of the captured rebels: 'poor fellows they murdered, burnt and robbed, but they were all under orders and look gentle and harmless enough, rather puzzled at it all. Amongst the rebels is the old woman witch-doctor, Nyanda. She is very old and very wicked according to our Christian ideas, but she is bitter because the white man has taken her freedom away and is trying to limit the wanderings of her people by rules and regulations . . . I feel sorry for her.'

We have a photograph of Kagubi and Nyanda taken about this time. Kagubi is lean and dejected, and his eyes are glazed with fatigue and defeat. But Nyanda manages to look both contemptuous and challenging as she leans back against the prison wall.

No doubt the prisoners were perplexed by the white men's long processes of the law which only ended in the March of 1898 with their conviction; they were hanged seven weeks later. It is almost impossible to read the account of their last days, written by a priest, without recoiling. He came to offer them religious instruction and baptism, and, although Kagubi at first refused to listen to him, he came to believe later that it might help him to avoid the gallows; somewhat pathetically he even offered his clerical visitor '10 head of cattle, his children, etc., if only I could get his sentence changed'. Nyanda on the other hand loudly and constantly rejected the priest's services; 'when told to keep quiet', he tells us, 'she refused and said she never would endure to be locked up . . . and began to dance and talk . . . called for her people, and wanted to go back to her own country—the Mazoe—and die there'. In a particularly gruesome part of the priest's account, we learn that his fruitful ministrations to her chief colleague a few days later were interrupted when Nyanda 'was taken out to the scaffold. Her cries and resistance when she was taken up the ladder disturbed my conversation with Kagubi very much, till the noisy opening of the trap-door upon which she stood, followed by the heavy thud of her body as it fell, made an end of the interruption.* Though very much frightened Kagubi listened to me and repeated he would no longer refuse to receive baptism. After he had made the necessary acts of faith, repentance, etc., I baptised him, giving him the name of the chief Dismas . . . Kagubi did not give the least trouble nor did he make any lamentation. He died . . . quiet and resigned, and, as I hoped, in good dispositions.'

After Kagubi had been pronounced dead the indefatigable pastor was able to record further success with six more con-demned men whom he 'had to rouse . . . from sleep next morning when I went to prepare them for baptism, and their end', and one can perhaps still sense something of their bewilderment as they were given the names of John Edward, Peter Canisus, Joseph Peter, Joseph Barnabas, Joseph Thadeus, and Joseph Thomas before being led to the gallows.

Such was the bizarre ending of the great Rhodesian rebellion, and a heavy silence fell now over the country. The fighting had cost 638 European dead and probably more than ten times that number of Africans, and it had put back the development of the country for many years. Just as the blame for the rebellion had been shared by blacks and whites, so this loss was common property. Yet something nevertheless had been gained from all its misery. The more pressing African grievances were remedied: a closer control for instance would now be exerted over punish-ments inflicted by district authorities while the system of forced labour or *corvée* was abandoned and replaced by a less vexatious form of direct taxation (although it must be admitted that for some time this was regarded as a demand for tribute rather than as a contribution to the communal welfare); the rebellions, moreover, besides compelling white Rhodesians to find new definitions for themselves had focused a spotlight on other legitimate aspirations of the Rhodesian Africans, and the fog of misunderstanding which had previously existed between the two

* It was said afterwards that the first two attempts to hang Nyanda failed, but after an 'informer' had explained to the hangman that he should first take away the snuff-box which rendered her immortal, she was successfully executed.

races was penetrated. The hatred experienced by both sides gave way to a new mood of reconciliation, and to a mutual wish for compromise and synthesis. The years of fighting had been a turning point in race relationships and from now on the future for Rhodesians—both black and white—was going to be totally unlike the past.

THE REFERENDUM

All through the afternoon of 6th November, 1922, the crowd had been growing outside the squat, iron-roofed, Bulawayo courthouse. Now at five o'clock it was calling for an official to tell them when the results of the referendum which had been held ten days earlier could be expected. Nearly everyone in the town was there. Except in front of the courthouse, the dusty streets were deserted and all business had come to a standstill; a gloomy store-keeper when asked how trade was going that day had answered with a glum 'one Chinaman'.

Most of the people in the crowd wore the red and purple ribbons of the Responsible Government Association, which stood for an independent self-governing Rhodesia. A fair proportion, however, sported the rosettes of the rival Unionist Party which wanted the country to join Rhodesia's giant neighbour, South Africa. The Unionist colours, if less lurid than those of the R.G.A. were also less comprehensible, and they had led Charles Coghlan to snort indignantly that the Unionist Party 'confound their impudence, has taken red, white, and blue, the imperial colours'.

A similar crowd had gathered that afternoon in the capital, Salisbury, to hear the result of this referendum which was to decide the destiny of Rhodesia, but the crowd at Bulawayo, the larger town, was more lively and obstreperous. It was mainly composed of European men and women, but a number of Africans were to be seen mingling with them, and they too were decked out in ribbons, whose appearance suggested that most of them were supporters of the R.G.A. 'The colour scheme appealed to them, for one thing', a journalist reported next day, and he went on to explain that 'since the fashion of the day was to wear a party colour, they were in the fashion. The more spectacular and the more fashionable red and purple of Responsible Government was with them the favourite blend.'

Presently the portly figure of Coghlan, the leader of the R.G.A. walked onto the courthouse verandah, and every now and then someone in the crowd raised a cheer for him. The excitement mounted when dynamite charges were exploded in the next block, for this was the agreed signal that the results had arrived in town and were being scrutinised. Then an expectant silence fell on the crowd as it settled down to wait for Mr Barnard, the Magistrate, to appear and read out the figures.

These white settlers had come a long way since the last embers of rebellion in Mashonaland had been stamped out twenty-five years earlier. They had brought English justice and peace to the country lying between the Limpopo and Zambesi, and because of their presence there, many thousands of people, who would otherwise have died from tribal raids and disease, were now alive; since the occupation Rhodesia's African population had grown from four hundred thousand to well over a million. These white Rhodesians were utterly different in spirit to their compatriots who had colonised the other British African territories. For one thing their country had not taken shape as a result of démarches presented by Whitehall to foreign powers: Rhodesia had come into existence only when Rhodes's pioneers outspanned their wagons at Fort Salisbury and began working the soil and prospecting for gold. These settlers were governed, not by the Crown, but by officials of a commercial undertaking. The conquest of their vast land and the burden of suppressing the rebellions of 1896 had not cost the British tax-payers a single penny. All the expense had fallen on the company's shareholders and on the Rhodesian settlers. What appeared to be unreasonable was that while their armed support was essential for the country's preservation, these settlers had no control over their governing body, and as other colonists of an earlier century had done, it was not surprising that they raised the cry of 'no taxation without representation'.

When peace returned to the great plateau in 1897 the settlers' first concern had been to pick up the threads of their lives again, which for the most part were associated with small-scale farming and mining. But then, during the past quarter century they had been able to marry the piled experience of Europe and its sense of the possible, to the Bantu virtues of patience, endurance, and easily aroused enthusiasm. They had combined the western discipline of the straight line and power over steel with the bridal opportunities of virgin Africa. Supported by Rhodes's generous backing the pioneers were enormous with energy as they forced the veld to conform to the English pattern. Everywhere the bush was hacked down and replaced by well-ordered farms and busy little tin-shanty towns. And slowly they had overcome their political problems. One was to find the means of substituting their own representatives for the Chartered Company's nominees as rulers of the country. The company had served them well enough at first, but in the new century it seemed to have outlived its usefulness, and many of the settlers had become sure that it was more concerned with the interests of its shareholders than with their own. So now they became involved in an acrimonious three-cornered dispute with the British Government and the company about the way Rhodesia should be ruled in the future, a dispute which was only settled by the referendum of 1922.

The first step was to gain legislative control. As early as 1899 the white Rhodesians had obtained the privilege of electing a minority of members to the Legislative Council, and during the next twelve years this number had been successively increased until in 1911 it exceeded the company's nominated members. But the Chartered Company still enjoyed unfettered executive power, and the political struggle during the next decade was concentrated on bringing an end to this anomaly and the substitution of a locally based administration.

During the Boer War and the First World War, however, the Rhodesians' fight for political progress was voluntarily suspended. Here in parenthesis we should note that in proportion to their numbers, the settlers' contribution to the British cause in both these wars exceeded those of any other parts of the Empire. It was a record which they repeated in the Second World War, and it was one in which Rhodesians still take pride. During the Boer War when the total white population was 10,000, 1,700 men joined up; during the First World War when the whites numbered

25,000 a quarter of them, as well as 3,000 African Rhodesians, enlisted. Their losses were heavy and when Winston Churchill as Secretary of State for the Colonies heard of the country's sacrifice, an observer noted that his eyes filled with tears. Implicit in the struggle to terminate company rule was the necessity to decide on the form its successor should take. Three possible choices lay before the Rhodesian electorate: they could opt to amalgamate with Northern Rhodesia and form a country stretching from the Limpopo to the Congo border which Coghlan scornfully called 'a new empire of Monomatapa'; secondly the settlers could attempt 'to go it alone' and create a self-supporting land-locked state; finally the Rhodesians could federate with the four states already in existence in South Africa. The suggested union with the 'black north', a project dear to Dr Jameson's heart, was the first alternative to be abandoned though it was briefly resurrected in 1953 when the ill-fated Central African Federation was formed. But federation with the south continued to be favoured by many Rhodesians, especially after Cape Colony, Natal, the Transvaal, and the Orange Free State combined to form the Union of South Africa in 1909. For the prospect represented many advantages to the small white Rhodesian population which was outnumbered fifty to one by Africans at the time, and which lacked the means to develop the country's natural resources.

In any case it had always been generally accepted that Rhodesia would eventually join a greater South Africa. The country after all had been colonised from the south, her laws were based on Cape law and her legal appeals were heard in Bloemfontein. Certainly Mr Rhodes had envisaged Rhodesia forming part of a South African federation, in which her British stock would redress the predominance of the Transvaal and keep the sub-continent within the imperial orbit. Admittedly President Kruger at Pretoria had long cherished a similar yet subtly different idea: he dreamed of a South Africa that embraced Rhodesia but was dominated by his own people: 'there shall be', he exulted, 'from Zambezi to Simons Bay, Africa for the Afrikanders'.*

* The term 'Afrikander' has now been largely replaced in this context by 'Afrikaner'.

Then with the ending of the Kaiser's war a new factor appeared in the great debate: General Smuts cast his influence on to the side of those who were working to bring Rhodesia into the Union.

Yet almost simultaneously a series of political events occurred which turned many Rhodesians against absorption by South Africa. For during the early nineteen-twenties the tide of Afrikaner nationalism was clearly beginning to run more strongly as General Hertzog followed President Kruger's example and began to preach a creed of 'Africa for the Afrikaners'. Rhodesians' distaste for developments south of the Limpopo increased too when the Union was shaken by a strike of European gold miners that soon blazed into open insurrection and which was only suppressed at the cost of many casualties. But above all it was the 'Britishness' of the Rhodesian settlers which most affected their attitude towards South Africa: as Coghlan told Churchill on one occasion, 'we in Rhodesia wished to have no part or lot (in the Union) which had apparently the constitutional right, and so far as the Dutch element was concerned, all the will, to cut us adrift from the British flag', and he went on to startle the new Secretary of State with an assurance that 'we will not part with the British flag without fighting'. For the Rhodesians sustained a loyalty to the Crown which was perhaps greater than that of any other exiled Britishers. At a time when the old belief in the virtues of everything British had scarcely been challenged, the Rhodesians had advanced into the future with their eyes always fixed on their forebears' past. In this loyalty Whitehall possessed a capital asset which no one living in the nineteen-twenties could have conceived would ever be squandered.

Added to their innate 'Britishness' and fear of being swamped by the 'Dutch element' of South Africa, the Rhodesians instinctively disliked the Union's native policy. It was more discriminatory than their's, and it was likely, they believed, to result in increasing bitterness between the races. In 1918 Vere Stent, who in 1896 had accompanied Cecil Rhodes to the first *indaba* in the Matopos, had counselled Rhodesians to keep out of the Union if they wished to avoid 'the pitfalls of racialism and the encroachment of Dutch disloyalists', and the same sort of advice was constantly being drummed into their ears by other men who had played important parts in the country's earlier history. Rhodes himself had laid down the dictum that there should be 'equal rights for every civilised man south of the equator', adding the explanation that his definition of a civilised man was 'a man whether white or black who has sufficient education to write his name, has some property or works, in fact is not a loafer.' This had been accepted as the basic criterion for enfranchising the Africans in Rhodesia, although it may be that many of their educated men and women were not sufficiently interested in politics to get themselves on to the Voters' Roll, and in the referendum of 1922 it was estimated that out of a total poll of 14,826, only sixty votes were cast by Africans.

A disinterest in politics was perhaps only part of the Rhodesian Africans' more general apathy. Their roots had been torn out by the rebellion, and afterwards their attitudes were scarcely more than a passive acceptance of the *status quo*. There was a tendency among them to abandon the ancient Karanga religion and adopt instead the faith of the stronger race which had defeated them. For paradoxically the results of Christian proselytism had been made more promising by an armed rising whose avowed objective was to deny Rhodesia the blessings of Christianity. The missionaries' prestige had been vastly increased by the white men's victory and they became the real rulers of many rural areas in the country. One of them pointed out that 'belief in superstition and witchcraft has received a severe blow' by the African defeat, while another missionary rejoiced that 'the storm which has just blown over, so far from having proved the destruction of Christianity in Mashonaland, has in no slight degree aided its propagation'.

Admittedly some members of the old African ruling families attempted to revive their countrymen's interest in Rhodesian politics and for a time it seemed that Lobengula's sons would lead another national reaction to European rule. But Njube, the generally accepted heir to the Matabele monarchy died in 1910, and his brother Ngubyena drifted into a sullen melancholia and withdrew from the leadership, while Nyamanda, the most promising of them all, became disillusioned after his failure to convince the delegates at the Versailles Peace Conference of the necessity of creating a Matabele homeland.

Even before the end of the Great War the white settlers in Rhodesia had begun to divide themselves in two factions: the Unionists who favoured joining South Africa and the Rhodesia Government Association which advocated independence.

The latter body, the R.G.A., was led by a successful Bulawayo lawyer named Charles Coghlan. Of Irish stock, Coghlan was born in South Africa in 1863 and only came to Rhodesia towards the end of the Boer War. He worked up a prosperous practice and had little wish to embroil himself in local politics. But Coghlan had a flair for reducing problems to their simplest forms, and in 1908 he was induced to enter the Legislative Council. From then on the supporters of Responsible Government had found their chief advocate, Coghlan became a statesman *malgré lui*, and in the steady flow of his irrefragable (though harshly delivered) logic the Rhodesian quest for independence found its accompanist.

Coghlan's biographer admits that his hero 'had not the physical advantages of an engaging or impressive person and attractive oratory', and his style of speaking was flatly condemned as 'uninspiring, his voice as heavy and lacking in flexibility, while he wanted or was heedless of the power of climactic peroration'. Yet Coghlan's courage and integrity were such that he came to be regarded with a respect and affection by contemporary Rhodesians which was second only to that accorded to Mr Rhodes himself.

Coghlan's square-cut face looks out from his portraits with the half-apologetic, half-complacent expression of a Galsworthy character rather than that of a political leader who could hold his own with men of the calibre of Winston Churchill and General Smuts. We obtain our clearest insight into his personality from the long letters he wrote to his wife during the absences abroad when he was negotiating self-government; they reveal a man who was apt to dismiss everything that did not fit into his own preconceived ideas, and who was determined not to be intimidated by the immensely strong influences opposed to him. Mingled with these traits was an engaging homeliness: it was perfectly in character for Coghlan to explode with fury once in England when he was charged 38*s.* for an umbrella which before the war had sold for 17*s.* 6*d.*, especially as he said he would find little use for it when he returned to Rhodesia.

The Union Party in Rhodesia was led by a second Bulawayo lawyer named Herbert Longden, who sincerely believed that the country possessed neither the population nor the resources to sustain independence. He was supported by a number of diverse but influential bodies of opinion. One of them was the British Government: it made no secret of its hope that Rhodesia would become South Africa's fifth province, as this would relieve the British taxpayer of any necessity of 'buying out' the Chartered Company when it abdicated control of the country. Thus, one confidential memorandum on the subject pointed out in 1914 that then, 'it would be for the Union to settle with the Company', and added that this would be 'an arrangement which would be most convenient for His Majesty's Government'. Five years later when the discussion was resumed Whitehall had not shifted its ground, and we find Coghlan noting that the R.G.A. had 'to reckon with an unsympathetic attitude on the part of the Imperial Government which would like to put us into the Union and have done with us'. And when the subject was raised again with Winston Churchill, Coghlan wrote that the new Secretary of State 'was out to get us into Union if possible, but damn him he will not succeed if I can help it'.

If Whitehall's attitude seems hard to correlate with later affirmations that its only real concern over Rhodesian independence was with the protection of the country's Africans, the reason for the support given by the Chartered Company to the Unionists at least had the virtue of ingenuousness: its directors believed they could dispose of their vested interests more profitably to a relatively affluent South Africa than to a newly independent state of Rhodesia. Big Business in South Africa which also backed Longden admitted that it did so because Union would be likely to ensure an endless supply of cheap labour from beyond the Limpopo to work the Rand gold mines; and Big Business was very influential in Rhodesia since it controlled the local press.

And so the chances that Coghlan would be able to persuade the electorate to reject Union seemed poor even to his most optimistic supporters, and even worse when the prestigious General Smuts, back from his triumphs at the Peace Conference and the formation of the League of Nations, threw his immense influence on to the side of the Unionists. Smuts believed genuinely that Rhodesian interests would be best served in absorption by her neighbour, but it was also suggested that he wanted Rhodesian support in the South African parliament: this was certainly Coghlan's estimate; after one of his passages with the South African Prime Minister he announced dismally that he had 'failed to make him understand that the question of Rhodesia was not a matter of the ins and outs of an ordinary contested election, but the matter of a people with a soul to be saved as well as a body to be kicked'.

From now on the struggle for the Rhodesian future was virtually a contest between Coghlan and General Smuts, and Smuts at this time was the most persuasive of propagandists—a man with a very good case to sell. He was a strange blend of mystic and practical politician. The mystic in him had developed the philosophy of Holism, and inevitably this made him advocate the creation of a greater South Africa as Rhodes and Kruger had done before him, and he appealed to this sentiment in messages like the one he sent to the electorate just before the referendum which read 'Rhodesia's destiny calls her to the great Union which is laying the foundations of the future South Africa.'

At the same time the practical politician in Smuts appreciated the need for a Rhodesian bloc in his own parliament which would contain the rising forces of Afrikanerism, and to gain it he made it known that Rhodesia would be treated very generously if she opted for Union.

When they were published his terms, among other things, offered Rhodesia ten seats in the South African parliament: this meant that 1,200 Rhodesians would have the same voting powers as 2,958 persons in the Transvaal. On a more material basis

Smuts promised to spend £5,000,000 during the next ten years on Rhodesian development, and the indignant Coghlan was given to understand that if he switched sides he could expect a seat in the new Cabinet. Smuts followed up his offer with a visit to Rhodesia, and although he made a show of avoiding politics the speeches he made at every opportunity were all subtle yet masterful pleas for Union. He mingled appeal to expedience with idealism and it was the sort of approach that Smuts could manage superlatively well.

Although it must have seemed that the cause of the R.G.A. had been torn to shreds, Coghlan fought back as 1921 gave way to 1922. He emphasised the Rhodesians' traditional loyalty to the British Crown: 'Keep your independence', he exhorted one audience. 'Never forget your duty to the Empire, to your brethren in the south, and to your king and country.' But privately he was depressed by the 'tremendous odds' against him, which he gloomily enumerated as 'the local Argus daily press, the South African press, the English press, the mighty Smuts and his magical personality, the unfriendly attitude of the Imperial Government, a party with unlimited funds at their back from Corner House,* the Joels, the Chartered Company and all the capitalists with axes to grind . . . and a campaign of organised lying.'

But in the end his approach to the electorate was more effective than Smuts'. He played on the almost obsessive pride Rhodesians took in their British heritage, and on their instinctive fear of Afrikaner nationalism. And he was assisted by several unexpected events. After Smuts' suppression of the Rand strike the Rhodesian Labour party stigmatised him as an enemy of the working man. Then a fear grew up in Rhodesia that Union would be followed by a flooding of 'poor whites' into their country which their immigration laws had previously excluded, and there was a strong suspicion that the promised development funds would be devoted to their settlement. Most important of all Smuts quite failed to reconcile two sections of the community to the idea of Union—the railway workers and the junior civil servants. They

* The headquarters of certain gold mining interests in Johannesburg.

believed that their pay and working conditions would be adversely affected by Union and that bilingualism would affect their chances of promotion.

In the end the votes of these two sections of the electorate turned out to be decisive, but their importance was still unrecognised by Coghlan when 'the day of days arrived, Friday 27th October 1922,' and the Rhodesians went to the poll to decide between their conflicting loyalties to Great Britain and South Africa. And now, ten days later, a quietness had fallen on the crowd outside the Bulawayo courthouse as Mr Barnard, with a paper in his hand, came through the door and on to the verandah. He read out that 8,774 votes had been cast for Coghlan and 5,989 for the Unionist Party. It was a clear majority and the destiny of a country had been settled by the votes of less than 15,000 men and women.* According to the Bulawayo *Chronicle* the result was wildly applauded: 'the cheering was loud and long' it reported, 'Hats were waved and thrown into the air', and fireworks left over from Guy Fawkes day were set off. In reply to shouted demands Coghlan came forward with a short speech which ended with a rousing 'For King and Empire—that is our motto', and Mr Moffat, John Smith Moffat's son, had something to say about the exciting prospects lying ahead of the country. Then the crowd slowly dispersed conscious that a page of history had been turned that day.

Rhodesia had set her course: she had chosen to model herself on British ideals rather than on expediency, and it had been an inherited liberal sentiment and an unlimited trust in the British people which had made her do so. The Imperial Government responded a shade less generously than might have been anticipated, but within the year internal self-government had been granted to Rhodesia and Coghlan had become her first premier. The settlers agreed to pay Whitehall £2,000,000 for the country's crown lands, a transaction which today seems a little strange when we have now grown used to emergent countries being

* And it could be argued of a subcontinent too, for it is doubtful whether with the Rhodesian electorate opposed to it the Nationalist Party would have come to power in South Africa after the Second World War.

generously provided with cash to support their 'freedom'. But then Rhodesia had never been a financial liability to the British taxpayer and there seemed no reason why the country should not pay for her independence.

But was she really independent? Not entirely. It had been agreed that 'because of the peculiar history of the country' her independence should be 'subject to certain limitations'. Yet this restriction caused little concern at the time. Rhodesia was certain that after the support afforded to the mother country in wartime, England would never treat her less generously than South Africa which it could be argued had far less claim on British gratitude.

And gradually her full *de facto* independence was accepted, as the British Government recognised that there was 'an established convention for Parliament at Westminster not to legislate for Southern Rhodesia on matters within the competence of the Legislative Assembly of Southern Rhodesia except with the agreement of the Southern Rhodesian Government.' As late as 1963 we find the then Secretary of State announcing that the country enjoyed 'complete internal self-government' and that Britain had 'long ago accepted the principle that Parliament at Westminster does not legislate for Southern Rhodesia except at her request.'

The mosaic of Rhodes's plan took form as the new white élite settled down to govern Rhodesia as a meritocracy. It was perhaps a meritocracy at its crudest, but at least it was an improvement on anything which had gone before in Mocaranga. The Africans in the country were fed now on fresh hopes, for it was accepted that voting rights would be extended to the mass of the people as they gained in education. Rhodesia was committed to the breathtaking ideal of black men and white men having equal access to learning, work, and opportunity. No one in the crowd straggling away from the Bulawayo courthouse that November evening in 1922 could conceive the spasm of reappraisal about plural societies which would rack the world forty years later, or that it was not perhaps Coghlan after all who had said the last word when the referendum result had been announced. Rather some people would come to believe that it belonged to Longden, his opponent instead. 'Rhodesia has made its choice', he had said, on learning of the figures, 'whether this is going to be a wise one or not, time alone will show. . . . I have no doubt that the ideal of Union will in the fullness of time be realised. I feel that Nature intended it. . . .'

EPILOGUE

A new élite attempted to take over in Rhodesia during the nineteen-sixties—the Communists.

African students in Rhodesia were lured by offers of scholarships to China, Russia, and other countries beyond the Iron Curtain. But at their destinations they discovered that instead of the Arts and Humanities, their courses consisted of political indoctrination, arson, and murder. When their training had been completed they were infiltrated back into Rhodesia, some of them unwillingly, others as fervent disciples of Communism. Their instructions were to commit acts of terrorism and to set up cells in rural districts where other potential rebels could be trained. It was envisaged that once these cells had been properly organised a campaign of intimidation and terror would in due time lead to the establishment of a Communist government in Rhodesia, and deny the country to the west.

These well tried tactics had proved successful already in many parts of the world like South-East Asia and there seemed no reason why they should not be equally effective in southern Africa.

The stooges of the aspiring élite were canoed across the Zambesi in well armed gangs. But they were distressed to discover that the Rhodesian Africans were implacably hostile to them, that the border country was desperately inhospitable, and that they would have to face alert and well trained security forces.

This book is not the place to discuss the unpublicised guerrilla war in the Zambesi valley against Communist terrorists (C.T.s in army parlance). But since one operation was typical of them all, and woke strange echoes of Rhodesian history it may be briefly considered here.

A large group of C.T.s crossed the Zambesi early in August, 1967. They were dressed in civilian clothes but carried automatic guns and grenades of Chinese manufacture. They belonged to the

S.A.N.C.* and Z.A.P.U.† political parties. Their crossing place was not so very far from where the Helmores had died one after the other more than a century before. From there the terrorists marched down the Botswana–Rhodesia border, dropping off small parties at intervals to infiltrate eastwards towards the great plateau. A nucleus of about forty men continued southwards, and then turned east, taking the same route past a succession of waterholes which Mzilikazi had used in 1838–9 when he marched to keep his rendezvous with Gondwana on Thabas Induna.

At 5.20 in the evening of 23rd August the terrorists clashed with two platoons of the Rhodesian African Rifles. A scrambling action followed in thick bush where visibility was not more than five yards. 'The C.T. tried to advance on us a couple of times', the senior platoon commander reported later, 'the exchange of firing continued and towards last light there was only sporadic firing which stopped at approximately 18.20.'

The Rhodesian losses were one private in the R.A.R. and one white policeman killed, and one officer, one policeman, and six other ranks wounded. All the insurgents were accounted for.

The Rhodesian policeman killed was twenty-three years old. He was the sixth member of his family to die for his country; one had been killed in the First World War, two in the Second, one had died with the Shangani Patrol, and one in an obscure scuffle with slavers in the Zambesi valley. He was a fourth generation Rhodesian. His name was Thomas Morgan Thomas.

* South African National Congress.
† Zimbabwe African Peoples' Union.

BIBLIOGRAPHY

Chapter 1. THE FIRST RHODESIANS

At present the evidence regarding the two hypothetical origins of the Bushpeople is about equally balanced: Professor Carleton Coon is a protagonist of a north African origin and expounds his theory in two most valuable books, *The origin of Races* (1962), and *The Living races of Man* (1965, New York, Alfred A. Knopf). Professor P. V. Tobias on the other hand comes down heavily and equally authoratively on the side of the 'Central African local hypothesis', and the student may wish to follow the arguments propounded in several papers such as those appearing in *Man*, 1957, 6., *Am. J. Phys. Anthrop.*, 1956 V, 14, 2; and *Ecology in S. Africa* (1965, The Hague, W. Junk).

The controversy has also been discussed by A. R. Willcox in his splendidly produced *The Rock Art of South Africa* (Johannesburg 1963) in which he ventilates the opinions of Professor Raymond Dart. George Stow in his pioneering *The Native Races of South Africa* (London, Swan Sonneschein & Co., 1905) goes no further than to suggest that the Bushpeople migrated from 'the distant unknown north', but Bleek (*NADA* 1928) draws attention to these people's supposed early contact with the Egyptians.

The Rhodesian publication *The Native Affairs Department Annual of Southern Rhodesia* (hereafter called by the more familiar *NADA*) has published several important articles about the Bushmen living in the country and articles by W. H. H. Nicolle and A. C. Campbell in 1959 and 1964 respectively record especially useful material.

Mrs Elizabeth Marshall-Thomas in her *The Harmless People* (Alfred A. Knopf, 1959) has provided us with one of the best accounts of the modern Bushman's ethos; in it she mentions the fact that they call themselves the *Zhu twa si,* adding that *twa* means 'just' or 'only' in the sense of '*just* the wind' or '*only* me'.

The unpleasant impression made by the Bushmen last century on European travellers is nowhere better reflected than in Vaughan-Williams *A visit to Lobengula in 1889* (Glasgow, Robert Maclehose & Co., 1946) where he writes that 'they were an evil-looking dirty lot, very small, the tallest not more than four feet six inches in height. . . . They had evil, animal-like faces, sometimes tattooed, and many had prominent teeth, said to be due to tearing meat off bones when small children. . . . They really were evil little devils, like wild animals, which they resembled in many ways. . . . The Boers shot them like vermin and they are now practically exterminated, except in the Kalahari and South-West Africa.' This description can be compared with Dorothea Bleek's more accurate delineation in which she writes: 'the Bushman is a good lover and a good hater, very loyal and very revengeful. He remains all his life a child, averse to work, fond of play, of painting, singing, dancing, dressing up and acting, above all things of hearing and telling stories.' Willcox sums up the Bushmen very well as a 'race of Peter Pans'. Silberhauer accounts for most Europeans' prejudice against the race by explaining that 'Bushmen are friendly people, but tend to be afraid of anything unknown, which includes strangers toward whom they are initially very shy.'

Tobias has dealt at length with the unusual physical traits of the Capoids in articles already quoted, and suggests that the dwarfing which they underwent, like that affecting other animal species, was favoured and strongly selected in Africa during the late Pleistocene, but he also mentions the possibility of dwarfing having been mediated by malfunction of the pituitary gland. Coon has summarised the Capoids' anatomical characteristics in *The Living races of Man*, and discusses the characteristic 'atelier Egyptienne', the common peda-morphic appearance, monorchy, large nipples, and unusual penile position. The presumption that the ancient Rhodesian Bushpeople showed aberrations similar to those of today is strongly supported by their artists' depictions. The phenomenon of infibulation is seen in many paintings, and is particularly noted by Willcox.

B. M. Fagan's *Ancient Peoples and Places, Southern Africa during the Iron Age* (London, Thames & Hudson, 1965) provides the general reader with an easily-read account of the area's prehistory, and emphasises the importance of the Bushmen's invention of the bow and arrow hunting technique. Willcox and Silberhauer both have a good deal to report about the arrow poisons used by modern Capoids in South Africa and Botswana.

Bushmen paintings in southern Africa were described by the Portuguese as early as 1721 (Willcox); the first report of rock engravings that I have come across is in Thomas Leask's diary of 1859, and almost certainly he was here describing those at Bumboosie.

By far the most important work on Rhodesian cave paintings is *Prehistoric rock art of the Federation of Rhodesia and Nyasaland* (edited Roger Summers, Univ. Press of Glasgow, 1959), and I have relied heavily on this magnificently illustrated book for descriptions and interpretations of the country's rock art. Elizabeth Goodall deals in this work with the paintings of Mashonaland, C. K. Cooke with the rock art of Matabeleland, and J. Desmond Clark has contributed a chapter on the paintings north of the Zambesi. Elsewhere Cooke has noted the occurrence of 2,000 painted sites in Rhodesia (*Proceedings and Transactions of the Rhodesian Scientific Association* Jan., 1964). Mrs Goodall describes up to fifteen superimpositions of style in a single cave; Cooke divides the Matabeleland paintings into five successive stages of which the last one is decadent and comparatively modern, and provides tentative dates for them all; he also puts forward the suggestion that the 'old masters' of Capoid art were peripatetic.

The interpretation of Bushman paintings will no doubt continue to exercise the imagination of their *aficionodos* for many years to come. Leo Frobenius has made many suggestions on this subject in two books published in German; Hans-George Bondi in *The Art of the Stone Age* (New York, Crown, 1961) draws attention to the similarity of the paintings of Africa and western Europe, while a contributor to his book, Erik Holm, has suggested that Capoid art attempts to express the essential unity of men and animals, and their interchangeability.

The related motivation that lay behind the paintings has similarly always been something of a mystery in Rhodesia. L. Cripps discussed the problem at length in *NADA* during 1941 (and also here made valuable reference to colours, age, sequence, and the materials used by the artists). The diversity of opinions advanced since then about the purpose of Capoid paintings only emphasises the complexity of the problem, and it provides a challenge to future observers of this rare art form.

Chapter 2. MONOMATAPA

A considerable bibliography of the Monomatapan period of Rhodesian history is available to the student. Much of it is based on G. McC. Theal's monumental researches which were to some extent at least inspired by Cecil Rhodes. The results appear in *Records of South-eastern Africa* (Cape Town 1899) and *History and Ethnography of Africa South of the Zambesi* (London 1910). Theal's pioneering work has been followed up by several modern scholars, notably D. P. Abraham, who by a brilliant exercise in relating oral tradition to Portuguese records, has unravelled much of the Monomatapan past, notably in articles appearing in *NADA* 1959, 'The early political history of the Kingdom of Mwene Mutapa' (U.C.R.N., 1962), 'Maramuca' (*Journal of African History*, 1961), and *The Historian in Tropical Africa* (O.U.P., 1964). Eric Axelson in *South East Africa, 1488–1530* (London 1940) has also given us a scholarly account of the Karanga Empire, while the more general reader will find accurate and easily read accounts of the era in Fagan's relevant contribution to *Ancient Peoples and Places* (London 1965), A. J. Wills' *An Introduction to the History of Central Africa* (London 1964), and J. D. Clark's *The Prehistory of Southern Africa* (London 1959). L. H. Gann's *A History of Southern Rhodesia* (Glasgow 1965) has, however, been far and away the most useful authority for this and all subsequent chapters of this book.

A great deal about the religious beliefs of the Karanga has been recorded in *NADA*, and especial mention must be made of J. Richardson's account in the periodical of 1942. Professor T. O. Ranger has emphasised the importance of the Mwari cult to modern Rhodesian history, notably in *The Zambesian Past* (Manchester 1966) and in *Revolt in Southern Rhodesia, 1896–97* which has so far only been available to me in the page proof edition.

The Karanga move from the Great Zimbabwe region to the Dande has been documented by Abraham and by Axelson in *The Portuguese in South East Africa* (Johannesburg 1960). For accounts of events and customs at the Monomatapan court, and of the internecine wars that broke it up, I have again drawn heavily on translations made by Theal and Axelson as well as on *Portuguese and Dutch in South Africa* by S. R. Welch (Cape Town 1691) and I also found the more contemporary *Ethiopia Oriental* by Joao dos Santos and *The Book of Duarte Barbosa*, both of which have been reprinted, very informative. De Faria's *Portuguese Africa* (1569, reprinted London 1745) provides us with many valuable insights into life in the Karanga Empire. H. A. Wieschoff's *The Zimbabwe-Monomatapan Culture* (Menasha 1941) is an excellent and scholarly examination of the period. The long quotation concerning

Changamire's usurpation of the throne is taken from Diogo de Alcancova's account translated by Theal, which also appears in Basil Davidson's most interesting *The African Past* (London 1964). Like so much else in this chapter the report of Nogomo's obsequies is owed to Abraham's research.

Chapter 3. THE PORTUGUESE CONQUEST

The period of Portuguese ascendancy in Mashonaland is still comparatively unknown even to Rhodesians. Many of the sources noted for Chapter 2 have again been used in writing the present account. Thus Fernandes' pioneering journey is documented by Axelson in *South East Africa.* The route he took has been discussed at length by W. A. Godlanton and J. F. Schofield in the *Proc. & Trans. Rhod. Scient. Assoc.* in 1945, 1949, and 1960, as well as by H. Tracey in *Antonio Fernandes* (Lourenco Marques 1940). The Silveira literature is considerable. Perhaps the best general account is that of Father W. F. Rea appearing in *Rhodesiana* (1959) but the interested reader is also referred to A. F. Loveday's *Three Stages of History in Rhodesia* (Cape Town 1961) and to S. R. Welch's *South Africa under King Sebastian* (Cape Town 1949). The latter also reports the course of the Baretto expedition at some length, while Theal gives a translation of Monclaro's narrative in *Records of South Eastern Africa.* A great deal of information about the expedition has also been taken from De Faria. Several articles discussing the sites of the Portuguese 'Fairs' in Rhodesia have appeared in *Proc. & Trans. Rhod. Scient. Assoc.,* while T. V. Bulpin has provided the more general reader with a colourful account of the Portuguese occupation and indeed of a wide span of Rhodesian history in *To the Banks of the Zambesi* (Johannesburg 1965). Modern archaeological research is at present revealing most valuable additional information about the Portuguese in Rhodesia.

Chapter 4. MZILIKAZI

I found E. C. Tabler's *The Far Interior* (Cape Town 1953) to be the most useful single authority for the Matabele period of Rhodesian history; it is a model of accuracy and carefully notes all the relevant source material. The Rozwi era has been elucidated for us by many archaeologists' papers, notably by Roger Summers and K. R. Robinson. Summer's contributions include *Inyanga* (Cambridge 1958), 'The

Southern Rhodesian Iron Age' (*Journal of African History*, 1962), and *Zimbabwe* (Cape Town 1963). Works by Robinson which have been particularly useful are *Khami Ruins* (Cambridge 1959) and his chapter on 'The Archaeology of the Rozwi' appearing in *The Zambesian Past* (Manchester 1966).

D. R. Morris has provided an excellent summary of the earlier Nguni history in *The Washing of the Spears* (New York 1965); A. J. Bryant's *Olden Times in Zululand and Natal* (London 1929) is the recognised authority for this period. For a record of the Matabele migration to Rhodesia I found *The Zulu Aftermath* (London 1966) by J. D. Omer-Cooper perhaps the most useful of many published accounts. Persistent tradition in Matabeleland insists that Dr Robert Moffat advised Mzilikazi about the fine cattle ground beyond the Limpopo near a prominent flat-topped hill, but this is highly unlikely although Moffat may well have counselled his friend to leave the Transvaal so as to avoid a clash with the Boers. The possible routes taken by Mzilikazi and Gondwana have been discussed in *NADA*, 1934 and 1935.

Moffat in *Missionary Labours in Southern Africa* (John Snow, London 1842) was one of the first writers to call attention to the existence of the Matabele nation. *Shaka Zulu* (London 1955) is a fine biography of the great man by E. A. Ritter, and an almost equally good life of Mzilikazi has been written by P. A. Becker, *Path of Blood* (London 1962).

Life in Matabeleland under Mzilikazi and Lobengula has been described in many accounts. Many of them are referred to in the next chapter's bibliography. T. Baines' remarkable contribution to our knowledge of Matabeleland twenty years before the British occupation is especially valuable and has appeared in the Oppenheimer series under the title of *The Northern Goldfield Diaries* edited in scholarly style by J. P. R. Wallis (London 1946). Leask's diary has also been made available in this admirable series (London 1954). Much information can be gleaned about the Matabele from *NADA*. F. C. Selous' *A Hunter's wanderings in Africa* (London 1881) did much to awaken contemporary European interest in the far interior.

Interesting accounts of the Zulu headring are given in *NADA*, 1925, and *The Washing of the Spears* already noted. The diary of the Jesuit missionaries at Lobengula's court has been translated by Mrs M. Lloyd and appeared in *Rhodesiana*, 1959. I have also found the following most useful: Tabler's reproduction of Major Stabbs' Journal (Cape

Town 1967), Neville Jones' *My Friend Kumalo* (1944), and *Rhodesian Genesis* (Glasgow 1953), and A. A. Campbell's *Mlimo* (Pietermaritzburg 1925).

Bishop Knight-Bruce has also made a useful contribution to our knowledge in *The Mashonaland Mission* (London 1949). He was a biased and somewhat bewildered traveller: One passage of his diary reads 'I do not know where we are going, nor where we are, except that we have crossed the Hunigani River. . . .' The Bishop opposed Rhodes's designs in the far interior for some years and wrote of the Rudd concession that 'such a piece of devilry and brutality as a consignment of rifles to the Matabele cannot be surpassed'; then he suddenly changed sides; the cause of his conversion is one of the minor mysteries of the Rhodesian story.

So far little about the Boer invasion of Matabeleland in 1847 has appeared in print. The student of this adventure is referred to Walker's article in *The Cambridge History*, Sir Robert Tredgold's splendid edition of Nobbs' *Matopos* (Salisbury 1956), and to E. C. Tabler's *Pioneers of Rhodesia* (Cape Town 1966).

The references to Mzilikazi's ill health are mostly taken from the missionary diaries which are more conveniently considered under the next chapter heading; but Leask's *Diary, The Recollections of William Finaughty* (ed. E. C. Tabler, Cape Town 1957), and *My Friend Kumalo*, already mentioned, have also been useful sources. The note about the lightning at the time of the king's death comes from Baines' diary and Jeannie Boggie's *First Steps in civilising Rhodesia* (Bulawayo 1940). There is some doubt concerning the number of wives and slaves slaughtered to accompany Mzilikazi's passage to the Matabele Valhalla; Mrs Boggie for instance speaks of three, but the Jesuit Fathers mention the number of three hundred. A good account of Mzilikazi's funeral is found in *NADA*, 1933, while the desecrations of his sepulchre are noted in two biographies of Rhodes written by J. G. McDonald (London 1928), and J. G. Lockhart and G. M. Woodhouse (London 1963).

Chapter 5. THE SECOND CHRISTIAN VENTURE

The candid journals which Dr Robert Moffat wrote during his three visits to Matabeleland are all of prime importance to the historian of missionary enterprise in Rhodesia. Together with his son's journal and some correspondence, they have all been published in the Oppen-heimer series (London 1945) with prefaces ably written by J. P. R. Wallis. Unfortunately these editions skirt some controversial matter and this somewhat detracts from their interest. The biography of Robert Moffat by Cecil Northcott (London 1961) makes a very fair assessment of his subject's contribution to the opening up of Central Africa. The Rev. T. M. Thomas wrote his own brisk account of the early days at Inyati (*Eleven Years in Central South Africa,* London 1872), but this book must be read with caution, as inevitably it is partisan. The Rev. J. Mackenzie's *Ten Years North of the Orange River* (Edinburgh 1871) contains some revealing passages about conditions at Inyati. My interest in the tragedy of the Linyanti missionaries was first aroused by E. W. Smith's biography of Roger Price which he called *Great Lion of Bechuanaland* (London 1957); gaps in the story were filled in from the correspondence of other missionaries kindly made available to me in the L.M.S. Archives, London, by Miss Irene Fletcher.

More information about the Inyati Mission was obtained from W. A. Elliott's *Gold from the Quartz* (London 1910), from Iris Clinton's *These Vessels* (Bulawayo 1959), and from the privately printed memoirs of Celt Thomas, son of the pioneer missionary. The note about Mzilikazi's interjections during the brethren's sermons comes from *The Recollections of William Finaughty* (ed. E. C. Tabler, Cape Town 1957). When Thomas's dismissal from the Society was under consideration, the directors of the L.M.S. were each presented with a volume containing the correspondence (running to 174 documents) of the younger Moffat, Sykes, Thomas, and other missionaries. Only the British Museum copy of this book has survived, perhaps because the others were deliberately destroyed. From it I have drawn many of the details of the quarrels which marred the first years of the Inyati Mission.

Chapter 6. MR RHODES

A tremendous bibliography of Cecil Rhodes is in existence.* I found the biographies written by the following authors to be the most useful in attempting to make a fair assessment of this remarkable man's character: Phillip Jourdan, William Plomer, Sarah Gertrude Millin, J. G. McDonald, and the most recent work coming from J. G. Lock-hart and C. M. Woodhouse. Rhodes's speeches collected by *Vindex*

* Over a hundred biographies or biographical sketches of Rhodes are available

(1902) give several little-known glimpses of the founder of modern Rhodesia.

I am greatly indebted to my friend Dr J. C. Shee for his help with this chapter and particularly for allowing me to make use of his original research into the origin of Rhodes's ill health. Shee's pertinent article in the *Central African Journal of Medicine*, 1965, is a model of medical detective work.

Descriptions of the concessionaires at Lobengula's court are to be found in the relevant Blue Books, Leask's Diary, Mrs Lippert's letters (Cape Town 1960), Charles Rudd's journal (London 1949), and Thompson's autobiography (London 1924) which was edited by his daughter, partly to give an explanation of his hurried departure from Bulawayo. H. M. Hole's *The Making of Rhodesia* (London 1926) has a very good account of the machinations that ended with the occupation of Mashonaland.

The best biography of Dr Jameson is still that by Ian Colvin (London 1923). Other accounts of the doctor's life have been more concerned with his raid into the Transvaal, so that his Rhodesian career has, in comparison, been neglected.

Chapter 7. THE PIONEERS

After writing his autobiography *Great Days*, Frank Johnson submitted the proof copy to Lord Malvern, and on his advice omitted the chapter dealing with the project to seize Bulawayo by an armed coup. The original manuscript, however, can be studied in the Rhodesian Archives, and I have drawn on it to describe this disreputable scheme which fortunately never got past the planning stage.

The march of the pioneers to Mashonaland is extremely well documented. Marshal Hole's *The Making of Rhodesia* (London 1926) still holds its place as one of the best accounts of the events leading up to the 'Occupation'. The protracted preliminary negotiations have been surveyed more recently by Philip Mason in *The Birth of a Dilemma* (London 1958). Neville Jones selected several of the pioneers' accounts of the march to Salisbury for *Rhodesian Genesis* (Glasgow 1953), but Major Leonard in *How we made Rhodesia* (London 1896) is perhaps our most useful of the contemporary reports. His book is racy in style (although sometimes interrupted by long lapses into homespun philosophy) but he draws vivid pen-pictures of most of the important personalities in the drama of 1890. Hardly anyone escapes his somewhat caustic criticism and his writing catches the pioneers' mingled and sometimes disconcerting strain of patriotism, facetiousness, and brutal self-confidence, a strain in them which Kipling recognised when he wrote

> We've laughed at the world as we've found it—
> Its women and cities and men—
> From Sayid Burgash in a tantrum
> To the smoke-reddened eyes of Loben (Dear Boys!)
> We've a little account with Loben.

The ramifications of the dispute between Rhodes and the Portuguese is never likely to be better elucidated than in P. R. Warhurst's *Anglo-Portuguese Relations in South Central Africa, 1890–1900* (London 1962) and in Eric Axelson's *Portugal and the scramble for Africa* (Johannesburg 1967). Colquhoun gives his side of the story in his autobiographical *From Dan to Beersheba* (London 1908); a revealing pen-portrait of Colquhoun by J. A. Edwards appears in *Rhodesiana*, 1963.

Reports of the Battle of Macequece appear in many books: Gann's *History* as always is accurate on the subject; Victor Morier's is the most useful of contemporary accounts and appears in *Rhodesiana*, 1965. Warhurst's book covers Heyman's battle, outside Macequece, as do sections in *Rhodesian Genesis* and Leonard's book. The Rhodesian Archives possess a good deal of useful correspondence relating to this action, and Sir Henry Loch's considered opinions about it can be read in Blue Book C–6495.

The Chartered Company's skilful propaganda succeeded in throwing most of the blame for beginning the Matabele war of 1893 on to Lobengula; he was represented as an unreconcilable savage who had been preparing to overwhelm the white settlers in Mashonaland, but was frustrated by Jameson's prompt preventive action. The effect of this propaganda was greatly helped by the published statements of local missionaries. Thus Father Prestage, S.J., states that he considered the Matabele régime to be one of 'iniquity and devilry' and soon after the Fort Victoria incident telegraphed to Cecil Rhodes 'I consider there is most just cause for punishing the Amandabeles at once. Without prompt punishment there is every possibility of the same atrocities recurring' (noted in *Rhodesiana*, 1960).

At the same time liberal circles in Great Britain condemned the war which William Blunt summed up grimly as 'slaughter for trade' (*Jameson's Raid* by E. Pakenham, London 1960).

In this chapter I have relied to a great extent on Professor Glass's reconstruction of the events leading up to the war in two fine papers entitled 'The Background to the Matabele War' (1959) and 'Sir Henry Loch and the Matabele War' (1964). But it is only fair to note that Professor Ranger's survey of the same subject in *Rebellion in Southern Rhodesia* differs somewhat in emphasis, being more critical of Dr Jameson and the Chartered Company.

The Downfall of Lobengula by W. A. Wills and L. T. Collingridge (London 1894) is the general source for all accounts of the war. I have also made use of Blue Book C–7555, *NADA*, 1959 and 1962, Hans Sauer's eminently readable *Ex Africa* (London 1937), and the biographies of Rhodes written by Millin and McDonald, to which reference has already been made.

Chapter 8. THE SHANGANI PATROL

In writing of the Wilson patrol I have relied very largely on the manuscript of the Court of Inquiry into Forbes's conduct which is lodged in the Rhodesian Archives (code number CT I/14/3). This reports the evidence of most of the officers serving under Forbes during the pursuit to the Shangani. African accounts of the battle near the Pupu creek are taken from oral evidence of two surviving Matabele warriors who fought in the action, from *NADA*, Pat Fletcher's diary, and the Napier papers (the two latter documents kindly made available to me by the sons of the participants, Peter Fletcher and Mark Napier respectively), A. V. Smit's reconstruction, and from Frederick Burnham's vivid but regrettably inaccurate biography *Scouting on two continents* (London 1926). There is a good deal to suggest in fact that Burnham was not ordered away from the patrol as he makes out, but deserted it with his brother-in-law Ingram when he saw the odds that Wilson's men would have to face. Forbes's own account of the disaster appears in *The downfall of Lobengula*, and his actions have been defended by Lieutenant-General E. A. Altham in a memorial privately printed in Winchester about 1927. The contemporary suspicions concerning the true cause of Raaff's death are recorded in *The African Review*, of 17th February, 1894. These suspicions are still entertained by Raaff's descendants in Rhodesia, but now they could only be proved by exhumation and an autopsy of the Commandant's remains.

Chapter 9. REBELLION

The earliest and still one of the most useful accounts of the outbreak of the Matabeleland rebellion is to be found in F. C. Selous's *Sunshine and Storm in Rhodesia* (London 1896). Ranger's book, already noted, is without doubt the best general report of the outbreak. Burnham has written at length about his experiences during the siege of Bulawayo in *Scouting on two continents,* but this book must be read with caution. A fine account based on African oral tradition about the Mashona rebellion has been provided by C. G. Chivanda (U.C.R.N., 1966).

For the account of the siege of Mazoe, I have drawn on articles by Dr R. C. Howland (*Rhodesiana,* 1963), Major Nesbitt, V.C. (*Outpost,* 1950), H. D. Rawlinson (*Outpost,* 1939), H. Pollet (*Rhodesiana,* 1957), and in a long letter by ffolliott Darling recorded in W. H. Brown's *On the South African Frontier* (New York 1899). Dr Howland kindly walked over the ground at Mazoe with me and clarified the whole episode in my mind.

The Matopos campaign enjoyed a brief period of publicity in late Victorian England; of the several accounts describing it, I found the following accounts particularly useful: F. W. Sykes' *With Plumer in Matabeleland* (London 1897), H. Plumer's *An irregular Corps in Matabeleland* (London 1897), and R. S. Baden-Powell's *The Matabele Campaign* (London 1897).

Details of the executions of Kagubi and Nyanda are taken from the *Zambesi Mission Records* (1898).

Chapter 10. THE REFERENDUM

Considering its importance to the future of southern Africa surprisingly little has so far been written about the Rhodesian referendum of 1922. I have based my description of the scene outside the Bulawayo courthouse on reports appearing in the *Bulawayo Chronicle*. Basic facts concerning the white settlers' struggle for independence appear in L. H. Gann's *History of Southern Rhodesia,* Walker's *History of Southern Africa,* and Volume VIII of *The Cambridge History of the British Empire.* The only biography of Sir Charles Coghlan to appear so far is *One Man's Hand* (London 1950) by J. P. R. Wallis, and from it I have taken several quotations. Claire Palley's scholarly *Constitutional History and Law of Southern Rhodesia* (Oxford 1966) is an invaluable source book for students of recent Rhodesian history which it carries up to the Unilateral Declaration of Independence. *The real Rhodesia* (London 1924) written by Mrs Tawse Jollie, who was Archibald Colquhoun's widow, gives a highly personal viewpoint of Coghlan's struggle, while 'A day of decision' (*Proc. C. A. Hist. Assoc. Conf.* 1966) concentrates on the political importance of the referendum result. My authority for the £2 million paid to Britain by the Rhodesian settlers is J. P. R. Wallis in *One Man's Hand.*

INDEX